UNDERSTANDING
& TEACHING
PRIMARY
ENGLISH

Dedicated to Claire (for enduring), Nick Swarbrick (for his friendship and guidance) and Mary Sutcliffe (for always inspiring).

MT

To all of the wonderful primary teachers I've been lucky enough to talk to, work with, and learn from over the years. Educational theories are fascinating, but it takes great teachers to bring them to life in the classroom.

JC

UNDERSTANDING & TEACHING PRIMARY ENGLISH

THEORY INTO PRACTICE

JAMES CLEMENTS & MATHEW TOBIN

Los Angeles | London | New Delhi
Singapore | Washington DC | Melbourne

Los Angeles | London | New Delhi
Singapore | Washington DC | Melbourne

SAGE Publications Ltd
1 Oliver's Yard
55 City Road
London EC1Y 1SP

SAGE Publications Inc.
2455 Teller Road
Thousand Oaks, California 91320

SAGE Publications India Pvt Ltd
B 1/I 1 Mohan Cooperative Industrial Area
Mathura Road
New Delhi 110 044

SAGE Publications Asia-Pacific Pte Ltd
3 Church Street
#10-04 Samsung Hub
Singapore 049483

Editor: James Clark
Senior assistant editor: Diana Alves
Production editor: Katherine Haw
Copyeditor: Clare Weaver
Indexer: Adam Pozner
Cover design: Naomi Robinson
Typeset by: C&M Digitals (P) Ltd, Chennai, India
Printed in the UK

Library of Congress Control Number: 2020947521

British Library Cataloguing in Publication data

A catalogue record for this book is available from the British Library

ISBN 978-1-5264-2658-1
ISBN 978-1-5264-2659-8 (pbk)

At SAGE we take sustainability seriously. Most of our products are printed in the UK using responsibly sourced papers and boards. When we print overseas we ensure sustainable papers are used as measured by the PREPS grading system. We undertake an annual audit to monitor our sustainability.

CONTENTS

ABOUT THE AUTHORS

James Clements is an experienced teacher, researcher, and education writer. He has worked with groups of schools, education organisations and governments in the UK and across the world. Prior to this, James was a primary teacher and school leader in central London. He is the author of *Teaching English by the Book*. James' principal areas of interest are children's development of language, the pedagogy surrounding language and reading comprehension, and how schools create rich reading cultures and authentic ways of supporting children's written communication.

Mathew Tobin was a primary teacher and school leader for many years before becoming a senior lecturer in Primary English and Children's Literature. He continues to work closely with school practitioners and pupils with a particular focus on raising standards in English. He is passionate about promoting the importance of Reading Teachers and the Reflecting Realities agenda and teaches these areas at both Undergraduate and Postgraduate level. Mathew is often invited to chair discussions and deliver keynotes around Children's Literature, and is involved in various book-judging panels. His own research interests include exploring the relationship between Children's Literature and landscapes and the pedagogical potential and benefits of a locality-based curriculum.

INTRODUCTION

The relationship between educational theory and classroom practice is symbiotic: both elements reinforce and enhance the other. As Orchard and Winch (2015) explain:

> The best teaching practice combines elements of technical know-how with knowledge of research and theory, including a conceptual map of the educational field. Practical wisdom of this kind enables teachers to act in practically appropriate ways in a variety of complex settings.

While developing this 'practical wisdom' is likely to be an important goal for students, trainees, and new teachers taking their first steps into the classroom, making sense of educational theory and its relationship with classroom teaching is a journey that will last for an entire career.

The teaching of English in the primary school is a subject underpinned by a long history of theory and research. This is derived from a range of different academic traditions from conceptual thinking around the literature used with children to practical classroom-based research on the efficacy of different teaching techniques. It draws on thinking conducted over centuries, from philosophical ideas dating back hundreds of years to findings from recent cutting edge cognitive science.

As teachers, engaging with this rich body of knowledge allows us to construct our own philosophy of education, helping us to make professional judgements and reflect on our own practice. It allows us to make 'best bets' (Major and Higgins, 2019) about what might work in our own classrooms, thinking critically about new initiatives, weighing up likely successes and potential challenges. Very rarely can an idea or technique from research be taken and directly used in the classroom. Often, it will need to be mediated to fit with the demands of a specific school or cohort, a teacher's beliefs and the educational ecosystem into which it will fit. As Wiliam (2017) explains:

> While educational research can never tell teachers, leaders and policymakers what to do – the situations they face are too varied and complex – it can suggest which practices are likely to have the greatest benefits for their students, and which are likely to be less effective. However, even where such guidance is supported by the preponderance of evidence, it is important to note that it may not be applicable to all situations. As a result, teachers, leaders and policymakers need to be critical consumers of educational research.

Another challenge in building practical wisdom is that, in educational research, nothing is ever set in stone. Research findings are often contested and navigating these opposing claims requires a strong degree of research literacy to evaluate different findings critically. In addition, theories evolve and grow as further studies are conducted. As professionals, being able to weigh up the claims of different pieces of research and integrate them into our existing schema is an important skill to develop.

But engaging with theory and research isn't the only way of developing the practical wisdom so important for teaching. There is a rich vein of knowledge that comes with experience in the classroom, both learning from other practitioners and from self-reflection, considering what is happening in our own classroom and the impact it has on the students we teach.

Using this book

As teachers first, and now as researchers, we have written *Understanding and Teaching Primary English: Theory Into Practice* to bring together these two aspects; demonstrating links between theory and practice across the breadth of primary English. While English is a holistic subject, with different areas supporting and complementing one another, for ease of navigation, we have divided the book into broad, interrelated sections:

- English in the Early Years
- Oracy and Spoken Language
- Reading
- Writing
- Vocabulary and Word Knowledge
- Curriculum, Planning and Assessment

Each section is structured into two parallel parts. The first part introduces the key theoretical ideas, sharing important research and signposting further reading. The second part looks at the implications for this theory in practice, offering illustrations and case studies of how different theoretical ideas might be enacted in the classroom. This approach is designed to help you move confidently between theory and practice, thinking critically about the validity and application of educational research, as well as considering the foundations on which classroom practice is built. Both parts include Reflection Points, to support you to consider your own opinions and practice.

We hope *Understanding and Teaching Primary English: Theory Into Practice* will help you navigate your path through the myriad possibilities that exist in primary English teaching. Upon this journey towards practical wisdom, it is important to foster your own philosophy and understanding of education: we hope our own experiences and readings inform and guide you on your way.

James Clements and Mathew Tobin

BIBLIOGRAPHY

Major, L.E. and Higgins, S. (2019) *What Works? Research and evidence for successful teaching*. London: Bloomsbury.

Orchard, J. and Winch, C. (2015) *What Training do Teachers Need?: Why theory is necessary to good teaching*. Salisbury: Impact.

Wiliam, D. (2017) 'Getting Educational Research Right'. RSA Medium. Available at: https://medium.com/@thersa/getting-educational-research-right-b77fbc82ef6e (accessed 17/06/2020).

PART 1

ENGLISH IN THE EARLY YEARS

READING IN THE EARLY YEARS: THEORY

THIS CHAPTER WILL

- Introduce the concept of emergent readers

- Explore the impact that early reading experiences have on later reading

- Consider the theoretical underpinnings of different precursors to reading

---

Introduction

As primary practitioners, understanding the gradual journey children take in becoming literate is imperative. These initial chapters on reading and writing in the Early Years have been included so that practice and pedagogy is informed by these developmental foundations (it is referred to as 'Early Years *Foundation* Stage' for good reason). All teachers benefit from understanding good Early Years practice.

It is important to note that the Early Years phase of education, in England, stretches from birth to the age of five. In England, the Early Years Foundation Stage (EYFS):

> ...sets the standards that all early years providers must meet to ensure that children learn and develop well and are kept healthy and safe. It promotes teaching and learning to ensure children's 'school readiness' and gives children the broad range of knowledge and skills that provide the right foundation for good future progress through school and life.
>
> (DfE, 2017)

These four chapters will explore the key landmarks on a child's journey to becoming literate. This chapter benefits from being read alongside Chapters 7 and 8, which are concerned with theory and practice in learning to read itself, including approaches to word reading.

An overview of the emergent reader

When children enter formal schooling, they will have already begun those initial steps to becoming a reader in their home and surrounding environments (McLachlan and Arrow, 2017). Yet, research has shown that the quality and quantity of these experiences will vary greatly (Goodman, 1986) with the greatest differences being connected to 'phonological awareness, vocabulary and oral language' (Buckingham et al., 2013). These, along with several other factors, will affect the child's reading readiness (see Tables 1.1 and 1.2).

With there being a direct correlation between early reading success and later academic success, it is our role to ensure that we give every child the chance to succeed (Langston, 2014; Court, 2017).

As *emergent readers*, each child will enter the Early Years setting – Nursery or Reception – at different developmental stages and, in relation to providing a supportive and engaging environment, we must provide developmentally appropriate activities, conversations and observations to assess and address them (Godwin and Perkins, 2002). Practitioners must keep in mind that a child's reading journey is a personal one and that a balance between a skills-based scaffolded approach and the enjoyment of books provides holistic, contextualised and meaningful reading experiences which convince children of the purpose and pleasure behind reading. This is imperative for future reading success.

Table 1.1 illustrates that the journey to independent reading is an individual one, which is affected by social and cultural factors often outside of a teacher's control. These begin from birth and continue throughout a child's entire schooling.

Table 1.1 Reading experiences and the emergent reader

	Rich Early-Reading Experiences	Poor Early-Reading Experiences
A growing understanding of the purpose of reading Experiences of the pleasures of reading	Children show an interest and 'motivation in text-based activities' (McLachlan and Arrow, 2017). They see the interconnectedness of speaking, listening and writing and feel confident in talking about and asking questions of texts. Reading experiences are associated with intimacy and emotions (Browne, 2012) as well as being informative. They see exploration of books as a group and independent activity which can be exciting and rewarding.	A disassociation between books and pleasure or having had limited experience of texts – both shared and independent – means convincing children of their value and purpose when entering the school setting. This can be time-consuming and have long-term effects on comprehension (Reese et al., 2010). Not valuing reading as a 'collective' experience could lead to a difficult transition into more formal early reading experiences (Clay, 1985).
Alphabetic knowledge, phonological and phonemic awareness	Children have reached the *logographic* stage where they recognise some words and letters by the shape or size but without any phonological association. They may be able to point to whole words 'like their name or a favourite key word/phrase in a book' and repeat it (e.g. *Fred, dinosaur, Oh no!*) (Frith, 1985). Others may enter the Early Years with *alphabetic* knowledge and know that letters represent sounds. They may understand that a word is made of different letters and associated sounds and be able to recognise and talk about environmental sounds too.	Limited experience in this area will affect later decoding abilities and children may access phonics instruction at a different rate to peers (Lonigan et al., 2000).
A broad and rich vocabulary	Supports comprehension (Stanovich, 1986) and gives them a 'taste for language' (Whitehead, 2010) which, in turn, will encourage them to make informed guesses when encountering new words when reading.	Learning new words becomes a slower process which, in turn, affects comprehension (Walberg and Tsai, 1983).
Concepts about print and how books work	Children realise that print in different forms carries meaning and serves a purpose in the real world: – logos and signs in their everyday lives (for example, shop signs or road symbols, names and individual letter shapes). They understand the directionality of a story; can turn pages in the right order and know how books are organised internally (e.g. front/back). They acknowledge that both pictures and print carry meaning even if they cannot fully access the latter.	Knowledge of the purpose of print (either pointed out to them or modelled) can affect other aspects of literacy development and is a predictor for later reading development (Scarborough, 1998 in Dobbs-Oates et al., 2015).
Semantic knowledge	When reading or listening to a text, the child is able to use their knowledge to 'reconstruct' the information in order to make meaning (Pendergast and Garvis, 2013).	Poor long-term memory and/or limited access to life experiences (going to the park, understanding what a letter, castle, lake is or what a cow, helicopter, train is) means that children's understanding and access to a text is limited, making comprehension a greater challenge.

Discovering children's identities as readers is imperative in the Early Years setting and supporting them in seeing themselves as readers should be central to any pedagogical approach. Whatever their background or experience, a strong, supportive relationship between child, carer and setting ensures that all children have the best chance of success in the literate world.

STOP AND REFLECT

Gee (2004) refers to literacy as being 'linked into ways of talking, thinking, believing, knowing, acting, interacting, valuing and feeling'.

How are we being asked to see the teaching of English here and how might it affect our pedagogy in the primary classroom?

Read Table 1.1 again, thinking closely about the different strands of early reading experience.

- What might the implications be for a child starting school who has not had the rich early-reading experiences outlined?
- How might a teacher or a school mitigate for this?
- What might be the implications for curriculum design?
- What might be the implications for classroom teaching?

Facilitative parents and conventional parents

For some children entering the Early Years setting, reading will already be associated with fun, pleasure and meaning making. Stories, information, songs, rhymes, jokes and forms of language play would have been shared throughout the day and be an integral part of bedtime routines. These shared, intimate experiences in which the adult is modelling the act of reading as something worth investing in will have a positive effect on the child's in-school attitudes and reading readiness (Langston, 2014; Dobbs-Oates et al., 2015). They will also provide opportunities to extend alphabetic knowledge, show how print and picture both carry meaning by 'pointing out words' and pictures and understand a book's format and story structure (Sawyer et al., 2014; Hume et al., 2015). Booktalk around picturebooks has especially been associated with improving language development, 'vocabulary and narrative skills' and reading fluency (Leech and Rowe, 2014).

In a US study which explored the relation between reading attitudes of parents and children in early childhood, Dobbs-Oates et al. (2015) placed the former in one of two categories: facilitative parents and conventional parents.

Table 1.2 Facilitative parents and conventional parents (adapted from Dobbs-Oates et al., 2015)

Facilitative Parents	Conventional Parents
• Believe that they should take an active role in teaching their child to read at home	• See schools as primarily responsible for teaching their children
• Understand the need to promote children's vocabulary, knowledge and morals through reading	• Report barriers to any shared reading experiences
• Engage in shared reading and language-based activities	

There is extensive research that shows the impact of parental attitudes to reading on their child's emergent literacies (Barker et al., 2011). This is known to be a notable predictor for children's knowledge of print and has a 'moderate relationship' to later decoding, spelling and comprehension (Dobbs-Oates et al., 2015). It follows then that supporting conventional parents to acknowledge and work on this should become part of the school's remit if we want to offer all children the best chance of success.

Parents need to see emergent reading as a process of modelling to their children the purpose and pleasures of reading and how it can help their child to make sense of the print-rich world in which they live (Godwin and Perkins, 2002). Pointing out print in invitations to parties, street signs, shop names, posters, information on mobile devices and computers models to children the purpose and function of print and how it plays a part in everyday communication.

There is a risk that the teaching of early reading can be conflated with word-reading: the process by which we decode the words off the page. Seeing the process of reading as merely barking at print rather than inviting them to listen to 'the tune on the page' (Godwin and Perkins, 2002) – a phrase defined as expression, intonation and pace – means that, for the emergent reader, purpose, meaning and enjoyment may be lost. Instead, there is more value in initial reading experiences that focus on parents promoting the enjoyment of reading by showing children how to hold a book, directionality of a story, and pointing to whole words on the page to show how they carry meaning. Pointing to pictures and naming objects in books could also lead to some purposeful discussion in which vocabulary and comprehension are enriched as part of the process. Parents are often told to read *to* their children but asking them to read *with* their children would present a more holistic, shared experience: a safe, three-way dialogue between text, adult and child in which talk is central.

Reading at home

There is extensive evidence relating an emergent reader's interest in reading with future reading achievement (Hume et al., 2015), and children spend far more time at home than they do at school. As a result, creating a safe, non-judgemental dialogue between parent, child and school must be seen as a priority which is then fostered and maintained throughout a child's schooling. A mutually supportive relationship between home and school, in which the child's reading successes are shared and celebrated, has been shown to improve both attitudes and results (Bus et al., 1995; Manz et al., 2010). This relationship is best initiated in the Early Years, where good habits can be formed, and parents are most likely to be engaged with school life.

STOP AND REFLECT

A school provides initial guidance for parents about how reading is taught and organised through a series of workshops for Nursery and Reception parents before the start of the school year, and advice and printable materials on the website, backed up with input from individual class teachers on open days and parents' evenings. Parents are talked through an advice sheet, suggesting the following key messages:

- When reading aloud to your child, make sure you're both comfortable and close and that you both can see the words and pictures with ease.
- When sharing a book, talk about the characters and what happens but also point to objects of interest. Name and talk about them, using props or sounds to create a more multi-sensory reading experience – this not only builds up a child's general knowledge but lays the foundations for comprehension.
- Before reading the book to your child, look through and consider any words which they might not understand. You might want to point this word out or say and give a simple definition before beginning the read.
- Guide them through the format of a book. It doesn't matter if your child does not pick up the language of a book at first, gradual repeated modelling will help. Note the cover, title, blurb, names of the author, illustrator and contents (when applicable). This will help prepare them for booktalk in the classroom.
- When reading a poem, non-fiction text, signs, stories, when appropriate encourage links to the child's own experiences. This can help develop deeper understanding and support your child to make connections between reading and their own lives.
- Don't get frustrated if your child wants to revisit books repeatedly. With each reading, they are becoming more confident with handling the text, absorbing both the language and grammar as well as narrative and character.
- Always make sure that books are available for your child to pick up and explore. This can be in a bookshelf or in a small, movable container.
- Sometimes try pointing to the words while you are reading at home. This allows the emergent reader to see how print works and prepares them for future reading instruction.
- Reading experiences at home should be done in safe, stress-free spaces. Children should see reading as something fun, enriching and rewarding.

Which of these key messages would be important in your setting? Are there any other key messages you would wish to add?

Phonological awareness in the Early Years setting

The relationship between limited early phonological awareness and vocabulary has been shown to affect later reading success (Goldstein, 2011; Buckingham et al., 2013). Both have their place in the Early Years, with the teaching of the former becoming more systematic and rigorous when children begin Phase 2 of *Letters and Sounds* (see Chapter 7 for more on this). Prior to the explicit teaching of systematic synthetic phonics in the Early Years, supporting children in becoming more sensitive to 'sound structures' (Mihai et al., 2015) is central. Identifying and playing with sounds around them is key to preparing children for later phonics instruction in which they can decode and segment words through grapheme-phoneme-correspondences.

Emergent readers' phonological progression will begin with moving from larger to smaller units of sound and this transition is the central literacy skill and focus of Phase 1 of *Letters and Sounds* (DFES, 2007). The *Letters and Sounds* teaching programme contains several overlapping approaches to provide coverage for this transition (see below), often through contextual, play-based, meaningful activities. This phase supports children in making sense of the noise of language (what Gopnik et al. refer to as the 'Tower of Babble' (1999)) and having both the confidence and skill to begin breaking down everyday sounds into smaller segments.

As children progress from word manipulation to syllables, to onset and rime and then to individual phonemes (through playing with the alliteration of initial sounds, rhymes in songs and words (Phillips et al., 2008; Whitehead, 2010)), the practitioner's role is to make what *Letters and Sounds* refers to as, 'principled, professional judgements about children's developing abilities' and identify/instruct accordingly. The following two tables illustrate the different components of phonological awareness and its 'growing complexity' (Mihai et al., 2015).

Table 1.3   Letters and Sounds: Phase 1 components and main purpose (adapted from *Letters and Sounds*)

Letters and Sounds: Phase 1 components and main purpose
Aspect 1 – Environmental sounds
Develop children's *listening skills* and awareness of sounds in the environment. Develop *vocabulary* and the identification and recollection of the *difference between sounds* to make up simple sentences and talk in greater detail about sounds.
Aspect 2 – Instrumental sounds
Experience and develop awareness of sounds made with instruments and noise makers; to *listen* to and appreciate the difference between sounds made with instruments; to use a wide *vocabulary* to talk about the sounds instruments make.

(Continued)

Table 1.3   (Continued)

Letters and Sounds: Phase 1 components and main purpose

Aspect 3 – Body percussion

To develop awareness of sounds and rhythms; to distinguish between sounds and to remember *patterns of sound*; to *talk* about sounds we make with our bodies and what the sounds mean.

Aspect 4 – Rhythm and rhyme

To experience and appreciate *rhythm and rhyme* and to develop awareness of rhythm and rhyme in speech; to increase awareness of words that rhyme and to develop knowledge about rhyme; to talk about words that rhyme and to produce rhyming words.

Aspect 5 – Alliteration

To develop understanding of *alliteration*; to listen to sounds at the *beginning of words* and hear the differences between them; to explore how different sounds are articulated, and to extend understanding of alliteration.

Aspect 6 – Voice sounds

To distinguish between the differences in vocal sounds, including *oral blending and segmenting*; to explore speech sounds; to talk about the different sounds that we can make with our voices.

Aspect 7 – Oral blending and segmenting

To develop oral blending and segmenting of sounds in words; to listen to *phonemes within words* and to remember them in the order in which they occur; to *talk* about the different phonemes that make up words.

It is interesting to note the real attempt of Mihai et al. (2015) to make sense of the progression from environmental to phoneme awareness. Table 1.4 provides a useful structure for the practitioner in recognising that there are many ways into taking crucial, early steps, although these are not seen as developmental milestones or 'distinct stages' (Mihai et al., 2015). It is the practitioner's role to assess the starting point of any child in their care and call upon a range of strategies to guide them through the Aspects and components.

Table 1.4   Phonological components (adapted from Mihai et al., 2015)

Phonological Components

Environmental sounds

Initial discussion of and introduction to sounds in the environment and the objects that make them offer a way into relating sounds and words. Additionally, children realise that sounds provide us with the language of the world that they live in.

Word awareness

Children demonstrate word awareness by isolating and identifying individual words that are spoken (Lane et al., 2002). Children also develop an awareness that some words are made up of two smaller words, as is the case with compound words (thunderstorm, football, moonlight). They listen for the separate words that have been joined together and identify what a word would sound like when one section is removed ('moon' 'light').

Phonological Components

Syllable awareness

Syllables refer to the sound segments within a word. The ability to discriminate syllables signals that a child is gaining an awareness of smaller units of speech sounds and this will assist with early decoding.

Rhyme awareness

Developing rhyme awareness refers to the ability to hear that some sounds have the same ending sound (e.g. light and tight).

Onset-rime awareness

Onset-rime awareness refers to separating one-syllable words into two parts: their onset or beginning sound, and their rime or ending.

Phoneme awareness

A phoneme is the smallest unit of sound in a language. Phonemic awareness is developed when children are taught the sounds associated with letters and combinations of letters.

STOP AND REFLECT

Read the information in the two tables again carefully.

- What are the similarities and differences between these two models of describing phonological awareness?
- What are the key differences?
- How might these translate to practical strategies for you to encourage children's early reading development?

Central and 'critical to the success' (DfES, 2007) of these approaches is the provision of opportunities for and the modelling of speaking and listening within a play-centred, language-rich environment. These encourage children to:

1. Listen attentively
2. Enlarge their vocabulary
3. Speak confidently to adults and other children
4. Discriminate phonemes
5. Reproduce audibly the phonemes they hear, in order, all through the word
6. Use sound-talk to segment words into phonemes

(*Letters and Sounds*, DfES, 2007)

Both Tables 1.3 and 1.4 highlight different aspects of developing phonological awareness. The Phase 1 model in *Letters and Sounds* is not one of progression. Children are not expected to move through the Aspects but rather to experience them flexibly. Practitioners should continue using them even when children begin formal systematic synthetic phonics instruction. Mihai et al.'s (2015) framework proposes increasingly complex ways into identifying and manipulating speech sounds when moving from larger to smaller speech sounds. Being aware of where children are within this structure provides a clearer understanding of the kinds of progress a child might make and can better support practitioners in their planning and pedagogy.

Modelling and teaching reading in the Early Years

Supporting the emergent reader to see pleasure and purpose in reading should be integral throughout the Early Years. To do so requires a daily reading programme (Whitehead, 2010). 'Programme' and 'pleasure' may seem oxymoronic, but this refers to the need for frequent, regular reading activities. These are modelled and discussed in a print-rich environment where children can explore texts in their own time, too. Shared and guided reading, storytime and booktalk all provide opportunities for the teaching and pupil application of 'specific skills strategies and knowledge' (Graham and Kelly, 2008), but it is important that, central to a teacher's pedagogy, is Meek's philosophy on the teaching of reading, paraphrased here by Goouch and Lambirth:

> It is not teachers alone or programmes that make a difference but the human connection between reader and text and teacher that consistently provides the reading lesson.

> (Goouch and Lambirth, 2011)

There will be children who enter the Early Years having had limited access to books and who will not see reading as an enjoyable and worthwhile activity. For this reason, modelling why so many of us choose to read is as important as developing the acquisition of emergent reading skills. This 'human connection' should remain central whenever a teacher is sharing stories, songs or rhymes with children. Talking together about the stories you encounter, together, builds long-lasting relationships between a child and a text, a child and their teacher and a child and their peers: they must see reading as something *worth* doing and that reading, with carefully selected texts, can be a way of understanding the world and their place in it (this is explored further in Chapters 9 and 10).

For this to happen, the teacher must ideally be a reader themselves with a broad knowledge of high-quality texts which go beyond the acquisition of word-reading skills and prioritise stories which develop empathy and understanding. Adults working in the Early Years set the template for a child's vision of what schooling looks like: it needs a practitioner who promotes positive attitudes to reading and celebrates it as a form of pleasure.

Conclusion

During the early years of reading, finding the balance between instruction and play is important. We need to acknowledge that both the psychological and physical environment have an impact on a child's emerging literacy skills. A pedagogy predicated upon a talk-rich community in which children share their ideas, opinions, observations and knowledge when encountering print in all forms is beneficial for all. There must be time each day for the teacher to model and foster emerging reading skills within pleasurable, interesting and meaningful contexts. Similarly, there must be time for the young reader to enjoy and explore print independently.

Time is always precious in the school setting but a 'quick win' reading culture (Goouch and Lambirth, 2011), in which children are charged through daily phonics instruction alone, will help no one and potentially damage children's attitudes to reading. As teachers, it is important to constantly bear in mind that children progress at different rates and that a successful reading classroom is one that takes into account each child's route, ability and attitude to reading.

IN SUMMARY

- Emergent reading refers to a child's initial steps into recognising and engaging meaningfully with the world of print. For many children this will start before they begin any formal education.
- Aspects of emergent/early reading include: developing a knowledge of the purpose of and pleasure in reading; gaining alphabetic knowledge, building phonological and phonemic awareness; developing a broad and rich vocabulary; considering concepts about print and how books work; and constructing semantic knowledge.
- Early Years settings can do much to support emergent readers before they begin the formal processes of learning to read. At this stage, building a positive attitude to reading is as important as developing the acquisition of emergent/early reading skills.
- Approaches to developing reading in young children in the EYFS should include teacher-led approaches (such as shared reading, reading aloud and guided reading), child-led approaches (such as independent and paired reading) and environmental factors, such as building a rich reading environment.

FURTHER READING

- *Teaching Language and Literacy in the Early Years* by Diane Godwin and Margaret Perkins is a nice introduction to the Early Years curriculum and still current. It brings together both theory and practice and offers guidance on planning.

- Ann Browne's book *Developing Language and Literacy 3–8* is an excellent introduction to early literacy in the classroom. The book is accessible and bridges that divide between the Early Years and primary.
- *Literacy in the Early Years: Reflections on International Research and Practice* edited by Claire McLachlan and Alison Arrow is an excellent series of research-based articles on early childhood literacy and the challenges that come with early literacy acquisition. Each article provides a clear and engaging insight into effective literacy practice within the Early Years setting.

REFERENCES

Barker, R. (2011) *Report of the Inquiry into Overcoming the Barriers to Literacy. All Party Parliamentary Group (APPG) for Education.* British Educational Suppliers Association (BESA). Available at: www.educationengland.org.uk/documents/pdfs/2011-appge-literacy-report.pdf

Browne, A. (2012) *Developing Language and Literacy 3–8* (3rd ed.). London: Sage.

Buckingham, J., Beaman, R. and Wheldall, K. (2013) Why poor children are more likely to become poor readers: The early years. *Educational Review*, 66(4): 428–46. doi: 10.1080/00131911.2013.795129.

Bus, A.G., Van Ijzendoorn, M.H. and Pellegrini, A.D. (1995) Joint book reading makes for success in learning to read: A meta-analysis on intergenerational transmission of literacy. *Review of Educational Research*, 65(1): 1–21.

Clay, M.M. (1985) *The Early Detection of Reading Difficulties* (3rd ed.). Auckland, New Zealand: Heinemann.

Court, J. (Ed.) (2017) *Reading by Right: Successful strategies to ensure every child can read to succeed.* London: Facet Publishing.

Department for Education (DfE) (2017) *Statutory Framework for the Early Years Foundation Stage: Setting the standards for learning, development and care for children from birth to five.* London: DfE.

Department for Education and Skills (DfES) (2007) *Letters and Sounds: Principles and practice of high quality phonics, Primary National Strategy.* [online] gov.uk. Available at: www.gov.uk/government/uploads/system/uploads/attachment_data/file/190599/Letters_and_Sounds_-_DFES-00281-2007.pdf

Dobbs-Oates, J., Pentimonti, J., Justice, L. and Kaderavek, J. (2015) Parent and child attitudinal factors in a model of children's print-concept knowledge. *Journal of Research in Reading*, 38(1): 91–108.

Frith, U. (1985) Beneath the surface of developmental dyslexia. In K. Patterson, J. Marshall and M. Coltheart (Eds), *Surface Dyslexia: Neuropsychological and cognitive studies of phonological reading* (pp. 301–30). London: Erlbaum.

Gee, J.P. (2004) *Situated Language and Learning: A critique of traditional learning*. London: Routledge.

Godwin, D. and Perkins, M. (2002) *Teaching Language and Literacy in the Early Years*. London: David Fulton.

Goldstein, H. (2011) Knowing what to teach provides a roadmap for early literacy intervention. *Journal of Early Intervention*, 33: 268–80.

Goodman, Y.M. (1986) Children coming to know literacy. In W.H. Teale and E. Sulzby (Eds), *Emergent Literacy* (pp. 1–14). Norwood, NJ: Ablex.

Goouch, K. and Lambirth, A. (2011) *Teaching Early Reading and Phonics: Creative approaches to early literacy*. Thousand Oaks, CA: Sage.

Gopnik, A., Meltzoff, A.N. and Kuhl, P.K. (1999) *The Scientist in the Crib: Minds, brains, and how children learn*. New York: Morrow.

Graham, J. and Kelly, A. (2008) *Reading Under Control*. London: David Fulton.

Hume, L.E., Lonigan, C.J. and McQueen, J.D. (2015) Children's literacy interest and its relation to parents' literacy-promoting practices. *Journal of Research in Reading*, 38(2): 172–93.

Lane, H.B., Pullen, P.C., Eisele, M.R. and Jordan, L. (2002) Preventing reading failure: Phonological awareness assessment and instruction. *Preventing School Failure*, 46: 101–10.

Langston, A. (2014) *Facilitating Children's Learning in the EYFS*. Maidenhead: Open University Press.

Leech, K.A. and Rowe, M.L. (2014) A comparison of preschool children's discussions with parents during picture book and chapter book reading. *First Language*, 34(3): 205–26. Available at: https://doi.org/10.1177/0142723714534220

Lonigan, C., Burgess, S. and Anthony, J. (2000) Development of emergent literacy and early reading skills in preschool children: Evidence from a latent-variable longitudinal study. *Developmental Psychology*, 36: 596–613.

Manz, P.H., Hughes, C., Barnabas, E., Bracaliello, C. and Ginsburg-Block, M. (2010) A descriptive review and meta-analysis of family-based emergent literacy interventions: To what extent is the research applicable to low-income, ethnic-minority or linguistically-diverse young children? *Early Childhood Research Quarterly*, 25(4): 409–31.

McLachlan, C. and Arrow, A. (Eds) (2017) *Literacy in the Early Years: Reflections on International Research and Practice*. Singapore: Springer.

Mihai, A., Friesen, A., Butera, G., Horn, E., Lieber, J. and Palmer, S. (2015) Teaching phonological awareness to all children through storybook reading. *Young Exceptional Children*, 18(4): 3–18.

Pendergast, D. and Garvis, S. (2013) *Teaching Early Years: Curriculum, pedagogy and assessment*. Crows Nest, NSW: Allen & Unwin.

Phillips, B.M., Clancy-Menchetti, J. and Lonigan, C.J. (2008) Successful phonological awareness instruction with preschool children: Lessons from the classroom. *Topics in Early Childhood Special Education*, 37: 284–97.

Reese, E., Suggate, S., Long, J. and Schaughency, E. (2010) Children's oral narrative and reading skills in the first 3 years of reading instruction. *Reading and Writing: An Interdisciplinary Journal*, 23: 627–44. doi:10.1007/s11145-009-9175-9.

Sawyer, B.E., Justice, L.M., Guo, Y., Logan, J.A., Petrill, S.A., Glenn-Applegate, K., Kaderavek, J.N. and Pentimonti, J.M. (2014) Relations among home literacy environment, child characteristics and print knowledge for preschool children with language impairment. *Journal of Research in Reading*, 37: 65–83. doi:10.1111/jrir.12008.

Stanovich, K. E. (1986) Matthew effects in reading: Some consequences of individual differences in the acquisition of literacy. *Reading Research Quarterly*, 21: 360–407.

Walberg, H.J. and Tsai, S.-L. (1983) Matthew effects in education. *American Educational Research Journal*, 20(3): 359–73.

Whitehead, M. (2010) *Language and Literacy in the Early Years 0–7* (4th ed.). London: Sage.

2

READING IN THE EARLY YEARS: PRACTICE

THIS CHAPTER WILL

- Consider practical approaches for teaching reading in Early Years settings

- Illustrate different principles from research and theory, making links to the classroom

- Explore the use of adult-initiated activities, child-initiated activities and the wider environment as vehicles to develop children's early reading

Introduction

The first steps children take to becoming readers happen long before they join school. It is the home environment and early childcare provision that will lay the foundations of future literacy. The more secure these foundations, the easier children are likely to find it to develop into keen and competent readers (Fisher, 2002). When each child joins formal education, whether in a Nursery or Reception class, or once statutory schooling begins, the range of experiences they have had will differ, as will their confidence and attitude to reading.

Chapter 1 was concerned with exploring the theories around emergent reading. This chapter builds on this, suggesting practical ways that young readers can be supported; starting from their previous experiences and interests. While the Early Years Foundation Stage (EYFS) in

England sets the standards and expectations for the period from birth to the end of the year in which a child is five, this chapter is primarily concerned with practical approaches in a school setting, in Nursery and Reception classes, as well as how links can be made with the home environment. As with the partner chapter on the theory of early reading, this chapter benefits from being read alongside Chapters 7 and 8, which are concerned with theory and practice around the Simple View of Reading.

Early reading in practice: Opportunities for developing emergent reading

This section considers six practical classroom opportunities for developing emergent reading skills and behaviours, outlining why they are important and illustrating each with examples drawn from practice:

1. Songs and rhymes
2. Reading aloud
3. Shared reading
4. Guided reading
5. Paired and independent reading
6. The wider reading environment

The importance of songs and rhyme

Phonological awareness is a blanket term that refers to the ability to hear, respond to and manipulate structures in sound. The broadness of the term is mirrored by the seven aspects of *Letters and Sounds* Phase 1 (DfES, 2007) and Mihai et al.'s model (2015). Phonemic awareness focuses on individual sounds (phonemes) in words and is best modelled in Aspect 7 of *Letters and Sounds* Phase 1, although there are opportunities to focus on individual phonemes in spoken and written words in the other Aspects. The transition from phonological to phonemic can be a challenge for some children and the continuation of these Phase 1 speaking and listening activities throughout the Early Years is imperative.

Knowledge of nursery rhymes, the enjoyment of identifying and playing with rhythm and rhyme and alliteration, and listening to and talking about familiar patterns of sound in the words they hear and see are crucial in developing a child's phonological awareness (Harrison, 2004; Langston, 2014). Building up a bank of songs, rhymes and poetry with the children is key (Browne, 2007). These areas have been shown to level the literacy field of the emergent reader (Bryant and Bradley, 1985; Bryant et al., 1989; Goswami, 1990).

Planning for the playful exploration of songs, rhymes and poems offers opportunities to recognise alliterative forms, broaden vocabulary and identify patterns in language (Graham and Kelly, 2008; Whitehead, 2010). Through engaging and meaningful contexts, teachers can provide opportunities for children to appreciate the interconnectedness of sounds, patterns in language and, eventually, print. *Letters and Sounds* refers to the 'overlapping' nature of the Phase 1 Aspects (DFES, 2007). If teachers are to provide emergent readers with the best start, then a similar overlapping approach should be taken with poetry (including nursery rhymes), rhyme and song. This goes a long way to ensuring that it is a constant presence in the daily routine of teaching and prevalent throughout all aspects.

STOP AND REFLECT

Revisit the seven Aspects of Letters and Sounds Phase 1:

- Environmental sounds
- Instrumental sounds
- Body percussion
- Rhythm and rhyme
- Alliteration
- Voice sounds
- Oral blending and segmenting

Where could songs, poems and nursery rhymes work well for helping children to develop these areas?

Can you think of nursery rhymes or songs with:

- clear rhyming patterns?
- notable alliteration?
- opportunities for body percussion such as clapping and clicking?

Reading aloud

There is substantial evidence to suggest an association between academic success and access to a rich range of language when a child is read aloud to (Wells, 1987; Godwin and Perkins, 2002; Langston, 2014; Merga and Ledger, 2019). Telling or reading a story to a class is a pleasurable experience for everyone involved and is something that some children may not have experienced before. It introduces them to the language of the written word and how its conventions can differ from the spoken (Langston, 2014). Sharing a variety of text types this way can show children, for example, how the style, tone and language of a postcard differs from the repeating structure of a cumulative picturebook or poem. Although these would not be explored in the same depth as with older children, introducing children in the EYFS to text types that are part of their everyday lives helps to bring a sense of purpose and meaning to the activity. In addition, high-quality texts can broaden their vocabulary and their early concepts of syntax and grammar.

Inviting children to listen to and enjoy a story, poem or an information text is a valuable activity in itself. While being a pleasurable, shared experience, it also provides several opportunities in which to support children's emergent reading skills. Through reading aloud, the teacher is a model for reading fluency, providing expression and intonation where appropriate and leaving children to focus on listening and looking (at the pictures).

STOP AND REFLECT

In *Exploring Children's Literature* (2019), Gamble suggests several ways to prepare for successful reading aloud:

- Think carefully about how you will introduce and recap each reading session to pique children's interest.
- Decide how the children will be seated.
- Think about the different characters in the book and the range of appropriate voices that could bring them to life.
- Set aside regular time for reading aloud to your class. Think about where this is best placed, so it doesn't get squeezed out due to time pressures.
- Maintain a balance between stopping reflection and keeping the story moving. Too many questions will disrupt the flow; pausing for an occasional question can build suspense.

What do you think are the merits of each of these bullet points and what skills might you need to develop to support this framework?

Although a more specific focus on the emergent reader's skills will be explored in greater depth during shared and guided reading, being read to aloud invites children to relate the spoken word with the written. Hearing the patterns and shape of language encourages them to join in with repeated phrases and instils in them the confidence to become an active member of this communal experience.

Repeated readings of the same book will support children to become familiar with the structure and entices them to join in with the rest of the class. In turn, this growing confidence and familiarity with the story and its structure can encourage readers to retell the story in their own words at a later stage and play with the language of the text; especially if copies of the book are made available (Perkins, 2015).

CASE STUDY 2.1

In a nursery setting catering for children aged 3–5, the nursery manager builds in three opportunities for listening to a story each day – in the morning, before children enjoy some fruit, straight after lunch before afternoon activities, and at the end of the day, once the room has been tidied up. The setting seeks to create and relate 'a sense of special' with story time, so they try different approaches including:

- **Children's choice:** the children are invited to suggest their favourite books to read – either books from the book corner or books from home.
- **A very special book:** much emphasis is given to the fact that the book is going to be exceptional (often one of the adult's 'favourite books' or 'a special book they've brought in from home').
- **Re-reading:** The adults will often return to old favourites or share different books in a series featuring the same characters. They might read the same book each day for several days, or come back to it after a longer break (much to the children's delight).
- **The big reveal:** the book will be delivered to the adult in an envelope or in a package and it is opened by one of the children (with a sense of excitement mounting all the time...).
- **Lights off:** Occasionally the lights in the hall/classroom are turned off and the book is read by torchlight (with one child invited up to shine the torch on the pages of the book). This is especially successful with books set at night or in a dark place, such as *Owl Babies* by Martin Waddell and Patrick Benson or *The Deep Dark Wood* by Algy Craig Hall and Ali Pye.

Where possible, follow-up activities linked to the book are provided, so children might have paint laid out to try their own dot paintings after listening to *The Dot* by Peter H Reynolds or the chance to create animals from playdough after *You Can't Take an Elephant on the Bus* by Patricia Cleveland-Peck and David Tazzyman.

While the activities and approaches to create a sense of excitement are a key part of helping children to be interested in books, ultimately, success depends on the adults in the setting having a strong and up-to-date knowledge of children's books and the diverse readership in their classroom. The importance of this is addressed further in Chapters 9 and 10.

Shared reading

Shared reading is a teacher-led activity that involves the whole class exploring a text which may be a large, physical copy, or a smaller copy presented on a visualiser or uploaded to a large screen so that both pictures and print are accessible to all. This way, the teacher can point out details in pictures as well as phrases, words and letters. These short, daily sessions will provide opportunities to practise early language and emergent reader skills (see Table 1.3) and prepare children for more formal instruction. It is hoped that from this collaborative adult-led experience, children will then practise and apply the same skills with peers and independently (Graham and Kelly, 2008).

During these short sessions, the teacher will focus on:

- concepts of print, including directionality, placement and purpose
- comprehension with regards to assessing understanding of what they hear and see within the text and using their knowledge of the world to make predictions and deductions
- extending the breadth and depth of their vocabulary through introducing new words in the print (Christ et al., 2014) or naming objects, concepts and ideas carried through the images
- phonological and phonemic awareness

These elements should be planned through meaningful contexts and a range of text types, some of which will lend themselves better to emergent reader skills than others. Choosing the right book for the right task is important and exploring early phonics alongside concepts of print will support readers to see meaning and purpose in the skills that they are learning (McLachlan and Arrow, 2017).

Although the focus will be on the teacher modelling the use of these early reading skills, there should be planned opportunities to 'challenge, scaffold and extend the children's skills' (Pianta, 2003). Purposeful discussions in which all are encouraged to take part should be regarded as a safe, enjoyable space for children to actively ask questions and share their own thoughts with the teacher and peers. Even those who are just listening carefully will find their vocabulary improved (Brannon and Dauksas, 2014): this is especially true for EAL children and those with limited reading experience (Graham and Kelly, 2008). Through peer support and modelling, this collaborative, social approach to learning can encourage risk taking in order to further extend their skill as a reader (Neaum, 2012; McLachlan and Arrow, 2017).

Multiple re-readings of the book during the week will provide the time and confidence to involve more children in the shared reading experience. While exploring early reading skills with high-quality texts, it is worth remembering that such skill-building exercises should still model the reading process as both interesting and pleasurable: a didactic, laborious approach could not only turn engaged readers off the process but also disengage those who have yet to find pleasure in it (Cremin et al., 2015).

CASE STUDY 2.2

In one Reception class, the teacher used *Christopher Nibble* by Charlotte Middleton for a shared reading session.

Over the course of the 20 minutes, the children had the opportunity to:

- **Explore early concepts of print:** Before reading, the teacher focused on the purpose of the front and back covers. She pointed to individual words when reading the cover, in order to reinforce for children the direction of the print ('Christopher Nibble in a tale of dandelion derring-do!').

- **Practise decoding of the text:** The teacher used key words from the book for children to practise their decoding as they read. The children joined in with words like *munch* and *puff* embedded in the illustrations. This was picked up in greater depth during whole-class phonics teaching and guided reading sessions.
- **Predict what might happen next:** The children were keen to make suggestions as to how Christopher would solve the dandelion shortage, suggesting buying some from the shops, eating other things, growing them and even stealing them from the neighbouring town!
- **Introduce unfamiliar words:** the children talked about the word 'tiniest', thinking about what it meant and why the author might have used that word rather than 'smallest'. The children also learnt what a cloche was, matching the word to the illustration and thinking about what it was used for in the story.

After reading, the book was left out for children to read independently or take home to share with their parents.

Small group guided reading

While the same principles as shared reading apply, guided reading focuses on a small group of four to six children who display the same progress or needs in reading (Goouch and Lambirth, 2011). These sessions run alongside all other forms of reading engagement offering a more focused exploration of emergent reading skills (if the group is ready). The teacher is there to listen and guide, supporting them to decode texts on their own. Working in smaller groups on a text also supports children in taking those initial steps towards independent reading, focusing on the skills needed to read and enjoy books on their own.

Speaking and listening is central to these sessions (Graham and Kelly, 2008), providing the scaffold for focused and structured discussion around understanding how the text works, and ensuring that there are no misunderstandings of content in relation to comprehension or phonological awareness. Within the short session, both the group and teacher have their own copy of the text in order to build up that sense of independent exploration while allowing the group to practise emergent reading skills. Whether this relates to print awareness, comprehension, the modelling of phonic strategies or any other reading skill will be dependent on a teacher's understanding of where each child is in relation to their reading progress. Because children learn and progress at different rates (DfE, 2017), guided reading groups can frequently change, as can the amount of time that adults spend with each group. Teachers need to be sensitive to the fact that some children will have greater stamina and interest than others, thereby ensuring that learning to read in the Early Years remains a fun, engaging experience.

CASE STUDY 2.3

After reviewing their curriculum, one school decided that while the guided reading session with the teacher was valuable, finding meaningful independent activities for the rest of the children presented a challenge.

It's the summer term in the two parallel Reception classes and guided reading is running three times a week for around thirty minutes. Children are divided into six groups of between four and eight children, and adults (teachers, teaching assistants, teaching students and reading volunteers) move from their other roles in the school to lead guided reading groups. The session includes time to read part of a book, with the adult listening to children to assess their fluency and any misconceptions they might have. There is then a discussion around the book, before the groups undertake an activity based on what they have read.

In addition to hearing children read and discussing the meaning of the text, within the teaching sessions adults have the chance to:

- emphasise emergent reader skills with a growing focus on the phonological and phonemic. For those children who have progressed further in either field, they can adapt their expectations accordingly
- guide children towards the concept that illustrations usually provide additional or conflicting information compared to the print
- point out language features such as capital letters, full stops and other forms of common punctuation, which can support children in building up concepts of grammar and how written sentences may sound different from spoken ones (DfE, 2020)
- find opportunities for assessing children's letter knowledge, both alphabetic and phonological. Correcting errors and repeating letter names can significantly support children's concept of print
- present questions to the group which encourage peer-to-peer interaction. These moments ask children to expand, extend and clarify their thinking

This approach depends on having enough well-trained and skilful adults involved in the teaching of reading. In addition to the organisational demands, significant energy has to be invested in training all adults taking part to teach reading well.

Paired and independent reading

In a study exploring peer-buddy reading behaviours in the preschool setting, Christ et al. (2014) showed that paired reading has a positive impact on the social engagement with texts and an improvement in 'several aspects of comprehension'. Browne, in reference to the work of Jerome Bruner, suggests that paired work and play provide an environment for more productive and sustained conversations in which ideas and concepts are shared and built on together (Browne, 2007).

Independent reading can often take place during times of transition or be available for children at any time during the day. These moments are important to the emerging reader since it could mean, for some readers, those initial steps into taking ownership over their own reading journey and for those used to exploring books at home, a moment of pleasure. Adults should still be there to guide and share books for the child to explore. During these times, it does not matter if the children cannot read all the words; the interaction and play is what is important, especially if it encourages children to want to take any books home. For children who speak English as an additional language, there are some books that come with multi-language CDs, such as *Lulu Loves Stories* and *Lulu Loves the Library* published by Alanna Max, which could be played in their home language.

CASE STUDY 2.4

One teacher, after finishing a read-aloud, made sure that multiple copies of the book were available for children to explore and share in their own time. When possible, she would also provide props to allow them to play and retell the story.

With some books, poems or nursery rhymes, she would provide a pack of small-world items (e.g. farm animals, vehicles, people) to give the opportunity for retelling and exploring.

She also found that laminated cut-outs of scenes and characters from books, or masks and dressing-up clothes in the role-play area allowed children to act out and retell these stories together, inside or outside, or on their own while exploring the language of the author. Her next step is to set up a system where these can be signed in and out for use in the home too.

The Early Years reading environment

The teaching of reading skills through shared and guided reading sessions should run alongside (and within) a socially active, print-rich reading environment. The teacher's role here is not only to ensure access to print but to create reading-rich opportunities in which children can talk, explore, play (Whitehead, 2010) and 'co-construct and communicate meaning' (Larson and Marsh, 2005) together. Frequent encounters with print in all its forms, especially within an interpersonal setting where children are encouraged to explore together, is beneficial to all, but especially for those from backgrounds in which such experiences and spaces are missing (Buckingham et al., 2013: 431).

When planning the Early Years literacy environment, it is helpful to consider two areas: *physical* and *psychological*. The former refers to quality, display of and access to materials, and the latter to opportunities for interaction and support (Guo et al., 2012). The relationship between both aspects is important; children need to see books and print as something more than 'the reading corner'. Print should also be seen as useful, relevant and purposeful to their daily lives both in and out of the classroom (Browne, 2007; Pendergast and Garvis, 2013). The physical environment should provide access to print in its various formats, including:

- alphabet charts
- picturebooks
- illustrated texts
- pop-up books
- lift-the-flap books
- touchy-feely books
- annuals
- comics
- magazines
- dual-language texts
- digital texts
- poetry books

These should sit comfortably alongside menus, brochures, signs and labels, as well as examples of adults' and children's writing. From a psychological perspective, planned activities, whether teacher led or child initiated, should take into account dialogic opportunities (either peer-to-peer or adult-to-child) in which children are encouraged to explore and retell stories that they know or have heard read to them in order to 'consolidate their understanding' (Browne, 2007).

Although books should be available around the classroom, serving different purposes, a centralised reading area, which is comfortable and exciting, would help associate pleasure and enjoyment with books (Browne, 2007). Displays of 'class favourites' (Goouch and Lambirth, 2011) should be regularly updated with the children able to see the covers and pick them up. These can include multiple copies of the shared text that has been explored during the week or the class storytime or even songs and poems that the children have enjoyed.

With regard to both the physical and psychological elements, it is important that teachers consider what reading material interests the children in their class. When considering books for reading instruction and reading for pleasure, a teacher must provide a selection which will hook children into reading and take into account different cultures and backgrounds, reflecting 'all those who live in the classroom space' (Goouch and Lambirth, 2011) and those of others. It is important that children from all backgrounds, cultures, and ethnic groups can see themselves reflected within the pages of a book. 'Connections to their own lives and experiences' (Whitehead, 2010) may encourage children to spend more time sharing, exploring and playing with books and, in turn, improve their chances of literacy achievement (Guo et al., 2012). The importance of diversity is further explored in Chapter 10.

STOP AND REFLECT

Spend some time auditing the books available to the children in your classroom.

- Are they a true reflection of the ethnic representation of the school and locality and of the country itself?
- Are different family structures represented in the books?
- Do the books available promote positive images of race, cultures, ages, physicality and genders?

Once you have audited the books available, think about how you could address any gaps. There is a good selection of picturebooks featuring characters from BAME backgrounds suitable for the Early Years available from The LetterBox Library. The Booktrust also has excellent themed booklists (search for both online). You might also consult with your local school library service, if you still have one in your area.

It is easier for children to find their lives and experiences reflected in picturebooks which tend to make up the majority of books available in the Early Years. They offer emergent readers a way into reading which would not be accessible through print alone and encourage children to look closely and spend time exploring. Picturebooks are as complex and subtle as they are accessible and engaging. They may have rhyming sequences or repeating refrains which encourage children to join in, thereby improving both confidence and ability (Browne, 2007).

STOP AND REFLECT

Look at the suggestions for creating a rich reading environment below.

- Which might be useful in your setting?
- Would any need adapting to meet the needs of your children or the pedagogical choices you would make?

Physical: Access to print and books

Aside from adults using books for instruction and sharing books for pleasure, ensuring that children have access to books to browse and look at independently is an important part of helping children to develop early reading behaviours. Reading and print interaction goes beyond books, however. Making sure that informative print is available to read and interact with at the same eye-level as the children helps them to notice both the text and its purpose.

The outdoor area can also be a place for echoing the environmental print that children encounter everyday outside the setting. Road signs, shop signs and symbols show that print comes in different formats and serves different, meaningful purposes. Having instructions available in areas in which play is promoted can provide authentic and meaningful reading opportunities (Perkins, 2015). A list of instructions in the garage outside, a shopping list or a set of simple guidelines on how to create a rocket in the small-world play area can help relate reading to real-life experiences.

Alphabet charts, not only in English, but in languages that reflect the different backgrounds of all children in the school, can be useful for prompting thought and discussion. Children can be encouraged to make their own alphabet charts too and these can be placed on display at their own height level. Wordbanks related to the topic and magnetic letters in which children can play with copying words that interest them or key words related to topic/text work can also be useful resources (and often a good link to play at home). Ideally, thematic books, alongside labels and key vocabulary, should be accessible throughout the classroom. They could be on display in the role-play area or available near the science table or small-world area. Slightly damaged books could be placed in a family box which could go out at the end of each term for parents to take home and keep. For those children not able to access the words on the page, having an audio version alongside the print one can be useful.

STOP AND REFLECT

Visit an EYFS setting or classroom, either your own or one that you know well. Record the text and books that are on display and then consider the following questions:

- Is text displayed at a child's eye height?
- Is an appropriate range of languages and alphabets on display?
- Is the outside area text-rich?
- Do children have access to a high-quality, up-to-date section of books to enjoy independently?
- Do the children have the opportunity to read in the role-play areas?
- Do the adults have a comfortable place in which to share books with children?

Conclusion

Preparing children to learn to read and supporting them to build positive attitudes towards reading and books is an important aspect of any EYFS setting. Sharing and talking about books supports almost every area of the curriculum, teaching children new things and introducing them to places, people and ideas far beyond their sphere of experience. It is also one of the most joyful things that can happen in an education setting. Chapters 1 and 2 have focused on children's reading development in the Early Years. Chapters 3 and 4 will consider the other side of the coin: the development of early writing. As Allyn has famously noted, 'Reading is like breathing in and writing is like breathing out' (2012).

IN SUMMARY

- The home environment and any early childcare provision are likely to form the foundation of children's attitudes and early dispositions to reading. Thoughtful provision in the EYFS, whether a Nursery setting or a Reception class, is vital in building on those steps.
- In an EYFS setting, effective provision for early reading might rely on several interlinked strands, including: the use of songs and rhymes, reading aloud, shared reading and guided reading, paired and independent reading, and the effective use of the wider reading environment.

FURTHER READING

- Both the *Reading and Writing Scales* provided freely by the CLPE are available on their website for download (search online). Built upon a huge catalogue of research, the scales 'describe the journeys that children make in order to become literate'. They offer both practical advice within the classroom while also supporting you recognising each child's reading and writing progress. Essential.
- Mary Roche's *Developing Children's Critical Thinking through Picturebooks* is an excellent investigation based on rigorous research and classroom practice on how practitioners can enable children to become critical thinkers through the use of picturebooks. An insightful and engaging read that opens up a truly dialogic reading community in the classroom that will benefit all children.
- Set within the Foundation Stage, Ann Browne's comprehensive guide *Teaching and Learning Communication, Language and Literacy* provides plenty of practical advice in supporting practitioners in creating an engaging and supportive learning environment. It not only explores how young children develop as learners in their own right but also how best to provide meaningful contexts for play-based learning.

REFERENCES

Allyn, P. (2012) Voices and Choices: The Secrets to Summer Reading and Writing Success. *HuffPost*, posted 26/07/2012.

Brannon, D. and Dauksas, L. (2014) The effectiveness of dialogic reading in increasing English language learning preschool children's expressive language. *International Research in Early Childhood Education*, 5(1): 1–10.

Browne, A. (2007) *Teaching and Learning Communication, Language and Literacy*. London: Sage.

Bryant, P.E. and Bradley, L. (1985) *Children's Reading Problems*. Oxford: Blackwell.

Bryant, P.E., Bradley, L., MacLean, M. and Crossland, J. (1989) Nursery rhymes, phonological skills and reading. *Journal of Child Language*, 16: 407–28.

Buckingham, J., Beaman R. and Wheldall, K. (2013) Why poor children are more likely to become poor readers: The early years. *Educational Review*, 66(4): 428–46. doi: 10.1080/00131911.2013.795129.

Christ, T., Ming Chiu, M. and Wang, X.C. (2014) Preschoolers' engagement with reading behaviours: A statistical discourse analysis of peer buddy-reading interactions. *Journal of Research in Reading*, 37: 375–408.

Cremin, T., Reedy, D., Bearne, E. and Dombey, H. (2015) *Teaching English Creatively* (2nd ed.). Abingdon: Routledge.

Department for Education (DfE) (2017) *Statutory Framework for the Early Years Foundation Stage.* Available at: www.gov.uk/government/publications/early-years-foundation-stage-framework--2

Department for Education (DfE) (2020) *Development Matters: Non-Statutory Curriculum Guidance for Early Years Foundation Stage.* London: DfE.

Department for Education and Skills (DfES) (2007) *Letters and Sounds: Principles and practice of high quality phonics, Primary National Strategy.* [online] gov.uk. Available at: www.gov.uk/government/uploads/system/uploads/attachment_data/file/190599/Letters_and_Sounds_-_DFES-00281-2007.pdf

Fisher, J. (2002) *The Foundations of Learning.* Milton Keynes: Open University Press.

Gamble, N. (2019) *Exploring Children's Literature.* London: Sage.

Godwin, D. and Perkins, M. (2002) *Teaching Language and Literacy in the Early Years* (2nd ed.). London: David Fulton.

Goouch, K. and Lambirth, A. (2011) *Teaching Early Reading and Phonics: Creative approaches to early literacy.* Thousand Oaks, CA: Sage.

Goswami, U. (1990) A special link between rhyming skill and the use of orthographic analogies by beginning readers. *Journal of Child Psychology and Psychiatry and Allied Disciplines*, 31: 301–11.

Graham, J. and Kelly, A. (2008) *Reading Under Control.* London: David Fulton.

Guo, Y., Justice, L.M., Kaderavek, J.N. and McGinty, A. (2012) The literacy environment of preschool classrooms: Contributions to children's emergent literacy growth. *Journal of Research in Reading*, 35(3): 308–27.

Harrison, C. (2004) *Understanding Reading Development.* London: Sage.

Langston, A. (2014) *Facilitating Children's Learning in the EYFS.* Maidenhead: Open University Press.

Larson, J. and Marsh, J. (2005) *Making Literacy Real: Theories and practices for learning and teaching.* London: Sage.

McLachlan, C. and Arrow, A. (Eds) (2017) *Literacy in the Early Years: Reflections on International Research and Practice*. Singapore: Springer

Merga, M. K. and Ledger, S. (2019) Teachers' attitudes toward and frequency of engagement in reading aloud in the Primary classroom, *Literacy*, 53(3): 134–142. doi: 10.1111/lit.12162.

Mihai, A., Friesen, A., Butera, G., Horn, E., Lieber, J. and Palmer, S. (2015) Teaching phonological awareness to all children through storybook reading. *Young Exceptional Children*, 18(4): 3–18.

Neaum, S. (2012) *Language and Literacy for the Early Years*. Exeter: Learning Matters (Early Childhood Studies Series).

Pendergast, D. and Garvis, S. (2013) *Teaching Early Years: Curriculum, pedagogy and assessment*. Crows Nest, NSW: Allen & Unwin.

Perkins, M. (2015) *Becoming a Teacher of Reading*. London: Sage.

Pianta, R. C. (2003) *Standardized Classroom Observations from Pre-k to 3rd Grade: A mechanism for improving access to consistently high quality classroom experiences and practices during the P–3 years*. New York: Foundation for Child Development.

Wells, G. (1987) *The Meaning Makers: Children Learning Language and Using Language to Learn*. London: Hodder and Stoughton.

Whitehead, M. (2010) *Language and Literacy in the Early Years 0–7* (4th ed.). London: Sage.

LITERATURE

Owl Babies by Martin Waddell and Patrick Benson

The Deep Dark Wood by Algy Craig Hall and Ali Pye

The Dot by Peter H. Reynolds

You Can't Take an Elephant on the Bus by Patricia Cleveland-Peck and David Tazzyman

Christopher Nibble by Charlotte Middleton

Lulu Loves the Library by Anna McQuinn and Rosalind Beardshaw

Lulu Loves Stories by Anna McQuinn and Rosalind Beardshaw

3

WRITING IN THE EARLY YEARS: THEORY

THIS CHAPTER WILL

- Introduce the concept of emergent writers

- Consider the principles and a model of progression for early writing drawn from research

- Explore the theoretical underpinnings of different precursors to writing

Introduction

A child's journey to becoming a confident and competent writer begins long before they have learnt to control the many aspects that make for effective communication through writing. This chapter seeks to investigate these foundations on which fluent writing will eventually be built, exploring the precursors to learning to write and considering the key landmarks on children's journeys to literacy. This chapter benefits from being read alongside Chapter 4, which addresses practical approaches to early writing, and Chapters 11 and 12, which are concerned with the theory and practice of learning to write later in primary school.

While this chapter might be of particular interest to teachers and students who work with children in their first years of schooling, it is important that all teachers understand those initial steps children take on their way to becoming writers. As with reading, it is important to note that the Early Years Foundation Stage (EYFS) stretches from birth to age five. It is far more than the Reception year of English primary schools and this chapter reflects that age span.

An overview of the emergent writer

From reading into writing, young children develop an understanding that not only does print carry meaning but that they too have the power to capture and share their own meanings and thoughts through the written word. Writing involves not only compositional aspects such as generating ideas, sequencing thoughts and sharing them with others but transcriptional skills too, such as spelling, punctuation, grammar and handwriting (which, in turn, relies on grip and fine motor skills). For the emergent, early writer, the process can seem a complex and potentially daunting one. The role of the teacher, then, is to show children that writing is something worth doing. As observer, facilitator and guide, the teacher will need to create a classroom climate that sees purpose, pleasure and personalisation as central to the writing process.

Understanding the purpose behind writing and displaying writerly behaviour themselves is something that children will have had differing experiences of before attending school, but the transition from simple mark making to intentional writing 'typically spans from 2 or 2 1/2 years of age to a little over 5 years of age' (Casbergue and Strickland, 2016). At home, they may have seen a parent take notes while on the phone, compose a shopping list, copy out an address for a birthday card to a distant relative or jot down important events on a family calendar. It is from these moments of authorship that the young writer begins to understand that our own print carries a range of purposes and meanings and, with the right materials and guidance, may be inspired to replicate what they have seen (Neuman and Roskos, 1997; Browne, 2007; Rowe and Neitzel, 2010; Langston, 2014).

Values and beliefs around the need for and purpose of writing will differ in every home as will the range of time spent modelling and instructing writing practices (Hall and Robinson, 2003; Wyse et al., 2018). Whatever the case, all children will bring some knowledge and understanding of writing to the early years classroom (Bissex, 1984 in Browne, 2012), but stages of development, attitudes and experiences will depend on the opportunities presented, shared and modelled to them in the home (McLachlan and Arrow, 2017).

A child's name can be that first 'bridge to literacy' (Davies, 1988), in which they make the connection between reading and writing. When they see their name in different places (on a clothes label, their bedroom door, a party invitation or written on paper by a family member), they begin to understand that it is formed only through a particular sequence of letter shapes. The repetitive encounters with their name show them that the shape and order or the marks that make up their name are important and they too may begin to play with this special type of mark making. From this, they begin to associate different shapes with letters and their corresponding sounds and spot those specific letter shapes and sounds in other places too. This initial experience of authorship, in trying to write their name, is revolutionary; it shows the child that some marks that they make can carry a special meaning that can be read by themselves and others (Browne, 2007).

The principles and progression of early writing

Before entering the Early Years setting then, children will have begun to build their own understanding of what writing is as a practice and have a range of opinions with regards to its 'functions and forms' (Bradford, 2015). Although early mark making may start off as a collection of dots, lines and shapes, often, by the time they are three, children 'are able to make that distinction between their intention to write and intention to draw' (Browne, 2007). Citing Clay (1975), Browne goes on to state that when this distinction is apparent, we are then able to assess their initial perceptions of print.

Recognising the developmental stage of writing that a child is at allows us to provide the right opportunities and environment in which to observe, facilitate and guide them. In practice, we should begin with investigating what knowledge of writing a child brings with them to the classroom and where this sits developmentally. In doing so, we are better placed to plan for and provide appropriate and engaging activities and environments in which to build upon those foundations. With this in mind, an exploration of early writing development can be helpful in providing us with the relevant knowledge and understanding needed to inform provision.

Writing development and writerly behaviours

As with reading, covered in the previous chapters, research suggests that children travel through a set of broad stages as they move from initial mark making to confident and independent writing. These are summarised below in Table 3.1, which has been amended from the *First Steps* model (Department of Education, Western Australia, 2013):

Table 3.1 Developmental stages of writing: adapted from *First Steps* (2013)

Stages of Writing Development	Writerly Behaviours
Role-play writing	Mark making:
	Children initially see no difference between drawing and writing but there is some awareness that making marks upon a surface can be a form of communication (Bradford, 2015). They may have seen adults writing/mark making and try to emulate this, although they have little to no idea of what these marks mean.
	Marks will be random and irregular and will consist of lines and curves. These may be repeated but have no phonetic function nor represent letters and will therefore be largely unreadable. This initial exploration into mark marking may involve using big chalk on a patio, a pen on paper (or wall!) or a paintbrush (or paint-covered hand!) and marks will be made out of interest and 'delight' rather than as a way of communicating (Casbergue and Strickland, 2016).

Stages of Writing Development	Writerly Behaviours
Experimental	Emerging, experimenting and playing: Marks on the page have begun to shift towards a more letter-like formation with some letters clearer than others. Known letters may be experimented with by altering their size, direction and order (Browne, 2007). These are often ones associated with a child's name since these are often most familiar to them. 'Mock letters' may also appear which closely resemble known letters and these may be collated to create 'mock words'. Although these have little relation to phonemic spelling, they are a growing indication of the process in which words are formed and that lines on the page bring meaning (Yang and Noel, 2006; Bradford, 2015; Casbergue and Strickland, 2016). Marks may be repeated and keep to similar patterns and forms. A growing awareness of the direction in which texts are written (left to right) is shown and from the top to the bottom of the page. Children may begin to understand that where something is written can define its meaning and purpose, such as a name at the bottom of a piece of writing or labelling a drawing by placing the title underneath (Yamagata, 2007 cited in Wyse et al., 2018). Knowledge of alphabetic principles will be limited and therefore not wholly applicable unless with guidance and modelling. Although they may not have the skill or desire to commit to any writing on the page, they are able to share, talk and dictate their ideas to another; such compositional skills will be more advanced than transcriptional ones.
Early writing	Transitional and personal: Children choose to write purposefully around what interests them. Writing their name on a picture may indicate that the work belongs to them or writing a list of items they want to have for Christmas might indicate a growing knowledge of purpose, audience and convention. Ideas for writing are generated by what they see in and out of the school setting and there is a growing sense of desire and independence in attempting the writing process. They have a developing knowledge of the alphabetic principle: that letters and therefore letter shapes, carry a sound (Ehri in Beech, 2005). This results in initial grapheme-phoneme awareness and the application of phonemic spelling which mainly results in the representation of consonants since they represent the beginning and end sounds of most words (Langston, 2014). For example, writing 'wolf' as 'wlf' when writing about *Little Red Riding Hood*. They may have begun to segment individual words with spaces, showing that they carry individual meaning. Although the writer can display some awareness of capitalisation, lower and upper case letters may be mixed and some letters reversed (Browne, 2007). There may be some initial exploration and application of simple punctuation. They can use a range of writing tools comfortably and are forming letters correctly. They have a growing awareness of capitalisation and simple punctuation.

(Continued)

Table 3.1   (Continued)

Stages of Writing Development	Writerly Behaviours
Conventional	Transcription, function, generation:
	The young writer has an awareness of how their writing, and the writing of others, are structured and has begun to plan and organise with greater thought.
	Automaticity of handwriting and spelling is emerging alongside punctuation due to a growing proficiency in phonetic knowledge and the ability to match sounds to their corresponding letters. They are using phonic strategies to spell 'simple, regular words and make plausible attempts' at more regular ones (Browne, 2007). Control of structure, punctuation and spelling means that spacing, grammar and semantics are mostly correct or that viable choices are being made.
Proficient	Independence:
	The writer has, through reading, listening, exploring and playing with various forms and writing conventions, adopted their own writing style.
	There is a strong sense of cohesion between ideas and both the writing process and the audience's reading is enjoyable and satisfying.

Although these stages of development, or 'milestones', are often achieved around the same age, this is not the case for everyone (Wyse et al., 2018). Nursery and Reception children will mainly sit within those first three stages of writing but relating ages with stages could confuse and convolute the journey each child takes. This, in turn, could limit and restrict teaching approaches and diminish the importance of tailoring provision. Browne (2012) presents us with two pedagogical approaches in which to support children on this journey. She refers to these as *developmental* and *traditional*, and they provide us with an overview of the teaching and learning of early writing within the foundation stages (Table 3.2).

Table 3.2   Traditional and developmental approaches to early writing: originating from Browne (2012)

Traditional approach	Developmental approach
A pedagogical approach set upon the belief that children can only write independently when they have the skills required to do so.	Teacher acknowledges what knowledge and understanding a child brings with them when entering the Early Years setting. Choices with regards to support, intervention and next steps are informed by their stage of development.
Writing opportunities following specific structures. Before the child can finish or move on to the next step, the teacher must check whether the work is 'right'; emphasis on copying adult models is sometimes present.	Opportunities for explorative, collaborative and independent writing and experimentation are presented from the outset with no dependence on or support from adults required (although it is available). Initial attempts are valued and celebrated as part of a writing community.
Teacher models and provides models of writing to the class. Correct spelling and handwriting are as important as letter formation.	Rather than focusing on spelling and handwriting, an environment predicated on purpose and audience is central to the writing ethos in order to engage and excite.

Traditional approach	Developmental approach
Teachers acknowledge that progression comes from a good knowledge of the alphabetic code and that this is best taught through direct instruction.	Teachers acknowledge that the writing process is a gradual one and that each child will progress at different rates with affecting factors including: • differing developmental starting points • difference in support/opportunities at home • attitudes towards choosing to take in writing activities at school
Teachers use shared writing to model and inspire early writers to want to write too.	Teachers use shared writing to model and inspire early writers to want to write too. Application of these skills can emerge in play.
Focus is on writing transcription (spelling, handwriting, grammar, punctuation, letter formation and spacing).	Focus is on writing composition (generating ideas, saying out loud what they are going to write, oral composition, sharing their ideas and writing with others).

STOP AND REFLECT

Think about your own experience of an Early Years setting. It might be from your own class, a school you know or your experience as a parent (or even a child).

• Does practice in the setting mirror either of Browne's approaches in the table above?
• Are there aspects that are drawn from both approaches?
• If you were leading the setting, which approach might you seek to employ? Why?

There are a number of functions that are demanded of the writer as they progress towards a conventional standard (Wyse et al., 2018):

• Planning what you are going to write before writing it down.
• Remembering what it is that you are going to write next.
• Remembering how to spell a word.
• Remembering to space words and letters.
• Recalling letter formation and letter size.
• Remembering any simple punctuation to separate sentences or ideas.
• Checking that what you have written so far makes sense.

For the emerging, early writer, the process of writing is cognitively demanding. Constantly being required to recall these functions will mean that aspects of composition will suffer. In focusing too much on *how to write*, the young writer may forget *what they want to write* and *why they want to write it*. Although transcriptional functions are best taught through direct instruction (Goswami, 2008), a safe, engaging space in which the emerging, early writer can experiment with and apply these skills must also be provided. Environments that provide purposeful, engaging contexts, 'facilitate enquiry' and 'respect performance' are more likely to motivate and inspire children to experiment with and actively apply those emerging skills (Hall, 1987, cited in Wyse et al., 2018). However, although these spaces might encourage children to apply those transcriptional skills, in order to have the freedom to create and compose, automaticity is needed.

In England, the *Statutory Framework for the Early Years Foundation Stage* (DfE, 2017) sets out the standards for writing that might be expected by the end of a child's Reception year:

- Children use their phonic knowledge to write words in ways which match their spoken sounds.
- They also write some irregular common words.
- They write simple sentences which can be read by themselves and others. Some words are spelt correctly and others are phonetically plausible.

(DfE, 2020b)

The Early Learning Goal for Writing focuses on transcriptional elements whose expectations rest between the behaviours of the transitional and conventional writer (Langston, 2014: 103). Although it may seem to acknowledge a more traditional pedagogical approach, the *EYFSP Handbook* does present a more developmental one in calling for a social, collaborative environment in which children should be encouraged to write through access to written materials that will 'ignite their interest' (DfE, 2020b).

Behind the Early Learning Goals are a range of context-rich, exploratory and highly social environments in which children have the space to experiment with and apply those skills which they will have been taught without fear of being corrected or a need to be guided. The writing examples that accompany these narratives tell us something about where the children are, developmentally, but it is the contexts, environments, time and space with which they choose to apply those skills that encourage progress.

STOP AND REFLECT

Exploring the STA's writing exemplification for expected outcomes (STA, 2014) presents us with an insight into the types of opportunities teachers can create in which children are inspired to apply and experiment with these skills. The document offers some rich examples of writing in the Early Years.

Read these statements taken from the exemplification and their relation to a developmental approach:

'Ben is in the role play area which is a hospital.'

'Oscar had spent 40 minutes building a giant's castle with a small group....' We need a notice now!" he announced, "I'm going to make it!" He organised himself in the writing area.'

'During her self-chosen learning time (Eleanor) went to the computer and independently produced this work.'

'The class had been making card and there was a selection of resources in the mark making area. Scarlet chose to go to this area and independently wrote an invitation to Miss Swaine.'

'The rich resources in the writing area inspired M to write her own version of the traditional tale...M proudly tells the practitioner, "I've written my own story, it's like the one in the book."'

Now, consider:

- How might each support children to become authentic writers?
- Which might be child-initiated and which adult-initiated?
- What role does the teacher/practitioner need to play in order for children to have these experiences?
- What role does the environment play?

The role of the teacher

The provision of early writing benefits from being exploratory and instructive. It is important that the teacher takes into account the emerging knowledge and understanding and prior experiences that each child brings into the classroom. As outlined in the 'Pedagogy' section in *Development Matters* (DfE, 2020a), the application and experimentation of established and new writerly behaviours should take place in meaningful and purposeful play-based contexts (Bradford, 2015). In order for teachers to provide an ethos and environment which best supports these expectations, they must attend to a range of responsibilities which have been separated into teacher as observer, teacher as facilitator and teacher as guide:

Teacher as observer

As observer, the teacher's role is to note how and if children are engaging with the classroom environment and in what ways this may need to be adapted to encourage and support them (Browne, 2012). This 'strategy' is the best way to collate 'evidence' in order to assess a child's development (Fisher, 2013). In observing children's engagement with print, either incidentally, through role play or at the writing table, the teacher needs to make choices and changes to these spaces with regards to appropriateness of resources and materials and whether they are engaging a range of children. Paying attention to what interests a child and how this can relate to writing presents you with the foundation of activities and dialogues upon which you can build and engage children with in the future.

Through observation, teachers consider the best moment to step into the role of guide or model in supporting the early writer and when is the best time to step back and allow them to experiment and play. Such interactions are talk based and look to engage the writer in the purpose and pleasure of writing. Feedback should be genuine and sensitive and build upon where they are, developmentally (Bradford, 2015). Focusing more on engaging the young writer in the purpose and pleasure of writing, support and guidance comes in the form of the teacher modelling or providing them with the tools and skills that could be applied independently the next time they write (Browne, 2007). For the emerging writer, this may be letter formation and phoneme-grapheme correspondences, or supporting them in clarifying their ideas rather than focusing on the role of punctuation: not all interventions need to focus on transcription.

Teacher as facilitator

The 'influence of environmental print' on early writers cannot be understated (Langston, 2014). It should play a functional use in the day-to-day running of the classroom: labels, names, key vocabulary words associated with what they are learning about, spaces and places, for example. Areas in which their own early writing attempts can be put on display can provide opportunities for children to see its potential and purpose and bring meaning to its role in the classroom (Casbergue and Strickland, 2016). In addition, they will see that it is valued and celebrated by those with whom they share the environment such as teachers and peers.

As an Early Years teacher, you may be the first to open the door to the purpose and pleasure of writing for many children in your class. Although the provision of a range of well-stocked resources cannot be underestimated, if creative, choice-centred opportunities are not provided then interest and engagement could be lost (Cigman, 2014; Cremin et al., 2015). Access to books that are tailored to class topics and a child's interests will, with adult support, introduce them to a variety of writing styles and story language, while complementary writing and role-play areas will present them with safe spaces to 'test their hypotheses about the forms and functions of writing' (Wyse et al., 2018).

In planning for writing opportunities, it is important to find the balance between traditional and developmental approaches. Acquisition of transcriptional skills is key and are best taught directly, but feedback should focus more 'on content and meaning' (Browne, 2007). The role of the adult should be to listen and interact and, when an opportunity presents itself, provide meaningful writing opportunities (Cigman, 2014). During these early developmental stages, our role is to 'work alongside children' (Browne, 2012) at an individual level, in groups and as a whole class, modelling being a writer too, thinking aloud, guiding their thinking, scribing ideas and narratives and facilitating writerly behaviours. These moments are centred on a sense of cooperation rather than instruction and should be celebrated as shared, exploratory experiences.

Teacher as guide

The importance of modelling to children what it is to be a writer cannot be understated. From displaying writerly behaviours to practising the functions expected of beginning writers, adults in the classroom can show children why writing is essential and convince them that it is something worth doing in their own time; positive attitudes to writing will do much to inspire those early, emerging writers to do the same.

Just as at home, the adult is observed by the child in a range of writing contexts. This may come in the form of making a note in a reading record, modelling in shared and guided writing or joining in role play. However, unlike home, the teacher has the role of making specific the choices they make when they write. In demonstrating being a writer, teachers can comment on what it is that they are writing, who they are writing for and this can bring a sense of purpose and inspiration to others. In modelling the act of writing, at any point during the school day, the teacher should think aloud, sharing their approaches to both transcriptional and compositional functions (Browne, 2007; Casbergue and Strickland, 2016). While the developmental approach can do much to enthuse children to write, gradually drawing attention to elements of transcription through modelling, thinking aloud and instructing is important if those emergent, early writers are to progress.

The third educator?

This phrase refers to an aspect of the Reggio Emilia approach, in which the learning environment is given equal importance to that of the two classroom teachers. A mirror of the teachers' own pedagogical beliefs, the Reggio Emilia classroom caters to the child's interests and, with a more developmental approach, it celebrates the importance of play, collaboration, talk and exploration and believes in learning through experimentation and problem-solving (Edwards et al., 1998). Vygotsky (1978) also places emphasis on the provision of meaningful and personally relevant learning opportunities that inspire, engage and motivate. In support of these beliefs, Cigman, (2014), Bradford (2015) and Wyse et al. (2018) each note that the best opportunities for writing come with the provision of active spaces, such as role-play and writing areas, that inspire, engage and support the early writer while building on what they already know with regards to the world around them and their developmental stages.

Role play can bring purpose and audience to the writing process as well as a range of formats and styles, especially when the adult is part of this and uses well-timed opportunities to model appropriate forms of writing (Browne, 2012). Themes which set the role-play area should be relevant to what is currently being explored in the classroom or to the interests of children in the classroom, while all writing resources here should be kept well stocked and clearly labelled (Hall and Robinson, 2003; Browne, 2007; Cigman, 2014).

Role-play areas are active, highly motivating social spaces that are best suited to the early learner (Hall and Robinson, 2003; Cigman, 2014; Cremin et al., 2015). Hands-on, child-initiated exploratory play provides the creative space for children to apply writing skills that they may have caught (through observing adults or peers writing naturally) or been taught, ensuring that these areas are authentic in their design and purpose, reflecting children's imaginative worlds and often drawing upon genuine experiences (such as a shop, doctor's surgery and, when outside, a garage or builder's yard). Good provision, regularly reviewed and changed when necessary, together with sensitive co-playing on the adult's part, will encourage children to spend more time there (Fisher et al., 2011) and, with the right resources, present greater opportunities for independent writing (Bradford, 2015).

Peers have a significant impact on writing development through demonstrating the language of play, enriching vocabulary and modelling purposeful and contextualised writing experiences. Those who know how and why you might need a shopping list when visiting the supermarket can share this knowledge with those who do not, modelling the different functions and purposes that writing can bring and providing meaning to the act of writing.

Early Years settings should provide dedicated areas for writing. With the right tools, these spaces offer children creative opportunities to experiment and apply skills without the concern of getting things right (Browne, 2007; Bradford, 2015). Available throughout the day, the writing area invites children to embellish and explore ideas and forms of writing independently no matter their developmental stage 'as part of their play' (Cigman, 2014).

Both writing and role-play areas offer something significant to young writers: a sense of ownership and purpose to the writing experience. This is at the heart of the characteristics of effective teaching and learning (DfE, 2017). These are spaces in which they are invited, not instructed, to write and they will see that not only is it a tool for sharing and making meaning but that its purpose can be fun and enjoyable too. These spaces succeed because language and choice are at the heart of it all (Lyle and Bolt, 2017).

STOP AND REFLECT

Think about an EYFS setting you know.

- Does the classroom provide meaningful and purposeful collaborative and independent contexts which encourage children to take risks and play with writing?
- Where could adult collaboration lead to broadening and supporting thinking? (Cigman, 2014)

As observer, you need to monitor how well your environment encourages social interaction and how children are using these spaces.

- How might your thoughts and views of writing and print be seen by the children you are working with?
- Do you value it too and for what purposes do children see you using it?
- While modelling and guiding children in more formal writing exercises, such as shared and guided writing, are you engaged with the children as a co-writer too?

When opportunities arise, it is your role, as an educator, to encourage them to share ideas and collaborate, to scribe and initiate active learning in which writing is personal, engaging and enjoyable.

Conclusion

Children arrive at school having had a wide range of writing experiences. Foundation Stage professionals need to acknowledge that each child's starting point will be different but that they should all see writing as something worth doing. Well-stocked classrooms with designated writing and role-play areas are essential. As facilitator, you are there to ensure space and time is given to promoting writing in and out of the classroom every day. Planned writing activities should be centred around topics and areas of interest and balanced alongside opportunities in which they can experiment with those skills taught formally.

IN SUMMARY

- Emergent writing refers to a set of precursors and behaviours that lead to writing. For many children, this will start before they begin any formal education.
- Approaches to early writing can be characterised as *traditional* or *developmental*.
- Provision for writing in the EYFS is likely to focus on teacher-led approaches (such as modelling and guiding through individual and group writing activities), child-led approaches (such as opportunities for child-initiated writing for 'real' purposes) and environmental factors, where the classroom and resources provide opportunities and inspiration for writing.

FURTHER READING

- Ann Browne's *Developing Language and Literacy 3–8* still remains an essential read for Early Years practitioners and primary trainee teachers. It constantly calls on relevant research while remaining accessible and engaging.
- Teresa Cremin and colleagues' *Teaching English Creatively* offers a range of ideas to develop imaginative readers, writers, speakers and listeners through creative approaches to teaching. The text is full of research-informed practice and written by a range of insightful and experienced voices.
- Claire McLachlan and Alison Arrow's article 'Literacy in the Early Years' published in the journal *International Perspectives on Early Childhood Education and Development* contains an in-depth collection of research around the topic of early childhood literacy. Each article explores the implications for educational practice and offers a wealth of further reading too.

REFERENCES

Beech, J.R. (2005) Ehri's model of phases of learning to read: A brief critique. *Journal of Research in Reading*, 28(1): 50–8.

Bissex, G. (1984) The child as teacher. In A. Browne (2012) *Developing Language and Literacy 3–8*. London: Sage.

Bradford, H. (2015) 'I can write...on my own!', in D. Whitebread and P. Coltman, *Teaching and Learning in the Early Years* (4th ed.) (pp. 154–68). Abingdon: Routledge.

Browne, A. (2007) *Teaching and Learning Communication, Language and Literacy*. London: Sage.

Browne, A (2012) *Developing Language and Literacy 3–8*. London: Sage.

Casbergue, R. and Strickland, D (2016) *Reading and Writing in Preschool: Teaching the essentials*. London: The Guilford Press.

Cigman, J. (2014) *Supporting Boys' Writing in the Early Years: Becoming a writer in leaps and bounds*. Abingdon: Routledge.

Cremin, T., Reedy, D., Bearne, E. and Dombey, H. (2015) *Teaching English Creatively* (2nd ed.). Abingdon: Routledge.

Davies, A. (1988) Children's names: bridges to literacy? *Research in Education*, 40: 19–31.

Department for Education (DfE) (2014) *EYFS profile exemplification for the level of learning and development expected at the end of the EYFS Literacy ELG10 – Writing*. Available at: https://assets. publishing.service.gov.uk/government/uploads/system/uploads/attachment_data/file/360534/ ELG10___Writing.pdf

Department for Education (DfE) (2017) *Statutory Framework for the Early Years Foundation Stage: Setting the standards for learning, development and care for children from birth to five*. London: DfE.

Department for Education (DfE) (2020a) *Development Matters: Non-Statutory Curriculum Guidance for Early Years Foundation Stage*. London: DfE.

Department for Education (DfE) (2020b) *Early Years Foundation Stage Profile Handbook*. London: DfE.

Department of Education, Western Australia (2013) *First Steps: Writing Map of Development*. The Department of Education WA. [online] Available at: http://det.wa.edu.au/stepsresources/detcms/navigation/first-steps-literacy/

Edwards, C.P., Gandini, L. and Forman, G.E. (1998) *The Hundred Languages of Children: The Reggio Emilia approach–advanced reflections* (2nd ed.). Greenwich, CT: Ablex Pub. Corp.

Fisher, J. (2013) *Starting from the Child: Teaching and learning in the foundation stage* (4th ed.). Maidenhead: McGraw-Hill Education.

Fisher, K.R., Hirsh-Pasek, K., Golinkoff, R.M., Singer, D.G. and Berk, L.E. (2011) Playing around in school: Implications for learning and educational policy. In A.D. Pellegrini (Ed.) *The Oxford Handbook of the Development of Play* (pp. 341–60). Oxford: Oxford University Press.

Goswami, U. (2008) *Cognitive Development: The learning brain*. Hove: Psychology Press.

Hall, N. and Robinson, A. (2003) *Exploring Writing and Play in the Early Years* (2nd ed.). London: David Fulton.

Langston, A. (2014) *Facilitating Children's Learning*. Maidenhead: Open University Press.

Lyle, S. and Bolt, A. (2017) What brings children to writing and energises their early writing efforts? In C. McLachlan and A.W. Arrow (Eds), *Literacy in the Early Years. International Perspectives on Early Childhood Education and Development*, vol 17. Singapore: Springer. Available at: https://doi.org/10.1007/978-981-10-2075-9_6

McLachlan, C. and Arrow, A.W. (Eds) (2017) *Literacy in the Early Years*. Singapore: Springer.

Neuman, S.B. and Roskos, K. (1997) Literacy knowledge in practice: Contexts of participation in young writers and readers. *Reading Research Quarterly*, 32(1): 10-32.

Rowe, D.W. and Neitzel, C. (2010) Interest and agency in 2- and 3-year-olds' participation in emergent writing. *Reading Research Quarterly*, 45(2): 169–95.

Standards and Testing Agency (2014) *EYFS profile exemplification for the level of learning and development expected at the end of the EYFS*. London: STA.

Vygotsky, L. S. (1978) *Mind in Society: The development of higher psychological processes*. Cambridge, MA: Harvard University Press.

Wyse, D., Jones, R., Bradford, H. and Wolpert, M. (2018) *Teaching English, Language and Literacy*. Abingdon: Routledge.

Yang, H.-C. and Noel, A.M. (2006) The developmental characteristics of four- and five-year-old preschoolers' drawing: An analysis of scribbles, placement patterns, emergent writing, and name writing in archived spontaneous drawing samples. *Journal of Early Childhood Literacy*, 6(2): 145–62.

4

WRITING IN THE EARLY YEARS: PRACTICE

THIS CHAPTER WILL

• Consider practical approaches for teaching writing in Early Years settings

• Illustrate different principles from research and theory, making links to the classroom

• Explore the use of planned activities, including shared and guided writing, and the wider environment as vehicles to support children's development as writers

Introduction

For many children entering Early Years provision, little distinction will have yet to be made between various forms and purposes of mark making (Cremin et al., 2015). Whether they are drawing or writing, their efforts will still be exploratory. It is important that EYFS settings provides children with the opportunities, resources and an environment in which they can see the purpose and pleasures of writing, in addition to beginning to understand the process.

The adult's role will be to enthuse, support and provide children with authentic context-driven writing activities during these early transitions, working as facilitator, observer and guide. They should model being a writer in front of pupils and alongside them, sharing their ideas and process (Cremin et al., 2015). Since composition begins long before transcription (Centre for Literacy in Primary Education (CPLE), 2016), playful and engaging ways to help children get their ideas onto the page (or wall, or sand pit, or floor) while 'easing the burden of transcription' by scribing for them at times, is a healthy way of enticing children into writing while also giving them the space and choice to play at writing themselves. As with reading (see Chapters 1 and 2), it is also important to be aware of the child's interests and socio-cultural background in order to find ways of hooking them into the writing experience (Pahl, 2007).

This chapter considers five areas of classroom practice, where opportunities exist for helping children to take their first steps as writers. Each section outlines the importance of this facet of EYFS practice, before illustrating with examples from the classroom. The five areas are:

1. Shared writing and guided writing
2. The wider role of the adult
3. The writing environment
4. Writing and role play
5. The relationship between home and school

Principle strategies for teaching: shared writing and guided writing

As with the teaching and learning of writing with older primary-aged children (see Chapters 11 and 12), shared writing and guided writing are valuable techniques in the Early Years setting. However, as this section will explore, they also need their own unique approaches, taking into account the age and developmental stage of the children concerned.

Shared writing

From awareness to proficiency, young writers will always benefit from a skilled teacher thinking and talking them through the writing process. Through questions and talk, each stage of writing development will call on different skills and behaviours being modelled; each shared experience is there to connect pedagogy with developed writerly behaviours.

Shared writing invites the whole class or large groups of children (Browne, 2007) to see the compositional process modelled through thinking aloud and transcription. It is a balanced process that should be used throughout Early Years and primary education and has long been referenced as effective in supporting children through collaborative, skill-focused modelling of the writing process (Evans, 2001). Consideration as to the length and coverage of each session, no more than 15 minutes, should always take into account the skills and needs of the children. Casbergue and Strickland (2016) present a simple yet informative structure to shared writing in the Early Years:

Step 1: *Hands-on inquiry that offers space for rich discussions and sharing of thoughts and ideas*:

How does it look in practice: *The initial shared writing step focuses on hooking children into the writing experience by creating activities that relate to their interests and encourage discussion. Casbergue and Strickland (2016) note*:

- talking around a whole-class text
- an activity that has taken place in the classroom or outside area
- an event that has involved or has interest to the children

Step 2: *Guided discussion in which phrases, words and ideas are generated and stored for the main writing activity. Dialogic, shared discussions are encouraged here: this is a social event (Evans, 2001; Fisher, 2016). Children see the teacher actively storing ideas through writing that can be collected and modelled on a sheet of paper big enough for all to see and able to be pinned up for accessible display at a later time.*

How does it look in practice: *The teacher records ideas and vocabulary children have used around the discussion. This may be*:

- things of interest in the text they have been exploring and ideas/language that has stemmed from this
- purpose and focuses for writing that might celebrate or further explore an activity
- memories and ideas stored for future use in the writing process

Step 3: *Writing aloud presents the opportunity for children to see the writing process modelled by an expert. Consider opportunities for the children to collaborate with you and contribute to the process. Instead of leading the writing at all times, create opportunities in which you step back and become the scribe, taking on the transcriptional elements so that they can enjoy the compositional elements (Browne, 2012). This may involve recalling and pointing to ideas, phrases and words collated during Step 2 or recalling events in Step 1 and allowing plenty of space for children to talk together about what comes next and what has been written already. You may wish to engage with these conversations, but the skilled teacher will interact not dominate.*

This step can be broken down further (Evans, 2001):

1. Teacher demonstrating/modelling the format while providing 'a running commentary'
2. Teacher including ideas and suggestions from the children through scribing and removing any transcriptive barriers
3. Teacher allows children to collaborate on whiteboards/with magnetic letters to assist them with letter shapes or images to support with the overall piece.

How does it look in practice: Writing aloud is a carefully planned opportunity for the teacher to model the following:

- The language of writing and how formal writing can differ from informal talk
- The opportunity for collaborative writing in which children might offer ideas, words and initial sounds for spelling
- Through thinking aloud children can see how the process of writing involves organising their thinking and modelling the importance of keeping the writing in relation to the content
- Showing early writers that marks on the page relate to sounds and that these collections of sounds join together to make words
- Early phonetic spelling
- Modelling the use of upper and lower case letters. Even though a focus in the early writer tends to be on the former, exposure will establish an earlier understanding and purpose (Casbergue and Strickland, 2016)
- Opportunities for children to point to and find specific letters and sounds or simple punctuation; time will then be given to associate this with other learning
- Using these moments to explore alternative spellings that the children have attempted (CLPE, 2016)

Step 4: Revisit and re-read. The idea of revisiting the shared writing over several days means that there is time to recap on skills and ideas learned and continually 'reorient' (Casbergue and Strickland, 2016) the children to the purpose of writing.

How does it look in practice: Shared writing has no set time or day to be completed but short segments over several days allows for a gradual, slow build-up of the writing process until completion. With each new session, time should be spent as follows:

- Reading through what has been written so far. Children can be invited to join in with the reading too
- A reading aloud of the completed text at the end and associating it with the original brief/objective reinforces that sense of writing for a purpose

Step 5: Exploration. In coming back to the initial draft, the teacher can create opportunities for children to bring their growing phonological knowledge to the writing, noting repeated letter sounds, patterns of letters or even whole words that they remember and what it is about them that make them memorable.

How does it look in practice: With the shared writing piece completed, discussions about the format of the text, letters and sounds, noting connections between early phonological awareness can help build connections between writing, reading and talking.

Step 6: Display and discuss.

How does it look in practice: Once the written piece is completed and has been explored, it should be made accessible to children at all times and at their height so that they can:

- revisit it at their own leisure and take pride in the collaborative nature of writing
- point to letters and sounds with peers and key words that they recall

- relate words, letters and sounds that they have been exploring to those that they see on the shared writing display
- use it as a potential for playing and exploring their own writing based on this, be it words, shapes or simple mark making/copying

Step 7: *Early steps towards independence*

How does it look in practice: *Now that the writing is complete, opportunities for children to attempt their own composition could be encouraged either with adults scribing or children mimicking the process should they show an interest at any point.*

CASE STUDY 4.1

For example, in one school's Nursery class, the children decided to write a thank you letter to a dad who came in to cook roti with the children.

Step 1: *After he had visited, the teacher wondered aloud how they could say thank you, and the children suggested writing a letter.*

Step 2: *The teacher collected children's ideas for things they might want to say and jotted them down on a large sheet of sugar paper. Suggestions included: 'thank you so much, Mr Sohail'; 'I loved rolling them out'; 'it was great fun' and 'I'm going to make them at home for tea!'*

Step 3: *The teacher scribed on a whiteboard, using as many of the children's ideas as possible and ticking them off as she used them, so children could see they were being used. She stopped and modelled reading aloud as she wrote, made several deliberate spelling mistakes, briskly saying 'I'm not sure how to spell that, but never mind, I'll have a go!'. Where children could identify the initial letter of a word, they were invited to come up and stick a magnetic letter onto the board 'to start the word off'. Two children were able to write a letter that she needed, so they came and added to her draft.*

Step 4: *In this case, as it was a very short thank you note, the writing was completed in one 10-minute session. However, the next day the teacher came back to the class to ask about how she could get the letter to Mr Sohail with a focus on the purpose of writing. Some children suggested posting it (something that provided a good opportunity to develop other children's knowledge and understanding of the world). The teacher 'found' a large envelope and together they wrote a simple address on the envelope. As a free-choosing activity later, some children made stamps for the letter.*

Step 5: *The teacher made use of the first draft of the letter when looking at initial sounds. She re-read the letter aloud again, asking children to put their hand up whenever they heard an /s/ sound.*

Step 6: The draft of the letter was displayed on the wall near the writing area and at their height so that children could come back to it, look at it and 'read' it should they wish to.

Step 7: Children were provided with paper, card and envelopes if they wished to write their own thank you letters or cards. There was a table available for them to work at, but some children chose to take their letters across to the carpet area to work on their laps using clipboards. Many children chose to make their own cards for Mr Sohail, others created cards for each other, and one even made a thank you card for the teacher.

During Step 4 there could have been an opportunity for children to fix real stamps to their envelope and post it in a real postbox with a member of staff or handed to their parent/carer at the day's end.

Throughout each step of the process, good-quality writing materials should always be made available to the children so that they can explore the process through play and in their own time (see further below for examples). Teachers often use large writing surfaces such as a flipchart, whiteboard or Interactive Whiteboard. The benefit of the flipchart paper lies in the fact that it can be moved at a later time to become more accessible to the young writer.

Guided writing

Shared writing focuses on the teacher as expert, modelling the processes to the class in a collaborative, social environment; guided writing builds on this work. These sessions provide opportunities for sustained writing practices in which early writers, with support, can apply or further explore what they have learned during shared writing sessions, in discussion with other adults through play (Cremin et al., 2015). It is recommended that supporting children according to ability, need and enthusiasm means that groups will be no larger than six (Bradford, 2015).

As with shared writing, these sessions tend to be brief, no longer than 20 minutes (Bradford, 2015), and can focus on making some of the shared writing practices more accessible or may focus on an aspect of composition and transcription. It may be that the adult educator is scribing a story for the group and encouraging them to use some descriptive language or transcribing a postcard or letter that the children have to write, referring to structure and layout. Rather than the focus being on the teacher, as it is with shared writing, the focus turns towards the pupil and opportunities for writing short pieces of text 'independently but with support' (Browne, 2007).

While supporting children during guided writing, the teacher can scribe using the same processes as with shared writing such as thinking aloud, planning out what they want to write and even beginning to use phonemic awareness for some initial spelling. Writing opportunities may include signs, labels, short stories and other activities related to themes, ideas and the children's interests. This should always relate to where they are in their writing development.

CASE STUDY 4.2

In the autumn term in one Reception class, children take part in a guided writing session each week, working on a short, motivating task with the close support of an adult. While the sessions are planned to support children's developing literacy from their different starting points, the EYFS team feel their real value is to get children used to working in the writing area and for every child to see that writing is for them.

In Tommy's session this week, the group are inventing a new mixed-up animal, inspired by a book they have become very interested in in the book corner: *Flip Flap Safari* by Axel Scheffler. Tommy decides he is going to draw a creature that has the head and body of a tiger and the legs of a zebra. After drawing his picture, his teacher supports him to label the parts 'tger' and zebrer', gently adjusting the way he holds his pencil to make his grip more comfortable. She then scribes some details for him: 'orange and black stripes'; 'black and white stripes'; 'sharp teeth' and 'fast legs'. Tommy is delighted with his animal and takes it home to show his parents. The next day, he returns to school with a 'half-lian-half-zebrer' he has drawn and labelled on his own.

The wider role of the adult

In the EYFS, part of an adult's role in developing writing will be through specific teaching, including shared and guided writing. However, much of their influence will happen through other approaches, some teacher-initiated but many child-initiated, with the adult on hand to observe, support, extend and offer positive feedback which reinforces the child's view of themselves as a writer. For further examples see the Active Learning section in *Development Matters* (DfE, 2020).

Modelling and scribing: The teacher as observer and guide

Choosing the right moment to focus a child's attention on concepts of print is important during those early writing years. Within an environment rich in print and books, this can be done in a range of engaging and meaningful ways that will ignite a child's sense of curiosity and interest. From Nursery to Reception there will be a gradual shift in focus from exploration and instruction with the idea of enjoyment and achievement always at the fore. Modelling, peer-modelling and scribing can all show early writers the process and conventions of writing for a range of purposes.

During Nursery, it may be that the adults in the room are scribing much of the content for children. It is important that you encourage aspects of composition in which there is open and engaging discussion about the structure of their stories and characters. These crucial moments model the connection between 'oral language and writing' (Cigman, 2014) and enable the early writer to see how their thoughts and ideas can be captured on the page. The more you invite such dialogic discussions, the richer the language and structure of writing will become. Scribing for children will also reduce much of the cognitive constraints in the early writer (Harste et al., 1984) and place them in a more engaging space to be creative and enjoy sharing and expressing their ideas (Cigman, 2014) while creating written pieces that are more readable to the child (Perera, 1984).

In addition, as with shared and guided writing, the adult scribe will also have the opportunity to draw attention to the structure of simple sentences, graphemes and phonemes, as well as letter formation which they can model and comment on. Children will be able to see how different texts are presented through their own oral composition and can take delight in creating and owning completed pieces. These moments not only help children see the connection between writing and reading but also acknowledge the concept that they too are part of a literary community.

During these Foundation years, writing opportunities should be part of a talk-rich culture in which adults can 'model, clarify, recast and enrich vocabulary and oral sentence structure, including the use of conjunctions to support and develop ideas' (CLPE, 2016).

The purpose of modelling and scribing

During the early years, it is important to remember that 'the physical act of writing can be a struggle for young writers who are still developing strength and coordination'. Not only could pushing children to complete an inappropriate extended writing activity cause discomfort but, in turn, discourage them from writing at all (Cigman, 2014).

Table 4.1   Opportunities for adults as scribes

Adult as scribe: Writing for children and with children presents opportunities for modelling the process in many ways. The approach can be supportive of both elements of transcription and composition.	Model the link between what we think and say and what their words look like when written down.

(Continued)

Table 4.1   (Continued)

Transcriptive opportunities	– Free the child from transcriptive aspects of writing which allows them to focus on composition and finding their writer's voice (Cigman, 2014).
	– With the adult scribing, there is space for exploring letter formation and orientation (Casbergue and Strickland, 2016).
	– Present opportunities for attention to be drawn 'to letter shapes (graphemes), letter sounds (phonemes) and punctuation' (Cigman, 2014).
Compositional opportunities	– Offer moments in which children can be part of the writing community and understand the joy that comes with seeing their words written down and hearing them read out aloud by others.
	– With the adult scribing, there is space for exploring ideas. Drawing attention to language choices, 'expanding on ideas and adding detail and description' when appropriate (CLPE, 2016).
	– Show the child that writing is more than just transcription and that their ideas and interests are important.
Compositional and transcriptional opportunities	– Reading aloud a child's work invites them to hear the 'tune and rhythms' of their writing while drawing attention to the structure of their phrases and choices of words (Cremin et al., 2015).
	– As with shared and guided writing, a 'shared engagement' in the process may leave opportunities for gentle reflection and discussion about improvement or next steps (Browne, 2007).

Teacher as facilitator

During the Early Years Foundation Stage, it is expected that young writers experience a range of writing forms such as: 'stories, non-fiction, rhymes and poems' (DfE, 2019), lists, captions, instructions, signs, directions, menus, labels, greeting cards and within 'a rich language and literacy environment' (CLPE, 2016). How adults introduce these experiences is important and a balance between pleasure, purpose and instruction must be planned carefully.

Alongside these compositional elements, planning regularly for transcriptional activities that promote early phonological awareness and relate it to written letters (graphemes) is essential. Encouraging early writers to hear those individual sounds in words and seeing what they look like in written form will help children with those first tentative steps into spelling. Both halves of the writing process are best explored through a range of strategies which are balanced between instruction, play-based exploration and experimentation indoors and outdoors, at home and at school. Shared writing, guided writing and independent writing opportunities should always be planned and prepared for and may often be connected (Browne, 2007). It is also essential that letter formation and phonics teaching are introduced early in order to invite and instruct children in how the alphabetic code works (CLPE, 2016).

Before planning for any writing, it is worth reflecting on its purpose. When we write in the real world, it is often for ourselves (a list or note to remind us of something) or for someone else who remains at a distance to us. Yet, as Browne (2012) states, when we ask children to write in the classroom they are often only writing for the teacher. If we are to convince early writers that this is a worthwhile skill to learn, then we need to plan for meaningful, worthwhile experiences whether that be signs for their outdoor garage or party invitations inspired by *Each Peach Pear Plum* by Janet and Allan Ahlberg. Inviting children to do this without adult support should be encouraged since it instils a sense of ownership and play (Dombey in Smidt, 2010).

In addition, when planning, remember that there is more room for supporting and exploring a child's writing ability in smaller groups rather than larger ones. It is important to present a range of activities that engage the children in and out of the classroom so that you have the space and time to work with those smaller groups who choose to write (Browne, 2012). These moments will present opportunities for you to talk through aspects of the process and provide the support and encouragement for them to develop and extend their ideas. This may involve enquiring about the marks they are making, asking them to comment on others' mark making/writing and their own.

Contexts for purposeful and engaging writing

For those who have only just begun making marks, much of their planned writing experiences may start in drawing; developing both gross and fine motor skills (Langston, 2014). These are, potentially, still narratives of a sort and important precursors to writing letters and words. These moments still provide important spaces for talk and creativity which can lead to writing in the future.

Table 4.2 Examples of contexts for creative writing

Indoors	– Creating labels, captions and speech bubbles around the classroom that might have the child's own name on (to be used as a morning register, dinner/packed lunch register) or draw attention to work that they have on display. Accompanying writing from the teacher may elaborate the mark making done or lend context.
	– Having a list of children's names in a tick-list register available for each child provides them the opportunity to role play the act of 'being teacher' drawing attention to letters and names. Children may wish to copy out their own names and their peers', looking for similarities or identical letters used.

(Continued)

Table 4.2 (Continued)

	– Laminated photos of each child with a space below them for them to have a go at writing their name with a marker pen. This can be repeatedly cleaned and attempted again.
	– A character from a story can leave written messages for the class (to be read by the teacher or collaboratively) and space can be left for children to reply. An example like this might be from a character from Daisy Hirst's *Natalie and Alphonse* books or one from a text that is being explored by the whole class. They could also take their own messages to other staff throughout the school – either admin, catering, teachers or TAs.
Outdoors	– On trips that take children out of the classroom/school area encourage them to look out for examples of writing, of signs, number-plates, posters, etc.
Both	– Create an alphabet book using photos of features from the local environment or what they can see as part of their surroundings.
	– Children collect objects or images of objects related to a theme or something that they are studying. These could be initial letter sounds (a display of items beginning with the 'b' sound), objects that share a commonality (the colour red) or objects/images related to a study topic (a small-world display of the landscape and characters from *We're Going on a Bear Hunt*). Children could then attempt initial letter labels or full labels using their own alternative spellings which would leave space for the teacher to address such spellings during shared writing.
	– Writing lists during role play or as part of an activity illustrates its purpose. This could involve going to a shop, writing down an order from a garage or a list of ingredients for cooking.
	– For emerging and early writers, opportunities that develop gross and fine motor skills will continue to be valuable. The CLPE (2016) provides the following useful examples: 'experimenting with arm movements with climbing and swinging, digging and pouring, work with streamers or scarves, play dough, threading, tweezer work.'
	– Drawing and mark making in and out of doors using a range of materials such as chalk on walls, chalkboards, slate or in tuff-trays; clipboards and paper with felt-tips, pencils, crayons, writing in sand with a finger or a feather; painting outdoors on wipeable perspex.
	– Setting up small-world play opportunities that build upon stories and rhymes explored in the classroom, or scenes that relate to the real world, presents children with the opportunities to collaboratively build up the language needed to amend and create their own stories for a later time (Cigman, 2014).

As an EYFS practitioner looking to support children's writing development, a key skill is knowing how to balance these different roles: observer, teacher, scribe and facilitator, recognising when to interact and support a child and when to step back and allow them to explore and work independently. Of course, adults are not the only resource that can help children to develop as early writers.

The writing environment

A case has already been argued for the role print-rich environments can play in enticing children into the world of reading in Chapter 2, and the same can be said of writing too. The environment's function in the classroom can be multi-purpose – from labels and messages to captions below photos of work, children and their families. Whatever its function, the CLPE (2016) makes it clear that if we are to have the best chance of engaging and enthusing all writers then we need to pay careful attention in ensuring these spaces reflect 'the cultural, social and linguistic diversity of the children': the more they see that writing is relevant to their lives outside of the classroom, the greater the chance that they will want to engage and own that practice. The same can be said of the stories, rhymes and songs that they encounter too: the more diverse and the broader the range of voices and purpose (to inform, instruct, persuade, entertain) the more meaningful and familiar the structures and settings (Cigman, 2014).

Research has shown that writing outside of school time has decreased and what writing there is, is mostly done using digital tools such as phones, tablets or computers (Dunn and Sweeney, 2018). It can be argued that it is important then that these tools are seen within the Early Years setting too. Touch-screen tablets can come in sturdy cases which means they could be used outside as well as in the classroom, and programs such as 'Book Creator' offer simple ways for children to create their own stories with minimal assistance. Other programs can invite drawing and mark making using fingers too. Both examples can support composition and transcriptive aspects of the writing process.

The practicalities of space, in which children can both access and practise writing, should also be considered. For many emerging and early writers, large surfaces (interactive whiteboards, whiteboards, large rolls of paper, tuff trays, table space and floor space outside) will present them with the opportunities to practise mark making with a range of tools without feeling cramped and in spaces that welcome a sense of collaboration and talk (Langston, 2014).

CASE STUDY 4.3

One school, drawing on the work of Cowley (2019) and Cigman (2014), carefully planned how the writing environment could support children's writing. They focused on gross-motor development, fine-motor skills and mobile writing opportunities, both inside and outside the classroom. Successful elements included the following:

- Rolls of paper for writing, drawing large maps and labelling. These could be placed up on a wall to use as a 'graffiti board' or spread out on whole tables so that children can collaborate and experiment using different writing materials together.

(Continued)

- Tuff trays filled with rice or sand in which children can use fingers, paint-brushes or sticks to draw lines and shapes. These might be initial letters, names, numbers or simple sensory exploration.
- Plastic tweezers for picking up marbles or small cotton balls and placing them in bowls/ice trays or along simple patterns.
- Threading activities can be found in abundance. Giant Alphabet Beads/Cubes can encourage children to focus on simple spelling patterns and their name, and support letter recognition.
- Hiding items (such as marbles and buttons) in playdough can be a good way to strengthen muscles in the hand. Opportunities for linking to topic work or a text read could also be enriching.
- Drawing shapes and patterns or mazes on card and inviting children to cut along the lines.
- Clipboards, spiral-bound notebooks, ready-made books, paper and suitable writing tools for observational writing, role play and mark making. Laminating paper/card means that they can be painted or drawn on outside and inside no matter the weather (remember bull-dog clips are very good at holding paper down).
- A mobile writing trolley stacked with whiteboards, clipboards, chalks, crayons and pencils can be used in and out of doors. If you wish the children to work with paint indoors or outdoors, you might consider using recycled hand-wash soap dispensers with slightly watered paint held in them: much less messy!
- If funding is available, a child's gardening tool bag can be used to carry pens and mark-making tools of their own choice and then placed back on the writing trolley when they have finished.
- Stampers and inkpads. Raised stampers with letters can be used to stamp in playdough with some not requiring ink. Stamps with images/characters in kinetic sand or playdough could encourage story telling too.

Writing areas

The provision of both opportunities and spaces for children to explore the writing process is important: risk and experiment are at the heart of children's progress. Writing areas are spaces that provide such opportunities, inside or out: they are often a staple in the Early Years setting and have a place in Key Stage 1 too. They are there to provide children with the opportunities to mark-make and attempt early writing motivated by things that are of interest to them free of critique, yet with guidance when appropriate (Bradford, 2015).

With regards to set up, writing areas can often be a table on which a range of writing materials and tools are available for children to choose from. In order to maintain a child's interest in the area, resources should be changed regularly and the impetus for writing there should cater for a child's interests. Setting up the area may also involve the class choosing what materials and writing activities may be of interest to them (Cigman, 2014). Having an area constantly available provides children with the frequent opportunity to mark-make and experiment with writing should they want to. Visiting adults can be there to 'act as an audience' (Evans, 2001; Cowley, 2019).

STOP AND REFLECT

Consider the following statements about EYFS writing areas.

Which ones do you agree with? Which ones do you think are the most important? Are there any that you disagree with?

Successful writing areas:

- allow children to choose what tools and materials they would like to use as well as the content
- are spaces in which adults write alongside children at times showing themselves to be models of writing (at times writing aloud) and interested in the process too
- are big enough spaces to allow for collaborative writing experiences and can be set up outside and inside when appropriate
- have room for children to either sit or stand when writing and to practise 'less refined gross and fine motor skills' (Cigman, 2014)
- are regularly maintained and updated: a tidy, well-resourced area says much to the child about a class's attitude to and interest in writing
- can provide purposeful opportunities for writing in which children can create work which has a place in and out of the classroom. This could come in the form of labels for displays, play areas and equipment in and out of the classroom bringing with it a sense of ownership and purpose
- use a variety of materials and tools, including the writing material's size, colour and texture as well as the implements with which they write (e.g. felt tips, crayons, pens, pencils, chalk, letter-stamps)
- make use of display boards that celebrate the writing or mark making that children do

It is important to understand that 'drawing is an important precursor to and part of emergent writing' (Wyse et al., 2018 citing Ferreiro, 1986; Levin and Bus, 2003; Yang and Noel, 2006; Lancaster, 2007; Yamagata, 2007). Initially, children may benefit from not being rushed into letter formation and early spelling and instead be shown the distinctions between print and pictures. This can be done by modelling both and explaining that they are 'writing' and 'drawing' when applicable.

Writing and role play

Role-play areas/home corners, and the peer-generated play-based talk that such spaces encourage, can provide a range of improvisational opportunities for marking making and writing (Evans, 2001; Dombey, 2010). These areas provide a safe, exploratory space for children to role play different people within a range of settings while learning and experimenting with the different tools we use to write (Browne, 2007). When writing in role-play areas, children can begin to see the nature and purpose of writing for different occasions and purposes. Here, they can experiment and explore with the process using a range of tools. The pressure of performance for the adult is considerably less but play nevertheless provides 'those familiar learning contexts' (Fisher, 2013; Swarbrick, 2013) opportunities for the teacher to observe a child's understanding of the process. The reflective educator can build on this during shared or guided sessions or when they are at the writing table (Swarbrick, 2013).

Table 4.3 Writing-rich role-play opportunities

Areas that:	– Provide opportunities for writing of different kinds and purposes (Hall and Robinson, 2003).
	– Setting up themed situations/settings that encourage a range of talk- and writing-based opportunities and hold a sense of purpose and meaning to a child's learning. These spaces and situations carry 'the capacity for extending and developing their knowledge' (Hall and Robinson, 2003).
	• Shops, stations, surgeries, libraries, spaces and places in books that have been explored or theme-based settings built around a child's interests (a palaeontologist's tent with a sand-based dinosaur dig next to it; a space-station in the construction area)
	– Allow for a range of roles to be played out – the more roles, the more chances for children to play and embrace longer moments of dialogue.
Resources that:	– Encourage talk and further exploration so that they build up the language and ideas to apply in their writing. These moments may involve being in role or re-enacting stories that they have heard (CLPE, 2016). These can be:
	• Story props, dressing up clothes, puppets, real-life items and toys that bring the setting to life.
Moments that:	– Allow the adult to 'play alongside children' (Browne, 2007). These spaces often provide talk, play and writing opportunities that may go unnoticed by children. Becoming 'part of the play' means that you can demonstrate and model without a didactic undertone (Hall and Robinson, 2003).
	– Invite children to be part of the process in creating the play space too. Discussing the play space collaboratively will allow you to highlight writing opportunities to the children.
	– Allow time for the adult to scribe if needed; especially in the Nursery in which skills may focus more on mark making.
	– Invite children from other classrooms to come and model being a more proficient writer, sharing approaches and skills that they have learned. This might involve remembering how to spell tricky words, modelling pencil grips, generating ideas or leaving finger spaces between words (Langston, 2014).

The relationship between home and school

Since research has suggested that later social and academic success rests upon the positive and purposeful literacy experiences provided in the home setting (Sylva et al., 2004; Street, 2013), it is important that Early Years practitioners work at developing close, supportive networks between home and school. For many parents, the prospect may seem daunting because of their own struggles and histories and some may believe that writing and reading are skills learned only when they begin school (Cigman, 2014). Brief workshops, close to pick-up time, can help guide parents through early writing progression. Care needs to be taken to lead parents away from an over-critical attitude which may be based on their own memory of school, and alternatives suggested. Resources could be placed or added to the packs mentioned in Case Study 4.4 below. Examples of writing activities and practice observed at school by parents are a powerful way of carrying such experiences home. These could be booktalk, role play, ideas for writing and mark making in and out of doors, as well as rich conversations between adult and child. The more parents see, the greater the chance there is of them practising similar, positive approaches in the home environment.

Supporting parental involvement during those initial years means providing them with a diverse framework that is both clear, manageable and purposeful and accommodating of their own confidence with literacy. While opportunities for writing and mark making around a child's interests are to be encouraged, children seeing the adults in their lives writing also illustrates purpose and meaning and these are just as powerful, if not more so, since they show intent and reason (Cremin et al., 2015). The more parents are involved and interested in the learning-to-write process, the greater the chance of that child's success.

Sharing with parents and carers the knowledge that children 'learn most effectively' when they see a purpose and function of writing (in all its forms) should help them recognise that much of their role outside of school is to model and guide them through the process (Browne, 2012). In doing so, their child has a greater chance of becoming more interested in the form and may want to join in, especially when these activities are relevant to them, be it writing and signing birthday cards to friends or writing a message on their parents' phone. It is, therefore, important that educators have a good knowledge of the range of writing practices that children meet in their homes (Cremin et al., 2015; Casbergue and Strickland, 2016). With this knowledge, appropriate activities can be recommended and opportunities suggested that parents may not have acknowledged as relevant (texting, posting on social media boards or writing lists are good examples). During these shared moments, parents need not only demonstrate but explain the purpose for their writing and invite their child to be part of the process too, whether suggesting what to write or picking out letters. This can be, for the emerging, early writer a far more powerful activity than sitting them down at a table and asking them to write a story.

CASE STUDY 4.4

One inner-city school, serving a large area of high-density social housing, worked hard to forge strong home-school links with regard to writing.

A simple writing pack was given to parents and carers. This contained materials and tools that would 'encourage children to experiment with writing for many different purposes freely and independently' (Cigman, 2014). Advice in the pack included:

- spending time with your child when they are mark making or attempting early writing and take an active interest
- if children are ready to attempt early writing, encourage them regardless of any spelling mistakes. Suggest corrections only when they are confident enough to accept critical feedback
- sharing conversations that they have had with their child about writing and about anything their child has spotted and recognised in and around their home, as well as environmental print on their travels

Parents were encouraged to share examples of their child's literacy engagement outside of school. These were recorded on sheets, on cards taken home, or as photographs taken on phones. This supported teachers to gain a richer understanding of the child's interests and literary world outside the school setting. A class post-box was set up for children to post pictures, scribbles, scribed letters and messages to parents or extended family. Some parents began to post letters to the child in the class post-box for them to read later in the day. Other parents encouraged children to mark on, sign and/or write in cards to other children in the class that were shared in the class post-box. Blank ready-made cards were provided by the school and available near the pick-up door so that parents and children were encouraged to take them. The emphasis was not on developing fine motor skills or spelling, but on acknowledging the purpose behind writing and its exciting role as a form of communication.

For the children who spoke English as an additional language, texts/books in their home language were borrowed from the local school library service. Parents were invited to send audio-files (using simple recording devices on the phone) of children's stories being read aloud or told at home so that these could be heard and shared in the classroom. Children were encouraged to share rhymes, songs and stories from their home culture, too.

Parents were welcomed to 'writing cafes' in which children would be writing in some form. Here, writing was led by play and exploration and this helped parents to see that writing can be both spontaneous and creative and not have to involve a strong sense of structure and focus. Parents would be invited to be part of the play and take part in some of the shared activities in and out of the classroom, at the writing area or the role-play area.

Conclusion

Chapters 3 and 4 have considered children's development in writing in the Early Years, looking at how all of the significant adults in a child's life, both at home and at school, can work to provide a solid base for future success. The next section of the book will move to consider the foundation that underpins written communication, both in the Early Years and in those that follow: spoken language and oracy.

IN SUMMARY

- For many children, their early attitudes towards writing are forged during their time in the Early Years, and their progress will depend on the support and opportunities they receive in their class or setting and at home.
- A strong Early Years practitioner will move between a number of different roles when helping children to develop as writers: observing, supporting, teaching, facilitating and scribing. Knowing when to employ each role is as important as an adult's skill at each.
- The writing environment can play an important part in children's development in writing, offering opportunities, reinforcement and stimulation for children working in this area.

FURTHER READING

- Julie Cigman's *Supporting Boys' Writing in the Early Years: Becoming a writer in leaps and bounds* is an important text on key issues in boys' literacy with plenty of personal details and examples about best practice.
- Sue Cowley's *The Ultimate Guide to Mark Making in the Early Years* is a practical guide to developing mark making in Nursery and Reception, managing to be refreshingly creative and highly accessible to both practitioner and parent.
- *The Excellence of Play* edited by J.R. Moyles is a key text in play theory in the Early Years with recent evidence and practical examples of how to implement high-quality play.
- Nick Swarbrick's chapter *The Place of Play in the Early Years Curriculum* in Wild and Street's *Themes and Debates in Early Childhood* explores the links between classic understandings of play and the modern curriculum in a book designed to support the development of critical thinking skills for practitioners and students in the Early Years.

REFERENCES

Bradford, H. (2015) 'I can write...on my own!', in D. Whitebread and P. Coltman, *Teaching and Learning in the Early Years* (4th ed.) (pp. 154–68). Abingdon: Routledge.

Browne, A. (2007) *Teaching and Learning Communication, Language and Literacy*. London: Sage.

Browne, A. (2012) *Developing Language and Literacy 3–8*. London: Sage.

Casbergue, R. and Strickland, D. (2016) *Reading and Writing in Preschool: Teaching the Essentials*. London: The Guilford Press.

Centre for Literacy in Primary Education (CLPE) (2016) *The Writing Scale*. London: CLPE.

Cigman, J. (2014) *Supporting Boys' Writing in the Early Years: Becoming a writer in leaps and bounds*. Abingdon: Routledge.

Cowley, S. (2019) *The Ultimate Guide to Mark Making in the Early Years*. London: Bloomsbury Publishing.

Cremin, T., Reedy, D., Bearne, E. and Dombey, H. (2015) *Teaching English Creatively* (2nd ed.). Abingdon: Routledge.

Department for Education (DfE) (2019) *Early Years Foundation Stage Profile Handbook*. London: DfE.

Department for Education (DfE) (2020) *Development Matters: Non-Statutory Curriculum Guidance for Early Years Foundation Stage*. London: DfE.

Dombey, H. in Smidt, S. (Ed.) (2010) *Key Issues in Early Years Education: A guide for students and practitioners* (2nd ed.). Abingdon: Routledge.

Dunn, J. and Sweeney, T. (2018) Writing and iPads in the early years: Perspectives from within the classroom. *British Journal of Education Technology*, 49: 859–69.

Evans, J. (Ed.) (2001) *The Writing Classroom: Aspects of writing and the primary child 3–11*. London David Fulton.

Fisher, J. (2013) *Starting from the Child: Teaching and learning in the foundation stage* (4th ed.). Maidenhead: McGraw-Hill Education.

Fisher, J. (2016) *Interacting or Interfering?: Improving interactions in the early years*. Maidenhead: Open University Press.

Hall, N. and Robinson, A. (2003) *Exploring Writing and Play in the Early Years* (2nd ed.) London: David Fulton.

Harste, J.C., Woodward, V.A. and Burke, C.L. (1984) *Language Stories and Literacy Lessons*. Portsmouth, NH: Heinemann Educational Books.

Lancaster, L. (2007) Representing the ways of the world: How children under three start to use syntax in graphic signs. *Journal of Early Childhood Literacy*, 7(2): 123–54.

Langston, A. (2014) *Facilitating Children's Learning*. Maidenhead: Open University Press.

Levin, I. and Bus, A.G. (2003) How is emergent writing based on drawing?: Analysis of children's products and their sorting by children and mothers: Israeli and Dutch preschoolers. *Developmental Psychology*, 39(5): 891–905.

Pahl, K. (2007) Creativity in events and practices: A lens for understanding children's multimodal texts. *Literacy*, 41(2): 81–7.

Perera, K. (1984) *Children's Writing and Reading: Analysing classroom language* (Reprinted ed.). Oxford: Blackwell.

Street, A. (2013) Equality and difference in the early years. In M. Wild and A. Street (Eds), *Themes and Debates in Early Childhood*. London: Sage.

Swarbrick, N. (2013) The place of play in the early years curriculum. In M. Wild and A. Street (Eds), *Themes and Debates in Early Childhood*. London: Sage.

Sylva, K., Melhuish, E., Sammons, P., Siraj, I. and Taggart, B. (2004) The Effective Provision of Pre-School Education (EPPE) Project Technical Paper 12: The Final Report – Effective Pre-School Education. Available at: www.education.gov.uk/childrenandyoungpeople/earlylearningandchildcare/evidence/a0068162/effective-provision-of-pre-school-education-eppe.

Wyse, D., Jones, R., Bradford, H. and Wolpert, M. (2018) *Teaching English, Language and Literacy*. Abingdon: Routledge.

Yamagata, K. (2007) Differential emergence of representational systems: Drawings, letters, and numerals. *Cognitive Development*, 22: 244–57.

Yang, H.-C. and Noel, A.M. (2006) The developmental characteristics of four- and five-year-old preschoolers' drawing: An analysis of scribbles, placement patterns, emergent writing, and name writing in archived spontaneous drawing samples. *Journal of Early Childhood Literacy*, 6(2): 145–62.

LITERATURE

Each Peach Pear Plum by Janet and Allan Ahlberg

Flip Flap Safari by Axel Scheffler

Natalie and Alphonse books by Daisy Hirst

We're Going on a Bear Hunt by Michael Rosen and Helen Oxenbury

PART 2

ORACY AND SPOKEN LANGUAGE

TALK, ORACY AND SPOKEN LANGUAGE: THEORY

THIS CHAPTER WILL

- Introduce key concepts and theory for understanding the role of talk in the primary classroom

- Consider the history and development of oracy and spoken language in primary education

Introduction

The 2014 National Curriculum in England acknowledges the role speaking and listening play as precursors to reading and writing:

> Spoken language underpins the development of reading and writing. The quality and variety of language that pupils hear and speak are vital for developing their vocabulary and grammar and their understanding for reading and writing.

> (DfE, 2013)

However, the importance of spoken language goes far beyond being merely a foundation for other areas of English. There can be few more important aspects of education than developing the ability to understand the ideas of others and to share your own thoughts, ideas and feelings. As the authors of the *Bercow: Ten Years On* report suggest, the effects of this area of children's development are far-reaching:

> Speech, language and communication skills are crucial to every person: for brain development in the early years and our attachment to others, for expressing ourselves and understanding others, for thinking and learning, for social interaction and emotional wellbeing, in school, as part of society and in the workplace.
>
> (ICAN/RCSLT, 2018)

As well as the social and emotional aspects of communication, spoken language is the means by which children engage with the rest of the school curriculum, the conduit through which they explore ideas and make sense of the world. As Alexander puts it:

> Reading, writing and number may be the acknowledged curriculum 'basics' but talk is arguably the true foundation of learning.
>
> (Alexander, 2008)

Perhaps not surprisingly, there is a strong correlation between children's spoken language skills and later academic success, both at primary school and beyond (Gross, 2011; Snowling et al., 2011). However, the impact of spoken language extends beyond its role as a foundation for academic achievement and the acquisition of literacy skills: it is linked to children's social development (Howe and Mercer, 2007), emotional development and their ability to self-regulate and manage their own behaviour (St Clair et al., 2011; Vallotton and Ayoub, 2011).

Aspects of oracy

Oracy and spoken language depend on a number of interrelated facets. One model suggests:

1. **Physical aspects of oracy**: control of vocal elements and body language that support different types of communication for different purposes
2. **Linguistic aspects of oracy**: the language demands of effective communication, including choice of words, syntax and grammar choices and the use of rhetorical devices such as humour and irony
3. **Cognitive aspects of oracy**: choosing the content and subject matter for talk, structuring and organising spoken texts and the range of cognitive skills that underpin talk for different purposes such as argument or explanation
4. **Social and emotional aspects of oracy**: a range of behaviours and competencies that allow different types of talk, both listening and responding to others and the confidence and self-awareness to contribute

(Mercer et al., 2014)

Sharing your thoughts is an inherently human activity, and recognition of the social and emotional aspects of oracy are especially important when children are asked to take part in the types of exploratory talk that is so important for learning. It takes individual confidence and a supportive environment for children to risk sharing half-formed ideas or suppositions aloud. These four aspects (above) provide the structure to consider classroom practice in Chapter 6.

Research and theory around spoken language in England

The role of talk and oracy in education has been widely debated for as long as formal education has existed. Opinions differ widely about its importance and its presence on the curriculum. The approaches that might be employed in the classroom have been the source of tension between different researchers and policymakers.

Much recent debate and theory in the area of oracy and spoken language has its roots in research from the 1960s and 1970s, most notably Barnes, Britton and Rosen (e.g. Barnes et al., 1969; Britton, 1970; Barnes, 1976) and Wilkinson (Wilkinson et al., 1965; Wilkinson, 1965, 1968). These theorists and researchers, many of whom were linked to both the National and London Associations for the Teaching of English (NATE and LATE), explored and articulated a number of ideas that still resonate today:

- How children learn through talk in different classroom contexts
- The importance of social context in supporting children's spoken language
- How pupils use talk to make sense of their experiences and lives
- Different structures for talk, including small group discussion and collaboration
- The role modelling and imitation play in children's language development
- A respect for local dialect forms and the language of the home in the school context and their role in enabling learning
- The need for careful thought to feed into clear policy around language development, both at school and national level
- Contexts where children's opportunities to talk are limited due to the dominance of teacher talk can inhibit children's learning

For these theorists, talk was not merely a way for children to articulate what they had learnt, it was *the vehicle by which they learnt*:

> ...we sharpen our understanding by telling or attempting to explain to others...[it is] access to that inner speech through which we organise our thinking.

> (Barnes et al., 1969)

Their work laid the foundations for theories of classroom talk that remain influential today.

Classroom talk: Theory to inform practice

Barnes (1976) suggests a useful distinction between *exploratory talk* and *presentational talk* in the classroom.

Exploratory talk describes the talk that children undertake to explore ideas and come to new understandings. This talk is often hesitant ('I wonder if…', 'It might be that…') as it involves trying out new ideas, assessing them in real time as they articulate them and eliciting the opinions of others.

In contrast, *presentational talk* is used to share more-polished thinking with others. Barnes and Todd (1976) describe this as:

> Final draft language [in speech or writing] is the contrary of exploratory: far from accompanying (and displaying) the detours and dead-ends of thinking, it seeks to exclude them and present a finished article, well-shaped and polished.

While it will not always represent children's definitive views and it might not always be correct, presentational talk comes from a place of greater confidence and understanding – it is a step beyond the 'playing with ideas' of exploratory talk.

Mercer and colleagues (e.g. Edwards and Mercer, 1987; Mercer and Littleton, 2007) suggest that exploratory talk can play a significant role in supporting learning across the curriculum, and that this 'interthinking' relies on a conscious awareness and specific teaching for children to enable this to happen (see Chapter 6 for more on this in practice).

STOP AND REFLECT

Think of a recent lesson you have taught, observed or planned. Jot down the opportunities that children had to talk:

- to one another
- to an adult
- to the whole class
- to a group
- to a partner

Now consider:

- Which of these would be classed as *exploratory talk* and which as *presentational talk*?
- Which was more prevalent in the lesson?
- How might these different purposes support the learning you were intending to happen or observe?
- How might they have supported children's wider development?

Dialogic teaching

Research documenting talk in schools stretching back to the 1970s suggests the prevalent types of discourse in classrooms are *Initiation-Response-Feedback* (IRF) or *Initiation-Response-Evaluation* (Sinclair and Coulthard, 1975; Burns and Myhill, 2004; Mercer and Dawes, 2014). These take the form of an initial (often closed) question by the teacher, a short response by the child and then confirmation/evaluation/feedback offered by the teacher:

Teacher: Who can remember where Toad lives?
Child: Toad House?
Teacher: Almost, it's Toad Hall.

IRF exchanges might follow this basic three-part pattern, but they can also lead to more complex exchanges, where an incorrect or unexpected response leads to further explanation from the teacher, and an invitation for a child to reformulate their answer or elaborate further on the subject (Molinari et al., 2013). However, at the heart of the exchange, it is the teacher who controls the discourse. While IRF can be useful as a pedagogical tool to check an individual child's understanding of a particular task or check children's existing knowledge and share it more widely (Gibbons, 2006), it does not provide a model for the exploratory talk that can be so useful for facilitating learning.

In his influential work on classroom discourse, Alexander (2001) organises classroom talk into five categories:

- **Rote:** the drilling of facts, ideas and routines
- **Recitation:** questions designed to elicit recall or work out answers from clues in the question
- **Instruction or exposition:** giving information and explaining facts, principles and procedures
- **Discussion:** the exchange of ideas with a view to sharing information and solving problems
- **Dialogue:** achieving common understanding through structured, cumulative questioning and discussion which guide and prompt, reduce choices, minimise risk and error, and expedite 'handover' of concepts and principles

While all of these types of talk are needed for specific purposes in the classroom, it is the final two, discussion and dialogue, that are most useful for helping children to think and reason, supporting the development of higher-order concepts through conscious and explicit focus (Mercer et al., 1999; Alexander, 2008).

Alexander suggests that:

Teaching which is dialogic rather than transmissive, and which provides the best chance for children to develop the diverse learning talk repertoire on which different kinds of thinking and understanding are predicated, meets five criteria.

(Alexander in Mercer and Hodgkinson, 2008)

Those criteria are:

- *Collective* in that teachers and children address learning tasks together, when there is a group or as a class
- *Reciprocal* in that teachers and children listen to each other, share ideas and consider alternative viewpoints
- *Supportive* in that children articulate their ideas freely, without the fear of embarrassment over 'wrong' answers, and help each other to reach common understandings
- *Cumulative* in that teachers and children build on their own and each other's ideas and change them into coherent lines of thinking and enquiry
- *Purposeful* teachers plan and state classroom talk with specific educational goals in view

(Alexander in Mercer and Hodgkinson, 2008)

These five criteria provide a model for the types of talk that might be employed in the primary English classroom to support children's learning.

Booktalk

Being able to find the space and time to share our thoughts and feelings around the literature that we read is not only a great way of promoting reading for pleasure but also celebrates that socially interactive experience, supporting rich talk in the classroom. The greater the formal and informal interactions we have around a text then the greater the opportunities for comprehension and understanding of both the text and each other. Chambers coined the term *Booktalk* in 1985 and sees it as a way of inviting and encouraging 'children to verbalise their literary experiences' (Eriksson, 2002), bringing them closer to the text and vice versa. Highlighting the centrality and nature of talk in readers' lives, it takes 'two forms': one is informal and the other is 'more considered' in that it follows a framework. The framework itself is built around 'levels of talk' that guides both teachers and children into becoming 'critically appreciative' and 'thoughtful readers' (Chambers, 1985, 2011).

Research suggests that children become more interested in and motivated to read the more that they talk about books with others (Wozniak, 2011; Hudson, 2016). This space and place for discussion in the classroom in both forms help to build that sense of a reading community and, in turn, provide opportunities for us to learn more about each other (Miller, 2014). Informal booktalk (or *book gossip* as Chambers calls it) might involve sharing recommendations, providing opportunities for children to broaden their reading repertoire: its aim is to encourage and empower intrinsic reading engagement and foster reading relationships. These encounters, alongside the formal approach explored below, 'encourage children to think in different ways' and ask 'more questions' about the text; digging deeper into the layers of meaning (Safford, 2014).

The Framework, a 'question-posing guide', was established as a way of emphasising the importance of teachers regularly providing and planning quality time for children to talk about books within a set time and group, and is a teaching strategy which focuses more on the 'nature' of talk (Chambers, 1985, 2011) with its foundations in Reader Response Theory – a concept that focuses more on the reader and their experience of the text. Chambers and his colleagues, in disseminating and reflecting upon their own dialogic reading practices with children, proposed a structure for individuals to share their thoughts and ideas about a book and a way in which to share those thoughts. The former is referred to as *The Three Sharings* and the latter as *Ways of Saying*. Together, they can support readers in thinking and talking about texts that they have read and, through dialogic discussion, build up a richer sense of meaning: Chambers refers to this as the 'Tell Me' approach. For more about this approach in practice, see Chapter 6 (p. 90).

Talk, spoken language and the curriculum

The importance of spoken language and its place on the curriculum has waxed and waned as a result of the statutory requirements placed on schools and the philosophies and enthusiasms of changing groups of policy makers.

The first National Curriculum for England, launched in 1989, organised the structure of English as a subject into three 'attainment targets': reading, writing, and speaking and listening, reflecting a commitment from the government of the day to the importance of spoken language in the classroom. This was supported by the central funding of the influential *Language in the National Curriculum Project* (LINC) (Carter, 1990). This project provided training materials to support teachers to develop their knowledge of language teaching and support effective classroom talk. However, tensions between policy makers and the project leaders over LINC's perceived sociolinguistic approach and the position it took in viewing Standard English as one of a variety within the richness of different English dialects, rather than a 'correct model' to which children should aspire, led to funding being removed. The work of the project remained influential among teachers and academics however, helping a sociolinguistic view of language teaching to flourish within the profession.

In the light of the Dearing Review (1994), a revised National Curriculum was introduced in 1995 which 'slimmed down' some of the curriculum content for primary schools to create 'discretionary time' in which literacy, numeracy and oracy were to be prioritised. In 1998, following a change of government, the National Literacy Strategy (NLS) was introduced with a clear focus on the teaching of reading and a formal, structured 'literacy hour'. This structure mandated a daily whole-class teacher-led 'interactive' element, which led to a model of classroom dialogue that relied heavily on IRF patterns of classroom talk (Coles, 2005). A new National Curriculum was launched in 1999. In addition to speaking and listening as a strand of English (comprising of *speaking, listening, group discussion and interaction, drama, Standard English* and *language variation*), this model took *communication* as a key skill that ran throughout the curriculum, where 'skills in speaking and listening include the ability to speak effectively for different audiences; to listen, understand and respond appropriately to others; and to participate effectively in group discussion' (DfEE, 1999). In 2003, the NLS was combined with the Numeracy Strategy to become the National Primary Strategy (DfES, 2003). Again, talk and oracy was somewhat overlooked in favour of a focus on reading and writing. While support materials such as *Speaking, Listening and Learning: working with children in Key Stages 1 and 2* (DfES, 2003) eventually followed, reflecting the structure of speaking and listening in the 1999 National Curriculum, the onus was on individual schools and teachers to find and utilise these resources, rather than them being an integral part of the framework.

The current 2014 National Curriculum for England employs the term 'spoken language' for this aspect of English. The framework claims to reflect '…the importance of spoken language in pupils' development across the whole curriculum – cognitively, socially and linguistically' (DfE, 2013). In early drafts of the framework, this spoken language element did not exist as a discrete element and instead was 'reflected and contextualised within the reading and writing domains' (DfE, 2013). In the final published version, the 2014 National Curriculum for England gives twelve 'statutory requirements' which apply to all primary years and 'should be taught at a level appropriate to the age of the pupils':

- Listen and respond appropriately to adults and their peers.
- Ask relevant questions to extend their understanding and knowledge.
- Use relevant strategies to build their vocabulary.
- Articulate and justify answers, arguments and opinions.
- Give well-structured descriptions, explanations and narratives for different purposes, including for expressing feelings.
- Maintain attention and participate actively in collaborative conversations, staying on topic and initiating and responding to comments.
- Use spoken language to develop understanding through speculating, hypothesising, imagining and exploring ideas.
- Speak audibly and fluently with an increasing command of Standard English.
- Participate in discussions, presentations, performances, role play, improvisations and debates.
- Gain, maintain and monitor the interest of the listener(s).
- Consider and evaluate different viewpoints, attending to and building on the contributions of others.
- Select and use appropriate registers for effective communication.

(DfE, 2013)

It has been argued that this brief additional section suggests that spoken language is not a significant priority for the curriculum (Mercer et al., 2014). This is especially evident when compared with the lengthy and detailed expectations for grammar and punctuation: instead, 'it undervalues the spoken language at Key Stages 1 and 2, and is over-concerned with formal, performance-based uses of the spoken language…' (Richmond, 2016).

STOP AND REFLECT

Considering the statements describing the statutory requirements for spoken language drawn from the 2014 National Curriculum above, consider:

- How might each statement differ in key stage 1, lower key stage 2 and upper key stage 2?
- Which statements might be priorities to focus on in your class?
- Which statements might need to be planned as specific learning opportunities and which might be addressed through the wider curriculum?
- How might different learners need to be supported to work towards meeting the different statements? How could we support children who speak English as an additional language (EAL), or children with speech, language and communication needs (SLCN), for example?

Aside from this initial set of statements, however, many of the expectations for reading comprehension and writing composition are interwoven with reference to spoken language. Table 5.1 illustrates this with the example of the Year 3 and 4 programme of study.

Table 5.1   Year 3 and 4 programme of study – spoken language elements

Reading comprehension statutory requirements	Pupils should be taught to develop positive attitudes to reading and understanding of what they read by:
	• listening to and discussing a wide range of fiction, poetry, plays, non-fiction and reference books or textbooks
	• preparing poems and play scripts to read aloud and to perform, showing understanding through intonation, tone, volume and action
	• discussing words and phrases that capture the reader's interest and imagination
	Pupils should be taught to understand what they read, in books they can read independently, by:
	• checking that the text makes sense to them, discussing their understanding and explaining the meaning of words in context
	• asking questions to improve their understanding of a text
	• participating in discussion about both books that are read to them and those they can read for themselves, taking turns and listening to what others say
Writing composition statutory requirements	Pupils should be taught to plan their writing by:
	• discussing writing similar to that which they are planning to write in order to understand and learn from its structure, vocabulary and grammar
	• discussing and recording ideas
	Pupils should:
	• read aloud their own writing, to a group or the whole class, using appropriate intonation and controlling the tone and volume so that the meaning is clear

When planning English as a whole, the teacher must be careful to acknowledge how talk and oracy are both important aspects of the curriculum in their own right and the medium through which learning happens. While the statutory requirements for spoken language outlined in the 2014 National Curriculum are not opposed to the rich dialogic patterns of talk that support deep learning in the primary classroom, it is clear that they rely on skilful teachers to mediate the statements and weave them together into a coherent classroom model.

Conclusion

Talk, both social and for learning, provides the foundation of English as a subject at primary school. As the *Cambridge Primary Review* noted:

> …talk – at home, in school, among peers – is education at its most elemental and potent. It is the aspect of teaching which has arguably the greatest influence on learning.

> (Alexander et al., 2009)

This chapter has considered some key theoretical implications drawn from research, reflecting on the types of talk that might be useful to support children's learning and the different cognitive, linguistic, physical and social elements that make up speaking and listening in school. In Chapter 6, these ideas will be explored through classroom practice, introducing ways of supporting children to communicate successfully both to share their ideas and to understand and make sense of the world around them.

IN SUMMARY

- Oracy and spoken language are crucial for the development of reading and writing; they are also important in their own right as they allow children to communicate their ideas with the world.
- Development in this area relies on a series of interlinked facets, including physical, linguistic, cognitive and social and emotional elements.
- While IRF remains the dominant model of discourse in many primary classrooms, exploratory talk and dialogic teaching can support children's learning in addition to their language development.

FURTHER READING

- Read *Exploring Talk in Schools* edited by Neil Mercer and Steve Hodgkinson for a thorough overview of the work of Douglas Barnes and a consideration of valuable types of talk in schools.
- For a detailed introduction to dialogic teaching, see *Towards Dialogic Teaching: Rethinking classroom talk* by Robin Alexander.

REFERENCES

Alexander, R.J. (2001) *Culture and Pedagogy: International comparisons in primary education*. Oxford: Blackwell.

Alexander, R.J. (2008) *Towards Dialogic Teaching: Rethinking classroom talk*. Cambridge: Dialogos.

Alexander, R.J. (Ed.), Hofkins, D. and Northen, S. (2009) *Introducing the Cambridge Primary Review*. Cambridge: University of Cambridge, Faculty of Education.

Barnes, D. (1976) *From Communication to Curriculum*. Harmondsworth: Penguin.

Barnes, D., Britton, J. and Rosen, H. (1969) *Language, the Learner and the School*. Harmondsworth: Penguin.

Barnes, D. and Todd, F. (1976) *Communication and Learning in Small Groups*. London: Routledge & Kegan Paul.

Britton, J. (1970) *Language and Learning*. Coral Gables, FL: University of Miami Press.

Burns, C. and Myhill, D. (2004) Interactive or Inactive? A consideration of the nature of interaction in whole class teaching. *Cambridge Journal of Education*, 34(1): 35–48.

Carter, R. (Ed.) (1990) *Knowledge About Language and the Curriculum: The LINC Reader*. London: Hodder and Stoughton.

Chambers, A. (1985) *Booktalk: Occasional writing on literature & children*. London: Bodley Head.

Chambers., A. (2011) *Tell Me (Children, Reading & Talk) with the Reading Environment*. Stroud: The Thimble Press.

Coles, J. (2005) Strategic voices? Problems in developing oracy through 'interactive' whole-class teaching. *Changing English*, 12(1): 113–23.

Dearing, R. (1994) *National Curriculum and its Assessment: Final report*. London: School Curriculum and Assessment Authority.

Department for Education (DfE) (2013) *The National Curriculum in England. Framework document*. London: DfE.

Department for Education and Employment (DfEE) (1998) *The National Literacy Strategy: Framework for Teaching*. London: DfEE.

Department for Education and Employment (DfEE) (1999) *The National Curriculum*. London: Her Majesty's Stationery Office (HMSO).

Department for Education and Skills (DfES) (2003) *Primary National Strategy Speaking, Listening and Learning: Working with children in Key stages One and Two*. London: HMSO.

Department for Education and Skills (DfES) (2006) *Primary National Strategy: Primary framework for Literacy and Mathematics*. London: DfES.

Edwards, D. and Mercer, N. (1987) *Common Knowledge: The development of understanding in the classroom*. Abingdon: Routledge.

Eriksson, K. (2002) Booktalk dilemmas: Teachers' organisation of pupils' reading. *Scandinavian Journal of Educational Research*, 46(4): 391–408.

Gibbons, P. (2006) *Bridging Discourses in the ESL Classroom: Students, teachers and researchers*. London: Bloomsbury Academic.

Gross, J. (2011) *The Contribution of Oral Language Skills to School Improvement and Outcomes for Children and Young People*. London: Office of the Communication Champion.

Howe, C. and Mercer, N. (2007) Children's Social Development, Peer Interaction and Classroom Learning. *Primary Review Research Survey 2/1b*. Cambridge: University of Cambridge Faculty of Education.

Hudson, A.K. (2016) Get them talking! Using student-led book talks in the primary grades. *Reading Teacher*, 70(2): 221–5.

ICAN/RCSLT (2018) *Bercow: Ten Years on – an Independent Review of Provision for Children and Young People with Speech, Language and Communication Needs in England*. London: ICAN/RCSLT.

Mercer, N. and Dawes, L. (2014) The study of talk between teachers and students, from the 1970s until the 2010s. *Oxford Review of Education*, 40(4): 430–45.

Mercer, N. and Hodgkinson, S. (Eds) (2008) *Exploring Talk in School*. London: Sage.

Mercer, N. and Littleton, K. (2007) *Dialogue and the Development of Children's Thinking: A socio-cultural approach*. London: Routledge.

Mercer, N., Warwick, P. and Ahmed, A. (2014) *Developing a toolkit to assess spoken language skills in the classroom: Final report of a project carried out in partnership with School 21 and funded by the Educational Endowment Foundation*. University of Cambridge.

Mercer, N., Wegerif, R. and Dawes, L. (1999) Children's talk and the development of reasoning in the classroom. *British Educational Research Journal*, 25: 95–111.

Miller, D. (2014) *Reading in the Wild: The book whisperer's keys to cultivating lifelong reading habits*. San Francisco, CA: Jossey-Bass.

Molinari, L., Mameli, C. and Gnisci, A. (2013) A sequential analysis of classroom discourse in Italian primary schools: The many faces of the IRF pattern. *British Journal of Educational Psychology*, 83(3).

Richmond, J. (2016) *English, Language and Literacy 3 to 19 – Principles and Proposals and Curriculum and Assessment in English 3 to 19: A Better Plan*. London: United Kingdom Literacy Association and Owen Education.

Safford, K. (2014) A reading for pleasure pedagogy. In T. Cremin, M. Mottram, F.M. Collins, S. Powell and K. Safford (Eds) *Building Communities of Engaged Readers: Reading for pleasure* (pp. 89–107). Abingdon: Routledge.

Sinclair, J.M.H. and Coulthard, M. (1975) *Towards an Analysis of Discourse: The English used by teachers and pupils*. Oxford: Oxford University Press.

Snowling, M.J., Hulme, C., Bailey, A.M., Stothard, S. and Lindsay, G. (2011) *Language and Literacy Attainment of Pupils during Early Years and through KS2: Does teacher assessment at five provide a valid measure of children's current and future educational attainments?* Better Communication Research Programme. London: Department for Education.

St Clair, M., Pickles, A., Durkin, K. and Conti-Ramsden, G. (2011) A longitudinal study of behavioural, emotional and social difficulties in individuals with a history of specific language impairment (SLI). *Journal of Communication Disorders*, 44(2): 186–99.

Vallotton, C. and Ayoub, C. (2011) Use your words: The role of language in the development of toddlers' self-regulation. *Early Childhood Research Quarterly*, 26(2): 169–81.

Wilkinson, A. (1965) The concept of oracy. *Educational Review*, 17(4): 11–15.

Wilkinson, A. (1968) The implications of oracy. *Educational Review*, 20(2): 123–35.

Wilkinson, A., Davies, A. and Atkinson, D. (1965) Spoken English. *University of Birmingham Educational Review* Occasional Publications No 2.

Wozniak, C.L. (2011) Reading and talking about books: A critical foundation for intervention. *Voices from the Middle*, 19(2): 17–24.

6

TALK, ORACY AND SPOKEN LANGUAGE: PRACTICE

THIS CHAPTER WILL

- Introduce a framework for considering oracy and spoken language in the primary classroom

- Share practical approaches for developing children's ability to communicate, focusing on the role of discussion and dialogic talk

- Illustrate different opportunities for spoken development through a range of case studies

Introduction

Oracy and spoken language are not only the foundation on which other aspects of primary English – reading and writing – are built. Spoken language is also the medium through which learning happens. As we have seen in Chapter 5, planned opportunities for rich exploratory talk and careful consideration of a range of different types of classroom talk are crucial for children's wider development and progress.

Chapter 5 explored the theory underpinning oracy and spoken language development in primary schools, and this chapter seeks to explore the implications of this in practice. As with the other paired chapters in this book, this chapter is intended to be read in conjunction with its complementary theory chapter, with the two elements of theory and practice supporting one another.

A framework for spoken language development

As it can be viewed as a biologically primary skill (Geary and Huffman, 2002; Geary, 2005), the great majority of children will naturally develop the ability to use spoken language. However, communicating confidently across a range of different contexts and for different audiences and purposes can be more challenging to master and is likely to demand specific teaching and attention across the curriculum. One reason for this is because oracy is not one discrete skill. Instead, being able to communicate confidently relies on a number of related attributes.

A useful model for an oracy framework is the one outlined in Chapter 5, created by Voice 21 with Oracy Cambridge (Mercer et al., 2014). The model suggests four aspects by which to organise the 'skills that enable successful discussion, inspiring speech and effective communication' (Voice 21, 2019). These are:

1. Physical aspects of oracy
2. Linguistic aspects of oracy
3. Cognitive aspects of oracy
4. Social and emotional aspects of oracy

While many frameworks for considering oracy and spoken language have been suggested (see Chapter 5), this model is appropriate for this practice chapter as it has been developed to 'balance detailed accuracy and complexity with clarity and practical usefulness' (Mercer et al., 2014). It also focuses on the skills and behaviours that underpin oracy across a range of contexts, rather than setting out the contexts for talk that might be expected (discussions, debates, presentations, etc.). In this regard, it is far closer to the model of teaching writing explored in Chapters 11 and 12, with a focus on conscious control of different aspects of language to meet the demands of audience and purpose, than to context-based frameworks such as the objectives drawn from the Primary National Strategy (DfES, 2006).

The curriculum model and pedagogical approaches schools employ when teaching reading and writing and across the wider curriculum need to provide opportunities for children to develop in each of these four areas. This could be through specific curriculum vehicles such as literacy circles or whole-class debates, or it could be, in a broader sense, through the way talk is organised and run in the classroom and school.

As we have seen in Chapter 5, Alexander (2001) organises classroom talk into five categories: rote, recitation, instruction or exposition, discussion and dialogue.

While all of these types of talk are needed for specific purposes in the classroom, it is the final two, discussion and dialogue, that are most useful in helping children to think and reason, supporting the *talking to learn* that follows *learning to talk*.

STOP AND REFLECT

Think about your last teaching session, whether you were working with an individual child, a group of children or a whole class.

- Which of Alexander's *categories for talk* did you employ?
- Were there any that you felt you could have employed?

Look at the scenarios below. Which types of talk might you use for each one?

- Teaching a group of Y1 children how to use capital letters and full stops in their writing
- Helping a class to learn a poem by heart
- Everyone in the class sharing their opinions about Bernard's parents in *Not Now, Bernard.*

Is there only one way of structuring the talk or could it legitimately be organised effectively in different ways?

Developing spoken language in practice

This next section will consider the four strands of Voice 21 and Oracy Cambridge's Oracy Framework (2019), illustrating each with case studies and outlining opportunities for discussion and dialogic teaching in practice.

1. Physical aspects of oracy

Effective spoken communication relies on a range of specific physical skills and behaviours. These encompass both vocal aspects and body language. Command of these, and having the ability to recognise when they might be employed, is a principal part of oracy. Table 6.1 outlines these aspects, giving examples from the primary classroom.

Table 6.1 Physical aspects of oracy: examples from primary classroom

Physical aspects of oracy: vocal aspects	Examples from the primary classroom
Controlling the volume of the voice so it can be heard	Children understanding the difference in volume required when speaking for different purposes. For example, consciously projecting voice loudly so everyone can hear when being part of a presentation about life in Victorian Britain, but speaking more softly when working in a small group to plan their presentation.
Regulating tone and pace to reflect the content and purpose of the task	Children recognising the need to speak slowly and clearly so everyone can follow their words when retelling the story of *Little Red Riding Hood* to a group of younger children. They might pause and speak even more slowly 'as...the...door...opens' to build tension, before speeding up to reflect the sense of excitement when the woodcutter rushes in.
Clearly pronouncing words so they can be understood	As well as attempting to pronounce their words clearly enough that they can be followed, children might have learnt some specific examples of terminology in maths that they find difficult to say (*parallelogram*, for example). Having had the chance to practise saying these tricky words aloud, they know to consciously enunciate them clearly, so their audience recognises the word.

Physical aspects of oracy: body language	Examples from primary classroom
Awareness and control of posture	Children have practised standing up straight with their heads held high when talking to the school as part of their class assembly on how the local area has changed over time. When talking in groups, however, they have been made aware of how they can show they are listening to others (leaning forwards, smiling, nodding, etc.).
Use of facial expressions, gestures and body language	When performing poems, children use different gestures to highlight parts of the poem, their body language reflecting their spoken language.
Making eye-contact when speaking and listening	Children think about how eye-contact can help to engage the audience when they are taking part in a whole-class debate about whether there should be a longer school day, making sure they are looking at the person they are debating with, rather than at the floor. When listening, they recognise that they do not need to make eye-contact at all times, but that it is a way of showing that they are thinking about what the speaker is saying.

While these aspects have been detailed individually in the table above, they are closely linked to one another and are likely to be taught and practised together: standing with shoulders back supports projecting the voice loudly and clearly, while awareness of hand gestures might help to add meaning and to draw attention to certain parts of their talk.

Opportunities for developing the physical aspects of oracy can be divided into two broad areas: ongoing teaching and attention and specific activities to develop children's control and confidence. In a language-rich classroom, where there are many opportunities for dialogue and discussion, children will have the chance to practise these behaviours. Teachers can support children by sharing expectations for different tasks ('In this session you'll be working in your groups so you'll need to show you're listening and thinking carefully about what other members of the groups say') and by building in opportunities for different types of talk to different audiences, from rich booktalk (see below) to regular 'show and tell' sessions, where children bring in something to talk about. Performing poetry and drama sessions also provide opportunities for developing the physical aspects of oracy.

CASE STUDY 6.1

As well as an opportunity to explore wonderful texts, performing poetry can be an excellent way of developing children's oracy skills. One school mapped the opportunity to learn poetry by heart and then perform it to an audience across the school three times a year, with a termly 'performing poetry week'.

Everyone in the school would perform a poem, but teachers could choose to organise this as whole-class choral performances; children working in groups or pairs to interpret a poem; or, with older children, learning a poem by heart and then performing it individually.

To support the teachers with the process of preparing a poem to be performed and with choosing a poem in the first place, a twilight inset was set aside each half-term for teachers to explore online resources such as Poetryline (CLPE.org.uk/poetryline) and Poetry by Heart (poetrybyheart.org.uk).

The project would culminate in a week of performances – assemblies to parents, classes performing to each other and performances being filmed to be shared across the school.

---

2. Linguistic aspects of oracy

The linguistic aspects of oracy are those concerned with language choices. Table 6.2 summarises these, illustrating them with examples.

Table 6.2 Linguistic aspects of oracy: examples from the primary classroom

Linguistic aspects of oracy	Examples from the primary classroom
Effective vocabulary choice	Children match the needs of their audience and purpose to the vocabulary choices they make. For example, when presenting the results in science lessons, they not only use scientific terminology (*evaporated, solution*), but also attempt to employ the formal language that might be found in presentations of this kind (*observed*, rather than *looked at; nutrients*, rather than *food*).

Linguistic aspects of oracy	Examples from the primary classroom
Language choices, including choice of register and choice of syntax and grammar	Children reflect on the language structures they choose to use, showing awareness of register and dialect forms. For example, they move into a more formal register when taking part in a whole-class debate about whether Charlie is brave or not when he disobeys a direct order in *Private Peaceful* by Michael Morpurgo.
Use of rhetorical techniques such as metaphors, deliberate understatement or hyperbole	Children are aware of different rhetorical devices that can be used for effect in speech. For example, they consider memorable phrases from history or literature and analyse the devices they use. When reading an abridged version of *A Tale of Two Cities*, the line 'It was the best of times, it was the worst of times' is introduced as an example of antithesis, setting two seemingly contrasting ideas against each other.

Vocabulary choice

Vocabulary choice is explored in depth in Chapter 14, considering both the theory surrounding vocabulary development and practical approaches for supporting this area in the classroom. Vocabulary development might focus on specific teaching activities (learning the word *assonance* when looking at poetry, for example), or it might be an ongoing focus, with teachers consciously introducing children to new words through techniques such as:

Target words

Children are given a set of essential words that they should try to use in a particular talk opportunity. These could be on a hand-out or displayed on the whiteboard. Once the meaning of the words has been discussed, children are encouraged to use them in their talk. For example, in Year 6 when looking at two newspaper reports with different perspectives on the same issue, children are encouraged to use the words *bias, intends, infers* and *editor*.

Amplifying and recasting

The teacher consciously models academic language, *amplifying* common terms to introduce potentially unfamiliar words ('…so we'll watch and see what happens, see what *occurs*'). When children talk, teachers can acknowledge their language use and then *recast* it, using different, less-common language ('Yes, that's right, he came towards the door, he *approached* the door).

Tricky word signal

The class has an agreed non-verbal signal that they can use to let the teacher know when she uses an unfamiliar word. This might be a hand on each shoulder or the time-out 'T' sign with two hands. If a child hears a tricky word, they make the signal. The teacher notices it and offers another word or simplifies the language they are using. For example:

Teacher: So, everyone needs to submit their project…
[Spots tricky word signal]
Teacher: So, each group should *hand in – submit* – their project by the end of the lesson.

Not only does this help children to find the meaning of potentially unfamiliar words, it encourages them to reflect on the language the teacher is using. Because the sign is non-verbal, the flow of the lesson isn't interrupted.

Techniques like these are useful when they become part of everyday discourse in the classroom; they explore layers of new words encountered until children build up a sense of where the new word can be used and how it fits with other words they know already.

Language choices

The language we employ is likely to depend on whom we are speaking to and our purpose for talk, in addition to any language patterns we employ linked to geographical area or social group. *Register* refers to the varieties of language linked to a specific purpose or use, employing different vocabularies or grammar patterns. For example, 'I look forward to our meeting on Tuesday 4th February' might be used in a formal email for a work context, while 'can't wait to catch up next week' might be more appropriate for a text message to a friend. *Dialect* is a set of words and grammatical structures linked not to purpose, but to user. These often have a basis in regional areas, but can sometimes become uncoupled from geography, such as what is termed 'estuary English' (Crystal, 2018) or Standard English. An awareness of these different varieties of language that we can employ and the ability to move between them forms a key part of oracy education.

The 2014 National Curriculum for England promotes the use of Standard English in the classroom. Standard English is defined as:

A very small range of forms such as *those books, I did it* and *I wasn't doing anything* (rather than their non-Standard equivalents); it is not limited to any particular accent. It is the variety of English which is used, with only minor variation, as a major world language. Some people use Standard English all the time, in all situations from the most casual to the most formal, so it covers most registers.

(DfE, 2013)

One issue with Standard English, especially in areas where local dialect forms are spoken, can be that Standard English is set up as being somehow 'better' than local forms of language – the dialects children might speak at home or with their family. Myhill et al.

(2016) suggest using the term 'language that we all understand', rather than 'Standard English', as it does not set one variation of language choices above another. It also has the benefit of encouraging children to think about their intended audience when speaking. If they use local dialect forms when creating a film that could be viewed by anybody, can they guarantee someone from another part of the country will understand their message? If they use a slang term that they use with their friends, would an adult necessarily understand what they were saying?

CASE STUDY 6.2

To help children to develop an ear for 'language that we all understand', one school used the British Library's 'British Accents and Dialect' site to share with children some different regional dialects from across the country. The children worked in groups to listen to different examples, some familiar and some unfamiliar, and to note some of the differences. They found differences with:

- Expressing negatives (I haven't; I cannae; I ain't; it's no possible; I divvent)
- Past tense (I went; I come back)
- Use of pronouns (those balls; them children; her'd go back along the road)
- Vocabulary (tired, knackered, cream-crackered, wabbit, done it)

They were then encouraged to think about which might be useful when talking to people who used the same dialect and which might benefit from being adapted when talking to a wider audience, where the speaker might choose to move to 'language that we all understand'.

Use of rhetorical techniques

Rhetorical devices are aspects of language that have been carefully chosen because they may resonate with a listener and prompt specific emotions. They can often be found in speeches, ranging from famous orations from history (the *anaphora* used in 'I have a dream...' or 'We shall fight...'), to Shakespeare (the *chiasmus* of 'Fair is foul, and foul is fair'), to many modern political speeches (the *epizeuxis* of 'education, education, education'). While learning about rhetoric might seem like an indulgence when probably very few children will have the need to give rousing speeches in their later life, learning about some of these features helps to reveal how language works under the bonnet, allowing children to explore its possibilities – a key part of great English teaching. Many rhetorical devices are also employed in literary works, so this helps to establish a grounding for secondary English literature lessons too.

3. Cognitive aspects of oracy

The cognitive aspects of oracy are those involved with thinking. The Voice 21 framework organises these into five linked aspects, outlined in Table 6.3.

Table 6.3 Cognitive aspects of oracy: examples from primary classroom

Cognitive aspects of oracy	Examples from the primary classroom
Selecting content	Children are able to select relevant content and build on the views of others. When presenting to the class about an aspect of Victorian life that they have researched, children are able to refer to other talks, building on the ideas of others. In a group discussion, they try not to repeat the ideas of others, instead building on or commenting on ideas that they have heard.
Organising structure	Children are able to reflect on and structure talk for different purposes. For example, recognising that a prepared speech arguing that single-use plastic should be banned at school might be structured differently from the back and forth of a debate about whether mobile phones should be allowed at school, even if the purpose of both is to persuade.
Clarifying and summarising	Children use questions to seek clarity from other speakers. They are able to summarise ideas to ensure that they understand. Summarising is one of the most useful metacognitive strategies we can help children to develop (Clements, 2017). In shared reading activities, children undertake a close reading of a section of *Flora and Ulysses* by Kate DiCamillo and then summarise to show their understanding. They then engage in a booktalk session (Chambers, 2011), exploring any aspects that they find puzzling.
Self-regulation of talk	Children are able to focus on their task, work within time constraints and show an awareness of the effectiveness of their talk. In a group writing task to collect ideas for an advert for new football boots, children are able to return to their brief, making sure that they discuss a name, possible tag lines and some of the key features they will try to draw out in their advert. Children are aware that they are spending too long on the name, so they decide to move on and return to that later, if time allows.
Reasoning	Here children give reasons to justify their own thinking, but also examine and challenge the ideas of others rationally. In a shared writing activity, children share their ideas for words to describe a character, explaining in order to support the suggestions they agree with and challenging those they do not.

Booktalk: cognition and talk in practice

In the English classroom, the strands that form the cognitive aspects of oracy can all be developed through *Booktalk* (Chambers, 1985).

Chambers' 'Tell Me' strategy (see Chapter 5, p. 74) provides teachers and children with a structure for thinking, talking and responding to texts as well as the thoughts of others. Not only does it offer opportunities for children to extend their vocabulary and language but it also invites them to share their ideas about a text and world-to-text associations beyond it. Equally, it invites them to listen to and interact with the thoughts of others in the group. This is not about, as Chambers (2011) puts it, guessing 'what's in the teachers' head'. Through this sense of collaborative meaning making, under the guidance of the teacher as expert, children begin to make complex and rewarding connections between themselves and the text, to other texts and text-to-the-world.

Kinds of saying

Booktalk is a 'communal activity' (Chambers, 2011). The act of sharing our thoughts, as well as listening to and building upon those of others, is an integral part of the Tell Me process and shows how it can be both 'private' (as we disseminate and share our own personal thoughts) and 'public' (when we share these thoughts with the rest of the group). Chambers breaks down these critical 'speech acts', ways of sharing our thoughts through talk, under the following headings:

Saying for yourself

This is a speech act that focuses on saying aloud an idea that you have in your head. You choose to share it with others as a way of clarifying your thinking and assessing whether what we are thinking makes sense to ourselves and others. Examples Chambers gives here are: 'How does this sound?', 'Let me try this on you' or 'I'm only thinking aloud'.

Consider: How can we best support children in sharing their thoughts and ideas? What kind of questions can we ask that will elicit rich responses and thinking?

Saying to others

When we have shared our thoughts with the rest of the group, it is our hope that they have fully understood what we were trying to communicate and, in turn, 'help us understand it better'. We can only know this if the listener 'reflects it back to the speaker'. The more we say and reflect, the more we enrich our understanding.

Consider: What makes someone a good listener? How can we support children to become better at this?

Saying together

Sometimes when reading and thinking about texts, we encounter an idea or a moment that might be too challenging for us to comprehend alone. What happens then is a 'conscious pooling' of thoughts and ideas between the group. At an individual level, each reader brings something to the text. This 'co-operative act' invites us to build meaning together and allows us to create a clearer picture of what the text might be saying.

Consider: What can we do to make sure that both the speaker has understood what they have said as well as the listener? How can the teacher 'consolidate' and confirm this shared knowledge and understanding?

Saying the new

The accumulation of the previous three sayings often result in speakers and listeners finding out something new about the text that they may not have seen or considered before: a 'revelation' as Chambers (2011) puts it. The idea of unearthing new meanings from the text is a richly rewarding and pleasurable experience.

Consider: What something new has been revealed and shared? What does the teacher 'say or do' with this?

The Three Sharings

With a concept of inviting different ways of responding to a text and to each other presented above, Chambers' *Three Sharings* presents us with a structure from which we can encourage these different *Kinds of Saying*. This process invites us to become more critical and exploratory in our booktalk and leads us towards a deeper reading and meaning of the text.

Sharing enthusiasms

This is separated into two different sections: 'likes' and 'dislikes'. The former invites us to share what we found pleasing, attractive, surprising and impressive about the text and what made us want to continue reading (Chambers, 2011). The latter invites us to share moments in the story that may have discouraged us from continuing. Often, this can be aspects or scenes which we found puzzling or challenging and if that is the case then such comments may find themselves moved into the following category.

Sharing puzzles (i.e. difficulties)

Sometimes there may be moments in the text that we did not understand. Through the four 'Sayings' we may later come to such an understanding, but for now they should be noted down. Additionally, the story may have several layers of meaning, some of which you could not find the answer to alone. Sharing these puzzles and difficulties can lead to a richer meaning and appreciation of the text.

Sharing connections (i.e. discovering patterns)

What patterns do we see in the narrative? Are phrases or images repeated and, if so, what significance might they bear? How about characters, plot, themes and motifs? Did we connect any of these elements to other stories beyond the text or even to our own experiences? In finding these connections or discovering patterns in the narrative we may enrich the meaning and our interpretation of the text.

Chambers (1985, 2011) tells us that neither sayings nor sharings come in any order of importance. Instead, they are 'guided by immediate need' rather than a prescribed structure. It is a model that provides us with a flexible scaffold in which to get the most out of the text and the talk connected to it in a critical yet deeply rewarding way.

4. Social and emotional aspects of oracy

As with much of the learning that happens in the primary classroom, effective oracy provision does not occur in a vacuum. Children are people with their own feelings and emotions. Speaking, whether to an audience or the back and forth talk of group work, is an emotional experience. When helping to prepare for this, the Voice 21 framework suggests four key areas, outlined in Table 6.4.

Table 6.4   Social and emotional aspects of oracy: examples from primary classroom

Cognitive aspects of oracy	Examples from the primary classroom
Working with others	Children are able to use their skills and knowledge of oracy to work on joint projects, group work and group discussion without adult input. For example, when working on a group project to design a new theme park, the children are able to go around the table, with everyone having the chance to suggest ideas, before trying to reach a consensus that is a genuine group decision.
Listening and responding	Building on the previous area, children are aware of their responsibility as a listener to take on board the ideas of others and then respond to them thoughtfully. Using scaffolds for talk that they have learned to use previously, they can then disagree and challenge one another's ideas politely. In booktalk sessions, children can express different interpretations of the poem *A Noiseless Patient Spider* by Walt Whitman, respecting each other's views.
Confidence in speaking	Children are confident when speaking in different situations ranging from a prepared talk about their favourite hobby to an audience, to sharing their ideas and defending them in a small group on a shared writing task in English.
Awareness of audience	Children are able to reflect on the likely needs of their audience and tailor the content and language structures they use accordingly. For example, choosing to include definitions of key words such as (*alliteration* and *assonance*) when making an oral report to parents about poems they have selected for a class anthology.

Listening, responding and working with others

Establishing a set of guidelines or expectations for discussion in a classroom is a useful step in structuring classroom talk and helping children to learn how to contribute meaningfully. Oracy Cambridge has created a set of free resources to help teachers to develop their own guidelines for discussion (search online for: *Oracy Cambridge resources*). Programmes with talk at the centre, such as Philosophy for Children (SAPERE, 2020), Circle Time (Mosley, 1996) or Helicopter Stories (Paley, 1991; Lee, 2015) can also provide a platform for children to develop rich classroom discussion.

Physical resources can also be used to help children to be aware of the types of talk that are being used in the classroom and their own contribution as a speaker.

CASE STUDY 6.3

One school explored the use of physical resources to help children to reflect on class discussion. They tried using two resources:

Connectable building blocks

These were used in two key ways. First, when speaking in small groups, individual children were allocated a different colour of brick. As each child contributed, their colour of brick was added to a growing tower. This enabled them to be aware of the flow of conversation and to actively reflect on and manage turn-taking. The second way these were used was by the teacher to record the types of talk being used in whole-class discussion. Different types of talk (agreeing, challenging, building on an answer, asking questions, asking for clarification) were allocated a different colour. As children made contributions, the teacher added a block to the tower. This enabled the children to reflect on the sort on discussion they had had, and also for the teacher to prompt if necessary ('We haven't had many questions yet. Does anyone have a question for Amira?').

Counters

Coloured counters were used to track children's contributions to group and whole-class discussions. Each child was given three counters and if they contributed, they 'paid' with one counter. For the children who were very keen to contribute, they had to learn to listen to others, wait for their turn and use their tokens wisely when they had something important to say. For those children less keen to join in, it was easy for the teacher to monitor discussion and intervene ('You've still got all of your counters left, Tom. Is there anything you'd like to say about the book?')

Confidence in speaking and awareness of audience

The social and emotional aspects of oracy are often seen as being 'natural abilities' and this is particularly true of confidence: some children are naturally shy, while others are happy talking to a large audience. While of course all children are different and all enter the class-room from different starting points, this aspect of oracy is one that can be developed and practised like any other.

Building confidence is likely to be a long-term project, involving a whole-school culture of talk. If opportunities to talk aloud are limited to specific termly or half-termly speaking and listening activities such as presentations and debates, then the curriculum is likely to be insufficient to help children become confident speakers. Instead, schools might:

Plan different opportunities to talk

Talking to (and with) different audiences, from a small group of friends to a full hall and for different purposes – from talking to your partner to see if you agree about the answer, to presenting the findings of your experiment – helps children to see that there are many different ways of being a successful speaker. Children can build on the scenarios they feel most comfortable with already, while developing their confidence in others through positive feedback.

Start from children's areas of confidence and interest

Having the chance to talk about things you know about or feel passionate about is a key way of building children's confidence. Showing a favourite toy from home, talking about your family or retelling your favourite story gives children the chance to be an expert. This means they do not have to worry about the content as it is already well known to them.

Make oracy activities *normal*

In a whole-school culture that values oracy, talk happens constantly. It is entirely nor-mal to share your ideas with a partner, talk in a small group, present your findings orally rather than through writing, or engage in booktalk after reading. If oracy is only about a big presentation at the end of a topic or a special debate where the tables have been moved, it can be overwhelming. Instead, talk needs to be the heartbeat that drives the curriculum forward.

Put drama and play at the heart of the curriculum

While putting on a performance to an audience can be useful for developing children's confidence, perhaps more beneficial is the play-based improvised drama (acting in role as a character, rather than performing a given role written by someone else). Working in role, whether following a formal model such as Mantle of the Expert (e.g. Heathcote and Bolton, 1995) or other play-based approaches (see Winston and Tandy, 2008), gives an opportunity to try out different types of talk and different ways of talking in a safe, imagined context. Working in role as the inhabitants of the graveyard deciding what they should do with Bod when studying Neil Gaiman's *The Graveyard Book* might be far less daunting for some children than a traditional whole-class discussion activity.

Conclusion

The development of speaking and listening is the foundation of English teaching. Not only does it enable reading and writing to happen, but it also allows children to find their own voice. This sense of being someone who has ideas that can be shared and to which other people might want to listen, provides a reason for the subject itself. We study English at school to learn how to communicate with others, to listen to the messages that others want to share with us through their talk and writing, reflecting on the language choices they make and the ones we might choose to make.

This chapter has explored a model for thinking about oracy built on four interlinked aspects: physical, linguistic, cognitive and social and emotional. While this is useful as frame for thinking and planning, each of these strands is interwoven closely with the others. Confidence in speaking will be affected by familiarity with the content of the talk and having had time to prepare the structure of the talk. Control of vocabulary and register will depend on an understanding of the audience and an awareness of their starting point. Managing the content of talk will depend on existing knowledge about the topic and an understanding of the language patterns that might best be employed in that situation. Like most areas of education, oracy skills develop through teaching, experience, and the opportunity to practise.

Of course, spoken conversation is not the only way we encounter new language. The next section will focus on another area which has a profound impact on children's language development, as well as a lifelong skill and hopefully a source of enjoyment throughout their lives: reading.

IN SUMMARY

- Oracy and spoken language development should be a key concern of the classroom.
- While oracy is vital for the development of reading and writing, spoken language development is important in its own right as it allows children to communicate their ideas with the world.
- There are many frames for thinking about spoken language in the classroom, but one useful model explores this aspect of education through four interlinked aspects: physical, linguistic, cognitive and social and emotional.
- While each of these aspects of oracy can be engaged with independently, successful development and good teaching and provision depend on the aspects working together.

FURTHER READING

- The structure of this chapter owes much to the work of the educational charity Voice 21. To find out more about their work and to read a range of publications to support the development of oracy, visit www.voice21.org.
- For a practical approach to developing a culture of spoken language across a school, see *Time to Talk* by Jean Gross.
- To find practical resources to support oracy and to engage with the theory that underpins them, visit www.oracycambridge.org and see *Exploring Talk in Schools* edited by Neil Mercer and Steve Hodgkinson.

REFERENCES

Alexander, R.J. (2001) *Culture and Pedagogy: International comparisons in primary education*. Oxford: Blackwell.

Chambers, A. (1985) *Booktalk: Occasional writing on literature & children*. London: Bodley Head.

Chambers, A. (2011) *Tell Me: Children, Reading and Talk*. Stroud: The Thimble Press.

Clements, J. (2017) *Teaching English by the Book*. Abingdon: Routledge.

Crystal, D. (2018) *The Cambridge Encyclopaedia of the English Language*. Cambridge: Cambridge University Press.

Department for Education (DfE) (2013) *The National Curriculum in England. Framework Document.* London: DfE.

Department for Education and Skills (DfES) (2006) *Primary National Strategy – a framework for literacy.* London: DfES.

Geary, D.C. (2005) *The Origin of Mind: Evolution of brain, cognition, and general intelligence.* Washington, DC: American Psychological Association.

Geary, D.C. and Huffman, K.J. (2002) Brain and cognitive evolution: Forms of modularity and functions of mind. *Psychological Bulletin*, 128: 667–98.

Heathcote, D. and Bolton, G. (1995) *Drama for Learning: Dorothy Heathcote's Mantle of the Expert Approach to Education.* Oxford: Heinemann.

Lee, T. (2015) *Princesses, Dragons and Helicopter Stories.* Abingdon: Routledge.

Mercer, N., Warwick, P. and Ahmed, A. (2014) *Developing a toolkit to assess spoken language skills in the classroom: Final report of a project carried out in partnership with School 21 and funded by the Educational Endowment Foundation.* Cambridge: University of Cambridge.

Mosley, J. (1996) *Quality Circle Time in the Primary Classroom: Your essential guide to enhancing self-esteem, self-discipline and positive relationships.* London: LDA.

Myhill, D., Jones, S., Watson, A. and Lines, H. (2016) *Essential Primary Grammar.* Maidenhead: Open University Press.

Paley, V.G. (1991) *The Boy Who Would be a Helicopter: Uses of storytelling in the classroom.* New York: Harvard University Press.

SAPERE (2020) Philosophy for Children website (accessed 11/01/2020).

Voice 21 (2019) *The Oracy Benchmarks.* London: Voice 21.

Winston, J. and Tandy, M. (2008) *Beginning Drama 4–11.* London: David Fulton.

LITERATURE

A Tale of Two Cities by Charles Dickens

A Noiseless Patient Spider by Walt Whitman

Flora and Ulysses by Kate DiCamillo

Not Now, Bernard! by David McKee

Private Peaceful by Michael Morpurgo

The Graveyard Book by Neil Gaiman

PART 3

READING

THE SIMPLE VIEW OF READING: THEORY

THIS CHAPTER WILL

- Introduce the Simple View of Reading

- Discuss the emergence of this theory's importance in the teaching of reading in English schools

- Consider the theoretical underpinnings of the two elements of the Simple View of Reading: word recognition and language comprehension

Introduction

While learning to communicate orally is something that the great majority of children will learn to do naturally, reading is a learned skill that requires both instruction and practice. As Lyon (1988) famously puts it, 'reading is not a natural process'. Turning marks on a page or screen into ideas that can be understood is a complicated business and theorists have suggested a variety of models to explain what happens when we read. One of the most influential is the Simple View of Reading; a model that doesn't suggest that reading is a simple process, rather it attempts to suggest a simple way of representing a complex process.

This chapter will introduce this model, considering the two interdependent strands: word reading and language comprehension. It will provide an overview of the history of the theory and outline how it has come to be so influential in English schools. This chapter is designed to be read in conjunction with Chapter 8, which considers its practical implications.

The Simple View of Reading

The Simple View of Reading (SVoR) model finds its origins in an article by Gough and Tunmer (1986) on 'decoding, reading and reading disability'. Questioning the relationship between decoding and reading ability, they posit that reading is the product of word recognition (recognising print) and language comprehension (the process by which words, sentences and discourse are interpreted). From this framework, the authors could better begin to understand those reading disabilities relating to either word recognition (dyslexia), comprehension (hyperlexia) or both. They argue that reading is the *product* of both the application of word recognition and linguistic comprehension (Gough and Tunmer, 1986). They present the formula like this:

Reading = Decoding × Comprehension

The acknowledgement of the wording 'product' here is important as it makes it clear in its definition that the formula for reading equates to competency in both areas in order for reading to take place. This can also be interpreted as 'making meaning from print' coming with both an understanding of how language works (vocabulary, grammar, comprehension alongside written and spoken discourse) and the ability to decode. Both elements, the framework argues, are interdependent yet require different teaching approaches in order for a child to attain reading fluency.

While the term *decoding* has become synonymous with *alphabetic decoding* (using phonic knowledge to match letters on the page to sounds), Gough and Tunmer (1986) used the term more broadly to describe reading the words on the page, as a later paper from Hoover and Gough explains:

> Skilled decoding is simply efficient word recognition: the ability to rapidly derive a representation from printed input that allows access to the appropriate entry in the mental lexical, and thus, the retrieval of semantic information at the word level.

(Hoover and Gough, 1990)

The decoding element of the SVoR is often referred to as 'visual word recognition' to ensure that both the phonological and orthographic routes to word reading are acknowledged (Stuart and Stainthorp, 2016).

The comprehension element of the SVoR refers to linguistic comprehension or language comprehension, understanding language in its broadest sense. This includes understanding everyday language and conversation, and also 'the ability to understand texts that were meant to be read. This skill is more difficult, and more complex, than understanding everyday spoken interactions or narratives' (Oakhill et al., 2015). Both of these strands will be explored in greater depth in this chapter.

The Simple View of Reading in England

How the SVoR came to be central to the teaching of reading within the National Curriculum (2013) is worth exploring briefly, as it helps put into perspective the reasoning behind a shift in the pedagogy of the teaching of reading since the publication of *The Independent Review of the Teaching of Early Reading* (also referred to as the Rose Review), in 2006.

From its inauguration in 1989, Rose states that the National Curriculum was said to have 'very little impact' on improving the standards of reading, and highlights, specifically, that much of this was down to a lack of focus on the teaching of word recognition skills, specifically, the quality of teaching with regards to phonics. When the National Literacy Strategy was adopted in 1998, bringing with it a rise in reading attainment (Rose, 2006), a more structured approach to the teaching of literacy was proposed through the Literacy Hour. With it came greater clarity on how to teach all of the elements of the reading process through the 'searchlights' model whose four-routes-into-reading approach placed the child in a more proactive, meaning making role.

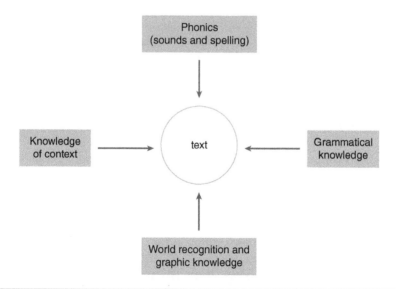

Figure 7.1   The NLS searchlights model of reading. (Image from *The Independent Review of the Teaching of Early Reading* (Rose, 2006))

This 'whole language/ top-down' approach, in which *analytic* phonics was one part of the meaning-making process, is described by Pullman as 'using all your mirrors when reversing a car' (Pullman, 2012). As can be seen in Figure 7.1, it acknowledges phonics as one of those mirrors but credits, equally, several other strands which a reader brings to the text (this is made clear by the direction of the arrows). Each strand is of equal importance; competence in one area may compensate for weakness in another. In 1999, *Progression in Phonics* was published in order to support a more systematic approach to the teaching of whole-class phonics through a seven-step approach, beginning in Nursery and ending in the final term of Year 1.

However, by 2005, the government found reading standards to still be below expected levels and Jim Rose was appointed by the Education and Skills Committee to investigate alternative approaches to the teaching of reading. His final report, *The Independent Review of the Teaching of Early Reading* (Rose, 2006), proposed the adoption of a systematic *synthetic* approach to the teaching of phonics within a new framework which would see word recognition and language comprehension as distinctly separate processes rather than parts of the whole. This framework drew on 'the Simple View of Reading' and can be seen in Figure 7.2 below.

This model was employed in the 2006 renewed Primary National Strategy (PNS) in which the teaching and learning of reading was to focus on a more vigorous, progressive phonics programme (Rose, 2006) within a language-rich environment that 'generates purposeful discussion, interest, application, enjoyment and high achievement' (2006). In the same year as the PNS, the Early Years Foundation Stage (EYFS) framework became statutory (unlike the guidance that proceeded it) and the published framework in 2008 noted, in the 'Communication, Language and Literacy' Early Learning Goals (ELGs), the application of 'phonic knowledge' in both a child's reading and writing.

Rose's argument for replacing the searchlights model with Gough and Tunmer's Simple View of Reading model was that it better supported teachers to recognise the process by which early readers progress into independent ones. Additionally, it allowed for greater focus on the discrete teaching of phonics before establishing a greater focus on comprehension.

When the DfE published *The Importance of Teaching* in 2010, the then Secretary of State for Education, Michael Gove, championed the use of systematic synthetic phonics above any other aspects of reading, echoing Rose's recommendations that this approach was 'the best method for teaching reading' (2006). *The Importance of Teaching* also introduced the phonics screening check (2012) to be administered at the age of six in order to assess the application of synthetic phonics and judge whether schools were on-track, nationally.

In the latest iteration of the National Curriculum (2014), the Simple View of Reading continues to be adopted with its emphasis on word reading (focusing on phonics) and language comprehension (linguistic processes such as grammar, vocabulary and knowledge of the world).

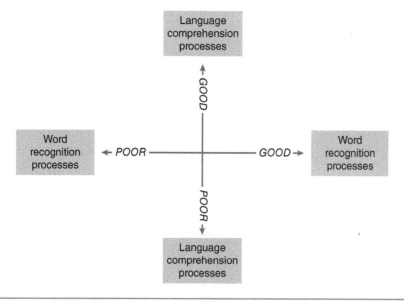

Figure 7.2   The Simple View of Reading (Image from *The Independent Review of the Teaching of Early Reading* (2006))

The teaching of early reading

The SVoR framework acknowledges the interdependent partnership between word recognition (decoding) and language comprehension (the skills/knowledge by which we make meaning from what we have read (written) or heard (oral)). Its simplicity should be seen as a point of entry when considering the complex nature of the reading process: the SVoR does not claim that reading is simple, rather it presents a simple model for approaching 'the broad landscape of reading' (Kirby and Savage, 2008).

As teachers, when we consider where children sit within the framework, we are better placed to support individual learning needs. Looking at the model (see Figure 7.2), we would recognise within the top left quadrant a child who understands a text read to them beyond the surface level, yet lacks the skills to read the words off the page themselves. Many children, when first beginning their schooling, start here, especially if they have had access to books and booktalk at home.

The child in the bottom left of the quadrant struggles to both apply any skills in order to decode the words off the page and, without support, understands little of the stories that they hear and explore. Conversely, a child in the top right quadrant is fluent in both strategies and may only struggle when challenged with specific domain knowledge (vocabulary/unfamiliar words). Finally, the child in the bottom right quadrant may be able to decode accurately but is able to make little meaning from the reading.

STOP AND REFLECT

Consider the four pupils in the scenarios below. Which quadrant of the SVoR grid in Figure 7.2 best describes their current reading behaviours and strengths?

Ciara

'I struggle to read easy books and when we are reading a book as a class, I can't really say what is happening in the story. I can't really talk a lot about stories that I have heard or things that have happened to me.'

Imisi

'I take a really long time to read and struggle over letters and sounds. I make a lot of mistakes when I am reading with the words. But when I am talking about the pictures or talking about what happened in the class reading book, I love it and am really good at answering questions and saying what is happening.'

Dafydd

'When I read I have no problem with sounding out the words. I use my phonics really well to break words down and read fluently without many mistakes. But when I have read a page and the teacher asks me what happened I can't say. Also, when the teacher is reading to the class, I don't really get what's going on.'

Gabriella

'I can read any book that I want. I can read most books without making any mistakes. I read with fluency and really enjoy talking about what is going on in the story. I like talking about why characters act the way they do and love talking about what has happened in a story when we read as a class.'

Ciara struggles in both aspects of reading. She cannot decode the words off the page and her comprehension is poor even when listening to a class story. (Bottom Left)

Imisi might struggle with his decoding, but his comprehension is excellent. He clearly loves listening to and talking about stories and a focus on his phonics will lend a greater balance to his reading skill. (Top Left)

Dafydd is competent at using his phonics to decode the words off the page but the meaning behind the story is lost. He would benefit from some quality booktalk in which some literal, entry questions give him the confidence to feel he can engage with the text. (Bottom Right)

Gabriella is comfortable with both decoding and comprehension. With greater fluency, she may be ready for early chapter books and will benefit immensely from books that excite and interest her while also providing some challenge in terms of vocabulary and content. (Top Right)

The Rose Review heralded a 'phonics first' approach to the teaching of early reading. As the Early Years Statutory Framework states, children are taught to use their 'phonic knowledge to decode' (DfE, 2017) and show their comprehension through a broad and rich talk-based curriculum. The Review proposes the following and, within the current curriculum framework, these pedagogical approaches to support children with their reading development are to be considered:

- The use of a range of different approaches when teaching either word recognition or language comprehension.
- The development of speaking and listening skills as central to the development of reading (and writing).
- A daily, discrete approach to the sequential teaching of systematic synthetic phonics in which letter-sound relationships are used to decode text into the sounds of spoken language.
- An approach which develops children's language comprehension (both spoken and written).
- All of the above to be embedded in an enjoyable, engaging, language-rich curriculum where children listen and speak attentively with clarity and confidence and are motivated to read and write within meaningful contexts.

We can see that the SVoR framework can support students and teachers in acknowledging the need to teach phonics and comprehension strategies separately from each other since they require different teaching methods. Finally, as was shown with Imisi, Gabriella, Dafydd and Ciara, the model provides us with a scaffold in which we can identify, broadly, gaps in pupils' reading needs. Not only does this acknowledge the fact that not all children will develop in both areas at the same rate but also lends greater focus to which aspect of reading we need to support pupils with.

The development of visual word recognition processes

Reading comprehension relies on the ability of the reader to recognise words on the page quickly and precisely (Perfetti, 2007). Research suggests that for early readers phonological decoding provides the principal foundation for learning to read words in English (e.g. Share, 1995; Ehri, 2005). But this is not the only pathway for word recognition. As children become more fluent and experienced as readers, research suggests that their reliance on phonological decoding lessens and they identify words directly from word to meaning (Coltheart et al., 2001; Harm and Seidenberg, 2004; Cunningham et al., 2020). Share (1995) suggests that during the process of translating graphemes to phonemes, children focus on the letters in each word and the sequences they most often appear in. Through reading experience, children build up a picture of the patterns of letters as they are combined and begin to understand how orthography maps to phonology. This knowledge can then be accessed on the next and subsequent encounters with the word, reducing the dependence on alphabetic decoding. This self-teaching process has been termed *orthographic learning* (Share, 2004) and is related to the concept of statistical learning, where proficient reading is viewed as requiring an understanding and integration of the statistical regularities present in the writing system (see Bogaerts et al., 2020).

STOP AND REFLECT

Try reading these words aloud:

tyrannosaurus   arachnophobia   Hawaii

Although they are complicated, multi-syllabic words, you probably didn't need to overtly phonically decode them. It is likely they are words you are familiar with and you were able to directly map from the word to the meaning.

Now try these words:

eustreptospondylus   ablutophobia   Kaumalapau

Each word is drawn from the same categories as above (a dinosaur, a specific fear, a place name), but as they are less common, it is likely you will have drawn on phonological decoding to turn them into spoken language before attempting to match them to the words you know already. Even experienced readers draw on both pathways when they read, although there is less reliance on the phonological pathway as reading experience gives them greater orthographic knowledge. For a child first beginning to read, they are likely to draw on phonological decoding far more frequently, but there are words that they might recognise using the morphological pathway right from the start of reading – their name, for example.

Now consider these words:

console   graduate   bass

To be able to read these accurately, following one of the word recognition pathways alone isn't enough. The first word could mean to make someone feel better or referring to a games-playing device. While visual word recognition is often possible without context, for heteronyms such as these, context is vital for accurate word reading.

While the SVoR separates the two strands of reading, it notes that skilled reading is the *product* of these two strands. Reading comprehension relies on visual word recognition, just as word reading can rely on language comprehension in the example above.

For both elements of the SVoR, a word's context matters. As Firth (1957) famously noted, 'you shall know a word by the company it keeps'.

Perfetti (1992, 2007) suggests that *lexical quality* – how precise and flexible a reader's knowledge of any particular word is – is a key reason for the importance of print experience as a factor in fluent reading. If significant cognitive resources are spent on the comparatively demanding process of phonological decoding, they cannot be directed towards comprehension. Once reading independently is fluent and automatic for a large percentage of words, cognitive space is freed for the challenging process of comprehension (Ehri, 2005; Oakhill et al. 2015).

While a small number of children might be able to teach themselves to read, working out the alphabetic code independently (Byrne and Fielding-Barnsley, 1989; Byrne, 2005), the great majority of children will require careful and deliberate teaching in the early stages of reading, and some children will continue to require significant and prolonged support to become fluent readers. Orthographic learning means that exposure to print is a powerful factor in children moving towards fluency as they absorb the statistical patterns that are inherent in written texts, but high-quality teaching is vital. Seidenberg (2017) suggests that well-timed and targeted instruction is effective because it 'accelerates the acquisition of this enormous data structure'. Explicit teaching of phonological decoding gives children the foundation for learning to read the printed word.

The pedagogical principles behind systematic phonics teaching

When *The Independent Review of Teaching Early Reading* (2006) was published, Rose singled out a systematic synthetic approach as the prime approach to the teaching of phonics within a broad, rich language curriculum. This then became the approach adopted in *Letters and Sounds* (DfES, 2007), which was offered as an alternative systematic, synthetic scheme to commercial products. Ofsted's *Reading by Six* report (2010) hailed it as central to reading success in Key Stage 1, supporting the argument that a time-limited approach to teaching phonics was key with the aim of all children to be fluent decoders by the end of Key Stage 1.

The term *systematic* is a reference to the pace and sequence in which phonics instruction is taught and the case for such an approach to the teaching of phonics is not new but its place, alongside the preference for a synthetic approach, is. Research (Ehri et al., 2001; Ehri, 2004; Stuebing et al., 2008; Graaff, et al., 2009; Vadasy and Sanders; 2012) suggests that a systematic approach, rather than an unsystematic one (in which phonics is taught but with no sequential structure), produces better results in reading accuracy.

Synthetic phonics, where grapheme-phoneme correspondences (GPCs) are introduced individually and then children are taught to blend them together to form words (*synthesising* them), was chosen as the route to decoding championed by the Rose Review. However, meta-analyses of studies into phonics instruction have not found a significant difference in effect size for synthetic phonics or analytic phonics, where children are introduced to whole words which are then broken down into their constituent GPCs (Ehri et al., 2001; Torgerson et al., 2006). While the effectiveness of the two approaches may require further research to provide a definitive answer, the synthetic approach to teaching GPCs seems to have the advantage as 'it is possible to control the learning environment more effectively and to ensure that each correspondence is taught explicitly and in an optimal sequence' (Castles et al., 2018).

Ehri herself, alongside five other speakers, would later attend and deliver a paper on Systematic Phonics Instruction at the DfES Phonics Seminar in London (2003), which examined the NLS's approach to the teaching of phonics. She stated that alphabetic knowledge, phonemic awareness and phonics, along with vocabulary, are key to word recognition. *The Sound Sense* report (Brooks, 2003), a summary of the proposals, highlighted that phonics was taught poorly by some teachers and not taught on a daily basis. Many of these papers, which would later feed into the Rose Review, stated that this related to inadequate teaching of early word recognition skills, specifically phonics.

Although the National Literacy Strategy (1999) was supported by two specific systematic approaches to the teaching of phonics in order to improve reading standards, both *Progression in Phonics* (DfEE, 1999) and *Playing with Sounds* (DfES, 2004) did not have the expected impact on reading attainment. Arguments for this relate to an analytic rather than a synthetic approach, as well as the pace, pedagogical approach and sequence in which phonics was taught. A more explicit, time-limited approach was needed and, therefore, a systematic synthetic approach to phonics was proposed as the primary approach to the teaching of decoding. The *Reading for Purpose and Pleasure* report from Ofsted (2004) supported this call for change, stating that in the best schools, teachers displayed good subject knowledge of phonics and taught it rapidly and early. Building on this, the Rose Review and the *Primary National Strategy Framework for Literacy* (DfES, 2006) ensured that a systematic, discrete approach to teaching phonics became the 'prime approach to teaching word recognition' (DfES, 2006).

In referencing Goswami and Bryant (1990), Medwell et al. (2017) confirm a correlation between phonological awareness in early readers and later reading success. Therefore, Ehri's (2004) argument for an early systematic approach rather than a late one seems especially pertinent in providing the best chance for reading success for those children who may have not begun school having had the same exposure to early reading as others.

What is meant by the Alphabetic Code and Phonological Awareness?

We have established that the teaching and learning of phonics, whichever approach is taken, is about the relationship between the sounds and symbols of our spoken and written language. The number of sounds in English is around 44, the exact number depending on the speaker's accent and dialect. The sounds are referred to as phonemes and the letter or groups of letters that represent the sounds on the page as graphemes.

STOP AND REFLECT

A simple way to remember the terms phoneme and grapheme is to consider the word roots of these two words with *phone* referring to sound or speech: 'telephone', 'headphone', 'microphone' and *graph* referring to letters, symbols; something written: 'graphics', 'calligraphy', 'autograph'. The English language, then, is heard and said through these grapheme-phonemic combinations and written using combinations of our 26 main graphemes – learning the relationship between both the spoken and the written language is the central tenet to teaching phonics.

The alphabetic code

When we consider how some sounds (phonemes) can be represented by more than one letter (graphemes), our alphabetic code can seem complex. A simple example introduced to children early on might be the phoneme /s/ when written as either 's' or 'ss', 'c' or 'sc': *set*, *sell*, *sit*, *loss*, *mess*, *kiss* all share the same phonetic /s/ sound but their grapheme correspondences are different. Later, further ways of representing the /s/ phoneme as it appears in the words *circle* and *science* will be introduced.

Exploring when these GPCs occur in both reading and writing is important since it encourages children to recognise and learn from the patterns of our language. In doing so, they are far more likely to confidently apply this understanding to their own reading and writing. Alongside GPCs, children are often taught the names of the letters of the alphabet. Where the names of the letters are taught first, they can provide a good introduction to letter sounds as most consonants contain the associated phoneme: (for example, /d/ in D, /f/ in F).

It has been suggested that the teaching of letter names can confuse children and sounds should be taught first (e.g. McGuiness, 2004), but more recent research suggests that teaching the name and sounds of a letter concurrently can support children's learning of sounds, as suggested above (Piasta et al., 2010). Regardless of what teachers may choose to teach, many children will arrive in the classroom with at least some letter name knowledge. Research suggests that children with good knowledge of letter names are more likely to be able to identify the sounds represented by letters (Burgess and Lonigan, 1998), although it has been argued that this could be due to a correlation with the positive home literacy environments: the children who arrive at school knowing the names of letters have also had other early literacy experiences that support learning to read (Share et al., 1984).

Phonological awareness

In order to learn the alphabetic code and understand the different units of sounds and their written equivalents, children need to develop a strong sense of phonological awareness: the ability to hear and distinguish the sounds of English – words, phonemes, syllables, and onset and rimes. A subset of phonological awareness is phonemic awareness, the specific ability to hear and manipulate phonemes, including the processes of blending and segmenting so important for phonological decoding.

A phoneme refers to the smallest unit of spoken sound within a word. They can be represented by more than one letter and many phonemes can be represented by different graphemes.

The key principle to a synthetic phonics approach is a rapid approach to the teaching of graphemes and their corresponding phonemes (GPCs) through the process of blending and segmenting. Blending is the process of 'sounding out' the individual phonemes in a word from left to right and then blending them together in order to make the word (often called *synthesising*). Segmenting is the reverse process and requires the listener to identify the individual phonemes within a word. It is a skill used to support early spelling.

The teaching of phonics begins with the introduction of single-letter sounds represented by a single-letter grapheme (referred to as the 'simple code') and then quickly moves on to sounds represented by more than one letter (referred to as the 'complex code' and including digraphs (letter-pairs /ai/ /ee/ /oo/), split-digraphs (letter-pairs separated by a consonant /cak_e/, /hug_e/) and trigraphs (three-letter combinations /ear/, /air/ /our/). These, and other phonemes, are taught alongside their grapheme-phoneme correspondence so that saying the sounds is taught concurrently alongside the writing of its graphemic counterpart.

STOP AND REFLECT

A key challenge in phonics teaching is modelling and teaching children to use pure sounds when sounding out and blending.

The most common sound used in English is the schwa (/ə/) – an unstressed vowel sound close to a short u (/ʌ/). While schwa use depends to some extent on accent, schwa sounds are found at different positions within many English words:

*   The start of a word (e.g. *along*, *o'clock*, *asleep*)
*   Within a word (e.g. b*e*fore, un*i*corn, med*i*cal)
*   The end of a word (e.g. butt*er*, sug*ar*)

The prevalence of the schwa in English leads to two main challenges in phonics teaching. First, it can make identifying the correct GPC tricky when spelling a word (so a child writes *wizud*, rather than *wizard*, for example). More significantly for beginning readers, a schwa is often added onto a letter sound, so /b/ is pronounced 'buh' rather than as a pure sound. This makes blending more difficult. An online search for 'articulation of phonemes Letters and Sounds' provides a useful video created by the then DfES. Most published phonics schemes will offer support materials too.

High frequency words / common exception words

There are many common words that children will encounter early in their reading and writing experiences such as *the, said*, and *we*. *Letters and Sounds* (DfES, 2007) refers to these as High Frequency Words (HFWs). While some of these will be decodable within the early phases of phonics instruction, some will contain GPCs that are less common or are yet to be taught. The document also refers to these as 'tricky' words. The National Curriculum refers to words whose GPCs are still to be introduced as 'Common Exception Words'. Because of the frequency with which they occur in texts, high frequency words are often taught within phonics sessions before they can be fully decoded by children.

The appropriateness of this approach is the subject of debate. It has been argued that teaching too many words explicitly as whole units might be damaging for children's early reading development, confusing their developing knowledge of letter-sound mappings, promoting 'a faulty decoding strategy'. This happens because memorising whole words seems logical and is relatively easy initially, leading to a false sense of security. But a whole word strategy may collapse eventually, depending on the child's vocabulary and visual memory skills. Meanwhile, the whole word strategy can harden into 'a habit that can be difficult to break' (McGuiness, 2004).

In contrast, Solity and Vousden (2009) argue that teaching of the 64 most common GPCs in English alongside explicitly learning the 100 most frequent words by sight, allows children to read aloud 90 per cent of words in texts they typically encounter. Further research (Shapiro and Solity, 2016) proposed that this approach was as effective as *Letters and Sounds* in outcomes for both reading and phonological awareness, suggesting that the presence of HFWs did not affect children's development of phonics knowledge. A similar finding was reached by McArthur et al. (2015) when studying older, struggling readers.

While this is an area that would benefit from further research, current research suggests that the judicious teaching of some HFWs is unlikely to hinder the development of children's phonological decoding and is likely to support their reading development by allowing them to read a greater variety of texts, supporting the process of orthographic learning. However, as Castles et al. (2018) note, 'children learning *sight words* should not be seen as analogous to them learning to read *by sight*'. Most systematic phonics schemes introduce a small number of HFWs, fast-tracking reading development through complementing phonological decoding, rather than replacing it. As a result, it is suggested that pupils are encouraged to apply their phonic knowledge to the part of the word that is phonically decodable (see p. 148 for a case study illustrating this).

Progression in phonics: Letters and sounds

With so many GPCs and high frequency words to teach, composing a systematic synthetic framework and choosing an order in which to introduce these would be a challenge for any teacher. Although the Rose Review provided a framework for assessing the effectiveness of the various synthetic phonics schemes available at the time, the DfES's *Letters and Sounds* (2007) has become the framework for many phonics programmes.

The programme was set out and structured within six phases which begins in Nursery/ Reception and should be completed by the time pupils finish Key Stage 1. Table 7.1 gives an overview of the teaching sequence and approach. The synthetic aspect of phonics teaching (blending and segmenting) begins in Phase 2 while Phase 1 focuses on developing children's speaking and listening skills in preparation.

Table 7.1   The six phases of phonics: focus, purpose, outcome

Phase duration	Focus	Purpose	Outcome
1 – Foundation Continuous throughout all phases with speaking, listening, exploring and experimenting with sounds and words seen as central	Playing, exploring and experimenting with rhymes, alliteration, environmental sounds, phonemes and recognising speech sounds in words. Begin to *orally* blend and segment while building up their vocabulary	To play and experiment with sounds and words with a focus on developing speaking & listening skills and phonological awareness	Pupils are prepared for a systematic approach, can speak with a clear voice and are aware of different speech sounds
2 – Foundation 6 weeks*	A systematic approach to synthetic phonics (blending and segmenting) with the relationship between GPCs introduced in weekly sets: Set 1: s, a, t, p Set 2: i, n, m, d Set 3: g, o, c, k Set 4: ck, e, u, r Set 5: h, b, f, ff, l, ll, ss HFWs introduced	To encourage pupils to blend and sound out letter sounds. Introduce them, explicitly, to segmenting with simple CVC words. They will also begin to attempt some words with two syllables although this may be a challenge	Children can blend and segment simple CVC words containing the 19 GPCs taught during this phase to support their reading and spelling
3 – Foundation 12 weeks*	A further 25 graphemes are introduced (now including 2 & 3 letter strings) so that children recognise one grapheme for each of the 44 phonemes Set 6: j, v, w, x Set 7: y, z, zz, qu Consonant digraphs: ch, sh, th, ng Vowel digraphs: ai, ee, igh, oa, oo, ar, or, ur, ow, oi, ear, air, ure, er HFWs continued alongside a chosen alphabet song	Pupils can apply blending and segmenting skills (using GPCs covered) in order to read and spell regular words as well as high frequency words	Pupils can confidently blend and segment CVC words using a further 25 graphemes and all taught phonemes. They will be able to read simple captions, two-syllable words and some HFWs that have been covered

Phase duration	Focus	Purpose	Outcome
4 – Foundation 4–6 weeks*	No new graphemes are introduced. This phase is used to consolidate understanding and read words which have adjacent consonants (CVCC)	Pupils consolidate and are confident in their knowledge of GPCs through blending and segmenting (CVC and CVCC words)	Pupils can read and spell CVC words as well as those with adjacent consonants (CVCC) and some polysyllabic words
5 – Year 1 A 30-week programme that runs throughout Year 1	Further GPCs introduced with a focus on alternative pronunciations for graphemes. Pupils encouraged to begin reading whole words as decoding becomes increasingly fluent. They begin to decode unfamiliar words silently	Pupils' knowledge of GPCs continues to broaden in order for them to see that most phonemes have different ways in which they can be spelled and that some graphemes can be represented by multiple phonemes	Recognising and blending graphemes will become quicker and more fluent with many pupils independently reading longer texts. Most GPCs will have been learnt and unfamiliar words will be decoded quickly and quietly. Unfamiliar words may be tackled through sounding out. Spelling will be phonemically sound although there may be inaccuracies with unfamiliar words
6 – Year 2	Strategies for word specific spellings and alternatives, ensuring automaticity in both reading and spelling	Pupils to become more fluent with their reading and more accurate with their spelling	Pupils can decode quickly and recognise most of the HFWs. Spelling of words may be phonemically correct (but may not be the correct spelling). Reading fluency (in relation to phonics) so that greater focus on comprehension can continue throughout Key Stage 2

*A suggested duration on the proviso that all approaches are systematic. It is important to acknowledge that some children will not be able to learn at this pace while others may have the aptitude to learn at a quicker one, with teachers differentiating accordingly.

Principles of high-quality phonics teaching

Each school will have its own set of principles and pedagogical approaches for teaching word reading. These will be drawn from the school's ethos and culture, the experience of staff and the school leadership team, and the needs of pupils and the wider school community. Additionally, pedagogical application will be informed by any phonics programme the school follows. Communicating these to all staff is crucial: effective teaching and learning in phonics relies on an understanding of the content to teach, why it is being taught and how this can be done most effectively. These principles for effective teaching might include:

Staff knowledge and understanding

- Careful planning with a discrete, structured, systematic approach that is consistently applied by all members of the team.
- Staff are proficient with all the terminology associated with the teaching of phonics and pronunciation of pure sounds.
- Staff agree on the use of key terms when teaching phonics (e.g. *blend, segment, common exception word, high frequency word, phoneme, grapheme, split digraph*).
- Staff do not need to stick with one programme but should ensure that the framework is covered and that reliable assessment opportunities and tracking are embedded: this should be implemented and led by an assigned member of staff and senior leaders.
- Pupils understand that blending and segmenting are reversible processes to help with decoding and spelling, with blending 'demonstrated both orally and physically' (Perkins, 2015) and see the links between decoding and spelling.
- Guidance is given to staff on how best to adapt the phonics programme/s for children who may have missed previous aspects or have special educational needs.
- Although the use of decodable books lends itself to opportunities for applying phonetic knowledge, this must not be at the cost of rich reading experiences with quality texts or a child's favourite book in order to continually foster a love of reading.

Classroom practice

- A language-rich environment in which a strong culture of speaking and listening should be at the foundation of all phonics teaching.
- Purposeful and genuine opportunities should be embedded throughout the curriculum, including reading aloud to adults, in which children are actively thinking and applying their phonic knowledge in meaningful and enjoyable situations.
- All phonics teaching builds upon a pupil's existing knowledge.
- Teachers should continually model correct enunciation when blending and segmenting of new GPCs in and out of phonics sessions when meaningful opportunities present themselves.
- Teaching sessions should be focused, brisk and multi-sensory in order to engage children in the learning.
- Opportunities in shared/guided reading and writing for the application of phonics skills should be carefully planned on a regular basis.
- Planning should follow the four cyclical elements of the recommended daily phonic teaching sequence: Revisit and Review, Teach, Practise and Apply.

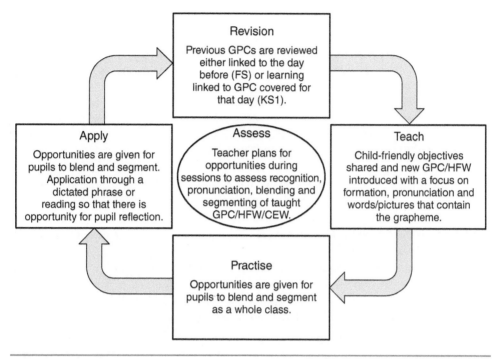

Figure 7.3 A Phonic teaching sequence based on the sequence in *Letters and Sounds* (DfES, 2007)

Monitoring and assessment

- When grouping pupils, don't be afraid to move them in order to support their needs.
- Teachers are responsive to pupils' needs and will accelerate or support depending on the individual child.
- Assessment is continual (some schemes suggest a dictation at the end of sessions to see how confident application of the new [and previous] GPCs are).
- Staff are continually looking for evidence of pupils' learning in their application of decoding when reading and spelling.

Exploring language comprehension

The Rose Review focused principally on the teaching of word recognition processes (explicitly phonics), saying little about language comprehension. Since the focus was on early reading, giving children the tools to decode words from the page was prioritised, so that when this was mastered, the development of comprehension would 'overtake' this aspect (2006). This image of two processes travelling together is an interesting one and, importantly, supports the idea that they are taught in tandem: the explicit teaching of phonics does not mean a lack of teaching with regards to language comprehension, especially when we consider that when children arrive at school, their oral comprehension will often be significantly ahead of their word reading skills.

Rose describes the difference between reading and language comprehension as 'access from eye rather than ear' which is understood 'whether it is spoken or written' (2006). Oakhill et al. (2015) add greater clarity to this definition:

1. Comprehending what someone is saying to us is easier than what is written, since we can ask the speaker questions for clarification and they can read our expressions and restate their point if they notice our lack of understanding.
2. Intonation matters and is far clearer in spoken language – be it eagerness, excitement, a question or an exclamation.
3. There is a noticeable difference between the form and style of language used in writing and speaking. We don't write the way we speak and we don't speak the way we write.
4. Context is far easier to access through the spoken word than the written. When we are talking to each other, we can add and amend information (or even point it out) in order to help the listener comprehend (i.e. 'you know the drinks machine over there by the doors, well it's been broken for ages'). When reading, however, the reader is required to consistently create a 'mental model' (Oakhill et al., 2015) of the situation, instruction or report, which is more taxing.
5. There is a difference in how much information is carried in the written and spoken word. Oakhill et al. (2015) point out that, when reading, information and details can be lost because of the amount of information we attempt to take in, whereas talking usually involves a lot less information for the listener to subsume anyway, generally keeping to key points.

It is clear here that we ask far more from a reader (or listener) when we present them with the written word (both through decoding and reading aloud) than we do when asking them to listen to everyday communication. In whatever format it takes, in the earlier years, language comprehension is often approached through talk and will invite the pupil to engage with the text on multiple levels. Guppy and Hughes (1999) define these levels as: 'reading the lines, reading between the lines and reading beyond the lines', and Browne's interpretation of these is useful:

*   Reading the lines – using phonic, graphic, contextual and syntactical strategies to make literal meanings
*   Reading between the lines – understanding the author's intentions and implied, inferential meanings

- Reading beyond the lines – reacting to the text, appreciating and valuing the author's meanings, understanding and evaluating the author's craft

(Browne, 2009)

As can be seen, as well as phonic knowledge, there are many other elements to consider when acknowledging what it is a reader does when they are reading for meaning. Decoding the words is simply not enough and, as the model above indicates, even when the words are read to you, there are still other aspects of comprehension that we need to consider and plan for if we want to ensure a pupil can make meaning from what they hear or read. Since Rose's definition of language comprehension encompasses both of these approaches, an appreciation of the 'discrete components' that we rely on to comprehend should be explored and considered.

What is meant by comprehension?

The Rose Review called for a shift from pupils completing comprehension exercises, which only tested knowledge, to one in which the teacher would teach a range of strategies that guided children to actively engage in the meaning making process (2006). In 2005, the DfE, as part of the Primary National Strategy, published three documents all titled 'Understanding Reading Comprehension' which defined the process and offered approaches, much of which remains relevant and applicable today. Although only alluded to in the Rose Review, they also ask for a shift in which we see the child as:

- an active agent in making meaning
- someone who calls on a range of strategies, 'cognitive, interpretive and problem-solving', to make meaning
- whose comprehension is built upon the total sum of their life experiences

(DfES, 2005)

Three models are worth exploring when it comes to understanding what is meant by reading comprehension. All three vary in their interpretation of what processes are involved when making meaning from the written word. A simplified version of Perfetti's 'blueprint' (1999) can be found in the Rose Review, Scarborough's Reading Rope (2009) is referenced by Oakhill et al. (2015), and the final model is Tennent's 'Components of Comprehension' (2015).

Each considers the components an accomplished reader needs in order to make meaning, at all levels, from the text:

Perfetti's Amended Blueprint:

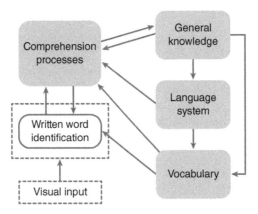

Figure 7.4 The components of the comprehension system. (Image from *The Independent Review of the Teaching of Early Reading* (Rose, 2006))

Shaded parts illustrate the elements of comprehension involved when making meaning from spoken discourse, whereas those in white only become part of the process when the written word is involved. Understanding each part of this framework helps us to appreciate the demands comprehension puts on the reader. This amended model asks us to consider the following:

- **General knowledge:** refers to the information that the listener/reader will need in order to help them recreate a mental representation of an event/moment/ character.
- **Language system:** refers to sentence structure and the acknowledgement and understanding of the different parts of speech. It can also refer to word order in relation to grammar as well as a sentence's relationship to those preceding it.
- **Vocabulary:** refers to the listener/reader's knowledge and understanding of words encountered within the context of what is being read or said. If a reader/listener comes across too many of these components, then understanding will be lost. Additionally, 'depth of word knowledge' is required in order to appreciate shades of meaning (Oakhill et al., 2015).

Applying all these components helps the reader build a mental model of what they are hearing or reading. However, two more recent 'blueprints' suggest that the processes involved in meaning are more complex still.

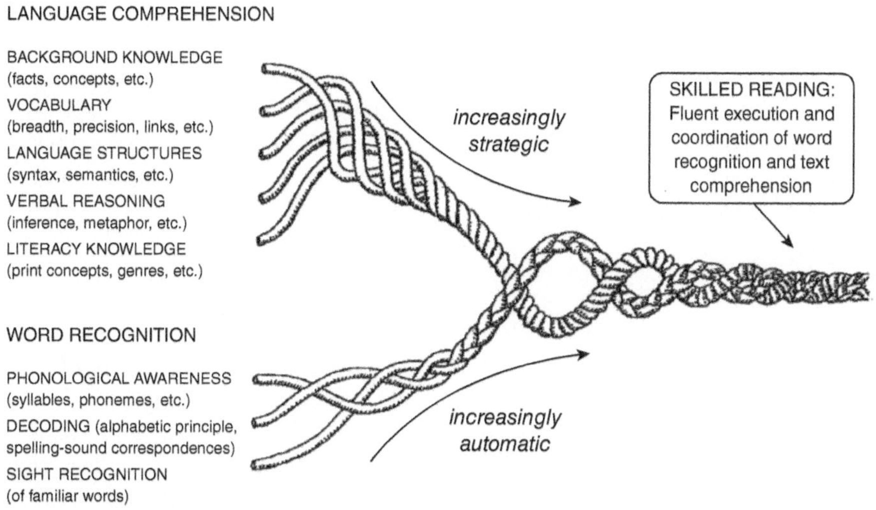

LANGUAGE COMPREHENSION
BACKGROUND KNOWLEDGE
(facts, concepts, etc.)
VOCABULARY
(breadth, precision, links, etc.)
LANGUAGE STRUCTURES
(syntax, semantics, etc.)
VERBAL REASONING
(inference, metaphor, etc.)
LITERACY KNOWLEDGE
(print concepts, genres, etc.)
WORD RECOGNITION
PHONOLOGICAL AWARENESS
(syllables, phonemes, etc.)
DECODING (alphabetic principle,
spelling-sound correspondences)
SIGHT RECOGNITION
(of familiar words)
increasingly
strategic
increasingly
automatic
SKILLED READING:
Fluent execution and
coordination of word
recognition and text
comprehension

Figure 7.5 The many strands that are woven into skilled reading (Scarborough's Reading Rope (2009))

Syntax
Vocabulary
General knowledge
Domain knowledge
Linguistic processes
Knowledge bases
The understanding of text
(Meta-)cognitive processes
Memory
Inference making
Comprehension monitoring

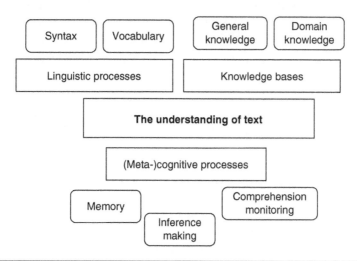

Figure 7.6 Tennent's components of comprehension (Image from *Understanding Reading Comprehension*, Tennent, 2015)

Scarborough's 'Reading Rope' (2009) has a direct correlation with Gough and Tunmer's Simple View model but since both these models consider similar components, they will be explored together under the headings provided by Tennent.

Domain knowledge

All three models agree that the reader's knowledge of the world is based on personal, 'social and cultural experience' (Tennent, 2015), with Tennent's model refining this down to 'domain knowledge': information known only to those who have specialised knowledge in that subject area (such as a knowledge of species of birds or trees). Domain knowledge in an area can bring greater depth to understanding.

Memory

Both Oakhill et al. (2015) and Tennent (2015) place emphasis on the importance of a teacher needing to understand the active role of working memory/short-term memory. Although distinct, both operate in the moment (seconds) and are involved in maintaining recent information (such as the previous sentence) while maintaining coherence with the narrative as a whole. Oakhill et al. (2015) illustrate how this can be useful when considering who is speaking (pronouns – e.g. 'they said'; 'she called') while Tennent (2015) explains how a 'poor working memory' can lead to poor comprehension since children may be unable to hold previous sentences in their heads or have the capacity to quickly access vocabulary. Long-term memory stores information related to semantics, vocabulary, narratives and personal experience which we can recall. Both short-term and long-term memory are vital cognitive processes with regards to comprehension.

Verbal reasoning/Inference

Reading between and beyond the lines, a process Tennent (2015) describes as 'filling in the gaps', is central to the business of making meaning and begins at a young age. Rich narratives invite the reader to go beyond the literal and often ask them to call on their prior knowledge from the text and their own lives to (among other things): deduce, empathise, predict, compare, clarify, question, analyse and summarise. This is known as inference. *Global coherence inferences* are inferences that are drawn from across the whole text: a reader might see the phrases 'the warriors streaked with woad', 'the centurion ordered his men forward' and 'the mud that covered the battlefield' and then be able to build a mental model of the scene (a battle between the Romans and Celts in Ancient Britain), even if this information hasn't been explicitly stated.

Local cohesion inferences are inferences made on a smaller scale, where a reader might need to resolve a pronoun (*He put on his hat – ah, that must be Jon's hat!*) or recognise where a noun phrase is standing in for a character ('his faithful steed' for Gringolet the horse, for example). Inferences require a personal response from the reader and can often result in an interpretation which is wholly unique to that child.

Comprehension monitoring

Tennent's heading makes explicit the process by which a reader is constantly checking that what they are reading 'makes sense' (Tennent, 2015). A good reader/listener, argue both Oakhill et al. (2015) and Tennent (2015), is always ensuring that understanding is there during the reading process and will either purposefully or automatically fill in gaps or re-read passages to check that meaning is maintained.

All these processes, under whatever heading they fall, illustrate how complex the process of reading is and, equally, how being skilled in these areas will have a significant impact on reading comprehension. As teachers, we cannot assume that a child understands all that they are hearing being read to them or reading themselves. The following section considers some approaches which could best support readers towards independence.

Principles of high-quality comprehension teaching

As teachers of reading, our goal is to support children to become active, engaged and skilled readers who are constantly monitoring and evaluating their understanding (Kispal, 2008; Oakhill et al., 2015). From the models above, it should be acknowledged that a range of strategies will need to be directly taught, supported and modelled so that children have both the skill and knowledge of how to apply them independently.

The importance of talk

The nature and importance of talk is covered in several chapters throughout this book: such is its significance. The Rose Review also highlights its centrality in raising standards in comprehension, citing the requisite of regular, quality booktalk within the classroom: a statement validated in the latest curriculum for England (DFE, 2013). This is supported by computational models, where oral language was a foundation for reading acquisition (Chang et al., 2020). Structured, planned discussion and dialogue around texts should allow for moments in which the teacher is facilitator, guide, modeller and fellow collaborator, so that they can support, show, explain and join in with the range of processes that go into making sense and meaning. Embracing these roles will allow you to get the most out of planned sessions whether they are guided reading, shared reading, whole class or one-to-one.

Making time for pupils to talk you through their thinking, explain their views and how they came to them could give you an insight into the application of those components that are all part of the meaning-making business. Encouraging children to 'talk through their thought processes' (Tennent, 2015) allows us, as teachers, a far greater access to the mental model that they have of the narrative and, equally important, allows us to plan for and model approaches if they are finding difficulties in applying specific comprehension strategies.

Additionally, a classroom in which meaning making is collaborative and pupils, dialogically, work together to gain an understanding of the text, encourages children to acknowledge that sometimes there are multiple, yet valid, interpretations of a question. Such spaces encourage reflection, the sharing of ideas and a collaborative approach to solving problems (Oakhill et al., 2015).

Modelling

A trio of Reading Comprehension booklets from the DfES (2005) offered some sound ideas for modelling comprehension strategies. Synthesising these strategies with the later work of Kispal (2008) and Tennent (2015) provides a useful framework for modelling approaches to answering comprehension questions:

- Thinking aloud in order to share thoughts and understanding of what has been read
- Asking questions aloud in order to illustrate comprehension monitoring
- Making explicit which processes you/they are drawing on when 'drawing an inference' (Kispal, 2008)
- Question and speculate on structure, style, language choices, characters and plot in order to encourage pupils to be more critically reflective
- Summarise either by skimming through short pieces, by paragraph or chapter

Modelling, though, is not enough; pupils must also be given time to practise these skills (Tennent, 2015), either on their own, in pairs or in guided sessions where scaffolding can be offered.

Questioning

The art of knowing when to ask questions, when not to and when to offer time and space for children to bring their own questions to the discussion, always needs careful consideration if the aim is 'to encourage metacognitive reflection' (DfES, 2005). In doing so, the skills required to successfully and actively engage in a text will become automatic. The DfES (2005), Kispal (2008), Oakhill et al. (2015), Tennent (2015), Tennent et al. (2016) and the EEF (2017) all offer a range of excellent strategies to support these skills with, in recent years, a greater focus on inferential reading. Below are some suggestions which have been framed around Guppy and Hughes' (1999) levels of reading:

- Reading the lines:

  o Closed questions can encourage a literal reading of the text and test recall as well as aspects of comprehension monitoring.

- Reading between the lines:

  o Open questions in which answers are drawn by combining a set of information in the text in order to deduce or make an inference. This is achieved through drawing on what is known in the text and their own knowledge.

- Reading beyond the lines:

  o Open questions that encourage an evaluative response to the text as an artefact considering word choice, style, themes, meaning. Inferences relating to the author's purpose (which we can only guess at) are possible here too.

Chapter 8 provides a case study illustrating different levels of questioning (p. 139), while Chapters 17 and 18 consider effective classroom questioning in greater depth.

Effective booktalk is not just about asking questions but encouraging pupils to clarify, reflect, elaborate, challenge or develop their thinking and while considering our own questions prior to comprehension activity, it is of equal importance to encourage, scaffold and support children in producing their own questions too. If you have been modelling good questioning for different purposes, then when children apply these question types themselves, they are beginning to read between and beyond independently.

In preparation for any comprehension activity there are several aspects to consider in order to ensure that all children are engaged and can access the reading/task:

- Pupils' prior knowledge and experiences:

  o When exploring a text are there themes, items, places, things that the children would benefit from knowing before starting the book? If you were sharing *The Jolly Postman* by Janet and Allan Ahlberg in EYFS, would every child know what a postman's role is or what a written letter looks like? Clarifying this prior to reading can reduce the cognitive load when it comes to understanding the text.

- Vocabulary:

  o Depth of vocabulary (knowing a word well and its shades of meaning) is directly related to comprehension success more so than breadth (knowing lots of words at surface level) and can support children in 'making inferences' (Oakhill et al., 2015). Knowing what a 'jolly' postman is and understanding the subtle difference between one that is happy, might give an indication of the infectious nature of the postman's good humour rather than a sense of contentment.

    o   While pre-reading the text in preparation for the session, consider whether there are key words whose meanings are important in maintaining comprehension. If so, then clarifying/discussing their meaning prior to the reading will reduce the cognitive load giving more space for comprehension. Modelling this, through the use of a quality dictionary, should encourage children to do the same.

- Text:

    o   Finding the balance between a text that is too challenging in terms of the components of comprehension and not challenging enough is important. It should also be engaging, interesting to the pupils reading it and, if applicable, provide 'opportunities for inferences to be made' (Kispal, 2008).

Conclusion

This chapter has sought to show that far from being simple, the process of becoming a skilled reader is a complex one in which word reading, as the Rose Review makes clear, 'is an essential part, but not the whole picture of what it takes to become a fluent reader' (2006).

While learning to read might be a complicated process, Gough and Tunmer's (1986) model of the Simple View of Reading does offer a clear and robust model for understanding how two distinctive, yet entwined processes combine to allow skilled reading. Each element of the SVoR requires different teaching approaches. Decoding will likely be taught in a systematic way, relying on explicit teaching of the alphabetic code and opportunities to put this growing body of knowledge into practice. Comprehension, whether reading comprehension or wider language comprehension, relies on oracy, experiences with rich, motivating texts and a purposeful, language-rich curriculum and environment which are tailored to the needs and interests of the children. For a teacher, remaining critical, evaluative and reflective when teaching reading is vital, always acknowledging the complexity of the process.

Chapter 8 will consider how this theoretical knowledge of the Simple View of Reading can be applied to classroom practice.

IN SUMMARY

- The Simple View of Reading is an influential model for describing the process of reading, first proposed by Gough and Tunmer (1986). Rather than suggesting that reading is simple, it suggests a simple way of describing a complicated process.
- According to the Simple View of Reading, skilled reading is the product of two interrelated elements: decoding (visual word recognition) and language comprehension. Both are required for proficient reading.

- The decoding strand of reading relies heavily on phonological decoding in the early stages of learning to read. As readers grow more fluent, they increasingly rely on an orthographic pathway to read words.
- Reading comprehension depends on the wider sphere of language comprehension – understanding spoken language and words read aloud, in addition to the words that can be read on a page or screen. Proficient comprehension relies on a growing lexical knowledge, as well as a knowledge of text structure, syntax, and background knowledge. These skills are best fostered through high-quality talk and texts.

FURTHER READING

- For a detailed overview of the research into teaching reading, including the Simple View of Reading, see *Reading Development and Teaching* by Morag Stuart and Rhona Stainthorp.
- To learn more about the development of visual word reading, from early phonological decoding to skilled mature reading, see *Ending the Reading Wars: Reading Acquisition From Novice to Expert* by Anna Castles, Kathleen Rastle and Kate Nation.
- For a comprehensive overview of theories of comprehension, see *Understanding Reading Comprehension: Processes and Practices* by Wayne Tennent and *Understanding and Teaching Reading Comprehension* by Jane Oakhill, Kate Cain and Carsten Elbro.

REFERENCES

Bogaerts, L., Frost, R. and Christiansen, M.H. (2020) Integrating statistical learning into cognitive science. *Journal of Memory and Language*, 115: 1–5.

Brooks, G. (2003) Sound Sense report. Available at: http://dera.ioe.ac.uk/4938/5/nls_phonics 0303gbrooks.pdf

Browne, A. (2009) *Developing Language and Literacy 3–8* (3rd ed.). London: Sage.

Burgess, S.R. and Lonigan, C. (1998) Bi-directional relations of phonological sensitivity and pre-reading abilities: Evidence from a preschool sample. *Journal of Experimental Child Psychology*, 70: 117–41.

Byrne, B. and Fielding-Barnsley, R. (1989) Phonemic awareness and letter knowledge in the child's acquisition of the alphabetic principle. *Journal of Educational Psychology*, 81: 313–21.

Byrne, B. (2005) Theories of learning to read. In M.J. Snowling and C. Hulme (Eds), *The Science of Reading: A handbook* (pp. 104–19). Malden, MA: Blackwell.

Castles, A., Rastle, K. and Nation, K. (2018) Ending the reading wars: Reading acquisition from novice to expert. *Psychological Science in the Public Interest*, 19(1):5–51.

Chang, Y-N., Taylor, J., Rastle, K. and Monaghan, P. (2020) The relationships between oral language and reading instruction: Evidence from a computational model of reading. *Cognitive Psychology* (in press).

Coltheart, M., Rastle, K., Perry, C., Langdon, R. and Ziegler, J. (2001) DRC: A dual route cascaded model of visual word recognition and reading aloud. *Psychological Review*, 108: 204–56.

Cunningham, A.J., Burgess, A.P., Witton, C., Talcott, J.B. and Shapiro, L.R. (2020) Dynamic relationships between phonological memory and reading: A five year longitudinal study from age 4 to 9. *Developmental Science* (preview/in print).

Department for Children, Schools and Families (DCSF) (2008) *Practice Guidance for the Early Years Foundation Stage*. London: DCSF.

Department for Education (DfE) (2010) *The Importance of Teaching*. London: TSO.

Department for Education (DfE) (2013) *English Programmes of Study: Key Stages 1 and 2 National Curriculum in England*. London: TSO.

Department for Education (DfE) (2014) *The National Curriculum in England: Complete framework for key stages 1 to 4*.

Department for Education (DfE) (2017) *Statutory Framework for the Early Years Foundation Stage*. London: DfE.

Department for Education and Employment (DfEE) (1998) *The National Literacy Strategy: Framework for Teaching*. London: DfEE.

Department for Education and Employment (DfEE) (1999) *Progression in Phonics*. London: DfEE.

Department for Education and Skills (DfES) (2004) *Playing with Sounds*. London: DfEE.

Department for Education and Skills (DfES) (2005) *Understanding Reading Comprehension 1, 2 and 3*. London: DfES.

Department for Education and Skills (DfES) (2006) *Primary Framework for Literacy and Mathematics*. London: DfEE.

Department for Education and Skills (DfES) (2007) *Letters and Sounds*. London, DfEE.

Education Endowment Foundation (EEF) Available at: https://educationendowmentfoundation.org.uk/public/files/Publications/Campaigns/Literacy/KS1_Literacy_Guidance_2017.pdf

Education Endowment Foundation (EEF) Available at: https://educationendowmentfoundation.org.uk/public/files/Publications/Campaigns/Literacy/KS2_Literacy_Guidance_2017.pdf

Ehri, L., Nunes, S.R., Willows, D.M., Valeska Schuster, B., Yaghoub-Zadeh, Z. and Shanahan, T. (2001) Phonemic awareness instruction helps children learn to read: Evidence from the National Reading Panel's meta-analysis. *Reading Research Quarterly*, 36(3): 250–87.

Ehri, L. (2004) *Systematic Phonics Instruction: Findings of the National Reading Panel*. Available at: www.researchgate.net/publication/234603429_Systematic_Phonics_Instruction_Findings_of_the_National_Reading_Panel

Ehri L.C. (2005) Learning to read words: Theory, findings, and issues. *Scientific Studies of Reading*, 9: 167–88.

Firth, J.R. (1957) A synopsis of linguistic theory 1930–1955. In *Studies in Linguistic Analysis* (pp. 1–32). Oxford: Blackwell.

Goswami, U. and Bryant, P. (1990) *Phonological Skills and Learning to Read*. Hove: Lawrence Erlbaum Associates.

Gough, P.B. and Tunmer, W.E. (1986) Decoding, reading, and reading disability. *RASE: Remedial and Special Education*, 7(1): 6-10.

Graaff, S., Bosman, A.M.T, Hasselman, F. and Verhoeven, L. (2009) Benefits of systematic phonics instruction. *Scientific Studies of Reading*, 13(4).

Guppy, P. and Hughes, M. (1999) *The Development of Independent Reading*: Buckingham: Open University Press.

Harm, M.W. and Seidenberg, M.S. (2004) Computing the meanings of words in reading: Cooperative division of labor between visual and phonological processes. *Psychological Review*, 111: 662–720.

Hoover, W. and Gough, P. (1990) The simple view of reading. *Reading and Writing*, 2: 127–60.

Kispal, A. (2008) *Effective Teaching of Inference Skills for Reading*. London: DCSF.

Kirby, J.R. and Savage, R.S. (2008) Can the simple view deal with the complexities of reading? *Literacy*, 42: 75–82.

Lyon, G. (1998) Why reading is not a natural process. *Educational Leadership*, 55(6): 14–18.

McArthur, G., Castles, A., Kohnen, S., Larsen, L., Jones, K., Anandakumar, T. and Banales, E. (2015) Sight word and phonics training in children with dyslexia. *Journal of Learning Disabilities*, 48(4): 391–407.

McGuinness, D. (2004) *Early Reading Instruction: What science really tells us about how to teach reading*. Cambridge, MA: The MIT Press.

Medwell, J. and Wray, D., with Minns, H., Griffiths, V. and Coates, E. (2017) *Primary English: Teaching Theory and Practice*. London: Learning Matters

Oakhill, J., Cain, K. and Elbro, C. (2015) *Understanding and Teaching Reading Comprehension*. Abingdon: Routledge.

Ofsted (2004) *Reading for Purpose and Pleasure*. London: Ofsted.

Ofsted (2010) *Reading by Six*. Manchester: Ofsted.

Perfetti C. A. (1992) The representation problem in reading acquisition. In P.B. Gough, L.C. Ehri and R. Treiman (Eds), *Reading Acquisition* (pp. 145–74). Hillsdale, NJ: Erlbaum.

Perfetti, C.A. (1999) Comprehending written language: A blueprint of the reader. In P. Hagoort and C. Brown (Eds), *Neurocognition of Language Processing*, p.169. Oxford: Oxford University Press.

Perfetti C.A. (2007) Reading ability: Lexical quality to comprehension. *Scientific Studies of Reading*, 11: 357–83.

Perkins, M. (2015) *Becoming a Teacher of Reading*. London: Sage.

Piasta, SB., Purpura, D.J. and Wagner, R.K. (2010) Fostering alphabet knowledge development: A comparison of two instructional approaches. *Reading and Writing*, 23: 607–26.

Pullman, P. in J. Henry (2012) Sir Jim Rose criticises children's authors in phonics row. *The Telegraph*, 17 June. Available at: www.telegraph.co.uk/education/educationnews/9335860/Sir-Jim-Rose-criticises-childrens-authors-in-phonics-row.html

Rose, J. (2006) *Independent Review of the Teaching of Early Reading*. Nottingham: DfES Publications.

Scarborough, H. (2009) Connecting early language and literacy to later reading (dis)abilities: Evidence, theory and practice. In F. Fletcher-Campbell, J. Soler and G. Reid (Eds), *Approaching Difficulties in Literacy Development: Assessment, Pedagogy and Programmes* (pp.23–38). London: Sage.

Seidenberg, M.S. (2017) *Language at the Speed of Sight*. New York: Basic Books.

Shapiro, L.R. and Solity, J. (2016) Differing effects of two synthetic phonics programmes on early reading development. *British Journal of Educational Psychology*, 86(2).

Share D.L. (1995) Phonological recoding and self-teaching: Sine qua non of reading acquisition. *Cognition*, 55: 151–218.

Share, D. (2004) Orthographic learning at a glance: On the time course and developmental onset of self-teaching. *Journal of Experimental Child Psychology*, 87: 267–98.

Share, D.L., Jorm, A.F., Maclean, R. and Matthews, R. (1984) Sources of individual differences in reading acquisition. *Journal of Educational Psychology*, 76(6): 1309–24.

Solity, J. and Vousden, J. (2009) Real books vs reading schemes: A new perspective from instructional psychology. *Educational Psychology*, 29(4): 469–511.

Stuart, M. and Stainthorp, R. (2016) *Reading Development and Teaching*. London: Sage.

Stuebing, K.K., Barth, A.E., Cirino, P.T., Francis, D.J. and Fletcher, J. M. (2008) A response to recent re-analyses of the National Reading Panel Report: Effects of systematic phonics instruction are practically significant. *Journal of Educational Psychology*, 100: 123–34.

Tennent, W. (2015) *Understanding Reading Comprehension: Processes and Practices*. London: Sage.

Tennent, W., Reedy, D., Hobsbaum, A. and Gamble, N. (2016) *Guiding Readers: Layers of Meaning a Handbook for Teaching Reading Comprehension to 7–11-year-olds*. London: UCL IOE Press.

Torgerson, C., Brooks, G. and Hall, J. (2006) *A systematic review of the research literature on the use of phonics in the teaching of reading and spelling* (Research Report RR711). UK Department for Education and Skills.

Vadasy, P. and Sanders, E. (2012) Two-year follow-up of a kindergarten phonics intervention for English learners and native English speakers: Contextualizing treatment impacts by classroom literacy instruction. *Journal of Educational Psychology*, 104: 4.

LITERATURE

The Jolly Postman by Janet and Allan Ahlberg

8

THE SIMPLE VIEW OF READING: PRACTICE

THIS CHAPTER WILL

- Further explore the Simple View of Reading

- Consider practical approaches to teaching the two elements of the Simple View of Reading: word recognition and language comprehension

---

Introduction

Chapter 7 introduced the theoretical underpinnings of the Simple View of Reading (SVoR), first proposed by Gough and Tumner (1986). This chapter is concerned with the implications of the SVoR for the teaching of reading, considering how this theory can be translated to the primary school classroom. As with previous paired chapters in this book, this chapter is designed to be read in conjunction with Chapter 7, which introduces the theory and research elements that underpin classroom practice.

While dependent on each other for skilled reading, the two elements of the SVoR – language comprehension and word recognition – require different diets of teaching, at least at first when children are beginning to learn to read.

Developing children's comprehension

In one sense it is impossible to 'teach' reading comprehension. Reading comprehension is what happens when we understand the words on the page or screen. As Tennent et al. (2016) note:

> We don't teach comprehension because comprehension is an outcome; rather, we teach strategies to support comprehension.

This understanding is likely to be constructed differently for different readers: arguably, comprehension depends as much on the reader as it does the text:

> A novel or poem or play remains merely inkspots on the paper until the reader transforms them into a set of meaningful symbols. The literary work exists in the live circuit set up between the reader and text: the reader infuses intellectual and emotional meanings into the pattern of verbal symbols, and those symbols channel his thoughts and feelings.
>
> (Rosenblatt, 1938)

The route to constructing meaning of any text will be different for different readers. One reader may be very knowledgeable about a subject and find it easy to incorporate new information from the text into their existing understanding. For another reader, without this background knowledge to draw on, the process might be far more difficult. One child might know the meaning of a key word, while another might have to use clues from the context to understand what is happening in a scene.

While 'teaching' comprehension might be impossible, it is certainly possible for teachers to support children to become better at drawing meaning from a text, 'guiding readers', in the words of Tennent et al. (2016). This section presents several practical ways that teachers can support children to develop their comprehension:

- Using specific comprehension strategies
- Developing children's background knowledge
- Building vocabulary
- Authentic booktalk, using rich questions
- Modelling inference and making meaning from a text
- Using text structure
- Comprehension monitoring

Each of these ideas could be employed across the different vehicles for teaching reading in primary school: shared reading in English lessons, specific shared reading sessions (sometimes termed *whole-class reading*), or small group/guided reading. As noted in

Chapter 7, Gough and Tunmer refer to 'language comprehension' in the Simple View of Reading (1986), rather than 'reading comprehension'. As a result, these approaches could be applied both to the texts that children read themselves and to the texts that are read aloud with children.

Using specific comprehension strategies

Drawing on the work of Duke and Pearson (2002) and Palincsar and Brown (1984), Tennent et al. (2016) suggest seven strategies to support the development of comprehension:

- **Predicting**: readers consider the text and make educated guesses about what might happen next or the consequences of particular actions
- **Questioning**: readers use questions to explore ideas and themes in a text
- **Clarifying**: readers check the meaning of words, phrases and ideas during and after reading
- **Summarising**: readers collate the main ideas or events in a text and briefly summarise them
- **Thinking aloud**: readers express their thoughts aloud, explaining and exploring their ideas as they go
- **Noting the text structure**: readers pay attention to structural features of the text, including the organisation, the language features used and the layout on the page or screen
- **Visualising**: readers form a mental picture of the action, characters or information shared by the text

The authors suggest specifically introducing children to these strategies, ensuring they are clear in what each looks like and why each is important. Children should then be encouraged to practise using them, both when reading with an adult and when reading independently.

A teaching session might focus explicitly on one or two of the strategies; for example, predicting what might happen next in a text at the start of a whole-class reading session or summarising the information in a section of a non-fiction book in a guided reading session. Alternatively, children may use each of the strategies as opportunities organically arise when reading a text. While these strategies might be introduced discretely, it is through having the opportunity to use them that children will become independent readers.

Occasions for practising these skills need to be planned thoroughly by the teacher, although it is likely that this will depend on the text being studied as much as the need to introduce and practise the full range of skills.

CASE STUDY 8.1

A Year 1 teacher is reading *Sloth Slept On* by Frann Preston-Gannon with a small group of children as part of a guided reading session. Before reading, she identifies the following opportunities for practising the different comprehension skills:

Predicting

- Looking at the front cover together and anticipating what might happen
- Before the penultimate page, what will the sloth think when he wakes up in the rainforest?

Questioning

A mixture of literal questions, questions that require inference, and personal response questions with no preconceived answer, including:

- What type of sloth have the children found? (literal)
- Why does the sloth ask for directions back to the zoo? (inference)
- What might you have done if you had found the sloth? (personal)

Clarifying

Reading stops to ensure children understand the meaning of 'ferocious' and 'exhausted', and that they have noticed the details on the father's newspaper.

Summarising

Two points to summarise: at the midway point to check children have understood the sloth facts and at the end to check they have understood the story.

Thinking aloud

Paired activity after several pages, where children read a few sentences and discuss their understanding.

Noting the text structure

Children stop to discuss the story and how this is similar to/different from other animal stories they have read. Also, to discuss non-fiction pages about sloths – is this a regular feature of picture books?

Visualising

In this case, the pictures provide a visual element to the book, but children are asked to visualise and then describe what happens next to the sloth.

While it is important to ensure that children are aware of the strategies they can use to draw meaning from a text, and then to return to practise them, it has been suggested that the positive impact of explicitly teaching comprehension strategies might lose effect over time, with a short focused burst of attention being as effective as a prolonged period of instruction (Elleman, 2017). A useful model for using comprehension strategies might be to introduce them to children as a toolkit for thinking, something they can draw on to help them understand what they are reading.

Developing background knowledge

In order to make sense of the new information in a text, children need to be able to synthesise it with their existing knowledge. This relies on both *general knowledge* and our specific *domain knowledge* about that particular topic. While prior knowledge of a subject does not guarantee understanding (Bransford and Johnson, 1972), it seems reasonable that there would be a threshold below which comprehension would become very difficult; an idea supported by research (O'Reilly et al., 2019).

In order to make meaning while reading the archery competition in Geraldine McCaughrean's retelling of *Robin Hood and the Golden Arrow*, a reader needs enough general knowledge about England in the Middle Ages to be able to picture the costume and setting. A specific knowledge of archery might help the reader to picture the competition and understand the words 'arrowsmith', 'fletches' and 'butts'. It should also be noted that the relationship between reading and background knowledge is symbiotic: it might be that the child learns about England in the Middle Ages from *Robin Hood and the Golden Arrow*. Alongside rich talk, one of the best ways to build general knowledge is to read widely.

While a teacher can support a child, an additional complication is that it is difficult to know beforehand what level of knowledge each child will bring to the text: this will vary widely from child to child. There are a number of practical approaches to building background knowledge to support children with comprehension:

Pre-teaching key ideas or information

If a text is going to be studied in depth as part of a whole-class or group/guided reading session, setting aside time to learn some of the key ideas that will be important for comprehension can be a good idea. This might take the form of:

- **looking at the book itself:** for example, thinking about other books in the series or books by the same author and asking how that might shape their expectations of the new text
- **a discussion:** some time spent discussing the setting or key characters in the book, such as looking at a map of the Mediterranean before reading *Black Ships Before Troy* by Rosemary Sutcliff

- **reading or listening to another book:** perhaps another story that is useful to know such as a reminder of the story of *Little Red Riding Hood* before reading *Little Red* by Bethan Woolvin or a non-fiction book about World War II such as *Evacuation in World War II* by Martin Parsons while reading Sonya Hartnett's *The Children of the King*
- **using multi-media resources:** a clip of a mole burrowing underground and then emerging from the soil before reading *The Wind in the Willows* or watching and listening to a recording of waves crashing onto a beach in preparation for reading *Storm Whale* by Benji Davies

Maintaining a broad curriculum

The pressures on teachers and schools to ensure that numeracy and literacy outcomes are met can sometimes lead to a curriculum where English and mathematics are prioritised over the rest of the curriculum. However, ensuring that children have access to a broad curriculum that introduces them to knowledge and concepts will support them with reading comprehension.

Building vocabulary

There is a close correlation between the breadth and depth of children's vocabulary and their ability to make meaning from an unknown text (Carroll, 1993). Classroom teachers can approach vocabulary teaching in two ways: explicitly through activities designed to introduce children to the meaning of new words and implicitly through encountering and remembering those words in an organic way.

Implicit vocabulary building

A simple (and enjoyable) way to develop children's vocabulary is through encouraging children to read as widely as possible in their own time and by reading aloud to them. This is especially true for rich and challenging texts or books that they might not choose to read themselves (Cunningham, 2005). Through giving children the chance to reflect on the words they encounter as they read independently, either in writing or through talk, children can learn new words from their reading.

CASE STUDY 8.2

A Year 3 teacher gave children a blank bookmark to record the words that they didn't understand as they read. Children recorded these and then every week they would take out their bookmarks and share their words with their classmates. The children would be given time to find out the meanings and the teacher would choose a sample of the words to share as a whole class.

Explicit vocabulary teaching

Teachers can directly support children's vocabulary development in a number of other ways:

- **Plan for repetition:** Cain et al. (2003) suggest that in order for a word to become part of a child's receptive vocabulary, children need to encounter a word a number of times in different contexts. Sharing other books or films and webpages on the same topic as the book being read can support this, as can explicitly teaching the meaning of words before or after they have been encountered in the class novel. Re-reading the same picture books or poems can also help children to develop an understanding of the meaning of a new word.
- **'Tiers' of words:** Beck et al. (2002) suggest dividing the words used in school into three tiers:
    - Tier 1 words are commonly used in spoken language (e.g. *house, speak, book, fast*)
    - Tier 2 words are found in more mature written texts (e.g. *discrete, infer, anomaly, seize*)
    - Tier 3 are technical words: the language of the curriculum (e.g. *polar, analogy, Cambrian*)

        Tier 1 words are usually learnt through talking and discussion, while tier 3 words are the words explicitly taught through subject-specific lessons at school. Teaching that focuses on tier 2 words gives children access to these useful words, supporting them as writers and readers.

- **Etymology and morphology:** Explicitly teaching children about words using morphology (the way different root words, suffixes, prefixes combine to make meaning) and etymology (the origin of a word and the 'families' of words to which they belong) can be a useful way of enabling children to work out the meaning of a word when they come across it independently. Knowing the Latin root 'pater/patr' means 'father' might help children to make sense of words such as 'paternal' or 'patron'. Knowing the prefix 'auto-' refers to the self might help children to understand the meaning of 'autobiography' or 'automatic'. Morphology or etymology could be applied as approaches to understanding the words children encounter independently or as an approach to teaching spelling or introducing new words.

For an in-depth exploration of vocabulary teaching, see Chapter 14: Building vocabulary and word knowledge.

Authentic booktalk using rich questions

Roche (2014) suggests that authentic booktalk – time to talk about and explore a text through discussion – is crucial for developing children's understanding, oral language and vocabulary. Additionally, Cremin et al. (2009) argue that this type of booktalk can also be a critical factor in supporting children to form positive attitudes to reading.

As discussed at length in Chapters 5 and 6, rich talk sits at the heart of good English teaching. When supporting children's comprehension, the quality of talk around the books, especially the teacher's questioning, will be one of the key ways that children learn to make meaning from a text.

In practice, a teacher can support authentic booktalk through:

Building time for booktalk

One challenge for a teacher is to build in time for legitimate booktalk of the type outlined in Chapters 5 and 6, rather than the *initiation-response-feedback* pattern of discourse that is often observed in classrooms. Scheduling time for children to talk about the books they are reading and the books that are read to them is vital. Making use of Chambers' *Three Sharings* (Chambers, 1993) is a good way to begin booktalk such as this:

- Was there anything you liked about this book?
- Was there anything you disliked about this book?
- Was there anything that puzzled you?
- Were there any patterns or connections that you noticed?

Planning sequences of questions

Planning questions to drive discussion around a text takes skill on the teacher's part. Effective questioning requires a clear rationale for why a specific question is being asked: is it to check a child's understanding? To promote thinking? To drive discussion?

As discussed in Chapters 17 and 18, effective questioning will draw on a mix of open and closed questions (Harrison and Howard, 2009), while also drawing on authentic questions; ones that allow for more than one answer, including responses that have not been anticipated by the teacher (Tennent et al., 2016).

Case Study 8.3 illustrates how a teacher might structure a sequence of questions, including using statements rather than questions to promote talk.

CASE STUDY 8.3

A Year 5 class is studying *The Pied Piper of Hamelin* by Robert Browning in a whole-class shared reading session. The teacher carefully plans the questions for the session beforehand to facilitate rich discussion, while also leaving opportunities for children to offer their own opinions and ideas. Below is the extract the children read followed by the teacher's set questions. These questions are accompanied by a brief commentary explaining the teacher's thinking.

(Continued)

Text: Lines 10–20 of *The Pied Piper of Hamelin* by Robert Browning

Rats!

They fought the dogs and killed the cats,

And bit the babies in the cradles,

And ate the cheeses out of the vats,

And licked the soup from the cooks' own ladles,

Split open the kegs of salted sprats,

Made nests inside men's Sunday hats,

And even spoiled the women's chats,

By drowning their speaking

With shrieking and squeaking

In fifty different sharps and flats.

Questions for discussion:

1. Is there anything that you liked and anything you didn't like about this stanza?

2. Is there anything that puzzles you about this piece of the text? What would you like to find out?

3. Can you make any connections from this text to other books or stories you know?

These first three questions are drawn from Chambers' 'Tell Me'. The teacher begins with the three questions so that children have an authentic opportunity to respond to the text and share their own thoughts and ideas. Phrasing the first questions as 'is there anything?' rather than 'tell me one thing…' means that a child has the option of giving the answer 'no'.

4. List all of the actions that the rats carried out in Hamelin.

This is a straightforward retrieval task that the children carry out in pairs. It gives the opportunity for every child to contribute to the lesson immediately, practises literal comprehension and gives the teacher the chance to check that everyone understands what has happened in the text. Opportunities may arise in which the teacher is called upon to explain the meaning of unfamiliar phrases such as 'salted sprats' or 'sharps and flats'.

5. In your opinion, what is the most unpleasant thing the rats have done?

This is a chance for the children to reflect and visualise the actions and then offer a personal judgement. This question provides room for children to politely defend their own ideas and respond to the opinions of others.

6. Why might Robert Browning have chosen to list all of these different actions?

Children will explore this question with a partner before joining a whole-class discussion. The teacher listens and accepts all answers, but uses the discussion to introduce the idea that by sharing a number of unpleasant things, the poet is telling the reader that things are awful in Hamelin. It is important for the reader to know this at the start of the story in order to understand the importance of the Pied Piper later on. The purpose of this question is different from the others in that it has an answer the teacher is working towards, but it is a crucial piece of understanding that the children need in order to make sense of the poem. In addition, the teacher is drawing attention to an interesting example of effective writing.

7. Do you agree with this statement: The rats in Hamelin behave like normal rats. Why/ why not?

This task gives the children the chance to show their understanding of the text without there being a preconceived answer (both arguments could be defended – that rats kill the cats, suggesting they are not normal, but many of their actions reflect typical rat behaviour). If children work independently to frame their arguments before discussing it as a group, jotting down their ideas on a whiteboard or thinking aloud, the teacher can use this to assess their understanding.

Modelling inference and making meaning from a text

Modelling how a reader makes meaning, whether through whole-class shared reading or small group guided reading, can be a powerful way of showing children how meaning can be drawn from a text. This is especially true of understanding which requires inference – by which we mean occasions where at least some information is left for the reader to read 'between the lines' – making sense of details that are implied in the text or making links to their knowledge beyond the book.

   This modelling can take the form of the teacher thinking aloud, providing a commentary as they read and/or drawing children's attention to words, phrases or ideas. They might stop to discuss a specific point or to ask a question, but the key aim is to share how they make sense from what they read, making both *global coherence inferences* across the text and *local cohesion inferences* where understanding relies on making links within the text – resolving pronouns (knowing that the 'she' is the girl's mother, for example) or appreciating the implications of a particular conjunction (using 'but' rather than 'and' to join two clauses together, for example).

CASE STUDY 8.4

A Year 3 teacher read the opening to *The Elephant's Child* from *Just So Stories* by Rudyard Kipling aloud to his class:

> In the High and Far-Off Times the Elephant, O Best Beloved, had no trunk. He had only a blackish, bulgy nose, as big as a boot, that he could wriggle from side to side; but couldn't pick things up with it. But there was one Elephant – a new elephant – an elephant's child – who was full of 'satiable curtiosity', and that means he asked ever so many questions.

As the teacher and children are reading it together, the teacher could comment on:

- The meaning of any unfamiliar of words

    I'm not sure what 'satiable curtiosity' is. I wonder if curtiosity is just a deliberate mistake by the author and he means curiosity. I know curious means wanting to find out about something, so perhaps it means he was very curious and always wanted to find things out. I'll read on and see if that fits with the story.

- Local cohesive inferences required to help the text make sense

    'He had only a blackish, bulgy nose, as big as a boot, that he could wriggle from side to side; but couldn't pick things up with it.'

    The author uses the conjunction 'but' here, so that means the two clauses run counter to each other – although he can wriggle his nose, it isn't a trunk that can pick things up.

- Inferences required to help the text make sense

    I don't think that this is a true story about a real elephant. The author says it is set in the High and Far-Off Times, which doesn't sound real to me. I think it is a made-up story.

Modelling the reading process might take place in shared reading, or small group/guided reading. It can be used in conjunction with the other strategies in this section such as questioning, comprehension modelling and explicit vocabulary teaching. It is important to note, however, that it is not desirable to do this every time a teacher reads to the class; the idea is to model reading sparingly with children, who then take these ideas to use independently in their own reading.

Using text structure

Meta-analysis of the effects of text structure instruction (Bogaerds-Hazenberg et al., 2020) suggest that children who are familiar with the range of conventions and structures of different kinds of texts, both narratives and the various non-fiction forms, are able to use this knowledge to support their comprehension, although the ability to apply this knowledge consistently to unseen texts and wider comprehension is not clear (Stevens et al., 2020). If there is a deviation from what is expected (the narrative arc of a story, for example, or the layout of a newspaper report), they notice this and check whether this is deliberate on the part of the author or a gap in their understanding.

Diagrams and visual support such as story or narrative maps can be a useful way of making the structure of text visible, showing children the organisation of a text, whether a narrative or non-fiction text. They may serve as a reminder of what needs to be included in writing or be used as a visual tool to enable discussion.

Comprehension monitoring

Comprehension monitoring is where a reader is able to recognise when they've understood something and when they haven't. This is an important skill for comprehension, allowing children to recognise when they may need to re-read a section, stop to think or ask for help. Oakhill et al. (2005) suggest that developing an awareness of whether new ideas fit with our existing knowledge base could support the development of critical thinking and help with learning across the wider curriculum.

Teachers can support children to develop this ability through drawing their attention to it in reading sessions and modelling it through shared and guided reading:

Hmm, the text says 'the door slammed shut'. But where is the Captain? Is she on the outside or the inside? I'm not sure, so I'm going to re-read that section again. Ah, she must be outside because it doesn't say anywhere that she made it through. I'm going to read on now and see what she does next.

Or:

I'm not sure what this last phrase means: 'he was incandescent with fury'. Fury is anger, I think. I'm going to read on and see if there's any other information that helps me. If not, I'll go and look up 'incandescent' or ask an adult if they know.

Other comprehension strategies, such as clarifying or summarising the text are helpful for comprehension monitoring, so helping children to embed these as a natural part of their reading behaviour can support them to make meaning when reading.

STOP AND REFLECT

Think about your own comprehension teaching (or other sessions you have watched), both standalone sessions and through the wider teaching of reading.

- Which of the approaches above do you recognise from your own teaching/observation?
- Which approaches might be useful that you haven't previously used or seen?
- What challenges might you face using these approaches?
- Can you see any possible tensions between any of the approaches? If so, why?

Teaching word reading

As addressed in Chapter 7, developing fluent word reading skills is important if children are to become confident, independent readers. This section will address the practical aspect of teaching word reading in the classroom.

Systematic synthetic phonics teaching

For the majority of teachers in English schools, the emphasis on word reading will come through the discrete and systematic teaching of synthetic phonics, often supported by a published scheme (see Chapter 7 for an exploration of this). An approach to the teaching of synthetic phonics might be considered systematic if:

- it teaches beginner readers of the alphabetic code and all 44+ grapheme-phoneme correspondences (GPCs) in written language and phonemes in spoken language to support both decoding and spelling
- the introduction of the GPCs begins with single letters and their corresponding sounds and progresses incrementally to more complex GPCs
- the processes of blending and segmenting are taught as reversible processes which will support reading (decoding) and spelling (encoding) and which should be taught as soon as the reading of CVC words is achievable
- reading and spelling strategies are implemented when introducing high frequency words (HFW) which contain less-common GPCs. The term associated with HFWs in the National Curriculum is Common Exception Words: these come under the umbrella term of HFW

In addition, systematic synthetic phonics teaching can include:

- discrete, direct, regular teaching (often on a daily basis)
- GPCs being taught systematically and rapidly (from Reception) with single letter phonemes taught first and then on to alternative sounds which will include more than one letter

- sessions that are pacy, engaging, multi-sensory, interactive and enjoyable
- pupils being given time and opportunities to apply their knowledge and understanding with purpose outside of these sessions throughout the curriculum so that fluency and accuracy becomes automatic
- giving pupils opportunities to practise with decodable texts that contain GPCs which they have been taught so that they can apply their knowledge
- children applying their developing phonic skills to a wide range of texts, including their own choice of books, online and multi-modal texts, and words from the environment around them such as shop signs and text on packaging
- giving pupils opportunities to write using GPCs which they have been taught so that they can apply their knowledge and understanding
- carefully monitoring and assessing the progress of each child so that teaching can be responsive to the learning needs of pupils who may need additional support

STOP AND REFLECT

Decodable texts are levelled books that are comprised mostly of GPCs that have already been taught alongside some high frequency words (e.g. *said, the*). In practice, decodable texts are likely to form only a small part of children's reading experiences, and most of the books children encounter will be ones that are read to them, but the use of decodable texts in early reading teaching is an aspect of phonics teaching that generates heated debate.

Advocates of decodable texts point out that these texts allow children to experience success at an early stage of learning to read and that the books give children a medium to practise their decoding, which is preferable to practising reading words in isolation.

Critics suggest that when language is limited to decodable words, it is difficult to create an enjoyable book – something that could have implications for children's enjoyment of reading and subsequent motivation to read. It is also argued that decodable texts prevent children learning to identify the patterns and probabilities of real language, including the occurrence of different GPCs in English and encountering new vocabulary.

Research into the use of decodable texts is limited, and the results of what has been conducted are mixed, suggesting positive effects for decoding (Mesmer, 2005), but greater fluency from texts that were levelled but not specifically designed to be decodable (Mesmer, 2009; Price-Mohr and Price, 2017). Other studies comparing texts with different levels of decodability found it made no significant difference to reading outcomes (Jenkins et al., 2004).

Castles et al. (2018) argue that while the use of decodable books might be useful at the beginning of learning to read, 'once children move beyond the very early stages of reading, the benefits of decodable readers are likely to be outweighed by their limitations. More research is needed to determine when this tipping point occurs.'

- When it comes to the teaching of reading, what might be some of the benefits and limitations of using decodable-only texts?
- How is this theory reflected in any experience you have had using decodable texts with children?

Use of phonics skills in context

In addition to the explicit teaching of phonics, children will benefit from opportunities to employ their developing phonics skills away from targeted phonics sessions. This includes making use of texts that have been written especially for that purpose.

CASE STUDY 8.5

A Year 1 teacher carefully plans her reading provision so that children will have the opportunity to consolidate and embed the GPCs that have been taught in whole-class phonics sessions across the week.

1. In a whole-class phonics session, children are introduced to a new GPC – the grapheme –ir (representing the phoneme /ɜ:/). The teacher leads a fast-paced session with the children on the carpet that:

   • introduces the GPC
   • gives children the chance to practise pronouncing it
   • shows the GPC in the context of some familiar words (girl, first, skirt, shirt, thirsty)
   • asks children to write the GPC on mini-whiteboards
   • challenges children to write the GPC in the context of a word, linking this new learning to GPCs already learnt (sir, bird, third)

2. In small groups, children use a decodable text called The Third Bird to practise identifying and reading the –ir grapheme. The focus of this session is not comprehension, although children have the opportunity to read and discuss the meaning of the text, but to reinforce the GPC that has been learnt.

3. In a whole-class reading session using Shh! We Have a Plan by Chris Haughton, the teacher draws children's attention to –ir grapheme on the second reading of the text (the first reading is purely to enjoy the story). This incidental opportunity helps children to see the link between the word reading they are taught explicitly and their wider reading for enjoyment.

4. Children write their own letters to the hunters from the book, asking them not to catch any more birds. This gives them a chance to practise using the –ir grapheme in the context of real writing.

5. For consolidation, children are given two tasks: a matching game based on the –ir grapheme to take home and practise, and the job of looking out for any other words they come across with the –ir grapheme, ready to report back in the next session.

Address precursors to word reading

It has been suggested that phonemic awareness – the ability to recognise the phonemes that make up words – correlates to later word reading skill. Activities such as joining in with songs and nursery rhymes can help with this knowledge. Stuart and Stainthorp (2016) suggest that reciting and playing with rhyming words support phonemic awareness as finding words that rhyme involves changing the onset of the word (*wall*-*fall*; *men*-*again*). They cite some activities that can help develop phoneme and letter awareness drawn from the work of Castles et al. (2009).

Table 8.1 Activities to develop phoneme awareness or letter awareness

Activity	Develops awareness of	Description
Card match	Phonemes	Match picture card beginning with the same phoneme
	Letters	Match cards with the same letter
Dominoes	Phonemes	Connect dominoes with pictures starting with the same phoneme
	Letters	Connect dominoes with the same letter
Bingo	Phonemes	Put tokens on pictures starting with the presented phonemes
	Letters	Put tokens on letters matching those displayed by the trainer
I Spy	Phonemes	Look at a picture book and find objects starting with a given phoneme
	Letters	Look at a picture book and find the hidden letters
Snap	Phonemes	Take turns with the trainer to place down cards and say 'snap' when two sequential pictures begin with the same sound
	Letters	Take turns with the trainer to place down cards and say 'snap' when two sequential letters are the same
Memory	Phonemes	Turn over pairs of face-down cards and find two pictures beginning with the same phoneme
	Letters	Turn over pairs of face-down cards to find two with the same letter

(From Castles et al. (2009) in Stuart and Stainthorp (2016))

While activities that support children's phonemic awareness can be helpful in providing them with a base before they begin to learn how to word read, it is important to note that this ability might well develop in tandem with word reading (Castles and Coltheart, 2004). As children learn specific GPCs and then have the opportunity to use them to read the words they encounter, they will further develop their phonemic awareness by reading and listening to books as well as talking to their peers and adults in a language-rich environment.

Approaching high frequency words (including common exception words)

While systematic phonics teaching helps children to learn the alphabetic code, it is not possible to teach them all of this knowledge immediately. Like everything, it takes time to learn. However, if children are to become independent readers as quickly as possible, they are likely to encounter some words that are not yet decodable at the first stages of a child's phonological development. While almost all words become fully decodable at a later stage, some *high frequency words* are valuable to learn to recognise before a child has the alphabetic code or etymological knowledge to make sense of their spelling (see p. 113 in Chapter 7).

CASE STUDY 8.6

A Year 2 teacher is working individually with a child who has recently joined her class. Having made assessments of the child's reading through reading with her, the teacher found that the child's word reading was not as secure as might be expected for her age.

The teacher and child are working through a systematic synthetic phonics programme to help the girl catch up with her peers. She is making good progress. In this short 10-minute session, the child is reading a decodable book (*At Sea*) in order to consolidate the 'ea' (/iː/) grapheme. The book contains the common exception word *said*, so the teacher supports the child to learn this word through:

- drawing attention to parts of the word that are phonically decodable based on the child's current knowledge. The 's' and the 'd' are easy to recognise, the tricky bit is the 'ai' grapheme representing the phoneme /ɛ/ (as in *head* or *bed*)
- pointing out where it sits within the sentence and its purpose. In this book it follows dialogue, explaining what each character says
- asking the child to write the word down in order to reinforce her knowledge of the letters in the word (and hopefully to support her spelling in the future)
- setting the girl a challenge: can she find the word *said* in her independent reading ahead of their reading session the following day?

Most published phonics schemes have these high frequency words to be learnt embedded throughout, and for English schools, they are prescribed in the 2014 National Curriculum where they are termed 'common exception words'.

Conclusion

Chapters 7 and 8 have focused on the Simple View of Reading, a model that suggests that the two elements of reading – word recognition and language comprehension – combine to enable a child to become a fluent reader.

While learning to read fluently is one of the key aims of primary school, effective teaching of reading needs to go further than this, supporting children to develop the attributes, behaviours and skills that come with being a reader in the broadest sense. In the next chapter, attention will move to a deeper view of reading, considering the benefits – educational, social and emotional – that come with choosing to read widely for pleasure. The theory surrounding this will be explored, before considering how schools and teachers can support this in practice.

IN SUMMARY

- The two elements of the Simple View of Reading – word reading and language comprehension – require different diets of teaching.
- Reading comprehension is not a skill that can be taught – it is the outcome of understanding the words on a page or screen. Different readers will make this meaning in different ways, but it is possible to help children to become more confident comprehenders through a range of teaching activities.
- Once children have learnt to decode accurately, one of the best ways to develop as a reader is to read. Through reading, children develop fluency, nurture their vocabulary and general knowledge, and practise making meaning from a text.

FURTHER READING

- For a comprehensive and practical overview of supporting children to develop their comprehension, see *Guiding Readers: layers of meaning* by Wayne Tennent, David Reedy, Angela Hobsbaum and Nikki Gamble.
- For most schools, explicit teaching of systematic synthetic phonics will be built around a specific programme, either a published scheme or one written by the school. *I Hear with my Little Ear* by Liz Baldwin suggests games and activities for supporting children's learning in this area that can be used alongside a school's existing approach.
- For a thorough introduction to teaching reading, including an in-depth exploration of the evidence around different approaches to teaching word reading and practical examples, see *Reading Development and Teaching* by Morag Stuart and Rhona Stainthorp.

REFERENCES

Beck, I., McKeown, M. and Kucan, L. (2002) *Bringing Words to Life: Robust Vocabulary Instruction*. New York: Guilford Press.

Bogaerds-Hazenberg, S.T.M., Evers-Vermeul, J. and van den Bergh, H. (2020) A meta-analysis on the effects of text structure instruction on reading comprehension in the upper elementary grades. *Reading Research Quarterly* (Advance online publication).

Bransford, J. and Johnson, M. (1972) Contextual prerequisites for understanding: Some investigations of comprehension and recall. *Journal of Verbal Learning and Verbal Behavior*, 11(6): 717–26.

Cain, K., Oakhill, J.V. and Elbro, C. (2003) The ability to learn new word meanings from context by school-age children with and without language comprehension difficulties. *Journal of Child Language*, 30: 681–94.

Carroll, J.B. (1993) *Human Cognitive Abilities: A survey of factor-analytic studies*. New York: Cambridge University Press.

Castles, A. and Coltheart, M. (2004) Is there a causal link from phonological awareness to success in learning to read? *Cognition*, 91: 77–111.

Castles, A., Coltheart, M., Wilson, K., Valpeid, J. and Wedgwood, J. (2009) The genesis of reading ability: What helps children learn letter-sound correspondences? *Journal of Experimental Child Psychology*, 104: 68–88.

Castles, A., Rastle, K. and Nation, K. (2018) Ending the reading wars: Reading acquisition from novice to expert. *Psychological Science in the Public Interest*, 19(1): 5–51.

Chambers , A. (1993) *Tell Me: Children, Reading and Talk*. Stroud: The Thimble Press.

Cremin, T., Mottram, M., Collins, F., Powell, S. and Safford, K. (2009) Teachers as readers: Building communities of readers. *Literacy*, 43(1): 11–19.

Cunningham, A.E. (2005) Vocabulary growth through independent reading and reading aloud to children. In E.H. Hiebert and M.L. Kamhi (Eds), *Teaching and Learning Vocabulary: Bringing research to practice* (pp. 45–68). Mahwah, NJ: Lawrence Erlbaum Associates.

Duke, N.K. and Pearson, P.D. (2002) Effective practices for developing reading comprehension. In A.E. Farstrup and S.J. Samuels (Eds), *What Research Has to Say About Reading Instruction*. Newark, DE: International Reading Association.

Elleman, A. (2017) Examining the impact of inference instruction on the literal and inferential comprehension of skilled and less skilled readers: A meta-analytic review. *Journal of Educational Psychology*, 109: 2.

Gough, P.B. and Tunmer, W.E. (1986) Decoding, reading, and reading disability. *RASE: Remedial and Special Education*, 7(1): 6–10.

Harrison, C. and Howard, S. (2009) *Inside the Primary Black Box: Assessment for learning in primary and early years classrooms*. London: GL Assessment.

Jenkins, J.R., Peyton, J.A., Sanders, E.A. and Vadasy, P.F. (2004) Effects of reading decodable texts in supplemental first-grade tutoring. *Scientific Studies of Reading*, 8(1): 53–85.

Mesmer, H. (2005) Text decodability and the first-grade reader. *Reading and Writing Quarterly*, 21 (1): 61–86.

Mesmer, H. (2009) Textual scaffolds for developing fluency in beginning readers: Accuracy and reading rate in qualitatively leveled and decodable text. *Literacy Research and Instruction*, 49: 20–39.

Oakhill, J., Hartt, J. and Samols, D. (2005) Levels of comprehension monitoring and working memory in good and poor comprehenders. *Reading and Writing*, 18: 657–713.

O'Reilly, T., Wang, Z. and Sabatini, J. (2019) How much knowledge is too little? When a lack of knowledge becomes a barrier to comprehension. *Psychological Science*, 30: 1344–51.

Palincsar, A.S. and Brown, A.L. (1984) Reciprocal teaching of comprehension-fostering and comprehension-monitoring activities. *Cognition and Instruction*, 1: 117–75.

Price-Mohr, R. and Price, C. (2017) Gender differences in early reading strategies: A comparison of synthetic phonics only with a mixed approach to teaching reading to 4–5 year-old children. *Early Childhood Education Journal*, 45: 613–20.

Roche, M. (2014) *Developing Children's Critical Thinking through Picturebooks*. Abingdon: Routledge.

Rosenblatt, L.M. (1938) *Literature as Exploration*. New York: Appleton-Century, 1938 (from: Revised edition, New York: Noble and Noble, 1968).

Stevens, E.A., Vaughn, S., House, L. and Stillman-Spisak, S. (2020) The effects of a paraphrasing and text structure intervention on the main idea generation and reading comprehension of students with reading disabilities in grades 4 and 5. *Scientific Studies of Reading*, 24: 5.

Stuart, M. and Stainthorp, R. (2016) *Reading Development and Teaching*. London: Sage.

Tennent, W., Reedy, D., Hobsbaum, A. and Gamble, N. (2016) *Guiding Readers: Layers of meaning*. London: UCL, Institute of Education.

LITERATURE

Evacuation in World War II by Martin Parsons

Just So Stories by Rudyard Kipling

Little Red by Bethan Woolvin

Robin Hood and the Golden Arrow retold by Geraldine McCaughrean

Shh! We Have a Plan by Chris Haughton

Ships Before Troy by Rosemary Sutcliff

Sloth Slept On by Frann Preston-Gannon

The Storm Whale by Benji Davies

The Children of the King by Sonya Hartnett

The Pied Piper of Hamelin by Robert Browning

The Wind in the Willows by Kenneth Grahame

9

BECOMING A READER: THEORY AND PRACTICE IN READING FOR PLEASURE

THIS CHAPTER WILL

- Introduce the theoretical underpinnings of reading for pleasure, including the importance of creating a genuine, authentic reading culture

- Consider practical approaches for promoting reading for pleasure in the primary school

Introduction

The Simple View of Reading, discussed in Chapters 7 and 8, provides a model for how we might go about teaching children *to* read. But being able to read is only one aspect of being a reader. If children can read, but never choose to read then they miss out on the benefits that being a reader can bring: academic, social, cultural and emotional. More than anything, they miss out on the pleasure that reading can bring – the enjoyment of being lost in a thrilling novel or the fascination of finding an unexpected fact from a website.

The first section of this chapter outlines the theory around reading for pleasure, introducing what research tells us about how schools can build an authentic reading culture. The second section looks at practical approaches for encouraging children to read widely for pleasure in the primary classroom.

Reading for pleasure – theory

The first section of the chapter will consider theory and research surrounding reading for pleasure and building a reading culture in the classroom.

Defining reading for pleasure

'Reading for pleasure' has become the recognised term for the reading that children choose to do of their own volition. Bearne and Reedy (2018) neatly define reading for pleasure as 'personal motivation and engagement in reading which leads to sustained voluntary reading'. This reading may happen in class or at home, but the key word is *voluntary*. Whether the text is fiction or non-fiction, paper or on screen, reading for pleasure is:

> Reading that we do of our own free will, anticipating the satisfaction that we will get from the act of reading. It also refers to reading that having begun at someone else's request, we continue because we are interested in it.
>
> (Clark and Rumbold, 2006)

The benefits of reading for pleasure

Research suggests a correlation between becoming a reader, someone who chooses to read in their own time, and a wide range of academic benefits, including:

- a correlation between reading engagement and reading attainment (Morgan and Fuchs, 2007; Petscher, 2010; Clark and de Zoysa, 2011; De Naeghel et al., 2012; McGeown et al., 2014; Torppa et al., 2019; Toste et al., 2020)
- better general knowledge (Cunningham and Stanovich, 1998)
- a possible effect on wider academic performance (OECD, 2002)
- increased performance in tests of spelling and mathematics (Sullivan and Brown, 2013)
- improved vocabulary and language development (Sullivan and Brown, 2013; Mar and Rain, 2015)
- a link between reading and self-confidence in reading (Guthrie and Alvermann, 1999)
- a link to both improved attainment and more positive attitudes to writing (Cremin and Myhill, 2012; Clark, 2014)

As Clark and de Zoysa (2011) note, the relationship between enjoyment in reading and reading attainment is not necessarily causal – it may be that stronger readers enjoy reading more, rather than that their enjoyment in reading is raising attainment: a hypothesis supported by Toste et al.'s meta-analysis (2020). Indeed, research by Van Bergen et al. (2018) disputes the relationship is even reciprocal, suggesting that children's reading ability determines the amount that young children wish to read. However, other research indicates that exposure to print is a factor in children's reading fluency (Stanovich and West, 1989; Mol and Bus, 2011).

Share's *self-teaching hypothesis* (Jorm and Share, 1983; Share, 1995) suggests that for beginning readers, a combination of conscious phonological decoding and repeated exposure to words enables children to self-teach through their independent reading. As they encounter more words in print on the page or screen, children's orthographic knowledge grows, lessening their reliance on phonological decoding and eventually supporting fluent reading. Later, as children progress from this early stage of decoding to become fluent readers, exposure to text might support vocabulary acquisition, background knowledge and provide them with the opportunity to practise applying the range of strategies for comprehension discussed in Chapter 8. It seems plausible that reading for pleasure would positively affect reading outcomes.

Perhaps due to these reported academic benefits, the 2014 English National Curriculum contains a number of references to reading for pleasure and pupils' wider reading, stating that:

> Pupils should be taught to read fluently, understand extended prose, both fiction and non-fiction, and be encouraged to read for pleasure. Schools should do everything to promote wider reading... [Pupils] should be reading widely and frequently, outside as well as in school, for pleasure and information.
>
> (DfE, 2013)

This focus is welcome even if, as critics argue, this rhetoric is not always reflected in other policy decisions, including the emphasis given to the testing of a narrow range of specific aspects of reading comprehension at Key Stage 2 or the introduction of a phonics check at the end of Year 1 (Bearne and Reedy, 2018). For further discussion on the role of national assessments, see Chapter 17.

Of course, academic progress isn't the only reason reading widely might be important. Research suggests that reading widely can support children to:

- develop empathy for others through their engagement with fictional characters (Nikolajeva, 2013)
- develop their awareness and understanding of their emotions and furnish them with a vocabulary to discuss these (Kumschick et al., 2014)
- promote a better understanding of the world (Howard, 2011)
- less predication to prejudice and stereotyping (Vezzali et al., 2012, 2015)
- develop their self and social identities (Moje et al., 2008)

Aside from these reported academic and social benefits, reading can also bring immense enjoyment. Pleasingly, reading for pleasure is an area where the research suggests a convergence between what is likely to be academically useful, what can support children's emotional development and awareness, and what might be a pleasant and enjoyable way to spend their time.

Supporting children to become readers seems like a key priority for a teacher in the primary classroom. So, how might this best be approached?

Encouraging reading for pleasure – theory

There is an obvious problem if we try to coerce children into undertaking the 'reading that we do of our own free will' (Clark and Rumbold, 2006). When considering modern approaches to parenting, Gopnik (2016) compares the difference between how a carpenter and a gardener approach their respective work and the same analogy might be useful here. Rather than approaching reading for pleasure like carpenters, attempting to chisel children into readers through ordering them to read or through bribing them with initiatives and rewards, we might be better approaching the task as a gardener. If we can set up the right conditions to make reading enjoyable and motivating; there is every chance that they will grow and flourish into readers. If schools can create a culture where reading is valued and celebrated, time is made on the curriculum for free voluntary reading and children are introduced to inspiring books and other reading materials, then success is very possible.

Cremin et al. (2014) offer a 'coherent strategy' for developing children's reading for pleasure, making eight recommendations for schools and teachers:

1. Take responsibility for developing reading for pleasure, alongside and as complementary to, reading instruction, and plan systematically to achieve this.
2. Widen their conceptions of reading and being a reader in the twenty-first century.
3. Develop as reading teachers: teachers who read and readers who teach.
4. Make space and time to build reciprocal reading communities in their classrooms that blur the boundaries between children's home and school reading worlds.
5. Expand their knowledge of:

   - literature and other texts
   - everyday reading practices and experiences
   - individual children as readers

6. Develop a reading for pleasure pedagogy that fosters inside-text talk and builds positive reading identities for all children.
7. Foster children's autonomy as readers who can exercise discrimination and choice within and beyond school.
8. Construct new, more equivalent reading relationships with families and community members, exploring the potential synergy between teachers', children's and parents' reading lives and practices.

These eight areas form the basis of the practice section of this chapter and reflect research by McGeown et al. (2012) which suggests that an intrinsic motivation to read (a desire to read drawn from genuine interest), rather than an extrinsic motivation (the promise of recognition, rewards or praise) is a more powerful factor in children becoming accomplished, confident readers. The importance of the teacher as a reading for pleasure role model is explored in greater depth in Chapter 10.

Approaches to developing an authentic reading culture – practice

This section considers four practical approaches to developing reading provision, each of which reflects Cremin et al.'s (2014) principles:

- Developing teachers' knowledge of children's literature and other twenty-first century reading practices
- Teachers promoting reading for pleasure alongside effective reading instruction and creating a responsive reading for pleasure pedagogy
- Schools forging reading relationships with families and the community
- The school community celebrating reading, encouraging children to grow into autonomous, motivated readers

Developing teachers' knowledge of children's literature

Keeping abreast of children's literature and other up-to-date reading material can be difficult within teachers' busy professional lives. However, as explored thoroughly in Chapter 10, teachers with a comprehensive knowledge of children's literature are well placed to make considered recommendations for children's' future reading, select texts that are useful and engaging in the classroom and can talk enthusiastically about books, supporting the development of an authentic reading community (Cremin et al., 2009).

STOP AND REFLECT

- How well would you rate your knowledge of children's literature and other reading materials, such as websites, periodicals and apps?
- Do you know which books and texts are popular with children in your class?
- Do you know which books and texts are popular with children across the country?
- Do the texts you share with children, both in English lessons and reading sessions, and those books children can choose to read independently, reflect the diversity of your school community and society as a whole?

Access to high-quality and up-to-date booklists, such as the CLPE's Corebooks (www.clpe.co.uk/corebooks) or reading the work of specialists in the field such as Nikki Gamble (www.exploringchildrensliterature.uk) can be a useful starting point to broaden teachers' knowledge, as can interacting with publishers, authors, book bloggers and other experts online and through social media.

Reading organisations such as the Booktrust and the Reading Agency are also excellent sources of information about books. The Reading Agency (www.readingagency.org.uk) features booklists and resource packs for many recent publications. The Booktrust's 'What to read after...' series suggests books that might be recommended after children have finished a popular series or book (www.booktrust.org.uk). The Booktrust Bookfinder (search online) offers an interactive way of searching for new books, allowing the filtering of texts by age and theme. The long and shortlists for children's book awards, such as the Carnegie Award, the Greenaway Award or the UKLA Children's Book Award are all great places to find new books too (search online for each).

Appointing a reading champion at school, responsible for promoting reading and sharing new books, can also be an effective way of raising awareness of reading, although for an initiative like this to be successful, they will need a medium to share their expertise that will not add too much to teachers' workloads.

CASE STUDY 9.1

One headteacher was keen to give teachers time to develop their familiarity with children's literature and other reading materials. One twilight staff meeting was set aside each half-term for teachers to browse a collection of recently published children's books and discuss those that could be shared in class.

Following this, a group of teachers set up a teachers' book group that met monthly to discuss a book or set of picture books. The school also put aside a space in the staffroom for teachers to display books they thought might be popular with other teachers. Teachers began leaving books with annotated sticky notes on them, suggesting who might enjoy them and what purposes they might be put to in the classroom.

A carefully planned text-based curriculum can also support teachers to embrace new or unfamiliar books. When planning an English curriculum (a topic discussed in depth in Chapters 15 and 16), care needs to be taken to balance teachers' freedom to choose books they wish to share while also outlining a core entitlement for all children across the school. A popular model is a long-term plan where each year is divided into a series of text-based units. Each unit has a selection of recommended texts that a teacher could use. If a teacher has a better idea for the text to use, they can make a conscious decision to ignore the recommendations and use their chosen one instead. An approach to curriculum planning such as this can support those for whom English isn't their specialism or particular area of interest or those who are new to text-based teaching, without inhibiting the text selection of experienced or confident teachers.

CASE STUDY 9.2

One school chose to encourage teachers to go beyond their old favourites by introducing a 'Brand New Book Fortnight' across the school. Each class teacher would choose a book published in the last year that hadn't been taught by the teacher before. A staff meeting was run by a librarian from the local Schools Library Service who brought in a range of children's books and encouraged teachers to read and discuss them. A fortnight of work would then be taught around their newly chosen book. This had the effect of encouraging teachers to take a chance on an unfamiliar book, broadening their repertoire and knowledge of children's literature.

After three years of the initiative, a curriculum audit found that many books that had begun as *Brand New Books* were now established in the curriculum.

Teachers promoting reading for pleasure alongside effective reading instruction

Cremin et al. (2014) suggest creating a responsive reading for pleasure pedagogy comprising several elements:

- Rich reading environments
- Regular reading aloud
- Time for booktalk and recommendations
- Time for independent choice-led reading

Rather than work in opposition to reading instruction, these elements should form a symbiotic relationship with learning to read: in order to read widely for pleasure, it is important to become a fluent reader. Conversely, as we have seen, wide independent reading is one of the most significant factors in supporting children's growing proficiency in reading. Reading for pleasure and learning to read are two sides of the same coin.

Rich reading environments

While this phrase is often used to describe the physical spaces where children read and where books are kept and displayed, the reading environment is far more than this. Chambers (1993) refers to 'the social context of reading': the choice of books available, the time allocated to reading in the classroom, the purpose(s) for reading, and even opportunities for experiences to reflect the mood of the reader. An attractive book corner or reading display may help the books look more appealing but the range of texts available is likely to be a more significant factor on children's reading for pleasure in the long run. This range should include texts that reflect children's interests as well as a breadth of genre and formats. Time to browse, discuss, choose and explore these texts are all significant factors when making the most of that reading space.

CASE STUDY 9.3

One teacher decided to make use of digital photoframes to display recommended reads from children in her book corners and bookshelves.

Once they had finished a book they had particularly enjoyed, children could be photographed holding up the book and a short one-line review written on a mini-whiteboard. These photographs were displayed on the photoframes for their classmates to see, encouraging others to seek out the books their friends had enjoyed.

Regular reading

Reading aloud turns enjoying a book into a communal activity that can be shared by everyone in the class. It allows everybody to share in the ideas and language of the same book, enabling conversation. Research suggests that listening to books being read aloud right through children's schooling is likely to be one of the most educationally useful things we can do as teachers, supporting language comprehension and vocabulary development (Westbrook et al., 2018).

Aside from the educational benefits, sharing a book as a class can be a joyful time of day where children have the opportunity to experience the pleasures books and reading can bring. Reading aloud can be a useful pedagogical tool, but if we are to use it as a catalyst for children becoming lifelong readers, making the time to listen to a story for pure enjoyment with no planned follow-up questions, analysis of language or written task is vital. While the ring-fencing of reading aloud for pleasure in an education system where reading is measured through performance in tests might seem like a luxury, it is in fact a form of 'advertising for literacy' (Leland et al., 2018). Embedding these pleasurable shared reading experiences could be the inspirational spark which starts a child on their own journey to becoming a reader themselves.

Reading aloud in class also offers opportunities to introduce children to authors and text types that they might not choose in their independent reading, as acknowledged in the 2014 National Curriculum for Years 5 and 6:

> Even though pupils can now read independently, reading aloud to them should include whole books so that they meet books and authors that they might not choose to read themselves.

(DfE, 2013)

Time for booktalk and recommendations

As discussed in Chapter 8, authentic booktalk is an integral part of good English teaching. In the context of reading for pleasure, booktalk allows children space to explore multiple interpretations of the same text and affords a way of sharing their opinions and listening to those of others, exploring meaning and preferences collaboratively. Drawing on the work of Chambers (1993), Maine (2015), Rosen (2018) and Roche (2015), McGonigle (2018) suggests some examples of questions and prompts to generate the type of booktalk that might encourage a thoughtful response to a text:

Reflecting

- Does anyone have something they want to say about the story?
- Tell me… was there anything you really liked or disliked about this book? Which character interested you the most?
- I really liked the part when…
- I thought… was an interesting character especially when…

Clarifying/speculating

- Does anyone have a question about the story? Tell me, did anything puzzle you or take you by surprise?
- Why do you suppose…?
- It confused me when…
- I'm not sure why… happened?

Connecting

- Tell me… have you read any other books like this, or has anything like this happened to you?
- It reminds me of…

Empathising

- What did we find out about how the characters were feeling?
- I understand how… felt, I would too because…

Evaluating

- What would you tell your friends about this book?

Analysing

- What is this story about?
- Why do you think the author wrote this book?

(McGonigle, 2018)

Independent choice-led reading

Time spent reading and browsing independently is a crucial component of a well-planned reading curriculum. Educationally, sustained independent reading is vital for building fluency and reading stamina. When considering children's reading for pleasure, this is the space where children can follow their interests and reading enthusiasms. Children's choice of text is crucial to becoming a reader (Clark and Rumbold, 2006; Gambrell, 2011) and while it would be desirable for every child to have this free-choice reading at home, research suggests that this is often not the case (Clark, 2014). For some children, independent free-choice reading will only happen regularly at school. If children do not have specific time to read independently at school, they simply will not benefit from this vital experience.

CASE STUDY 9.4

A Year 6 teacher noticed that some children in her class were reluctant to take a chance on unfamiliar books, instead always choosing the same type of book or a book from the same narrow band of series or authors.

   She created a book loyalty card for each child. Over the course of a month, each child was set the challenge of reading five different types of book, collecting a stamp for each. The categories were:

- a novel by an author you've never read before
- a picture book
- a book of poetry
- a non-fiction book about a topic you don't know much about
- a book recommended to you by someone else in the class

If the children collected all five stamps, they would win an *Adventurous Reader* certificate, presented in assembly.

   The initiative worked well because it ran over a short period of time and it still allowed plenty of choice within the categories. Children could also choose not to take part (although they all did). At the end of the month, the children were free to return to the books they had read before if they wished. In fact, the teacher reported that many children became far more willing to take a chance on an unfamiliar book or try different genres of book.

Schools forging reading relationships with families and the community

International reading studies suggest that children who are supported in their reading at home are much more likely to enjoy reading and tend to achieve more highly at school generally, with parental engagement being a greater influence than level of parental education, family size and socio-economic background (Flouri and Buchanan, 2004). It has been suggested that the positive effect of parents being involved with children's reading at primary school can still be seen at the age of 15 (OECD, 2012).

The ideal relationship between professionals at school and parents at home should be reciprocal, with communication and learning passing from one to another. Schools can harness the enthusiasm of families by providing guidance, advice and resources to make reading at home as enjoyable and successful as it can be. And parents can provide teachers with insight into their home literacy practices, information around their children's interests and reading habits and any potential barriers and opportunities they encounter at home.

CASE STUDY 9.5

After some reflection as a staff team, one school felt that communication with parents and carers about reading was restricted to key times in a child's school career. There was plenty of communication in Reception, when children started at the school and the strategies for teaching reading were explained, along with how home-school reading worked. Then there was a flurry of communication at the start of each year, which gradually petered out.

The school was determined to ensure regular contact with parents around reading, reinforcing the message that listening to children read at home and reading aloud to children, no matter how old or confident they were at reading, were hugely valuable things to do. School leaders were also aware that it was not always possible to get messages about reading to every family, with some being hard to reach due to their relationship with the school, time commitments with work, study or caring for younger children, and challenges posed by some parents' literacy and language proficiency. The school implemented a number of initiatives, monitoring each for success and impact on children's reading:

- Regular communication – the school sent letters, text messages and held monthly storytime coffee mornings for parents. Regular reminders to read widely (and that included comics, magazines and websites) were affixed to children's weekly homework. In addition, there was a fortnightly 'reading surgery', where a staff member would be available for parents to drop in to talk about any issues regarding reading. The deputy head, who often ran this, would walk around the site at the start of the day inviting specific parents to attend too.
- Each term, class assemblies began with an 'advertisement' for reading with children. A small group of children would talk about why reading at home was so important and how much they loved reading with their families. These assemblies would normally see the majority of parents and carers attend, providing a good audience to share this message with.
- Parents were invited to regular drop-in mornings to watch storytime in their child's class. This was useful for parents of older children to see how much Key Stage 2 pupils enjoyed being read to. Afterwards, a display of motivating books would be on show in the hall for parents to browse.

(Continued)

- The school library was open after school on three days each week for families to come and choose books together. Parents commented that seeing their children choose a book with excitement made them more likely to sit and share it with them.
- These initiatives focused on parental engagement with reading both with their children and as a way for them to share their thoughts and concerns about reading at home. The school's priority was to try and engage parents with their children's reading lives and to explore a range of ways in which they could support their child in becoming a lifelong reader.

The school community celebrating reading

If children are to become readers, it is likely that learning to read fluently, ring-fenced time to read, reading role models at home and at school, and a curriculum that introduces children to books that they are interested in with time for genuine booktalk, will be the driving factors in making this happen. However, there is a danger that the discourse around reading for pleasure focuses on more superficial elements: reading competitions, book corners and displays, or special reading events. Looking beyond these to authentic reading experiences is necessary, otherwise reading for pleasure becomes 'little more than an act of institutional window dressing in our highly performative culture' (Cremin, 2016).

While special events and competitions can help to create a buzz about reading (and can be lots of fun, which is no bad thing in primary school), it is likely that the ongoing factors of a curriculum that gives children the chance to encounter great books and a staff team who inspire children to read will have a greater impact on children's attitudes to reading in the long term. Special care should be taken when offering extrinsic rewards for reading such as stickers or collecting points. While these can be initially motivating, they are only valuable if they lead to children choosing to read when the reward is not on offer. Research suggests that rewarding behaviours with an extrinsic prize can lead to a lack of motivation when the reward is not on offer (Deci et al., 1999); something that also appears to be true of reading (McGeown et al., 2012).

Clements (2017) suggests four key questions to consider when judging whether a reading for pleasure initiative is likely to be worthwhile:

1. Is the initiative actually about reading? Will it help children to become better readers or help them to see the enjoyment in reading?
2. Is it equitable? Can all children access the initiative to the same degree? Events that involve dressing up or contributing money can be difficult for some families.
3. Does it help children to see the intrinsic value and enjoyment in reading? Collecting stickers, rewards and points can be motivating, but are only valuable if they inspire children to read when they are eventually not on offer.
4. Is there likely to be any lasting effect on reading in the school beyond the actual initiative? Is the amount of effort expended on the event worth it in terms of the impact on children's reading?

(Clements, 2017)

Conclusion

If children are to become confident, fluent readers then time spent reading independently for pleasure is likely to be a significant factor in their development. For some children, this will happen naturally because of their inclination to read. For others, the reading habit will come from home. But for some children, it is a rich reading culture at school that will be their only way into the world of books and reading. This is crucial because, as the teacher and author Donalyn Millar explains:

> Reading changes your life. Reading unlocks worlds unknown or forgotten, taking travellers around the world and through time. Reading helps you escape the confines of school and pursue your own education. Through characters – the saints and the sinners, real or imagined – reading shows you how to be a better human being.

(Miller, 2009)

IN SUMMARY

- There is a strong correlation between children choosing to read, time spent reading widely and a range of positive outcomes, both educational and social. It is also helpful to show children that reading can be an enjoyable activity in its own right. This is especially important for children who might not have the opportunity or support to read widely outside of school.
- Choosing to read for pleasure and learning to be a confident, fluent reader are two sides of the same coin – each supports and strengthens the other.
- Schools and teachers can support children to become readers through building an authentic reading culture, where promoting wider reading is given the same focus as learning to read. This can happen through teachers becoming knowledgeable about children's literature and being willing to act as reading role models; curriculum time dedicated to reading aloud, independent free-choice reading and booktalk; meaningful reciprocal relationships being made between school and home; and celebrations of reading being used to raise the profile of books and reading.

FURTHER READING

- For accessible overviews of reading for pleasure, see *Reading for Pleasure: What we know works – Research from the Power of Reading project* from the Centre for Literacy in Primary Education and *Building an Outstanding Reading School* by James Clements, both freely available through an online search.

- For an in-depth introduction to the theory underpinning reading for pleasure pedagogy, read *Building Communities of Engaged Readers* by Teresa Cremin, Marilyn Mottram, Fiona M. Collins, Sacha Powell and Kimberly Safford.
- To find practical examples of how schools and teachers have created rich reading cultures, visit The Open University's *Research Rich Pedagogies* site (www.researchrichpedagogies.org/research/reading-for-pleasure).

REFERENCES

Bearne, E. and Reedy, D. (2018) *Teaching Primary English: Subject knowledge and classroom practice*. Abingdon: Routledge.

Centre for Literacy in Primary Education (CLPE) (2014) *Reading for Pleasure: What we know works – Research from the Power of Reading project*. London: CLPE.

Chambers, A. (1993) *Tell Me: Children, Reading and Talk*. Stroud: The Thimble Press.

Clark, C. (2014) *The Literacy Lives of 8–11-year-olds: 2005–2013*. London: National Literacy Trust.

Clark, C. and de Zoysa, S. (2011) *Mapping the Interrelationships of Reading Enjoyment, Attitudes, Behaviour and Attainment: An exploratory investigation*. London: National Literacy Trust.

Clark, C. and Rumbold, K. (2006) *Reading for Pleasure: A Research Overview*. London: National Literacy Trust.

Clements, J. (2013) *Building an Outstanding Reading School*. Oxford: Oxford University Press.

Clements, J. (2017) *Teaching English by the Book*. Abingdon: Routledge.

Cremin, T. (2016) Reading for Pleasure: Just window dressing? *Cambridge Primary Review Trust* blog. Available at: https://cprtrust.org.uk/cprt-blog/reading-for-pleasure-just-window-dressing/

Cremin, T. and Myhill, D. (2012) *Writing Voices: Creating Communities of Writers*. Abingdon: Routledge.

Cremin, T., Mottram, M., Collins, F., Powell, S. and Safford, K. (2009) Teachers as readers: Building communities of readers. *Literacy*, 43(1): 11–19.

Cremin, T., Mottram, M., Collins, F., Powell, S. and Safford, K. (2014) *Building Communities of Readers: Reading for pleasure*. Abingdon: Routledge.

Cunningham, A. and Stanovich, K. (1998) What reading does for the mind. *American Educator*, 22(1 and 2): 8–15.

De Naeghel, J., Van Keer, H., Vansteenkiste, M. and Rosseel, Y. (2012) The relation between elementary students' recreational and academic reading motivation, reading frequency, engagement, and comprehension: A self-determination theory perspective. *Journal of Educational Psychology*, 104: 1006–21.

Deci, E.L., Koestner, R. and Ryan, R.M. (1999) A meta-analytic review of experiments examining the effects of extrinsic rewards on intrinsic motivation. *Psychological Bulletin*, 125: 627–68.

Department for Education (DfE) (2013) *National Curriculum in England: Primary Curriculum*. London: DfE.

Flouri, E., and Buchanan, A. (2004) Early father's and mother's involvement and child's later educational outcomes. *British Journal of Educational Psychology*, 74(2): 141-53.

Gambrell, L. (2011) Seven rules of engagement: What's most important to know about motivation to read. *The Reading Teacher*, 65(3): 172–8.

Gopnik, A. (2016) *The Gardener and the Carpenter: What the new science of child development tells us about the relationship between parents and children*. London: The Bodley Head.

Guthrie, J.T. and Alvermann, D.E. (1999) *Engaged Reading: Processes, Practices, and Policy Implications*. New York: Teachers College Press.

Howard, V. (2011) The importance of pleasure reading in the lives of young teens: Self-identification, self-construction and self-awareness. *Journal of Librarianship and Information Science*, 43 (1): 46–55.

Jorm, A.F. and Share, D. L. (1983) An invited article: Phonological recoding and reading acquisition. *Applied Psycholinguistics*, 4: 103–47.

Kumschick, I.R., Beck, L., Eid, M., Witte, G., Klann-Delius, G. and Heuser, I. (2014) Reading and feeling: The effects of a literature-based intervention designed to increase emotional competence in second and third graders. *Frontiers in Psychology*, 5: 1448.

Leland, C.H., Lewison, M., and Harste, J.C. (2018) *Teaching Children's Literature – it's critical*. New York: Routledge.

Maine, F. (2015) *Dialogic Readers: Children talking and thinking together about visual texts*. Abingdon: Routledge.

Mar, R.A. and Rain, M. (2015) Narrative fiction and expository nonfiction differentially predict verbal ability. *Scientific Studies of Reading*, 19: 419–33.

McGeown, S.P., Norgate, R. and Warhurst, A. (2012) Exploring intrinsic and extrinsic reading motivation among very good and very poor readers. *Educational Research*, 3/54: 309–32.

McGeown, S.P., Putwain, D., Geijer Simpson, E., Boffey, E., Markham, J. and Vince, A. (2014) Predictors of adolescents' academic motivation: Personality, self-efficacy and adolescents' characteristics. *Learning and Individual Differences*, 32: 278–86.

McGonigle, S. (2018) *Creative Planning with Whole Texts*. Leicester: UKLA.

Miller, D. (2009) *The Book Whisperer: Awakening the inner reader in every child.* San Francisco, CA: Jossey-Bass.

Moje, E., Overby, M., Tysvaer, N. and Morris, K. (2008) The complex world of adolescent literacy: Myths, motivations, and mysteries. *Harvard Educational Review*, 78(1): 107–54.

Mol, S.E. and Bus, A.G. (2011) To read or not to read: A metaanalysis of print exposure from infancy to early adulthood. *Psychological Bulletin*, 137: 267–96.

Morgan, P. and Fuchs, D. (2007) Is there a bidirectional relationship between children's reading skills and reading motivation? *Exceptional Children*, 73(2): 165–83.

Nikolajeva, M. (2013) Picturebooks and emotional literacy. *The Reading Teacher*, 67(4): 249–54.

OECD (2002) *Reading for Change: Performance and Engagement Across Countries: Results from PISA 2002.* New York: Organisation for Economic Co-operation and Development.

OECD (2012) *PISA – Let's Read Them a Story! The Parent Factor in Education.* New York: Organisation for Economic Co-operation and Development.

Petscher, Y. (2010) A meta-analysis of the relationship between student attitudes towards reading and achievement in reading. *Journal of Research in Reading*, 33(4): 335–55.

Roche, M. (2015) *Developing Children's Critical Thinking through Picturebooks.* Abingdon: Routledge.

Rosen, M. (2018) *Poetry and Stories for Primary and Lower Secondary Schools.* London: Michael Rosen.

Share, D.L. (1995) Phonological recoding and self-teaching: Sine qua non of reading acquisition. *Cognition*, 55: 151–218.

Stanovich, K.E. and West, R.F. (1989) Exposure to print and orthographic processing. *Reading Research Quarterly*, 24: 402–33.

Sullivan, A. and Brown, M. (2013) *Social Inequalities in Cognitive Scores at Age 16: The role of reading.* CLS Working Paper 2013/10. London: Centre for Longitudinal Studies.

Torppa, M., Niemi, P., Vasalampi, K., Lerkkanen, M., Tolvanen, A. and Poikkeus, A. (2019) Leisure reading (but not any kind) and reading comprehension: A longitudinal study across grades 1 and 9. *Child Development.*

Toste, J., Didion, L., Peng, P., Filderman, M. and McClelland, A. (2020) A meta-analytic review of the relations between motivation and reading achievement for K–12 students. *Review of Educational Research*, 90.

Van Bergen, E., Snowling, M.J., de Zeeuw, E.L., van Beijsterveldt, C.E.M., Dolan, C.V. and Boomsma, D.I. (2018) Why do children read more? The influence of reading ability on voluntary reading practices. *Journal of Child Psychology and Psychiatry*, 59(11).

Vezzali, L., Stathi, S. and Giovannini, D. (2012) Indirect contact through book reading: Improving adolescents' attitudes and behavioral intentions toward immigrants. *Psychology in the Schools*, 49: 148–62.

Vezzali, L., Stathi, S., Giovannini, D., Capozza, D. and Trifiletti, E. (2015) The greatest magic of Harry Potter: Reducing prejudice. *Journal of Applied Social Psychology*, 45: 105–21.

Westbrook, J., Sutherland, J., Oakhill, J. and Sullivan, S. (2018) 'Just reading': increasing pace and volume of reading whole narratives on the comprehension of poorer adolescent readers in English classrooms. *Literacy*, 53(2): 60–8.

10

TEACHERS AS READERS – UNDERSTANDING THE IMPORTANCE OF CHILDREN'S LITERATURE: THEORY AND PRACTICE

THIS CHAPTER WILL

- Explore the importance of teachers' breadth and depth of knowledge of children's literature

- Reflect upon the importance of choice and diversity of literature we encounter and share

- Consider a range of approaches in supporting teachers to become avid readers of children's literature and bring the joy of reading into the classroom

Introduction

It can be easy to forget how influential we are as role models for the children under our care; if we are to support them in becoming lifelong readers then we must consider investing in improving both their skill in reading and their desire to read (Applegate and Applegate, 2004). The following chapter builds on what has been said in Chapter 9 but focuses further on the Reading Teacher as expert, facilitator and guide. Your knowledge, engagement and enthusiasm along with knowing each child as a reader are deeply influential with regards to a child's own reading habits and engagements (Gambrell, 1996; Applegate and Applegate, 2004; Collins, 2014) and play a powerful part in shaping a classroom's ethos.

If we acknowledge the correlation between a teacher's knowledge of children's literature and their confidence 'in the teaching of reading and writing' (Cox and Schaetzel, 2007; Cremin et al., 2008) then it becomes concerning when evidence suggests that many training teachers and established practitioners are not avid readers of children's literature.

Furthermore, children's literature constantly finds itself 'embroiled' in pedagogical debates around its function as a tool for the teaching of reading and other curricular areas (Cremin et al., 2008a; Arizpe et al., 2013).

Finally, 'overburdened' curricula, and a preoccupation with the teaching of the skill of reading rather than actively promoting 'a love of reading' (Merga, 2016), can dominate teachers' thinking and attitudes to the detriment of and a delight in a knowledge of children's books.

Studies have shown that motivated and inspired readers read more and, therefore, perform better in comprehension, knowledge, fluency, vocabulary and writing (Krashen, 2004) as well as 'stimulating...their social, emotional, and aesthetic development' (Chou et al., 2016). It seems sensible then to consider our own position in supporting them to become readers who have both the will and the skill to read.

The 2014 National Curriculum for English in England has a welcome emphasis on promoting reading for pleasure (explored in depth in Chapter 9); in consequence, teachers are more responsible than ever for fostering lifelong readers (Merga, 2017). Therefore, it seems to go against the grain that there should be such a focus on learning to read and less upon *why* we read. The business of guiding children to become lifelong readers means teachers making the distinction between the teaching of reading and both enabling and inspiring children to read for their own pleasure (Atkinson, 2017). Central to that enablement is a teacher's breadth and depth of knowledge with regards to children's literature in all its forms (Collins, 2014). This chapter will explore how we can support ourselves as training and practising teachers to fall in love with reading.

Teachers as readers – theory

Central to reading success is motivation, defined as 'the individual's personal goals, values, and beliefs with regard to the topics, processes, and outcomes of reading' (Guthrie and

Wigfield, 2000; Clark and De Zoysa, 2011). Motivation theory makes a clear distinction between intrinsic and extrinsic motivation and a brief understanding of both will not only help us reflect on our approaches but also on our attitudes towards fostering a positive reading culture (Applegate and Applegate, 2004; Guthrie et al., 2007).

Intrinsic motivation is 'an internal desire to complete a task' (Breadmore et al., 2019) because the reader, in this case, associates reading with a positive experience and sense of enjoyment and confidence on a personal level. Books are associated with a sense of curiosity, enjoyment and are valued; 'intrinsic readers' (Becker and McElvany, 2010) take pleasure in the 'emotional and cognitive' engagement (Wang and Guthrie, 2004) and challenge that reading can bring, and 'seek out' reading-related activities such as book sharing (Sainsbury and Schagen, 2004). Intrinsic readers have a 'positive self-concept' of themselves as readers (Clarkson and Sainsbury, 2008).

On the other hand, extrinsic motivation relates to completing a task for some future reward. This could be working towards improving grades; gaining attention and credit from peers/parents/teachers; reading as a source of recognition; compliance as a way of avoiding punishment or as a source of competition (Wang and Guthrie, 2004). 'Extrinsic readers' (Becker and McElvany, 2010) tend to have a 'negative self-concept' of themselves as readers and will 'avoid' reading (Clarkson and Sainsbury, 2008), especially after the reward has been gained. They may also 'see reading as a school job' and something not worth investing in outside of the classroom walls (Miller, 2012).

STOP AND REFLECT

Think of the children in your current class or a class you have worked with in the past.

- How many children would fall into the category of intrinsically motivated readers?
- How many would be extrinsically motivated readers?
- Are there occasions where you think that giving children an extrinsic motivation to read might not support them to see the intrinsic pleasure in reading?
- What might be the signs that a child is either intrinsically or extrinsically motivated within a particular context?
- Can you think of any actions you could take to support children's intrinsic motivation?

Although the main body of research above is focused on understanding children as readers, there is much here that we can learn about teachers as readers too. It stands to reason that our own motivation and attitudes also need acknowledging and reflecting upon: how do we see ourselves as readers and are these perceptions going to encourage children to be intrinsic readers too? If we, as teachers, are not intrinsically motivated to read and do not enjoy reading, or see ourselves as readers, then such beliefs may be mirrored in our classrooms (Strommen and Mates, 2004).

Reading teachers

If, as evidence suggests, children are motivated to read through the desire to 'explore', 'observe' and 'learn', then teachers should embrace these factors too when considering their role as Reading Teachers of children's literature (Gambrell, 1996; Wray et al., 1999; Applegate and Applegate, 2004; Cox and Schaetzel, 2007; Patrick et al., 2007; Cremin et al., 2009). 'Vigorous theoretical support and research' (Brooks, 2007) shows a correlation between teachers who valued and practised reading for pleasure and an increase in 'best practice' with regards to the effective teaching of reading and writing (Dreher, 2003; McKool and Gespass, 2009).

What value is there then in children's literature and why should training teachers and those in the field devote a large portion of their time to it? The answer to this links closely to the earlier comment on the need for educators to see children's literature as something more than a pedagogical tool, in which a text is mined for meaning or lexical form or used as a time filler (Cremin, 2007 in Goouch and Lambirth (2011); Cox and Schaetzel, 2007; Arizpe et al., 2013). Stories for children are much more than this. For example, they:

- invite readers to grow and develop emotionally and socially by presenting them with the opportunity to self-reflect and self-construct (Benton and Fox, 1985; Garces-Bascal et al., 2018)
- allow readers to step into the shoes of others and experience the world through different eyes, developing a strong sense of empathy and understanding of different cultures
- can offer a form of escape, a way of relieving stress, of improving our general knowledge and knowledge of ourselves (Dugdale and Clark, 2008)
- invite a 'greater insight into human nature and decision-making' and meaning-making (Dugdale and Clark, 2008 citing Bruner, 1996)
- invite readers to become part of a community in which they share their thoughts, opinions and feelings about the stories together (Dreher, 2003; Centre for Literacy in Primary Education (CLPE), 2015)

In the comprehensive 'Teachers as Readers: Building Communities of Readers' project run by the UKLA and involving 1,200 primary teachers, it was found that teachers relied on a limited range of children's literature. Choices were dependent on what they had encountered as children themselves or on best-selling children's authors. Few could cite more than a handful of picture-book authors/illustrators, poets (Cremin et al., 2008; Cremin et al., 2009) or diverse writers and illustrators. This becomes problematic when we consider the need for teachers to support readers in finding texts that children might like and how reading for pleasure flourishes in environments in which teachers' own intrinsically motivated reading identity is central to bringing young readers and stories together (McCarthey and Moje, 2002; Dreher, 2003; Merga, 2017; Goodwin, 2017). An 'extensive knowledge of children's literature' is imperative if we are to motivate every child in becoming and continuing to be a reader who reads for their own enjoyment throughout their primary years and beyond (Cremin et al., 2008a).

Reading Teachers, 'readers who teach and teachers who read' (Commeyras et al., 2003), are ideally placed to create a reading culture in their classroom that will foster intrinsic motivation for reading. The research by Clark and Foster (2005), Lockwood (2008), Cremin et al. (2008b) and Collins (2014) proposes that a broad knowledge of reading materials with regards to range, genre, voices, accessibility, content and form (e.g. websites, comics and e-readers) is key – with the proviso that the Reading Teacher also pays attention to the financial remit that they are bound by. The impetus behind the 'literate lives' of teachers means that they are constantly engaging with and learning from what stories have to offer. They ask questions of the text and encourage children to do the same (Kaufman, 2002). By sharing and reflecting openly on their own reading experiences, tastes and interests, Reading Teachers are seen and valued as readers by the children in their care. This is characterised by teachers and children engaging in 'meaningful language experiences', both formal and informal, around texts and showing an interest in one another's reading life (Clark and Foster, 2005; Arizpe et al., 2013). These teachers also use their knowledge to guide children with their reading choices, and prioritise time for independent reading and booktalk (Brooks, 2007; Miller, 2012; Collins, 2014).

Effective Reading Teachers know their children's reading interests, preferences and habits, alongside their ability, in order to support and motivate them to continue finding pleasure in reading (Clark and Foster, 2005; Brooks, 2007; Clark and Phythian-Sence, 2008; Lockwood, 2008; Cremin et al., 2008b). By being informed of the different reading backgrounds and reading cultures in a child's home, they accommodate and support where appropriate and possible: this allows the individual and the class to celebrate these differences by ensuring they have enough multicultural books available that authentically present 'mirrors and windows' (Bishop, 1990) into children's lives.

STOP AND REFLECT

Consider how you would answer the questions below. How well do you match the characteristics of a 'Reading Teacher' according to the research? Where do your strengths lie? Where might you have room to improve?

- How deep is your knowledge of children's literature, including:

  - Contemporary children's literature?
  - Poetry for children?
  - Picture books?
  - Literature reflecting a diverse range of characters and experiences?
  - Literature by authors from a diverse range of backgrounds?

- To what extent do you seek to find out about the reading lives of the children you teach?
- How do you share your own reading experiences and reading life with the children in your class?
- What strategies do you use to guide children's reading choices, introducing them to texts that they might not otherwise encounter?

The aesthetic Reading Teacher

Applegate and Applegate (2004) explain how it is those teachers who value and promote reading from an aesthetic perspective (who become 'absorbed in the text and live through the experience of others' (Rosenblatt, 1978)) who are most influential in the classroom since they create 'a sense of excitement' around the text and are passionate about how reading 'enhances and enriches their lives' (Gambrell, 1996 cited in Applegate and Applegate, 2004). The reading attitudes and behaviours that teachers embrace, therefore, affect their classroom practice (Chou et al., 2016).

Applegate and Applegate (2004) conjecture that if teachers are not 'engaged readers' then they cannot hope to motivate the children in their class to read. This has been validated by both Morrison et al. (1999) in a study involving 1,900 elementary teachers and with Cremin et al. (2007–8) in a study involving 1,200 primary teachers. Both pieces of research reinforce the concept that the more engaged teachers were in the aesthetic reading of children's literature, the greater the chances of using and promoting reading circles and pupil engagement and in going on to become 'effective literacy teachers' (Collins, 2014).

Developing our knowledge of children's literature

The research conducted by Cremin et al (2008b) shows that teachers rely on a limited canon of authors, poets and illustrators, and this means that their ability to make 'informed recommendations' for all readerly identities is equally limited. If our reading world is narrow, then it is likely that the stories we put into the hands of children under our care is limited too. This is especially important to acknowledge and reflect on if we consider that children's literature does much to shape children's views of the world around them (Arizpe et al., 2013).

If we are to encourage teachers to read more children's literature, then we can learn much from the research around what motivates young readers too. Clark and Phythian-Sence (2008) highlight the importance of 'choice, interest and self-awareness' in examining reading behaviours and the centrality of engagement as a form of motivation; this is important to remember when we consider the potentiality of social networks for Reading Teachers later in the chapter.

Making an 'informed and meaningful' choice as to which children's book you want to read next brings its own pleasure (Schraw et al., 1998; Clark and Phythian-Sence, 2008). You might pick up a book based on a number of factors: its cover, the familiarity of the author or the fact that it was recommended by someone. The fact that the choice is yours is what is empowering and is what might motivate you to pick up another book. 'Ownership and self-determination' are key.

Choice then remains central to the success of reading for pleasure both in the child reader and the Reading Teacher; choice with regards to finding the right text for the right child but also choice with regards to your choosing to read rather than occupying yourself with something else. In a time in which social media is prevalent across a range of platforms, choosing to make time to read children's literature is perhaps a greater challenge for training and working teachers than ever before and yet such motivation for both teacher and child is central to future reading success (Ross, 2000).

Children's literature for all

Choice then is an intrinsically motivating factor for us as adults. But, as teachers, we have a duty to consider the choices we offer the children in our classrooms too. Only then, in making reading meaningful and 'relevant', are we able to provide every child with the opportunity to become a lifelong reader (Hefflin and Barksdale-Ladd, 2001). Substantial research shows children being motivated to read if they have access to literature which reflects their own realities, be they related to gender, race, need or culture (Bishop, 1990; Colby and Lyon, 2004).

Hope's definition of diversity is a useful one to work from here:

> Diversity is an umbrella term that recognises a common need that underpins the exploration and representation of people from a wealth of backgrounds with varied experiences and lifestyles that construct our concept of society at large.

> (Hope, 2017b)

Celebrating both similarities and differences is vital; it helps us to relate and empathise with others and affirms our place and our culture in the world while respecting and acknowledging those of others (Rosenblatt, 1978; Colby and Lyon, 2004, Harper and Brand, 2010; CLPE, 2019). Part of our role as Reading Teachers is to support children to become more tolerant and accepting towards differences in the world around them while constantly reflecting upon our own 'beliefs, attitudes and practices relating to diversity' in the reading classroom (Colby and Lyon, 2004).

Our reading choices then need to consider what realities they reflect. As Hope (2017a) continues:

> When we discuss literature for children and adults we have to be aware of a historical precedent that has tended to reflect only a very narrow demographic in terms of class, race, sexuality and physicality.

With this in mind, we are required to be more critical of the literature we choose to read and share with children. In reading, we need to also be critical of our own entrenched cultural and social beliefs and privileges since we can carry and pass these on to the children in our classrooms too (Colby and Lyon, 2004).

In coining the term, 'Mirrors, Windows and Sliding Glass Doors', Bishop (1990) suggests that literature has the potential to 'transform human experience': the Mirror reflects our lived experiences back at us; the Window presents us with views into other lives which might be 'familiar or strange', 'real or imagined' and the Sliding Glass Doors invite us to 'become part of whatever world has been created or recreated' (Bishop, 1990). Bishop goes on to state that since 'mirrors' have a way of affirming our place within the world, then for some children to never see themselves in the literary world would not only be harmful but also present those who are constantly found in literature with 'an exaggerated sense of self worth'.

This should prompt us to diversify our reading and carefully assess the literature that we have in our classroom and whether it challenges or entrenches harmful, stereotypical concepts (Cochran-Smith, 2000; Hefflin and Barksdale-Ladd, 2001; Colby and Lyon, 2004; Larson and Marsh, 2005; Arizpe et al., 2013). Not only does this help the children we teach 'understand the principles of tolerance, inclusiveness, diversity and respect for all' but also challenges our own concepts in these areas and goes a long way to help us 'unlearn' narrow world-views (Cochran-Smith, 2000; Hefflin and Barksdale-Ladd, 2001; Pirofski, 2001; Campbell et al., 2016).

Reading Teachers, role models and relationships

> Unless a school is staffed by people who enjoy books and enjoy talking to children about what they read then it is unlikely that they will be very successful in helping children to become readers.

> (Chambers, 1973)

The literature that we place into the hands of children has the potential to invite a sense of joy and pleasure but also has the potential to challenge, affirm, comfort and invite them to see their place in the world: the same goes for Reading Teachers. Our own interactions with children's literature, and with the children who encounter it, is one that should motivate and engage all readers from all backgrounds. But these challenges and opportunities can only occur if a teacher is equally passionate about reading and places value in widening their knowledge of children's literature and considers its accessibility in the classroom.

Reading is 'fundamentally a social phenomenon' (CLPE, 2015; Chambers, 2011) and so finding others who want to share these reading experiences with you and being part of a community is important. Social media has made it easier than ever to be a part of a Reading Teacher community who can not only recommend great literature but also affirm your own beliefs about the power and importance of children's literature (Kwek et al., 2007; Collins, 2014). What is important is to reflect upon your own reading behaviour, attitudes and beliefs and whether they are best set to give children the opportunity to succeed in reading themselves and go on to be aesthetic, intrinsically motivated readers or not. Taking the time to care about and show an interest in each readerly identity in your classroom is central to building up that reading community. Who you are as a reader and who you are as a teacher of reading are not mutually exclusive identities; they are one and the same and pupils will be quick to see this (Whatley, 2011). With this in mind, it is important to consider what kind of model you think is the best one to help children succeed and what behaviours you both show and cater for in the classroom.

The teaching of reading throughout the Early Years and primary phase will always be a contentious site with regards to that balance between the skill to read and the will. While timetabling and precedence will largely be in the hands of school leaders and governmental initiatives/policies and although teachers' time is as constricted and busy as it has ever been, our own beliefs as Reading Teachers 'truly matter'(Applegate and Applegate, 2004). We have a profound effect on the literate lives of children, and it is through our actions in the classroom that this effect is enabled. The next section of this chapter will consider the ideas explored above in the context of practice.

Teachers as readers of children's literature – Practice

There are four core aspects to a pedagogy of reading for pleasure, and a Reading Teacher, or the *Enabling Adult* as Chambers (2011) sees them, that are key: talk around books, independent reading time, reading aloud and recommendations (Clark and Phythian-Sence, 2008; Safford, 2014), all of which become more challenging to promote if the teacher is not a reader of children's literature.

Teachers who are both knowledgeable and critically reflective of the literature they read will be better placed to foster an aesthetic reading environment. How 'visible' this environment is, how it is presented and what it provides readers is 'key to the engagement' of your class (Safford, 2014; CLPE, 2015) and Chambers (2011) provides an excellent model from which to build a sense of understanding as to what this looks like:

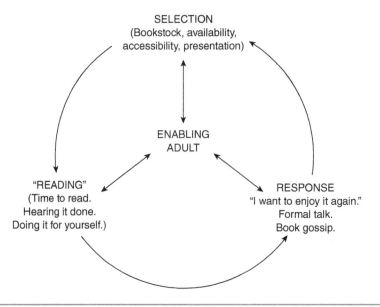

Figure 10.1 Chambers' (2011) Reading Circle

These three elements hold equal importance and rely upon that knowledgeable, active Reading Teacher as the enabler (Safford, 2014). In Chambers' model (see Figure 10.1), we can also see that the dual-headed arrows from the hub show that practice and experience inform the professional and vice versa. Each is part of an ongoing cycle that the Reading Teacher uses to improve and inform future choices that they make for themselves and for the children in their class. It relies upon us not only increasing our knowledge of children's literature and refreshing the environment but also reconsidering and revisiting the young readers in our class and adapting to their change and interests too (Safford, 2014).

When children see us in this role as informed, aesthetic reading teachers who find reading as something sociable, entertaining, pleasurable, rewarding and challenging then we have a greater chance of them emulating the same attitudes and beliefs in the classroom (Strommen and Mates, 2004; O'Sullivan and McGonigle, 2010; Arzipe et al., 2013).

Much of this journey starts with your own reflections as to what makes you the Reading Teacher that you are today. It is important to reflect upon what informs your own reading choices and the routes you took into reading.

Table 10.1 offers some guidance as to exploring these aspects of your readerly identity and proposes some next steps.

Table 10.1 Ways of exploring readerly identity

'Know yourself as a reader' by writing your own reading autobiography (Chambers, 2011; Lesesne, 2017)	One of the initial activities that you can do is to create a roadmap that explores your reading journey from your earliest memories to now (Cliff Hodges, 2010). Here, you could reflect upon the books that made you the reader you are today as well as the barriers which impaired your reading journey or halted it completely. What books instilled in you a joy of reading? What experiences or texts halted your reading for pleasure? What stops you reading books for pleasure now? In doing so, we are better equipped to acknowledge biases and pitfalls in our own reading journeys. Sharing these with the class will allow children to see you as not someone who just 'talks about reading' but also their 'reading life' (Bisplinghoff et al., 2003; Jennett, 2017).
Become a Reading Advocate (Jennett, 2017)	Take responsibility for exploring new children's book releases and share these with your colleagues, class and children's parents (Chambers, 2011, suggests a space for recommending books in staff meetings). Dreher (2003) suggests having a 'box of good books' or a 'book exchange' available for staff with each teacher selecting three to read and share reviews throughout the term. Many publishers have free downloadable catalogues and providing colleagues/peers time to browse through and indicate texts of interest to them can be useful. Follow annual children's book awards, reviews or specialists and enthusiasts in order to broaden your knowledge of new releases (Ross, 2000).

(Continued)

Table 10.1   (Continued)

Maintain a Reading Journal	Value the text as a reader and not as a teacher (Collins, 2014). Being able to delve through your own 'reading history' is a pleasure in itself (Chambers, 2011). Begin to model and curate your own reading of children's literature, writing a few passages that you would like to remember or responses that you want to recall. Share these responses with the children in your class but the process should never become burdensome (Bisplinghoff et al., 2003; Chambers, 2011; Merga, 2016).
Advocacy and Access for Reflecting all Realities (Arts Council England, 2003)	Check what books you have available in your own classroom. We all need to take action in improving our own knowledge around diverse children's literature. Our schools and classrooms will be better for it and present a truer and richer depiction of the world (Jennett, 2017; Ramdarshan-Bold, 2019; CLPE, 2019). Follow the CLPE's annual #RelectingRealities report to find good practice, publishers who care passionately about this and authentic representations. For minimal cost, become a member of Letterbox Library whose online catalogue and database of recommendations have been promoting 'inclusive and representative quality children's literature', 'specialising in culturally diverse and non-gender-stereotyped books since 1983' (CLPE, 2019; Hope, 2017a).
Reading is a shared, social experience so look out for supportive communities	Social media may have its pitfalls but the reading community in some spaces is a welcome and welcoming one. Look for blossoming reading communities with plenty of teachers, librarians, parents, authors and illustrators. You could use platforms such as Twitter and Goodreads to become part of this community. More than ever, authors and illustrators are more contactable (being on platforms like Instagram and Twitter) and gracious with their time. Following them can create important connections for you and the class. In addition, joining a group of like-minded teachers to discuss books and strategies for promoting reading can be a useful way of broadening your experience. The Open University and UKLA Teachers' Reading Groups are a network of groups that run across the country and can be found through an online search.
Reading Aloud for Pleasure (Safford, 2014)	The latest National Curriculum advocates for the reading aloud of whole texts (DfE, 2013) and this again offers you the chance to introduce children to new and exciting writers, illustrators and poets while helping children associate you with being a reader. Although established authors have their place on the class bookshelf, new voices could encourage children to venture into new reading territories especially when these texts are read 'with expression and emotional connection' (Merga, 2016). This is even more important with older primary children since research has shown that fewer than 50% of parents read aloud to their child when they get to Year 6 (Lockwood, 2008).

Finding the time to read independently for pleasure has always been a problem for teachers. Being part of a community helps. Both schools and initial teacher training programmes could build in some time to present teachers with this space. Sometimes, time is all that is needed to kick-start that passion and desire, and remind readers that reading children's literature can be pleasurable for its own sake (Merga and Ledger, 2018). In terms of visualising this as something manageable, Lesesne's (2017) model, adapted from Anderson et al. (1988), does make the goal seem more realistic:

- 'Reading 15 minutes each day = 105 minutes a week
- 105 minutes a week = 5450 minutes read a year
- This results in 20 books per year read in 15 minutes a day'

'Being a reader' not only means 'reading for yourself' but also making the time to do so (Chambers, 2011). Although he refers here to the context of a teacher providing these moments for their pupils, we must also consider it for ourselves, for our own time and pleasure, as well as for our class.

The Reading Teacher environment

In defining his environment and what 'determines' its potency and potentiality, Chambers (2011) separates the physical classroom surroundings (setting) from the personable and private (set) and considers the former more influential than the latter. While the setting might seem obvious (displays, seating, book availability), the set is vaguer but refers to, in part, our 'mental and emotional attitudes', our relationship with other readers in the class and accumulation of past experiences and knowledge – even our current mood (Ross, 2000).

Sharing your own latest acquisitions and recommendations will always appeal to the class while showing them that you are a part of their reading world (Jennett, 2017). Teachers may share the front cover, blurb, why they decided to purchase it and read an extract to hook potential readers in (Miller, 2012).

CASE STUDY 10.1

How we present literature to the class is important; any attractive bookshop display is testament to the skill of presenting books in an enticing manner. One school decided to follow the advice of Chambers (2011) in creating an exciting and engaging reading environment, including the following:

- Some teachers presented a review card next to the book on display while others kept their own personal texts in a teacher box next to their table for children to sign in and check out just like a library.

(Continued)

- Other teachers rotated their displays to keep the children's interest and engagement with the reading corner space. Some chose to have weekly, fortnightly or termly authors, illustrators, publishers and award winners or thematic shelves and spaces to offer readers new reading experiences or build on their interests. As Lockwood (2008) notes, it is important that you know what is available to the children on your bookshelves so that you can support them in making 'appropriate reading choices'.
- As Reading Teachers, staff were sure to find the time to join children in browsing (Allyn, 2012). Exploring the cover, blurb and initial pages modelled to the children how to go about choosing a book. Staff were sure to emphasise how much their reading choice was affected by their mood and personal taste (Clark and Phythian-Sence, 2008), reminding children it is fine to have different opinions and tastes from friends and classmates (and even teachers!).

A Reading Teacher has the knowledge of texts to foster a rich conversation with others around what informs their reading choices (Ross, 2000). Listen to what children are saying as they make their own choices; guide those who may ask or need it, but also learn to observe and listen while they browse on their own or with a friend, so that you can better support them in their future browsing sessions.

Show the children that you are an equal in this community. Inviting children to recommend books to you as well as their peers is also valuable, as are those shared reading experiences in which children may choose to read together or you might choose to read alongside another child or a small group for pleasure alone. These moments will not just create an inviting, relaxed environment but also encourage children to read for longer through their own choice (Cremin et al., 2009; Safford, 2014; Chou et al., 2016).

STOP AND REFLECT

Think about your current classroom or a classroom setting you know well. Considering the ideas presented above:

- What works well for modelling, promoting and sharing books and texts?
- Are there any areas where you could develop your practice?
- What potential barriers are there to becoming a Reading Teacher? How might these be overcome?

Conclusion

This chapter has explored how Reading Teachers not only enable children to experience the joys and pleasures of reading but how they can discover and enjoy those pleasures for themselves (Allyn, 2012). Being a Reading Teacher matters and having the qualities, knowledge and skills mentioned in this chapter should not be additional but something that is worth advocating for (Clark and Rumbold, 2006; Safford, 2014).

Much success for children as readers comes down to how much they read and what they read: that intrinsic motivation coupled with aesthetic reading experiences. The same can be said for the hallmarks of a Reading Teacher too (Chambers, 2011). Sharing our own 'experience, preferences and enthusiasms' (CLPE, 2015) as both a reading model and reading equal, and being part of the reading community in the classroom will go a long way in comvincing children of investing in becoming a lifelong reader.

Reading connects and dissolves boundaries (Bisplinghoff et al., 2003). It invites us to grow by becoming part of a greater whole; it can provide us with mirrors and windows into our lives and those of others, traversing across seas and oceans to other lands and realms yet still connect us all through the singular commonality of what it is to be human.

Reading can do more than just affirm our place in the world, it can challenge us all to be critical and reflective of the societies in which we live and help us see how we can all make a change for the better together. Literature, as Bruner (1996) reflects, renders the world 'less fixed' and 'more susceptible to recreation' (cited in Chambers, 2011). It shows us that things can change, that knowledge which was once beyond our grasp is there for the taking and that it invites us to imagine, to escape, to be free. If you value and understand this then that passion and knowledge will convince the most reluctant reader to join you on their own reading journey without scheme or scaffold.

IN SUMMARY

- Teachers and other adults who work in schools can be influential role models for children, supporting them to see that reading is for them and inducting them into the business of being a reader. Choosing to become a Reading Teacher – a teacher who reads and a reader who teaches – can have a resonance far beyond simply teaching children to read.
- Reading Teachers consciously develop their own knowledge of children's literature, in addition to sharing their own reading lives with children and showing a genuine interest in the reading lives of the children in their class.
- Research suggests that children are motivated to read if they have access to literature which reflects their own realities, including gender, race, need and culture. It is vital that every effort is made to ensure children have the opportunity to see themselves and their own lives, as well as the lives of others different from them, reflected in the books they encounter at school.

FURTHER READING

- Teresa Cremin and colleagues' *Building Communities of Engaged Readers* is the leading UK-based body of Teachers as Readers research. From an overview of the approach to a chapter-by-chapter breakdown of steps that schools and teachers can take to improve and build upon their Reading for Pleasure pedagogy – it is indispensable.
- *Teachers as Readers: Perspectives on the Importance of Reading in Teachers' Classrooms and Lives* edited by Michelle Commeyras, Betty Shockley Bisplinghoff and Jennifer Olsen works as a helpful and more personally reflective series of journals from a range of teachers in the United States. They share their own reading journeys and reflections and the steps they made to improve their attitudes and practice.
- Based upon her extensive knowledge and experiences in the classroom, Donalyn Miller's *The Book Whisperer: Awakening the inner reader in every child* is a welcome insight into how to create a classroom awash with a pleasure for reading. She understands the value of building a community of readers and shares how she sets about ensuring that all children in her classroom are readers for life. Practical with plenty of tried and tested strategies.
- For greater discussion about considering the books children can access in the class library and what realities they are promoting, read *Whose Worlds are we Sharing with Children?* by Mat Tobin (freely available – search online).
- As a resource bank of best practice, the Open University's *Research Rich Pedagogies* is an outstanding website full of classroom-based and research informed ideas that are frequently based upon the theories explored in this chapter.

REFERENCES

Allyn, P. (2012) Taming the wild text. *Educational Leadership*, 69(6): 16–21.

Anderson, R.C., Wilson, P.T. and Fielding, L.G. (1988) Growth in reading and how children spend their time outside of school. *Reading Research Quarterly*, 23: 285–303.

Applegate, A.J. and Applegate, M.D. (2004) The Peter effect: Reading habits and attitudes of preservice teachers. *Reading Teacher*, 57(6): 554–63.

Arizpe, E., Farrell, M. and McAdam, J. (2013) Opening the classroom door to children's literature: A review of research. In K. Hall, T. Cremin, B. Comber and L. Moll (Eds), *International Handbook of Research on Children's Literacy, Learning and Culture* (pp. 241–58). Chichester: John Wiley and Sons.

Arts Council England (2003) *From Looking Glass to Spy Glass*.

Atkinson, P. (2017) *Promoting Reading for Pleasure*. Leicester: UKLA.

Becker, M. and McElvany, N. (2010) Intrinsic and extrinsic reading motivation as predictors of reading literacy: A longitudinal study. *Journal of Educational Psychology*, 102(4): 773–85.

Benton, M. and Fox, G. (1985) *Teaching Literature: Nine to Fourteen*. Oxford: Oxford University Press.

Bishop, R.S. (1990) Mirrors, windows and sliding glass doors. *Perspectives: Choosing and Using Books for the Classroom*, 6(3): ix–xi.

Bisplinghoff, B.S., Commeyras, M. and Olson, J. (2003) *Teachers as Readers: Perspectives on the importance of reading in teachers' classrooms and lives*. Newark: International Reading Association.

Breadmore, H., Vardy, E., Cunningham, A., Kwok, R. and Carroll, J. (2019) *Literacy Development: Evidence Review*. London: Education Endowment Foundation.

Brooks, G. (2007) Teachers as readers and writers and as teachers of reading and writing. *The Journal of Educational Research*, 100(3): 177–91.

Bruner, J. (1996) *The Culture of Education*. Cambridge, MA: Harvard University Press.

Campbell, B., Dubitsky, A., Faron, E., George, D., Gieselmann, K., Goldschmidt, B., Skeeters, K. and Wagner, E. (2016) The top five reasons we love giving students choice in reading. *English Leadership Quarterly*, 38(3): 6–7.

Centre for Literacy in Primary Education (CLPE) (2015) *Reading for Pleasure, What We Know Works*, London: CLPE Brief.

Centre for Literacy in Primary Education (CLPE) (2019) *Reflecting Realities – A Survey of Ethnic Representation within UK Children's Literature*, London: CLPE Brief.

Chambers, A. (1973) *Introducing Books to Children*. London: Heinemann.

Chambers, A. (2011) *Tell Me: Children, Reading and Talk with The Reading Environment*. Stroud: The Thimble Press.

Chou, M.J., Cheng, J.C. and Cheng, Y.W. (2016) Operating classroom aesthetic reading environment to raise children's reading motivation. *Universal Journal of Educational Research*, 4(1): 81–97.

Clark, C. and De Zoysa, S. (2011) *Mapping the Interrelationships of Reading Enjoyment, Attitudes, Behaviour and Attainment: An exploratory investigation*. London: National Literacy Trust.

Clark, C. and Foster, A. (2005) *Children's and Young People's Reading Habits and Preferences: The who, what, why, where and when*. London: National Literacy Trust.

Clark, C. and Phythian-Sence, C. (2008) *Interesting Choice: The (relative) importance of choice and interest in reader engagement. Review*. London: The National Literacy Trust.

Clark, C. and Rumbold, K. (2006) *Reading for Pleasure: A Research Overview*. London: National Literacy Trust.

Clarkson, R. and Sainsbury, M. (2008) *Attitudes to Reading at Ages Nine and Eleven: Full report.* Available at: www.nfer.ac.uk/media/2106/raq01.pdf (accessed 12/01/2021).

Cliff Hodges, G. (2010) Reasons for reading: why literature matters. *Literacy*, 44(2): 60–8. doi: 10.1111/j.1741-4369.2010.00552.x.

Cochran-Smith, M. (2000) Blind vision: Unlearning racism in teacher education. *Harvard Educational Review*, 70(2): 157–90.

Colby, S.A. and Lyon, A.F. (2004) Heightening awareness about the importance of using multicultural literature. *Multicultural Education*, 11(3): 24–8.

Collins, F. (2014) Enhancing teachers' knowledge of children's literature and other texts. In T. Cremin, M. Mottram, F.M. Collins, S. Powell and K. Safford (Eds) *Building Communities of Engaged Readers: Reading for pleasure* (pp. 52–66). Abingdon: Routledge.

Commeyras, M., Bisplinghoff, B.S. and Olsen, J. (2003) *Teachers as Readers: Perspectives on the Importance of Reading in Teachers' Classrooms and Lives*. Newark: International Reading Association.

Cox, R. and Schaetzel, K. (2007) A preliminary study of pre-service teachers as readers in Singapore: Prolific, functional or detached. *Language Teaching Research*, 11(3): 300–16.

Cremin, T. (2007) Revisiting reading for pleasure: Delight, desire and diversity. In K. Goouch and A. Lambirth (Eds), *Understanding Phonics and the Teaching of Reading: A Critical Perspective* (pp. 166–90). Maidenhead: McGraw Hill. (ONLINE)

Cremin, T., Bearne, E., Mottram, M. and Goodwin, P. (2008) Primary teachers as readers. *English in Education*, 42(1): 8–23.

Cremin, T., Bearne, E., Mottram, M. and Goodwin, P. (2008a) Primary teachers as readers. *English in Education*, 42(1): 1–16.

Cremin, T., Bearne, E., Mottram, M. and Goodwin, P. (2008b) Exploring teachers' knowledge of children's literature. *Cambridge Journal of Education*, 38(4): 449–64.

Cremin, T., Mottram, M., Collins, F., Powell, S. and Safford, K. (2009). Teachers as readers: Building communities of readers. *Literacy*, 43(1): 11–19.

Department for Education (DfE) (2013) *The National Curriculum in England: Key stages 1 and 2 framework document*. Available at: www.gov.uk/government/publications/national-curriculum-in-england-primary-curriculum.

Dreher, M.J. (2003) Motivating teachers to read. *The Reading Teacher*, 56(4): 338–40.

Dugdale, G. and Clark, C. (2008) *Literacy Changes Lives: An advocacy resource*. London: National Literacy Trust.

Gambrell, L.B. (1996) Creating classroom cultures that foster motivation. *The Reading Teacher*, 50(1): 14–25.

Garces-Bacsal, R.M., Tupas, R., Kaur, S., Paculdar, A.M. and Baja, E.S. (2018) Reading for pleasure: Whose job is it to build lifelong readers in the classroom? *Literacy*, 52(2): 95–102.

Goodwin, P. (2017) Becoming a reluctant reader. In *Reading by Right: Successful strategies to ensure every child can read to succeed*. London: Facet Publishing.

Goouch, K. and Lambirth, A. (2011) *Teaching Early Reading and Phonics: Creative approaches to early literacy*. Thousand Oaks, CA: Sage.

Guthrie, J.T., Hoa, A.L.W., Wigfield, A., Tonks, S.M., Humenick, N.M. and Littles, E. (2007) Reading motivation and reading comprehension growth in the later elementary years. *Contemporary Educational Psychology*, 32(3): 282–313.

Guthrie, J.T. and Wigfield, A. (2000) Engagement and motivation in reading. In M.L. Kamil, P.B. Mosenthal, P.D. Pearson and R. Barr (Eds), *Reading Research Handbook* (Vol. 3, pp. 403–22). Mahwah, NJ: Erlbaum.

Harper, L.J. and Brand, S.T. (2010) More alike than different: Promoting respect through multicultural books and literacy strategies. *Childhood Education*, 86(4): 224–33.

Hefflin, B.R. and Barksdale-Ladd, M.A. (2001) African American children's literature that helps students find themselves: Selection guidelines for grades K–3. *The Reading Teacher*, 54(8): 810–81.

Hope, J. (2017a) Reflecting readers: Ensuring that no one is excluded. In J. Court (Ed.), *Reading by Right: Successful strategies to ensure every child can read to succeed* (pp. 107–26). London: Facet Publishing.

Hope, J. (2017b) Reading the future. In J. Court (Ed.), *Reading by Right: Successful strategies to ensure every child can read to succeed* (pp. 189–209). London: Facet Publishing.

Jennett, M. (2017) *Getting Everyone Reading for Pleasure*. Available at: www.letterpressproject.co.uk/media/file/reading-4-pleasure-10561.pdf (accessed: 29/01/2020).

Kaufman, D. (2002) Living a literate life, revisited. *English Journal*, 91(6): 51–7.

Krashen, S. (2004) *The Power of Reading: Insights from the research* (2nd ed.). Westport, CT: Libraries Unlimited.

Kwek, D., Albright, J. and Kramer-Dahl, A. (2007) Building teachers' creative capabilities in Singapore's English classrooms: A way of contesting pedagogical instrumentality. *Literacy*, 41(2): 71–8.

Larson, J. and Marsh, J. (2005) *Making Literacy Real: Theories and Practices for Learning and Teaching*. Thousand Oaks, CA: Sage.

Lesesne, T.S. (2017) Listening to their voices: What research tells us about readers. In J. Court (Ed.), *Reading by Right: Successful strategies to ensure every child can read to succeed*. London: Facet Publishing.

Lockwood, M. (2008) *Promoting Reading for Pleasure in the Primary School*. London: Sage.

McCarthey, S.J. and Moje, E.B. (2002) Identity matters. *Reading Research Quarterly*, 37(2): 228–38.

McKool, S.S. and Gespass, S. (2009) Does Johnny's reading teacher love to read? How teachers' personal reading habits affect instructional practices. *Literacy Research and Instruction*, 48(3): 264–76.

Merga, M.K. (2016) 'I don't know if she likes reading': are teachers perceived to be keen readers, and how is this determined? *English in Education*, 50(3): 255–69.

Merga, M.K. (2017) What would make children read for pleasure more frequently? *English in Education*, 51(2): 207–23.

Merga, M.K. and Ledger, S. (2018) Teachers' attitudes toward and frequency of engagement in reading aloud in the primary classroom. *Literacy*, 53(3): 134–42.

Miller, D. (2012) Creating a classroom where readers flourish. *Reading Teacher*, 66(2): 88–92.

Morrison, T.G., Jacobs, J.S. and Swinyard, W.R. (1999) Do teachers who read personally use recommended literacy practices in their classrooms? *Reading Research and Instruction*, 38: 81–100.

O'Sullivan, O. and McGonigle, S. (2010) Transforming readers: Teachers and children in the Centre for Literacy in Primary Education Power of Reading project. *Literacy*, 44(2): 51–9.

Patrick, H., Ryan, A.M. and Kaplan, A. (2007) Early adolescents' perceptions of the classroom social environment, motivational beliefs, and engagement. *Journal of Educational Psychology*, 99(1): 83–98.

Pirofski, K.I. (2001) Race, gender, and disability in today's children's literature. In *Multicultural Pavilion Research Room*. Available at: https://bit.ly/390dt2D

Ramdarshan-Bold, M. (2019) *Representation of People of Colour Among Children's Book Authors and Illustrators*. Available at: www.booktrust.org.uk/what-we-do/programmes-and-campaigns/booktrust-represents/representation-of-people-of-colour-among-childrens-book-authors-and-illustrators/

Rosenblatt, L.M. (1978) *The Reader, the Text, the Poem: The transactional theory of the literary work*. Carbondale, IL: Southern Illinois University Press.

Ross, C.S. (2000) Making choices: What readers say about choosing books to read for pleasure. *The Acquisitions Librarian*, 13(25): 5–21.

Safford, K. (2014) A reading for pleasure pedagogy. In T. Cremin, M. Mottram, F.M. Collins, S. Powell and K. Safford (Eds), *Building Communities of Engaged Readers: Reading for pleasure* (pp. 89–107). Abingdon: Routledge.

Sainsbury, M. and Schagen, I. (2004) Attitudes to reading at ages nine to eleven. *Journal of Research in Reading*, 27(4): 373–86.

Schraw, G., Flowerday, T. and Reisetter, M.F. (1998) The role of choice in reader engagement. *Journal of Educational Psychology*, 90: 705–14.

Strommen, T. and Mates, F. (2004) Learning to love reading: Interviews with older children and teens. *International Reading Association*, 48(3): 188–200.

Wang, J.H.Y. and Guthrie, J.T. (2004) Modelling the effects of intrinsic motivation, extrinsic motivation, amount of reading, and past reading achievement on text comprehension between U.S. and Chinese students. *Reading Research Quarterly*, 39: 162–86.

Whatley, L. (2011) 'That's how my students feel!' In M. Commeyras, B. Bisplinghoff and J. Olson (Eds), *Teachers as Readers*, pp.55–63. Available at: www.uilis.unsyiah.ac.id/oer/files/original/01532 b0c1b2aff17e99ce310617569c1.pdf

Wray, D., Medwell, J., Fox, R. and Poulson, L. (1999) Teaching reading: Lessons from the experts. *Reading*, 33: 17–23.

PART 4

WRITING

11

THE TEACHING AND LEARNING OF WRITING: THEORY

THIS CHAPTER WILL

• Consider the key theoretical research underpinning the teaching of writing

• Introduce four principal ways of viewing the act of writing, applying these to the context of the primary school

• Discuss the external factors that can drive schools' provision for the teaching of writing

Introduction

This chapter presents the theoretical underpinnings concerning the teaching of writing in primary schools, considering how we define and conceptualise writing, the principal theories that have shaped how writing is approached in the English education system, and some of the external drivers (both current and historical) that have influenced classroom practice with regard to writing. Chapter 12 addresses the practical aspects of teaching writing, exploring how the concepts discussed in this chapter might affect the teaching of writing in the classroom.

Theoretical foundations for teaching writing

What do we mean when we talk about teaching a child to write? This section will consider four interrelated ways of viewing writing in order to answer this seemingly simple question:

- Writing as communication
- Writing as a social act
- Writing as a set of genres
- Writing as a process

Writing as communication

At its heart, the teaching of writing is about communication. Our aim is for children to learn to control language in order to share exactly what they want to say, whether to entertain, inform or persuade. As Chamberlain (2016) elegantly explains:

> Rooting our writing in an understanding of purpose, and how it relates to our everyday spoken languages, makes a solid connection between how we really use language and why and how we commit oracy (the ability to express oneself fluently/grammatically in speech) to the page, virtual or real. By building foundations of writing based in oracy and in the everyday, writing is demystified: it is not started with a foray into the world of fancy vocabulary and poetic notions. Instead, it is functional and real, where vocabulary matters because of its accuracy and preciseness.
>
> (Chamberlain, 2016)

While there are inevitable (and necessary) differences between spoken and written communication, seeing these two things as interlinked domains is vital for children learning to write.

Linked closely to this is the idea of *metacognition*: an awareness of our thinking and learning and the desire to take responsibility for improvement and progress. Analysis of research suggests that these traits can have a significant impact on children's learning in general (Dignath et al., 2008; de Boer et al., 2014), but that this might be particularly significant in writing, where the ability to reflect on what message a created text communicates and how effectively it does this, then make changes in the light of this awareness, is key to development as a writer (Tracy et al., 2009; Fisher et al., 2010). Another aspect of metacognition is children being able to identify as a writer themselves, someone invested in the process of learning to communicate through writing:

If we can encourage children to see themselves as a writer, someone who shapes words and language to create a particular effect then not only are they more likely to write well, but they are likely to be motivated to want to improve their writing. If children are writing for us, their teachers, because they have to, then the responsibility for improving lies with us to cajole them into becoming better. If they are writing for themselves, because they see themselves as a writer, then they are far more likely to want to learn to control the language they use.

(Clements, 2017)

However the teaching of writing is organised in a primary classroom, effective communication through control of the different facets of writing should be central.

Writing as a social act

Cremin and Myhill (2012) describe writing as a social act as 'the dominant theoretical view of writing at present' stating that '…when we write, we are participating in a social practice which is shaped by social and historical understandings of what writing is and what texts should do' (Cremin and Myhill, 2012). Much of the teaching of writing in schools is concerned with teaching children to create pieces of writing that are situated within these practices. As a result, the writing that children produce at school is often assessed and valued against agreed social norms for what makes a good piece of writing. These features might include:

- whether the text fulfils its intended purpose
- the structure of the text
- use of Standard English forms
- accurate spelling
- recognised punctuation
- clear presentation (whether writing, typing or other multi-model aspects)

Access to these social norms is often presented as children's entitlement. Almost all professional jobs require at least some ability to communicate through writing, and the education system that children must navigate is one in which their skills and knowledge in almost any subject will be assessed through writing. The ability to communicate by adopting these conventions gives all children the opportunity to be academically successful. As the 2014 National Curriculum in England states:

A high-quality education in English will teach pupils to speak and write fluently so that they can communicate their ideas and emotions to others…pupils who do not learn to speak, read and write fluently and confidently are effectively disenfranchised.

(DfE, 2013)

While this view can be contested, with numerous critics arguing that these social norms represent a way of consolidating the power of one dominant social group over others (e.g. Crowley, 1991), schools and teachers operate within a curriculum and associated assessment system that are aligned to these expectations. Although the emphasis given to each strand will depend on the school, teacher and curriculum followed, learning to write at primary school is often about fulfilling certain external demands with achievement judged by an adult against these expectations. This means that 'schooled-literacy' (Cook-Gumperz, 2006) is often valued above other forms of writing children might choose to undertake; for example, those that adopt different forms such as writing online for social reasons or the crossover between writing, talk and play of younger children (see Chapter 4).

The idea of writing as a social act extends beyond achievement in writing depending on a child understanding a set of negotiated conventions for the writing produced at school. Writing itself is an inherently social practice, and the skills and competencies that children develop in writing at school and home will be applied across different contexts, used to achieve a range of social goals, each based on the ideologies of the social setting in which it occurs (Street, 1984). The writing skills children learn do not exist in a vacuum, they are context-dependent, requiring writers to be aware of the social context, identify what would constitute successful participation in that context, and then apply this awareness when creating their text (Gee, 2004; Barton, 2007). What is acceptable and desirable in a text will differ depending on each of these factors: a formal letter of thanks makes very different demands than a message sent to a friend while playing an online computer game.

Helping children to understand the context and demands related to any piece of writing is key to helping them develop as a writer.

Writing as a set of genres

If writing as a social act is the dominant theoretical view of writing, the use of specific genres has been the dominant pedagogical approach to writing in English classrooms for several decades. The approach draws on the work of M.A.K. Halliday and other genre theorists, which identified a number of key text types (originally both spoken and written) that were significant and useful for children to understand (Rose, 2011). It was suggested that genres of writing that shared a purpose often shared key features, including structures and language features: grammar in its broadest sense. A genre-based approach to teaching writing involves explicitly teaching the features of these different text types. The influence of the National Primary Strategy (DfES, 2006) led to this approach becoming a popular approach used in many English schools and this was further consolidated through commercial schemes of work and approaches to teaching writing that were based around prescriptive lists of success criteria or providing examples of 'what a good one looks like' (sometimes referred to as 'WAGOLL').

The wider field of genre theory is broader and more nuanced than that of the Primary Strategy, recognising that genres are constantly changing social constructs that share key features because this helps them to communicate ideas and knowledge effectively (Rose, 2008). Genres of writing haven't been created; rather they have grown organically and have been found and classified, not produced. Written, spoken and multi-model text genres are liable to change and look different depending on context and use rather than being one fixed set of conventions for a different purpose (Swales, 1990; Freedman and Medway, 1994).

The principal criticism made of a genre approach to writing teaching is that it can lead to formulaic teaching, a transmission model where knowledge of the correct structure of a text resides with the teacher, and work produced is valued based on how well it fits with this preconceived set of attributes, rather than drawing on children's existing skill at communicating (Wyse and Jones, 2001). Used flexibly, learning about the features of specific genres can give children an understanding of the purpose of a text and provide a model with which to arrange their own ideas, learning about the appropriateness of different language features for particular purposes and audiences. The key is flexibility, as Myhill and Fisher (2010) note: 'as writers develop, they have to learn not simply about formulaic patterns of text types but how genres are socially situated and mediated by their context'. How this might be approached in the classroom is explored in Chapter 12.

Writing as a process

For some children (and indeed some teachers), writing is about the end product. It is these completed drafts that are marked, assessed and shared, after all. Over the last 30 years, however, it has come to be understood that it is the *process* of writing, the business of shaping language and ideas into this final form, that is so useful to focus on when teaching children to write.

Graves (1983) is credited with developing the process approach, often referred to as 'the writer's workshop'. This model of teaching writing has been influential across the UK, Australia and the USA, and informed many curriculum models and teaching strategies that have followed (Wyse, 2017). Graves describes several 'essentials' to a successful writing process model:

- The adequate provision of time for children to write
- Children's choice of writing topic
- Working towards a published end product
- The teacher supporting the child with composition and transcription through writing workshops and 'mini-lessons' based on teacher's assessments of common misconceptions or issues that need addressing

The integrated three-phase model of planning for writing first outlined in *Raising Boys' Achievement in Writing* (UKLA/Primary National Strategy, 2004) draws on Graves' process approach, outlining three stages for the teaching of writing:

- Phase 1 – familiarisation with the genre
- Phase 2 – capturing ideas and planning
- Phase 3 – writing and presenting

The phases are organised so that children:

> …become confidently **familiar** with the features of the chosen text type. Ideas for writing will be **captured** in a variety of ways, but this part of the process is where the class is likely to benefit from talk, drama or role play activities which will support their grasp of the whole text structure (for example, role play to aid personal narrative or persuasive argument). Writing in many forms may be part of the process from the start, but once there has been extensive experience of the text features, the process of teacher **demonstrating**, modelling and guiding writing is used to **support** successful sustained and **independent** writing.
>
> (UKLA/Primary National Strategy, 2004, bold in original)

This influential model formed the basis of the revised National Primary Strategy and remains a popular structure for organising the teaching of writing in English primary schools.

The influence of both Graves' work and the three-phase model can be seen in the writing composition element outlined in the 2014 National Curriculum. The curriculum suggests a process approach to writing, suggesting the following steps:

- Plan: collecting ideas and mapping out the piece of writing
- Draft: writing the first draft, following their plan, but deviating from it where they have a better idea
- Evaluate: considering the strengths and weaknesses of the first draft
- Edit/Redraft: an opportunity for children to make improvements to their first draft in the light of the evaluate stage

By explicitly teaching children how to approach each of these stages, children can learn to shape a piece of writing until it communicates their intended message effectively. Just as with considering different genres of writing, care needs to be taken not to apply any particular process or set of stages too strictly. While explicit stages provide a useful way of thinking about how a child might move through the writing process, they can lead to an overly rigid approach to writing. Real writing is unlikely to neatly follow this linear route every time. As Myhill (2018) notes:

> What is clear is that this process of moving from ideas in the head, to words on a page, through to a finished piece is a messy process, or a recursive process, as the cognitive psychologists would term it. Expert writers, such as professional writers, don't plan their writing, write it, and then revise it: the generation of ideas, production of text and evaluation of text appear to be constantly interacting throughout the writing process. A beautiful messiness!

However, we might expect children taking the first steps to becoming writers to be different from these expert writers. As Berninger et al. (1996) suggest:

> …in skilled writers, planning, translating and revising are mature processes that interact with each other. In beginning and developing writers, each of these processes is still developing and each process is on its own trajectory, developing at its own rate.

Balancing the demands of composition and transcription can also place demands on a child's working memory, making it difficult for them to effectively manage each of the different elements (Myhill and Fisher, 2010). A process approach, with specific teaching of different elements combined with opportunities to practise and to bring them together, can help children to develop holistically as writers.

In a review of programmes to support the teaching of writing, Slavin et al. (2019) found 'considerable consensus in how to teach writing', noting three common features:

- Cooperative learning: working together collaboratively gives students opportunities to give and receive feedback on their writing, supporting them to evaluate how effectively they have communicated their intended message and providing a real audience for their writing. Cremin and Myhill (2012) refer to this collaborative approach as 'a community of writers'.
- Writing processes: Following the steps to plan, draft, revise and edit compositions outlined above was found to be beneficial across the programmes studied. Slavin et al. (2019) suggest that these steps help students who are more reluctant to write to take risks from the outset, understanding that they will have the opportunity later to improve their writing.
- Motivation and joy in self-expression: Slavin et al. (2019) note that 'good writing starts in the heart, with an urge to say something of importance'. This desire to write, to share ideas, is a critical part of understanding writing as communication, rather than as replicating a pre-conceived set of standards. It depends on authenticity and purpose.

STOP AND REFLECT

Consider the four interlinked frames for thinking about the teaching of writing:

- Writing as communication
- Writing as a social act
- Writing as set of genres
- Writing as a process

Which of these have you encountered before? Are any new to you? Which inform your own view of writing in the primary classroom?

In Chapter 12, we will consider some practical approaches for how a balance can be struck between following a process that helps children to articulate their thoughts clearly and embracing the 'beautiful messiness' of writing.

External influences on the teaching of writing

While ideas drawn from theory are likely to have an influence on how writing is taught in primary schools, it is other external factors such as the National Curriculum and national assessment that are likely to shape the practical business of teaching writing. In English primary schools, these will include:

* the 2014 National Curriculum
* statutory assessment of writing at Key Stage 1 and Key Stage 2
* Ofsted
* a school's own curriculum model, including published schemes

Writing in the 2014 National Curriculum

In the 2014 National Curriculum (DfE, 2013), writing is presented as three interrelated elements: transcription (spelling and handwriting), composition (articulating ideas and structuring them in speech and writing) and grammar and punctuation (understanding and using these features in writing). The statements for teaching writing are organised by year group in Year 1 and Year 2. Across Key Stage 2, the Programme of Study is grouped into Year 3 and Year 4, and Year 5 and Year 6.

Unlike the National Primary Strategy, writing in the 2014 National Curriculum is not organised around a set of different text types. Instead, there is a focus on children learning to tailor their writing for audience and purpose. The writing composition element outlined in the new curriculum suggests a process approach to writing with the following steps:

* Planning
* Drafting and Writing
* Evaluating and Editing
* Proof-Reading
* Reading Aloud and Sharing

Although it is clearest at Key Stage 2, this process of planning-writing-improving-sharing runs through every key stage and year group, from a child saying a sentence aloud before writing it in Year 1 to a Year 11 student proof-reading his answer during a GCSE examination.

The 2014 National Curriculum places considerable emphasis on the technical aspects of writing: spelling, grammar and punctuation, and these, along with an emphasis on vocabulary development, are intended to help children to communicate their ideas effectively. Specific focus is given to this in Chapter 13. The National Curriculum's grammar and punctuation expectations are outlined by year group in a separate appendix. An accompanying glossary provides details of the terminology used.

Statutory assessment of writing

While children's writing will be assessed both formatively and summatively throughout their time at school (see Chapter 17), the formal statutory assessments that take place at the end of Key Stage 1 and Key Stage 2 English in primary schools can be a key driver in the manner that schools approach teaching writing.

The nature of these assessments has changed greatly over the last decade. Until 2012, there was a writing test at the end of Key Stage 2 made up of a short and longer writing task (2003–2012) that was externally marked. At Key Stage 1, children's writing was assessed by the teacher, based on the National Curriculum, but often drawing on Assessing Pupil Progress sheets (DfES, 2006): a set of objectives drawn from the Primary Strategy. Children were awarded a national curriculum level, based on an overview of the quality of their writing. Judgements, both from writing tests and through teacher assessment, were 'best-fit', a system where writing was judged holistically and strength in one area of writing could compensate for weakness in another.

In 2011, ahead of the introduction of a new curriculum, a review of assessment at Key Stage 2 was launched. The Bew Report (2011), as it was known, recommended removing the writing test at Key Stage 2 due to concerns about its reliability as an assessment measure. It was replaced with teacher assessment for writing and a separate grammar, punctuation and spelling (GPS) test to assess these transcriptional aspects of writing.

The 2014 National Curriculum saw national curriculum levels removed as a measure. In 2016, interim frameworks for teacher assessment at Key Stage 1 and Key Stage 2 were released by the DfE (DfE, 2016). These provided a set of statements against which children's achievement in writing would be judged. At both Key Stage 1 and Key Stage 2, there were three performance descriptors:

- 'Working towards the national standard'
- 'Working at the national standard'
- 'Working at greater depth within the national standard'

The most significant change from the previous system of levels is that these performance descriptors were not to be used in a best-fit way:

> To demonstrate that pupils have met the standard, teachers will need to have evidence that a pupil demonstrates consistent attainment of all the statements within the standard.

> (DfE, 2016)

While based on the content of the 2014 National Curriculum, the great majority of the statements that made up the 2016 interim teacher assessment frameworks were linked to spelling, punctuation, grammar or handwriting. For 'working at the national standard' at Key Stage 1, these elements made up all twelve criteria. At Key Stage 2, nine out of ten statements focused on transcription elements of writing.

The interim teacher assessment frameworks were heavily criticised by teachers and teaching unions (e.g. Gazzard, 2016; NUT, 2016) and, after a public consultation process, changes were made in 2017. The revised framework sought to address criticisms around the lack of flexibility that had led to strong writers who may have struggled with one aspect of writing (spelling or handwriting, for example) being awarded a standard that didn't fully reflect their competence as a writer. The revised framework stated the principal changes were:

- A more flexible approach – teachers can now use their discretion to ensure that, on occasion, a particular weakness does not prevent an accurate judgement of a pupil's attainment overall being made. The overall standard of attainment, set by the 'pupil can' statements, remains the same.
- Revised 'pupil can' statements – a greater emphasis on composition, while statements relating to the more 'technical' aspects of English writing (grammar, punctuation and spelling) are less prescriptive. All changes are in line with the attainment targets for the Key Stage 2 programme of study.

(Standards and Testing Agency (STA), 2017)

Critics of the teacher assessment system have suggested that the more flexible approach makes comparisons between schools difficult, as the 'particular weakness' can be interpreted differently (Ward, 2017). The longer standing criticism of whether a set of statements can accurately capture a child's attainment in writing (Christodoulou, 2016) and whether an approach like this promotes a reductive approach to the teaching of writing, seeing it as a set of skills to be acquired and demonstrated (Cremin and Myhill, 2012), remain. These issues are explored more fully in Chapters 17 and 18.

Despite the STA's statement that 'the frameworks are not a formative assessment tool: they are not intended to guide individual programmes of study, classroom practice or methodology' (STA, 2017), the high-stakes assessment system in England means that the teacher assessment frameworks are likely to have an impact on how writing is taught, especially at the end of key stages.

Ofsted and the teaching of writing

As is the case with all subjects, the English schools' inspectorate, Ofsted, state that inspectors do not expect to see writing taught in any particular way:

Inspectors must not advocate a particular method of planning, teaching or assessment. It is up to schools themselves to determine their practices and for leadership teams to justify these on their own merits rather than by reference to the inspection handbook.

(Ofsted, 2018)

Historically, Ofsted has produced subject-specific reports collating findings from school inspections, although this has not been the case since 2011. The last documents of this type were *Moving English Forward* (2012) and *Barriers to Literacy* (2011). These reports suggested that effective writing teaching contained the elements below:

- Lesson plans were clear and realistic about the key learning for pupils within the limited time available in individual lessons.
- Teaching was flexible and responded to pupils' needs as the lesson developed.
- Tasks were meaningful, giving pupils real audiences and contexts where possible.
- Pupils were given adequate time to think, plan, discuss, write, and test out ideas.
- Teachers make good use of oral work in order to improve writing, including presentations and class debates and make links with reading.
- Good use of drama sessions can also lead to an improvement of children's vocabulary and expression.
- Children make good progress where systematic phonics is incorporated into writing lessons.
- Schools make good use of ICT facilities and resources to enrich pupils' writing.

(Ofsted, 2011 and 2012)

How each of these broad statements will be interpreted and implemented depends on the beliefs and approaches to teaching writing employed by different schools and teachers. Perceived ideas of what Ofsted might be looking for should not be a driver for organising the teaching of writing.

STOP AND REFLECT

Consider the points for effective writing teaching drawn from Ofsted's inspections above.

- Which of these do you agree should form part of a school's writing pedagogy?
- How many of these match with your own approach to the teaching of writing?
- Are there any that are currently under-represented in your practice that might be useful to consider?

A school's curriculum

Every school is different and, while the structure and organisation of a particular school's curriculum will reflect the demands of the National Curriculum and any national assessments, how these elements are interpreted and implemented will also differ. A school's writing curriculum encompasses both what children are expected to learn *and* how the learning is organised, including other experiences that will lead to writing. Chapter 15 addresses different curriculum models for a school's English curriculum in detail.

Some schools will create their own bespoke writing curriculum, others will use an existing structure such as the Primary Strategy and then make changes depending on their context, and others will make use of a published scheme. Some schools will have a heavily centralised curriculum model, with content and skills mapped for each year group, while in other schools the responsibility for deciding what is taught in each class will lie with individual teachers.

The model of teaching writing followed by any individual teacher is likely to depend on their own beliefs and ethos, the nature of their school's model for teaching writing and any statutory demands from the curriculum or assessments.

In the next chapter, we will consider some practical approaches that help to illustrate the theoretical ideas introduced in this chapter.

Conclusion

While the teaching of writing can be viewed through different interlinked viewpoints, in practice, the model of teaching writing followed by any individual teacher is unlikely to depend solely on their own beliefs and ethos. It will also depend largely on the nature of their school's model for teaching writing, any school-wide systems, approaches and schemes that they follow, and any demands placed on children by national or local curriculums or statutory assessments.

Whatever theoretical frame we adopt to think about the teaching of writing in primary school, it remains amongst the most important areas we can support children to master. In the next chapter, we will consider some practical approaches that help to illustrate the theoretical ideas introduced in this chapter.

IN SUMMARY

- At its heart, writing is about communication. Control of the different elements – composition and transcription – , so children can share their ideas, should sit at the heart of teaching writing.
- Writing is a social act– it depends on an understanding between the reader and the writer. While pieces of writing created for particular purposes are likely to share similar structures and language

features (often defined as *genres*), these features and what it means for them to be executed effectively depends on why it has been written and who it has been written for.

- A *process approach* to writing, where emphasis is given to the act of creating a text and communicating a specific meaning, not just the outcome, can support children to learn to write.

FURTHER READING

- For a comprehensive theoretical overview around the teaching of writing, see *Writing Voices: Creating Communities of Writers* by Teresa Cremin and Deborah Myhill.
- To learn more about the development of writing and the implications for this on curriculum development and teaching, see *How Writing Works: From the invention of the alphabet to the rise of social media* by Dominic Wyse.
- To find out more about the teaching of writing, including practical approaches to teaching writing, see *Inspiring Writing in Primary Schools* by Liz Chamberlain.

REFERENCES

Barton, D. (2007) *Literacy: An Introduction to the ecology of written language* (2nd ed.). Oxford: Blackwell.

Berninger, V.W., Fuller, F. and Whittaker, D. (1996) A process model of writing development across lifespan. *Educational Psychology Review*, 8(3): 193-218.

Bew, P. (2011) *Independent Review of Key Stage 2 testing, assessment and accountability: Final Report*. London: HMSO.

Chamberlain, L. (2016) *Inspiring Writing in Primary Schools*. London: Sage.

Christodoulou, D. (2016) *Making Good Progress? The future of assessment for learning*. Oxford: Oxford University Press.

Clements, J. (2017) *Teaching English by the Book: Putting literature at the heart of the primary curriculum*. Abingdon: Routledge.

Cook-Gumperz, J. (2006) *The Social Construction of Literacy*. Cambridge: Cambridge University Press.

Cremin, T. and Myhill, D. (2012) *Writing Voices: Creating Communities of Writers* . London: Routledge.

Crowley, T. (1991) *Proper English: Readings in Language, History and Cultural Identity*. London: Routledge.

de Boer, H., Donker, A.S. and van der Werf, M.P. (2014) Effects of the attributes of educational interventions on students' academic performance: A meta-analysis. *Review of Educational Research*, 84(4): 509–45.

Department for Education (DfE) (2013) *The National Curriculum in England: Framework Document*. London: DfE.

Department for Education (DfE) (2016) *Interim teacher assessment frameworks at the end of Key Stage 2*. London: TSO.

Department for Education and Skills (DfES) (2006) *Primary National Strategy – a framework for literacy*. London: DfES.

Dignath, C., Buettner, G. and Langfeldt, H. (2008) How can primary school students learn self-regulated learning strategies most effectively? A meta-analysis on self-regulation training programmes. *Educational Research Review*, 3(2): 101–29.

Fisher, R., Jones, S., Larkin, S. and Myhill, D. (2010) *Using Talk to Support Writing*. London: Sage.

Freedman, A. and Medway, P. (Eds) (1994) *Genre and the New Rhetoric*. London: Taylor & Francis.

Gazzard, E. (2016, 24 February) One primary teacher's open letter to the government: 'The standards expected are now untenable' *Times Educational Supplement*. Available at: www.tes.com/news/one-primary-teachers-open-letter-government-standards-expected-are-now-untenable

Gee, J.P. (2004) *Situated Language and Learning*. London: Routledge.

Graves, D.H. (1983) *Writing: Children and teachers at work*. London: Heinemann.

Myhill, D. and Fisher, R. (2010) Editorial: Writing development: Cognitive, sociocultural, linguistic perspectives. *Journal of Research in Reading*, 33(1).

Myhill, D. (2018) *Writing and Rewriting*. Available at: http://www.teachersaswriters.org/general/writing-and-rewriting/ on 17 April 2018.

National Union of Teachers (NUT) (2016) *The Crisis in Primary Assessment: Report of a NUT survey of primary teachers and head teachers*. London: NUT.

Ofsted (2011) *Removing Barriers to Literacy*. London: Ofsted.

Ofsted (2012) *Moving English Forward: Action to raise standards in English*. London: Ofsted.

Ofsted (2018) *Ofsted Guidance: Ofsted inspection myths*. London: Ofsted.

Rose, D. (2008) Writing as linguistic mastery: The development of genre-based literacy pedagogy. In R. Beard, D. Myhill, J. Riley and M. Nystrand (Eds), *Handbook of Writing Development* (pp.151–66). London: Sage.

Rose, D. (2011) Genre in the Sydney School. In J. Gee and M. Handford (Eds), *The Routledge Handbook of Discourse Analysis* (pp. 209–25). London: Routledge.

Slavin, R.E., Lake, C., Inns, A., Baye, A., Dachet, D. and Haslam, J. (2019) *A Quantitative Synthesis of Research on Writing Approaches in Key Stage 2 and Secondary Schools*. London: Education Endowment Foundation.

Standards and Testing Agency (2016) *Teacher Assessment Frameworks at the End of Key Stage 1 and Key Stage 2*. London: DfE.

Standards and Testing Agency (2017) *Teacher Assessment Frameworks at the End of Key Stage 1 and Key Stage 2*. London: DfE.

Street, B. (1984) *Literacy in Theory and Practice*. Cambridge: Cambridge University Press.

Swales, J. (1990) *Genre Analysis*. Cambridge: Cambridge University Press.

Tracy, B., Reid, R. and Graham, S. (2009) Teaching young students strategies for planning and drafting stories: The impact of self-regulated strategy development. *The Journal of Educational Research*, 102(5): 323–32.

UKLA/Primary National Strategy (2004) *Raising Boys' Achievement in Writing*. Leicester: UKLA.

Ward, H. (2017, 15 November) 'Clear as mud': Teachers react to KS2 writing assessment changes'. *Times Educational Supplement*. Available at: www.tes.com/news/clear-mud-teachers-react-ks2-writing-assessment-changes

Wyse, D. (2017) *How Writing Works: From the invention of the alphabet to the rise of social media*. Cambridge: Cambridge University Press.

Wyse, D. and Jones, R. (2001) *Teaching English, Language and Literacy*. London: Routledge.

12

THE TEACHING AND LEARNING OF WRITING: PRACTICE

> ## THIS CHAPTER WILL
>
> • Consider practical approaches for teaching writing in the primary classroom
>
> • Illustrate different writing processes that could be employed by children and teachers
>
> • Explore the use of shared writing and guided writing as key pedagogical approaches to teaching writing

Introduction

At its heart, writing is about communication. Even texts seemingly written for personal use such as diary entries or to-do lists have been written to share a message with our future selves. Much of the writing we do however, and almost all of the writing we ask children to do at school, is for an external audience. The ability to write clearly and lucidly makes this communication possible. It gives children a voice that they can use to share ideas, argue, delight or entertain. This gift is too important to be left in the hope it will evolve naturally. To give every child a voice, writing needs to be taught carefully and deliberately.

Chapter 11 discussed the theoretical aspects of teaching writing in the classroom, before considering the external factors that can shape how writing is taught, including the National Curriculum and national assessments. This chapter focuses on how theories around writing can be utilised in the primary classroom, suggesting a model for effective teaching of writing. It will focus on two key aspects drawn from research: using a process model for teaching children to write and considering the key teaching strategies for modelling writing. At the heart of both sections is a key concept drawn from the writing theory chapter: writing's role as a form of communication and the focus on children seeing themselves as writers.

Writing as a process

The work of Graves (1983) has been influential in helping the teaching of writing to be viewed as a process, moving from an initial idea or purpose for writing to a finished, published piece. This view is reflected in the model outlined in the English National Curriculum (DfE, 2013), which organises the stages of the process as:

- Plan: collecting ideas and mapping out the piece of writing
- Draft: writing the first draft, following their plan, but deviating from it where they have a better idea
- Evaluate: considering the strengths and weaknesses the first draft
- Edit/redraft: an opportunity for children to make improvements to their first draft in the light of the evaluate stage

These stages are likely to be fluid and recursive, with writers moving backwards and forwards between different stages and spending longer on certain elements depending on the purpose and context to the writing. Individual writers are also likely to favour different approaches though, with some favouring making a detailed plan and then writing based on that, and others preferring to get something down onto the page and then polish it through the editing process. For these reasons, it may be more helpful to think of 'writing process**es**', as there are many different paths to creating a piece of writing.

In the reality of the classroom, teachers will find that timetable demands and the nature of their school's curriculum mean that children often work through the stages of the writing process as a group, being taught and supported with each stage explicitly, rather than being given freedom to move through the stages freely. For teachers of writing, there is always likely to be a tension between the degree of freedom that children can be given and the requirement to model and teach each stage.

Plan

At its most reductive, the planning stage can become a simple paper exercise: completing a template or writing frame, drawing a visual map of the text or making a list of useful words. While these activities can be useful for helping children, these are just part of the broad domain of planning. In its broadest sense, the planning phase is about furnishing children with ideas and giving them something to write about. Table 12.1 outlines what planning might be in its broadest sense.

Creating a piece of writing involves a balance between compositional elements (developing the ideas and choosing the language) and the transcriptional elements (the physical skills of putting those ideas onto a page so they can be understood). The author Philip Pullman refers to these two aspects as 'making it up and writing it down' (Pullman, 2017). In the planning phase, emphasis will probably be given to the compositional aspects – forming ideas and thinking about language – although there are times where transcriptional elements might be useful to plan (for example, texts with a specific structure, such as letters, newspapers or some types of poems, or practising forming a particular letter for very young writers).

Table 12.1 What form might planning take?

An experience	An educational visit, a special visitor to school, the chance to experience a sensation such as plunging your hands into icy water before writing a story set in the Arctic or looking carefully at a flower before writing a poem can all give children something real to write about. This enables them to consider small details and gives them fuel for their writing. While experiences might be organised at school, drawing on children's out of school writing experiences and cultural backgrounds can be a powerful factor in helping and inspiring children to write (Parr and Limbrick, 2010; Chamberlain, 2015).

Research	Some types of writing, especially when writing to inform, require specific knowledge – something for children to write about. Balancing the demands of what to write about with how to write it can be challenging, so some research of subject/domain-specific learning can be useful before writing.
A written text	Picture books, novels, stories and poems can all provide a valuable frame for planning writing. This could be through a scaffold providing direct inspiration (writing a class book called *The Very Hungry Tadpole*) or as a catalyst for writing (writing a police statement from the crab in *This is Not My Hat* by Jon Klassen).
Films and images	Film can be a powerful and motivating planning tool for writing, providing 'a cradle to support the development of different, yet related, concepts' (Parker and Pearce, 2002). A short film can be used to model narrative structure, with children freed from the demands of reading. The visual nature of film can support children's descriptive writing and can allow children to explore how a writer depicts a character through actions and dialogue, rather than explicit description. This is also true of still images, whether photographic or taken from a text.
Templates and models	There are many different written frameworks for supporting children to plan a text. These may be based on texts, such as the 'Story Mountain' or 'Story S', or graphic in nature, such as a balanced argument graphic organiser or story map. In addition to supporting children to plan the language they might use, these tools help children to think about the structure of texts – a difficult facet to consider when they are busy in the process of writing. These might also be extended to using writing frames for children to write into directly, prompting their writing in the moment of drafting and removing the fear of the blank page (Lewis and Wray, 1997).
Spoken language rehearsal	The opportunity to rehearse ideas, words and grammar choices through spoken language before committing them to written language is hugely valuable (Fisher et al., 2010). This may be through a formal programme such as Talk for Writing (Corbett and Strong, 2011), through informal opportunities to talk with a partner or through the simple process of saying a sentence aloud before committing it to the page. The relationship between speaking, planning and writing is explored in Chapters 5 and 6.
Drama	Drama can have a hugely positive effect on children's writing, allowing them to explore a character or scene before writing. This gives them the same reservoir of ideas and language to draw on that comes from a real experience, helping them to add depth and detail to their writing (Barrs and Cork, 2001; Cremin and McDonald, 2012). This type of drama is very different from the performance-orientated drama of 'putting on a play' (see Case Study 14.3, p. 253).
Play	Linked closely to drama, is the important role of play. Not only does it give young children a means of exploring their feelings and making sense of the world (see Chapters 1 and 2), but it allows them to explore ideas and language structures, giving them an opportunity to experiment with language before and during writing (Fisher et al., 2010). It can also provide a motivating context for writing, especially where children write in role as part of their play.

At the end of the planning stage, a child should feel confident that they are ready to begin writing.

Draft

Once children have something to write about, they can begin to draft. At this phase of the writing process, the aim should be for children to concentrate on communicating their ideas on paper or screen, trying out new ideas and techniques in their writing, making ambitious vocabulary choices, and employing different sentence constructions – encouraging children to write without fear, understanding that some of their writing will work well, while other choices may not. If writing is approached as a process, with the children as writers experimenting with language and ideas, then writing doesn't need to be perfect at this stage, as subsequent stages follow in which the writing can be refined.

At this stage, children can draw on the ideas from the planning stage, but are not bound to their original plan – they can deviate from it when they wish if they have a better idea. Research suggests that understanding this freedom (and having the confidence to act on it) is an aspect of becoming a skilled writer (Dombey, 2013).

Children will approach this phase differently, with some choosing to work methodically, making revisions as they go and others working quickly and then checking their writing later. Research suggests that frequent opportunities for extended writing are important for developing children's writing stamina and ability to write cohesively across a longer piece (Cunningham and Allington, 1999; McGraham and Harris, 2005) although how long children can write for depends on their age, confidence with writing and the nature of the task itself. This regular practice helps children's transcriptional skills become automatic, so that they can focus more on the compositional elements of writing (McCutchen, 2000).

CASE STUDY 12.1

A teacher with a mixed Year 1/Year 2 class noticed that children were sometimes reluctant to use words they didn't know how to spell in their first drafts, instead opting for safer, less-ambitious choices. Another group of children would get stuck on a particular word and spend so long trying to write it that they would lose the thread of the sentence.

The class were taught to quickly write an attempt at a tricky word, jotting down an approximation and then underlining it before carrying on with their sentence. Then they could find the word later and look it up or it would be picked up during the feedback process. As a result, children were happier to try and use a more varied vocabulary and the drafting process was far more fluent. It also helped to reinforce the idea that the first draft did not need to be perfect and that there would always be an opportunity to return and make improvements later.

Evaluate

Evaluating is the process of checking that the writing communicates what the writer intends and does so as effectively as possible. It will certainly include a child's own evaluation, but can also refer to feedback from others, such as peers or an adult. While this may be a discrete phase, it is also likely to happen constantly through the writing process, with the child reflecting and making changes in the light of this.

A suggested model for evaluation and feedback is outlined in Chapter 18 (see Case Study 18.3, p. 324). Feedback for writing might include:

1. A chance to evaluate independently
2. Peer evaluation and feedback
3. Initial oral feedback from an adult
4. Extended written or oral feedback from an adult

Between each phase, a child should have the opportunity to make changes to their work in the light of the evaluation, acting on the feedback to make revisions to their work. Evaluations and feedback from teachers and support staff should be formative, suggesting possible improvements to the writing, but this is likely to be more valuable when the adult takes the role of an editor, helping children to articulate their ideas and guiding them towards appropriate language choices, rather than simply correcting errors. While this stage should be focused on improving children's work, evaluation by adults and peers should also be celebratory, validating and praising the parts of the writing that work well or show particular flair or creativity. The most important aspect of any evaluation is that children have the opportunity to act on and use it to improve their writing. This is why feedback is probably most useful at the draft stage, when the class have an opportunity to edit or redraft their work in the light of assessment, rather than once a piece of writing is completed.

As with other stages in the writing process, evaluation benefits from explicit teaching and modelling, with time built into the teaching sequence.

Edit/Redraft

The editing and redrafting phases offer children the opportunity to revise their work, identifying mistakes (misspelt words and misplaced punctuation) and opportunities for improvement (the choice of word, a different sentence structure, a new idea added). Editing should be seen as refining and modifying work so that it communicates a child's ideas as clearly and effectively as possible, not simply checking for mistakes. This can be one of the most challenging phases of writing for children, and like the initial writing itself, most children will need to be taught *how* to edit and redraft their work and understand its purpose and value. This might be through shared and guided writing or as a standalone editing exercise.

While it is possible to teach children how to revise their work, one of the biggest challenges is helping children to develop the motivation to do this. For many children, revising their work can be a chore – they have already finished their writing and now they have to go back to it. This is where approaching the teaching of writing as a 'community of writers' is so important (Cremin and Myhill, 2012). If we can encourage children to see themselves as a writer, someone who shapes words and language to create a particular effect, then not only are they more likely to write well, but they are likely to be motivated to want to improve their writing too.

In the words of Berger (2003), children become 'craftsmen… someone who has integrity and knowledge, who is dedicated to his work and is proud of what he does and who he is. Someone who thinks carefully and does things well'.

Some practical techniques for helping children to learn to edit are:

Shared editing on the whiteboard

Taking a child's work (or a piece especially written by a teacher) and then modelling the process of revising it. This approach would follow the same principles as effective shared writing (see p. 219), but starting with an existing draft to improve. During this activity, the teacher can model both changes to language and the physical process of how to look for things to change and how to change them, all the while thinking aloud and making the decisions explicit so children can apply them to their own writing.

Sharing questions or prompts

Giving children a set of prompts or questions can help children to work through a draft systematically, making revisions as they go. Useful prompts might include:

- Does this sentence make sense?
- Have I included full stops and capital letters?
- Are any bits unclear? If so, what do I need to change so they say what I want to say?
- Are there any parts I could move around or remove?

Pens, pencils and PCs

The medium that children write in will affect how they make changes and improvements. Writing in one colour pen and then using another to edit and make changes allows a teacher to see where editing has happened. Many schools also use coloured highlighters for teachers and children to identify effective elements and sections of the text that could be improved. Writing drafts in pencil is also useful, as writing can be erased and changed, although some schools are reluctant to do this as it leaves no evidence of the editing process. If a record of the effect of editing is necessary, then a photograph of the piece can be taken after the initial draft is finished. Then the child can work on their original and the difference between the photograph and the final draft is the evidence of editing. Creating written work on a computer provides a motivating way for children to learn to edit their work as they can make changes, rewrite text and move sections easily. Ofsted (2012) notes that the use of ICT programmes for writing and editing are effective (and sometimes underused) resources for teaching children to write.

Reading aloud

Asking children to read their work aloud, with younger children pointing to each word as they read, can be a useful way of helping them to identify where words are missing or what they have written doesn't say what they intended. They may read quietly under their breath or read aloud to a partner or table group.

Marking alongside a child

Providing written feedback can be useful in developing children's writing, but sitting with a child and making the corrections together helps them to see where the writing could be improved. They can then make the changes immediately, with teacher support if necessary. This 'live marking' might be organised through a guided writing session or through finding an opportunity to sit with a child individually. This approach is time-consuming, so will probably be used sparingly in a busy classroom, but can be very effective where a specific child is finding a particular concept difficult.

Editing stations

This refers to the practice of setting up different areas in the classroom, each with a different focus and then children moving between them in a carousel, having a short period of time to focus exclusively on that aspect of editing. This can be an effective way of helping children to concentrate on one thing and not to be overwhelmed by the editing process, but care must be taken not to artificially separate the different aspects of revising their writing: for example, spelling is closely linked to vocabulary choice and the use of specific language features such as different conjunctions will be linked to the purpose and audience for the writing.

CASE STUDY 12.2

At the start of Year 4, a teacher introduced editing stations to help his children to learn to make improvements to their biographies of Julius Caesar. Five tables were set up, each with a different focus:

- Coverage of the key events in Julius Caesar's life
- Using rhetorical questions (the learning objective that day)
- Reading aloud for sense

(Continued)

- Correcting spelling
- Checking punctuation

The children moved from table to table, spending five minutes at each, focusing on that particular aspect. They were encouraged to work with their peers and there were adults stationed at the 'reading for sense' table and 'key events' table to offer support. At the end of the session, children shared the changes they had made with their peers and some examples were shared on a visualiser/interactive whiteboard.

The approach worked well, and the teacher has planned to keep the reading aloud, spelling and punctuation tables each time, and to change the focus of the other two tables to reflect the learning focus. Over time, the teacher hopes that rather than physically moving around the room, children will be able to work through the different focuses, learning to check and edit their own writing.

As children are learning to become writers, time spent thinking and becoming aware of each stage and its different demands is likely to be useful. This is an aspect of *metacognition*, an awareness of one's own thinking and learning, that research suggests is important for children becoming confident writers with an awareness of audience and purpose (Tracy et al., 2009).

CASE STUDY 12.3

A Year 2 class is going to write a new letter to be included in a class version of *The Jolly Postman* by Janet and Allan Ahlberg. After the class read the book, they talked excitedly about the different types of letter that feature in the story. The teacher has set aside three lessons for the children to work through the writing process, thinking carefully about the demands of each stage. Her intention is for the whole class to move through the phases together, but with enough flexibility for children to work in a way that supports them to produce the best writing they can. This is how two children in the class approach the phases.

Plan

The teacher asks the children to work with a partner to decide who their letter will be from and who it will be to. Shabir and Sian work together. Shabir decides he will write a letter from Robin Hood to the Wicked Witch asking her to stop taking frogs from the pond in the forest. Sian decides she's going to write a letter from Sleeping Beauty to Goldilocks inviting her to a 'waking up party'.

After sharing their ideas, the children are given a simple writing frame to jot down their ideas. This includes space for an address, a greeting and then some key ideas and key vocabulary choices. Shabir works through the frame carefully, responding to each prompt with a mixture of words, phrases and pictures to remind him what to write – just as the class have practised together in Year 1 and Year 2. He talks to the other children on his table to try and work out the tricky spelling of 'endangered'. Sian is keen to get writing her letter, so she quickly jots down an address and the names of her characters. Then her hand goes up and she asks if she can start. Her teacher asks her a few questions to check that she has some ideas to write about and then invites her to begin.

At the end of the session, the teacher stops the children and shares some of their ideas – both for the letters and some of the key words and phrases they might choose to use. Children are welcome to borrow ideas from each other and some jot down new phrases onto their plans.

Draft

The next day, the children come in and begin to write their drafts. Most of the class (including Shabir and Sian) work independently, but a small group work with the teacher. Shabir writes the address and 'Dear Wicked Witch' and then begins writing his letter. As he goes, he ticks off each section of his plan once it is written. Meanwhile, Sian picks up where she left off yesterday, saying each sentence aloud under her breath before she writes it. When she comes to a word she isn't entirely sure how to spell, she writes it as well as she can and then underlines it with a wavy line, so she knows to come back and check it later. This stops her from losing her flow and getting stuck on the word, forgetting the rest of her sentence. Both children write on every other line so there is space for them to make changes later without the page becoming overly cluttered.

Sian finishes quickly and looks through her writing, trying to find any missing words or things that wouldn't make sense to a reader. Shabir uses all of his writing time, using a rubber to make changes as he goes.

At the end of the 30-minute session, the teacher calls the children to the carpet. She puts a piece of writing by one of the children from her group under the visualiser and the class reads it together, commenting on the elements they particularly like (a good line about the magic porridge pot overflowing 'like a volcano') and spotting a couple of small mistakes (including the wrong 'too').

Evaluate and edit

After the session, the teacher looks through the children's work and jots some notes for feedback on a whole class feedback sheet (see p. 324). She identifies that many of the class are still not confident with using the progressive forms of verbs to show actions in progress, so she plans a short session looking at this.

The next day, the children come into class to find their draft letters on their tables. They join the teacher on the carpet for a short lesson looking at the progressive form of verbs. The teacher has created several examples of writing where the verb forms don't

(Continued)

quite capture what the writer is trying to say. She shares these on the whiteboard and the children help her to correct them (for example, 'I write to you' is changed to 'I am writing to you'). Then the children move to their tables to see if they can find any examples where they could make changes to the verb forms they've used to make things clearer. Several children manage this and the teacher stops everyone to share these with the class and to celebrate. The children then have 15 minutes to work through their writing, correcting any errors they spot and making improvements or additions to their letters while the teacher works with a small group who needs more support with this task. The children use blue pencils for this, so the teacher can see their changes.

Shabir spots an opportunity to add some more description to his letter (describing the frogs' croaking as 'deafening'). Sian works with the teacher to read through her work. Together they break some of her longer sentences (with clauses joined together with 'and then') into shorter sentences and then work to ensure that the sentences are correctly punctuated with full stops and capital letters.

At the end of the session, the children have an opportunity to share their letters with a partner, who offers some positive feedback and acts as a proof-reader to spot anything the writer has missed.

Redraft and publish

Not every piece of writing the class does is redrafted, but this time their letters are, ready to be included in a class book. Before the redrafting session, the teacher reads through the class' writing, sorting it into three piles. The first is writing that children are ready to redraft. This group includes the children she has worked with, plus a group of children who produced writing that represents the best they can produce at the moment. A second pile is made of the work of children who will benefit from some written feedback. Here, the teacher works through, correcting key spellings and offering brief points for them to act on before they redraft. The third pile contains a small collection of written work which the teacher thinks could benefit from further redrafting. This includes two children who need support to write in complete sentences and two very confident writers who the teacher can challenging by modelling some more formal ways of phrasing their ideas and challenging them to make precise vocabulary choices.

In the next lesson, Shabir and Sian begin redrafting onto special letter paper, taking care to reflect any changes or feedback into the final draft, as well as presenting their writing as carefully as they can. Once they are all finished, the letters are bound into a class book. The book is delivered to the deputy head, who pops into the class one afternoon to tell Year 2 how much she enjoyed reading them.

Strategies for teaching writing

As Cremin and Myhill (2012) note, in the next lesson, 'unlike learning to talk, which almost all of us learn naturally through our social interactions, writing is a more deliberative activity which has to be learned. Critically… it is an activity which has to be taught.' While much of the vocabulary and language structures children employ in their writing come from exposure to spoken language and through the books that they encounter, learning to put them together to communicate ideas and create a particular effect takes deliberate teaching. This section considers two key strategies for teaching writing: shared writing and guided writing.

Shared writing

Shared writing, where the teacher and children work together to compose a written text, has been shown to be an effective way of teaching writing (Laycock, 2011). The teacher scribes, either on paper or a screen, and everyone contributes their ideas to the process. This might be done through children being invited to share an idea for the next line when they have one, through the chance to talk to a partner first and then make a suggestion, or through writing in a notebook or on a mini-whiteboard and then sharing these ideas. During the session, the teacher moves between this 'joint composition' where they make use of children's ideas and 'demonstration writing', in which they write and think aloud (Cremin and Baker, 2010). When demonstrating, the teacher models the writing process themselves, articulating their thoughts aloud as they write, demonstrating how a writer makes important decisions about the words and phrases they use and how they organise them.

At its most effective, shared writing follows some key principles:

- Children are clear about the audience and purpose of the text being created so they can think about how the words and language choices they make can fit this.
- Throughout the session, the teacher constantly 'thinks aloud', modelling the writing process and making writerly behaviours explicit to the children.
- The teacher makes links between the content, structural features, language and grammatical and punctuation features required to make the text coherent and clear.
- The teacher doesn't just model the initial writing, but also the drafting process, showing the children how writers make changes to their work as they write (and afterwards) in the light of later ideas and observations.

Research suggests that some teachers can be reluctant to lead shared writing sessions in front of a class, worrying that they might make an error or fail to produce a piece of writing that is good enough. This can lead to teachers using a pre-prepared example text with children (Grainger, 2005; Turvey, 2007). While a pre-written model text can be useful, seeing the actual writing process happen in front of them, watching a teacher make a mistake and then seeing how they behave when they notice and correct it are invaluable for developing writers. Shared writing also allows children to make suggestions, having their voice and ideas valued. Often, children will contribute ideas that are equally valid but take the writing in different directions and one will be chosen after discussion and negotiation. It is important for children to learn that often the decision facing a writer is not between one correct and one incorrect option; instead, they may have to make a choice between two equally valid options.

CASE STUDY 12.4

A Year 3 teacher has planned a shared writing session with her class based on the Pixar Shorts film *Piper*, which tells the story of a sandpiper who overcomes her fear of the waves at the seashore. The teacher watches the film first and jots down some ideas for useful words and phrases just in case they are needed in the session.

The class watches the film through once and the children are given a chance to talk about it with a partner, summarising what happened and discussing their favourite parts, with a focus on the little details they noticed.

Then the class begins a shared write of a short, novelised version for children. The teacher's aim in the sessions is to be more than a scribe – she leads the writing, modelling to the children how a writer works as a craftsman, shaping words and phrases in order to communicate a specific idea or create a particular effect.

She begins by asking how they could set the scene, starting with some action.

Josh:	How about 'the waves lapped onto the shore'?
Teacher:	Good, I love 'lapped'. It tells you exactly what happened. I'm going to change 'onto' to 'against' as that's what we tend to say. Are there any shiny details we could add here?
Sam:	There's white stuff on the waves. Is it bubbles?
Teacher:	Great, let's describe the bubbles. 'The waves lapped against the shore, bubbles floating on top'. Can anyone help me improve on that?
Aoife:	The bubbles are like the froth on hot chocolate.
Hanna:	Yeah, we could say 'The waves lapped against the shore making bubbles like hot chocolate froth.'
Teacher:	Great. And let's swap the word order a little and use that idea as a metaphor to make it sound a little more poetic. How about: 'The waves lapped against the shore leaving hot chocolate froth behind them.' How's that for an opening line? We can come back to it later to see how it flows into the next sentence. Now what comes next…

As the session continues, the teacher goes back to make changes in the light of later ideas. In this case, 'lapped' is changed later as the group decides it makes the waves sound too gentle and they want to share the idea that they are strong enough for the baby piper to be afraid of.

Guided writing

Guided writing is where a teacher works directly with children, focusing on a specific element of writing. This might be a shared writing task together, the children carrying out a focused writing exercise or children working on their own pieces of extended writing, with the teacher on hand to offer targeted support as they write. While guided writing often refers to a teacher working with a small group of children, it is possible to apply the same writing principles when working with any number from an individual to a whole class.

CASE STUDY 12.5

At one school, an audit of the English curriculum showed that far more time was spent on the teaching of reading than writing, even though assessment data showed that achievement in writing was weaker than reading. The school decided to reorganise the curriculum to redress the balance. Historically, all classes had a session of guided reading after lunch for 30 minutes. Once each week, children would read with an adult in a small group while other children undertook independent reading activities. The school kept guided reading in this slot for the first half of each term, and then swapped the focus to guided writing using the same model and time slot for the second half of each term. This gave teachers an additional opportunity to support children's writing development in a small group.

Guided writing is most effective where the children working together have a shared need or focus in their writing development. These groups should not be static, however. Rather, the most effective model is one where constant assessment allows for flexible groupings, with children joining together to form a group when it will benefit their progress as a writer (Parr and Limbrick, 2010). This might include introducing a new purpose for writing, such as writing a formal letter (perhaps using the passive voice to show detachment and learning how to lay out a letter); it might involve learning to use a new language feature, such as beginning sentences with capital letters or using an embedded clause to add additional information; or it might be a specific writerly behaviour to practise, such as proof-reading their own writing.

The collaborative nature of guided writing means that children can discuss ideas and learn from their peers. The small group gives the teacher the chance to check children's understanding, something that can be difficult when working with the whole class. It also provides an opportunity for 'live feedback' (see Chapter 18), where a teacher can offer advice or address any misconceptions a child may have, showing them how to make an improvement or how a specific language feature works. This system of modelling a concept and then immediately giving a child the opportunity to use it in their writing can be a powerful way of supporting children's development as a writer.

Shared and guided writing

Both shared writing and guided writing can be planned for different parts of the school curriculum: they may be used as part of whole-class English lessons, as standalone sessions to teach a particular learning objective, or as part of small group work. What is vital is that these two methods are focused on modelling good writing and making the sometimes-mysterious business of writing explicit. Effective writing teaching must also be carefully planned so that responsibility for applying what they have learnt in shared and guided reading sessions transfers to children (Graham et al., 2012; Graham et al., 2016). Modelling how to write well is only truly effective if children can demonstrate their newly acquired skills and knowledge in their independent writing.

STOP AND REFLECT

Read over the principles for effective shared and guided writing in the previous sections and compare them to your current model for teaching of writing.

- Are there enough opportunities for children to see the writing process being modelled?
- Do children have the chance to contribute to shared writing, having their ideas shaped into effective writing by a skilled writer?
- Do children have the opportunity to see a mature writer make mistakes and then address these?

Are clear links made between the concepts that are taught in shared and guided writing sessions and children's own independent writing?

Conclusion

Chapters 11 and 12 have addressed the teaching of writing, focusing on writing as a social act and as a way of communicating a child's ideas to the wider world. The next chapter will consider the role that grammar and punctuation play in children's writing development, exploring both the theory and the practice of effective teaching.

IN SUMMARY

- While most children will learn to communicate with spoken language through their social interactions, effective communication through writing benefits from being taught explicitly.
- Writing can be viewed as a set of processes. Although every writer will have their own preferred approach to writing, which may change with the circumstances and text, teaching children to follow a recursive process can support their development as a writer.
- Teachers can support children to develop the different aspects of writing through modelling, and making use of opportunities for shared writing and guided writing.

FURTHER READING

- For a comprehensive exploration of the perspectives of children, teachers and professional writers on the pedagogy of writing, see *Writing Voices: Creating communities of writers* by Teresa Cremin and Debra Myhill.
- To explore practical approaches to teaching writing in the primary classroom and for advice on creating an environment where writing can flourish, see *Inspiring Writing in Primary Schools* by Liz Chamberlain with contributions from Emma Kerrigan-Draper.
- To consider the act of writing as craftsmanship, see *An Ethic of Excellence: Building a culture of craftsmanship with students* by Ron Berger.

BIBLIOGRAPHY

Barrs, M. and Cork, V. (2001) *The Reader in the Writer*. London: CLPE.

Berger, R. (2003) *An Ethic of Excellence: Building a culture of craftsmanship with students*. Portsmouth, NH: Heinemann.

Chamberlain, L. (2015) *Exploring the out-of-school writing practices of three children aged 9–10 years old and how these practices travel across and within the domains of home and school*. Published thesis. Milton Keynes: The Open University.

Corbett, P. and Strong, J. (2011) *Talk for Writing across the Curriculum: How to teach non-fiction writing 5–12 years*. London: David Fulton.

Cremin, T. and Baker, S. (2010) Exploring teacher-writer identities in the classroom: Conceptualising the struggle. *English Teaching: Practice and Critique*, 9: 8–25.

Cremin, T. and McDonald, R. (2012) Drama: A creative pedagogic tool. In D. Wyse and R. Jones (Eds), *Creative Teaching* (pp. 83–97). London: Routledge.

Cremin, T. and Myhill, D. (2012) *Writing Voices: Creating communities of writers*. London: Routledge.

Cunningham, P.M. and Allington, R.L. (1999) *Classrooms that Work: They can all read and write*. New York: Longman.

Department for Education (DfE) (2013) *The National Curriculum in England. Framework Document*. London: DfE.

Dombey, H. (2013) *Teaching Writing: What the evidence says*. Leicester: UKLA.

Fisher, R., Jones, S., Larkin, S. and Myhill, D. (2010) *Using Talk to Support Writing*. London: Sage.

Graham, S., Bollinger, A., Booth Olson, C., D'Aoust, C., MacArthur, C., McCutchen, D. and Olinghouse, N. (2012) *Teaching Elementary School Students to be Effective Writers: A practice guide*. Washington DC: NCEE.

Graham, S., Bruch, J., Fitzgerald, J., Friedrich, L., Furgeson, J., Greene, K., Kim, J., Lyskawa, J., Olson, C.B. and Smither Wulsin, C. (2016) *Teaching Secondary Students to Write Effectively*. Washington, DC: NCEE.

Grainger, T. (2005) Teachers as writers: learning together. *English in Education*, 39(1): 75–87.

Graves, D.H. (1983) *Writing: Children and teachers at work*. London: Heinemann.

Laycock, L. (2011) Shared reading and shared writing at Key Stage 1. In P. Goodwin (Ed.), *The Literate Classroom* (3rd ed.). London: David Fulton.

Lewis, M. and Wray, D. (1997) *Writing Frames*. Reading: RLIC.

McCutchen, D. (2000) Knowledge, processing, and working memory: Implications for a theory of writing. *Educational Psychologist*, 35(1): 13–23.

McGraham, S. and Harris, K.R. (2005) Improving the writing performance of young struggling readers and writers: Theoretical and programmatic research from the center on accelerating student learning. *The Journal of Special Education*, 39(1): 19–33.

Ofsted (2012) *Moving English Forward: Action to raise standards in English*. London: Ofsted.

Parker, D. and Pearce, H. (2002) *Story Shorts – using film to teach literacy*. London: DfES.

Parr, J. and Limbrick, L. (2010) Contextualising practice: Hallmarks of effective teachers of writing. *Teaching and Teacher Education*, 26: 583–90.

Pullman, P. (2017) *Daemon Voices*. Oxford: David Fickling Books.

Tracy, B., Reid, R. and Graham, S. (2009) Teaching young students strategies for planning and drafting stories: The impact of self-regulated strategy development. *Journal of Educational Research*, 102: 323–32.

Turvey, A. (2007) Writing and teaching writing. *Changing English*, 14(2): 145–59.

LITERATURE

Piper (Pixar Shorts, 2016)

The Jolly Postman by Janet and Allan Ahlberg

This is Not My Hat by Jon Klassen

13

TEACHING GRAMMAR AND PUNCTUATION IN CONTEXT: THEORY AND PRACTICE

THIS CHAPTER WILL

- Explore theoretical approaches to grammar, both in how this area is framed in discussion and how it might be approached in schools

- Make links between grammar and punctuation, writing and children's broader communication development

- Suggest practical approaches for teaching grammar and punctuation in the primary classroom

Introduction

Grammar, punctuation and spelling are sometimes viewed as merely secretarial aspects of writing, somehow distinct from the creative business of composition. In fact, control of grammar and punctuation sits at the heart of our ability to communicate. Appreciating the messages these elements of language convey can be crucial for language comprehension and the ability to consciously control grammar and punctuation enables a writer to communicate effectively, sharing their message in a way that is best suited to their audience and purpose. As Myhill and Fisher explain:

> Words, phrases and clauses are not simply neutral grammatical structures which are naturally acquired, they are the essential semiotic resource for meaning-making in print or on screen. The choice of a verb, the shape of a sentence, the connotation of a metaphor each subtly shift and nuance the potential meaning in a text in the same way that paralinguistic features such as body language, intonation and emphasis do in speech.

> (Myhill and Fisher, 2010)

The grammatical choices a writer makes are an intrinsic part of the message they share with their audience and these aspects affect how effectively the writer is able to communicate their ideas. Grammar and punctuation are an integral part of both written and spoken communication.

As a result, this chapter seeks to build on previous sections on reading comprehension and writing, making links between these broader areas of English teaching and the specific domains of English grammar and punctuation.

Approaches to teaching grammar and punctuation – theory

The first section of the chapter will consider theory and research surrounding the teaching of grammar and punctuation.

Ways of thinking about grammar and punctuation

There are many different views around the teaching of grammar and punctuation in education, and these opinions and beliefs tend to drive the practical approaches teachers and policy-makers take towards this area of English teaching.

As grammar can be an abstract and complicated area to think about, people often resort to metaphors when discussing it. As Cushing (2019) notes, the metaphor we select can have an impact on the way grammar is taught in the classroom:

> …certain metaphors can have radical implications for classroom practice in grammar pedagogy, in highlighting positive aspects of grammar and framing it as a resource for making meaning, as opposed to a set of tightly constrained rules and regulations.

> (Cushing, 2019)

Cushing outlines that these metaphors range from 'grammar as the building blocks of language' to 'grammar as the rules that should inform our language use'. The 'grammar as rules' metaphor suggests a prescriptive view of grammar and punctuation, where different choices are clearly right or wrong and children must be taught the grammar they *should* use. By contrast, the 'grammar as building blocks' metaphor denotes the role grammar and punctuation play in constructing and sharing meaning, implying that there is unlikely to be just one way of being correct, but that each writer chooses from a range of options. People with this view are far more likely to approach grammar in a descriptive way, studying language in a number of different situations and thinking about the choices a writer can make.

STOP AND REFLECT

Which of the metaphors above most closely resembles your own view of grammar? Or are there other metaphors that you would use? Perhaps:

- Grammar as a rulebook?
- Grammar as the skeleton of language?
- Grammar as the nuts and bolts of language?
- Grammar as a puzzle?
- Grammar as glue?

Would the metaphor you would use change depending on the situation in which you are using it?

Another area where attitudes to teaching grammar and punctuation can differ is the balance between discrete and embedded language teaching. *Discrete grammar teaching* refers to the practice of children learning an aspect and, rule, of grammar from a teacher, textbook or worksheet, without a link to a text. *Embedded grammar teaching* is where grammar or punctuation are taught as they naturally occur in the books the children read, in spoken language and as they are used in writing. In reality, it is likely the English language teaching that happens in most classrooms draws on both of these approaches.

If writing is primarily about communication, then grammar is concerned with creating the meaning that makes that communication possible. David Crystal writes:

Grammar is the study of how sentences mean. 'Knowing about grammar' means studying how we construct sentences, and in particular how we manipulate the parts of a sentence in order to give satisfactory expression to whatever meaning we have in mind...Grammar has evolved to enable us to express the most profound and subtle nuances of meaning. It can make all the difference to the meaning of a sentence if we make a slight change in word order, alter a word ending, put an extra word in, or leave one out. So often, the exact point being made lies in the detail.

(Crystal, 2004)

To be able to make choices, a writer needs a good understanding of grammar and punctuation and a feel for how different features can be used. A descriptive approach to language teaching doesn't suggest that all language choice is merely a matter of opinion. Children need to be taught where things are right and where they are wrong: in prose writing, punctuation such as full stops or question marks demarcate the end of each sentence, rather than at the end of each line, for example. But much English language teaching is about choice and the impact those choices have on meaning. Once children know that punctuation should be put at the end of sentences to demarcate them in a continuous piece of prose such as a story, then they can learn about the difference changing the punctuation mark makes to meaning:

- Alice threw the ball.
- Alice threw the ball?
- Alice threw the ball!

(Of course, this example presents language learning as being pleasingly linear. Anyone who has taught children to punctuate sentences will know that the reality is often far more recursive.)

Grammar and punctuation – research findings

Repeated research suggests that discrete, prescriptive grammar teaching with a focus on terminology – for example, undertaking a set of exercises about subordinate clauses from a textbook – has little impact on children's writing (Elley et al., 1975; Andrews et al., 2004; Myhill and Watson, 2014). If grammar is something distinct from reading and writing and is not viewed as an integral part of communication, then its contribution to written communication appears to be limited. However, it should be noted that this is the impact measured on the quality of writing. If the aim of teaching is to transmit a body of knowledge around grammar, then discrete teaching of individual concepts may well be very effective.

Of course, discrete grammar sessions are not the only model for English language teaching. Myhill and her colleagues suggest an approach where grammar teaching is embedded within reading and writing teaching, where the language choices authors have made and the choices young writers *could* make are discussed and explored. This model found positive effects on all children's writing for teaching, with 'a more marked positive effect on able writers' (Myhill et al., 2012).

The 2014 National Curriculum and statutory assessment

The 2014 National Curriculum (DfE, 2013) and the accompanying changes to the national assessment system place a greater emphasis on grammar, punctuation and spelling than either the previous national curriculum (DfEE, 1999) or the National Primary Strategy (DfES, 2006): the previous drivers for the teaching of English in primary schools. In addition to the statutory requirements set out within the programmes of study for different year groups, Appendix 2 of the 2014 National Curriculum details the content to be introduced in different year groups. In 2015, a new assessment system for writing was introduced including a separate grammar, punctuation and spelling test (GPS test), which is statutory at Key Stage 2 and optional for Key Stage 1 pupils. Elizabeth Truss, an Education Minister at the time, described the rationale for the tests:

> Many children struggle with the basics of the English language at primary school, then don't catch up at secondary school. That is why employers bemoan the poor literacy of so many school and college leavers. This new test will mean that children are again taught the skills they need to understand our language, and to use it properly, creatively and effectively.

> (DfE, 2013)

The 2014 National Curriculum doesn't stipulate a model of formal, discrete grammar teaching, instead stating that the grammar content is merely 'the structure on which to construct exciting lessons'. In fact, the introduction to the vocabulary, grammar and punctuation appendix suggests a very different approach from formal grammar teaching:

> The grammar of our first language is learnt naturally and implicitly to interactions with other speakers and from reading…Building this knowledge is best achieved through a focus on grammar within the teaching of reading, writing and speaking.

> (DfE, 2013)

However, research indicates that the curriculum and GPS test have not only led to a greater focus being placed on the teaching of grammar and punctuation in recent years, but that there is more discrete formal grammar teaching on teacher's timetables. In addition, the format of the Key Stage 2 GPS test seems to have influenced the content and approach to teaching English language through the types of tasks set and the published resources available (Stafford, 2016). As a result, students arrive at secondary school conceiving grammar as a set of technical features, rather than as a tool for writing and discussing texts (Cushing, 2018).

Criticism of the GPS test and the subsequent focus on the emphasis on knowledge of grammar and the direct teaching of terminology grammar (e.g. Wyse and Torgerson, 2017) questions whether learning the metalanguage of grammar (the specific technical terms outlined in the National Curriculum) will have the desired effect on children's writing, leading them to use language 'properly, creatively, and effectively'.

A creative pedagogy

The practice section of this chapter will draw primarily on a descriptive approach to grammar and punctuation, suggesting that teachers start from actual language use in real texts and spoken language and view grammar and punctuation as the foundations from which meaning can be built. Myhill et al. (2016) suggest seven key principles for 'a creative pedagogy for teaching grammar':

1. Always link a grammar feature to its effect on the writing
2. Use grammatical terms, explaining them through examples
3. Encourage high-quality discussion about language and effects
4. Use authentic examples from authentic texts
5. Use model patterns for children to imitate
6. Support children to design their writing by making deliberate language choices
7. Encourage language play, experimentation and risk-taking

These principles inform the practice section of this chapter.

STOP AND REFLECT

- Which of the elements of Myhill et al.'s creative pedagogy for teaching grammar are strengths of your existing practice?
- Are there any that are new to you or that you might wish to use more in the classroom?

Approaches to teaching grammar and punctuation – practice

This section considers three practical approaches to teaching grammar and punctuation, each of which reflects Myhill et al.'s principles.

- Using rich texts as a model for language
- Explicit teaching of language features
- The impact of wider reading

Using rich texts as a model for language

An effective way to teach children to be aware of and to control different language features is to share the particular feature illustrated by a rich text. This might be looking at one specific feature, for example using *Time for Bed, Fred* by Yasmeen Ismail to model the difference between statements, questions and commands or *Little Red Riding Hood* to meet the Year 2 requirement for exclamation sentences beginning with *what* or *how* and then employ a verb ('What big teeth you have, Grandma!'). The advantage of using a real text is that it shows children not just how a language feature works, but why. Why might an author structure their words in a particular way and what effect might this have on the message they are communicating?

While drawing one individual element of grammar or punctuation from a text can be useful, the greatest benefit of using a rich text comes from seeing different language features working together for effect.

CASE STUDY 13.1

A Year 6 class was working on writing for suspense, creating scenes where they created a sense of apprehension for their reader. As a class novel, they were listening to *Uncle Montague's Tales of Terror* by Chris Priestley and the teacher decided to share an extract from his short story *Climb Not* with the class:

> 'This time there could be no doubt. Joseph distinctly heard a low moan, as if some kind of animal were at the foot of the tree, but no kind of animal he recognised – unless a bear had escaped from the zoo.
>
> Then it occurred to him it might be Jess; that she might be badly hurt and moaning with the exertion of having dragged herself back.
>
> 'Jess!' he called. 'Is that you, girl?'
>
> But it was not Jess. Whatever was making the noise was no longer at the foot of the tree, but had begun to climb it. He could hear the sound of something thudding into the bark and then dragging itself up, as if a soldier were scaling the tree using grappling hooks. He saw with mounting nervousness that the branches below him were shaking as whatever it was approached.
>
> Joseph wondered if it was old Mr Farlow trying to frighten him, but even as he clung to this feeble straw of hope the thing swished into view. He could not make out any features on the black shadow that was climbing faster and faster towards him, save for the huge curved claws that it used to grip the bark.'

(Continued)

After listening to the whole story, the children were asked to think about how they felt when Joseph was at the top of the tree. One child explained that his 'heart was beating fast and he wanted to listen and didn't want to listen at the same time'. After reading this section again, the children were asked to work in pairs to identify how the author creates a sense of excitement. The children suggested the use of different sentence lengths – long sentences for description, followed by short dramatic sentences (*It was not Jess.*); the use of precise and powerful verbs (*thudding, shaking, dragging*); and the repetition of adverbs (*faster and faster*). The children then discussed how these choices work together to make the reader's heart beat faster. The teacher was then able to make the teaching point that it isn't just the story and the ideas that affect the reader: it is also the way they are written – the grammar and vocabulary choices – that combine to create a particular atmosphere.

Where an author has chosen *not* to use a language feature can be useful too. For example, *Giraffe and Frog* by Zehra Hicks has direct speech, but the words aren't demarcated by inverted commas. Some time spent adding the punctuation in and then writing some further dialogue can be a motivating way for children to practise using a particular feature. This is also true of exercises such as changing the tense of a text. Reading a story written in the present tense, whether for older children such as *Whispers in the Graveyard* by Theresa Breslin or for younger readers such as *Hoot Owl: Master of Disguise* by Sean Taylor and Jean Jullien can help them to think about how the verb forms differ from action happening in the past. After rewriting some sentences from the story to change the tense, they can begin to write their own story trying to maintain a consistent tense.

Explicit teaching of language features

While research suggests that discrete grammar teaching may have a limited impact on the quality of children's writing, a session spent learning for example, what a fronted adverbial is and then completing an exercise to practise using this feature, might be an effective way of ensuring that children are able to identify these language features ready for a test. The high stakes nature of national assessment and the structure of many published resources and textbooks for teaching grammar means that this approach is understandably popular in classrooms.

Discrete grammar teaching is more likely to have a positive effect on writing if it empha- sises the choice a writer might make, rather than concentrating on 'correct use'. For example, considering how different determiners would change the meaning of a phrase:

- *A* car is coming
- *The* car is coming

- *That* car is coming
- *My* car is coming
- *Her* car is coming
- *No* car is coming
- *Every* car is coming

And then how a different determiner means a change to other words in the phrase:

- *Some* cars *are* coming

While each of the choices is grammatically plausible, each suggests a very different meaning. Children might invent a scenario for each of 'a car is coming', 'my car is coming' and 'no car is coming' or they might draw or act out the difference between them. This kind of playing with language can be both enjoyable and help different concepts to stick.

CASE STUDY 13.2

A Year 5 teacher asked her class to investigate the impact of different modal verbs on meaning. She gave her class a list of modal verbs (*can, could, might, may, must, shall, should, will, would*) and in groups they discussed the level of certainty and possibility each conveyed, ranking them in order of strength. The class was then asked to each write a verb on a piece of paper. These were put into a hat. Someone in the class would choose a noun and then the class spent some time pulling out a verb and applying a different modal verb to make a sentence (to much hilarity). For example:

- *The headteacher may melt*

- *The hamster will burp*

- *The monster might tickle*

- *The ice-cream van could cry*

The game became such a favourite that the children used to ask to play it at the end of the day.

Of course, to be truly useful for writing development, children will benefit from an opportunity to use the feature they have learnt about in their own writing to create a specific effect or to develop their writing somehow. That particular feature then becomes part of their writing arsenal, ready to be deployed at the right time. The sooner this can happen, the better, preferably while it is fresh in a child's memory. One successful way is using a three-step approach, where discrete language teaching is sandwiched between a real text and a child's own writing:

1. Analyse the feature being used in an authentic text – if being taught about noun phrases in Year 2, the children might look at a text where these are used to good effect and discuss why the author might have chosen to use them.
2. Discrete teaching of the feature – the teacher explains what the feature is, how it works and why it might be used, drawing on the text the children have read for examples. The children might complete some brief exercises to consolidate what they have learnt.
3. The children have the chance to use the feature in their independent writing. This might be a new piece of writing or the chance to go back and edit an existing piece, making use of what they have learnt in the previous session (see Chapter 12).

CASE STUDY 13.3

A Year 2 teacher made use of the three-stage model of grammar teaching when introducing expanded noun phrases to her class.

Step 1: The class read Super Happy Magic Forest by Matty Long, enjoying the illustrations on the whiteboard using a visualiser. After reading, they discussed the book using Chambers' Three Sharings (Chambers, 1993 (see p. 139)).

After discussing the story, the teacher showed the children the phrase 'agreeable fishing spot' and explained that it was a noun phrase, a phrase organised around a noun (*spot*) where the other words in the phrase provide the reader with more information about the noun in a concise way. She compared this with a longer way of sharing the same information (a nice spot where you can go fishing) and the children talked about the advantages and disadvantages of using both. The children were asked to look for other noun phrases in the text (*Old Oak; an epic quest; the bravest warriors in all the land*).

Step 2: The teacher explained that a noun phrase might consist of some different elements:

*   A word that tells you which thing it is (*a* car, *the* chocolate, *those* apples)
*   An adjective to tell you about the thing (a *sparkling* crown, a *tiny* dog)
*   Words that tell you where or when (the car *in the garage*, the snack *before lunch*)

The children then worked in groups to write some noun phrases of their own for characters in pictures from *Super Happy Magic Forest*.

- Blossom: a greedy unicorn
- Trevor: the mushroom on the path
- King Goblin: the joyful creature sitting on the throne

Step 3: The next day, the children began planning their own quests, focusing on inventing some new heroes. After modelling her planning with the class as a piece of shared writing (see p. 219), taking suggestions for her characters, the teacher worked with the children to write several noun phrases for each character. As an extension, she also devised a noun phrase for the class' setting (the Mega Jolly Mountain of Fun). The children then went off to devise their own characters for their quest. As they invented their characters, they tried to write an expanded noun phrase for each, explaining something about them. This enabled the teacher to see if they understood what expanded noun phrases were, but more importantly it was useful for the children's writing. When they came to write their quests, they would have some ready-made phrases to put into their story, adding variety rather than repeating the character's name each time.

The impact of wider reading

As discussed in Chapter 9, many of the words, language patterns and grammar knowledge children develop will not need to come from explicit teaching, but instead from spoken conversation and the books that they read and have read to them. Aside from very formal situations, spoken English tends to be different from the grammar of English that is so valued in schooled-literacy (Cook-Gumperz, 2006). This means that books are often the key source of different language models, both for individual words and exposure to different grammatical constructions and sentence structures (Elley, 1976). The more children read, the more likely they are to come across new words and new ways of organising them: grammar in its broadest sense. In addition to the amount of time that children are exposed to print, Clements (2017) suggests that the *range* of books children read is equally important. Supporting children to make adventurous choices and read books drawn from a wide range of different genres and text types allows them to experience different types of writing. As observed in Chapter 9, initiatives to promote reading for pleasure can often focus on the amount children read, rather than the types of books they choose to read. Barrs and Cork (2001) identify three kinds of texts that are particularly valuable for teaching writing (see Table 13.1).

Table 13.1 Valuable texts for writing (adapted from Barrs and Cork, 2001)

Traditional tales	The clear and regular narrative patterns support an understanding of story structure and the repletion of key language and archetypal characters allows for a familiarity to build up across texts.
Rich and lyrical texts	These contain 'poeticised speech', which enables children to appreciate how figurative language can be used to communicate different effects.
Emotionally powerful texts	These can draw children into a story, causing them to empathise with characters that they have come to care about.

Each of these texts is likely to have different language patterns for children to draw on, both consciously and unconsciously. Other forms, such as poetry, a range of non-fiction (both in books and online) and magazines and children's newspapers all provide valuable models for language as well as being engaging and, we hope, enjoyable.

Much of the benefit of reading widely will not be immediate; the language patterns and vocabulary often take many years to embed, slowly accumulating like the strata of rocks beneath the ground. But it is a worthwhile endeavour because it is these layers that eventually form the foundations for children's written and spoken communication.

Conclusion

It takes time to learn the grammar of English and it may take many years to reach the point where we have control over the forms of language we choose to use, matching them to our purpose, intentions and ideas. While much of that learning will be implicit, with children absorbing language patterns from spoken language and reading, it is likely that most children will benefit from learning about the different choices they can make, selecting grammatical patterns and language features that allow them to best express themselves.

Learning about grammar and punctuation is clearly more than learning a set of rules. It is through the context of rich English lessons that children will develop their knowledge and ability to use different language features to express themselves. Chapter 15 will draw all four language modes together (speaking, listening, reading and writing), outlining how they complement each other when planning units for the teaching of English.

IN SUMMARY

- While grammar and punctuation can be viewed as technical aspects of English, distinct from composition, they remain integral to effective communication. Control of grammar and punctuation allows children to communicate their ideas clearly and powerfully.

- Research shows little impact of discrete formal grammar teaching on children's writing, but this approach has become popular due to the 2014 National Curriculum and accompanying assessment.
- A creative pedagogy for English language, where grammar teaching is embedded within reading and writing teaching, has been shown to have a positive impact on children's written communication, as well as supporting them to learn the grammar elements of the National Curriculum.

FURTHER READING

- For a practical introduction to teaching grammar, see *Essential Primary Grammar* by Deborah Myhill, Susan Jones, Annabel Watson and Helen Lines.
- For a thorough and rigorous overview of key grammatical terminology and ideas, see *Rediscover Grammar* and *Making Sense of Grammar*, both by David Crystal.
- *How to Teach Grammar* by Bas Aarts, Ian Cushing and Richard Hudson provides an excellent overview of classroom grammatical concepts and how they might be introduced to children.

REFERENCES

Andrews, R., Torgerson, C., Beverton, S., Freeman, A., Locke, T., Low, G., Robinson, A. and Zhu, D. (2004) The effect of grammar teaching (sentence combining) in English on 5 to 16 year olds' accuracy and quality in written composition. In *Research Evidence in Education Library*. London: EPPI-Centre, Social Science Research Unit, Institute of Education.

Barrs, M. and Cork, V. (2001) *The Reader in the Writer*. London: Centre for Language in Primary Education.

Chambers, A. (1993) *Tell Me: Children, Reading and Talk*. Stroud: The Thimble Press.

Clements, J. (2017) *Teaching English by the Book: Putting literature at the heart of the primary curriculum*. Abingdon: Routledge.

Cook-Gumperz, J. (2006) *The Social Construction of Literacy*. Cambridge: Cambridge University Press.

Crystal, D. (2004) *Making Sense of Grammar*. London: Pearson.

Cushing, I. (2018) Grammar policy and pedagogy from primary to secondary school. *Literacy*, 53(3): 170–9.

Cushing, I. (2019) Resources not rulebooks: Metaphors for grammar in teachers' metalinguistic discourse. *Metaphor and the Social World*, 9(2): 155–76.

Department for Education (DfE) (2013) *National Curriculum in England: Primary Curriculum.* London: DfE.

Department for Education (DfE) (2013) *Press release: New grammar, punctuation and spelling test will raise children's literacy standards.* Available at: www.gov.uk/government/news/new-grammar-punctuation-and-spelling-test-will-raise-childrens-literacy-standards

Department for Education and Employment (DfEE) (1999) *Primary National Curriculum – handbook for primary teachers in England.* London: QCA.

Department for Education and Skills (DfES) (2006) *Primary National Strategy – a framework for literacy.* London: DfES.

Elley, W.B. (1989) Vocabulary acquisition from listening to stories. *Reading Research Quarterly*, 24: 174–87.

Elley, W.B., Barham, I.H., Lamb, H. and Wyllie, M. (1975) The role of grammar in a secondary school curriculum. *New Zealand Council for Educational Studies*, 10: 26–41.

Myhill, D. and Fisher, R. (2010) Editorial: Writing development: Cognitive, sociocultural, linguistic perspectives. *Journal of Research in Reading*, 33(1): 1–3.

Myhill, D. and Watson, A. (2014) The role of grammar in the writing curriculum: A review of the literature. *Child Language Teaching and Therapy*, 30(1): 41–62.

Myhill, D., Jones, S., Lines, H. and Watson, A. (2012) Re-thinking grammar: The impact of embedded grammar teaching on children's writing and children's metalinguistic understanding. *Research Papers in Education*, 21(2): 139–66.

Myhill, D., Jones, S., Watson, A. and Lines, H. (2016) *Essential Primary Grammar.* Maidenhead: Open University Press.

Stafford, K. (2016) Teaching grammar and testing grammar in the English primary school: The impact on teachers and their teaching of the grammar element of the statutory test in spelling, punctuation and grammar (SPaG). *Changing English*, 23(1): 3–21.

Wyse, D. and Torgerson, C. (2017) Experimental trials and 'what works?' in education: The case of grammar for writing. *British Educational Research Journal*, 43(6): 1019–47.

LITERATURE

Giraffe and Frog by Zehra Hicks

Hoot Owl: Master of Disguise by Sean Taylor and Jean Jullien

Little Red Riding Hood

Super Happy Magic Forest by Matty Long

Time for Bed, Fred by Yasmeen Ismail

Uncle Montague's Tales of Terror by Chris Priestley

Whispers in the Graveyard by Theresa Breslin

PART 5

VOCABULARY AND WORD KNOWLEDGE

14

BUILDING VOCABULARY AND WORD KNOWLEDGE: THEORY AND PRACTICE

THIS CHAPTER WILL

- Introduce key theoretical approaches to vocabulary development

- Explore the concept of word knowledge, focusing on *orthography, morphology* and *etymology* and the implications of these concepts on vocabulary and spelling

- Consider practical approaches for supporting children's vocabulary development and proficiency in spelling in the primary classroom

---

Introduction

While individual words are just one part of the rich tapestry of language, vocabulary – the body of words used in a language – has become a much-discussed area of education, presented by some researchers as a proxy for wider educational attributes (Hirsch, 2013) and by politicians as the key to addressing social inequality (Greening, 2017a).

This chapter will consider the importance of vocabulary development for primary-aged children, drawing on the research background in this area before linking this to classroom practice. It will also consider the concept of *word knowledge*, linking vocabulary with *orthography, etymology* and *morphology* to support vocabulary development and spelling.

It is important to note that while vocabulary development and word knowledge are important, they are just one part of a child's broader language development. As a result, this chapter should be considered alongside Chapters 5 and 6, which are centred on the importance of spoken language and language development in a more holistic sense.

Vocabulary development: theory

Words are the building blocks of language, one of the raw resources that we draw on for communication. Our vocabulary, both *receptive* (the words which we understand) and *expressive* (the words which we can use to communicate), gives us the means to understand new ideas and make sense of the world in which we live; the ability to communicate with others and to express our feelings. Research suggests that the language skills that children develop when they are younger can have a long-lasting effect on their education (Law et al., 2009; Hoffman et al., 2013; Law, et al., 2017; Pace et al., 2017).

Perhaps not surprisingly, research suggests that a child's level of word knowledge and vocabulary size correlate strongly with reading comprehension and wider reading development (Quinn et al., 2015; Spencer et al., 2017a; Chang et al., 2020) as well as other wider academic outcomes (Baumann and Kame'enui, 1991; Spencer et al., 2017b). These factors are the 'word-consciousness' foundation that prepares us for later written communication (Graves, 2006). As teachers, we know vocabulary isn't just important for children's reading and writing, it is a key factor in their ability to access a whole range of subjects. Beyond academic life, recent studies also suggest a link between vocabulary development at the start of schooling and behaviour and emotional wellbeing and mental health in adolescence (Westrupp et al., 2019).

STOP AND REFLECT

If we say we *know* a word, what does that actually mean? Do we know a word if we can read it? If we can understand it when someone uses it in conversation? If we can explain its meaning to someone else? If we can use it ourselves in a sentence? If we can use it across different contexts? If we know when *not* to use it? If we can write it? If we can spell it?

The seemingly simple concept of knowing a word proves to be quite complicated. Perhaps the answer to each of these questions depends on what we wish to do with the word?

Below are four words. How well do you *know* them?

chair   temperate   ennui   hebetate

Could you:

- read them aloud confidently?
- spell them?
- use them in a sentence?
- use them in more than one sentence?
- give a synonym or near-synonym of them?
- explain their meaning to someone else?

In order to understand a word in a text, would you need to be able to answer 'yes' to all of these questions? How much knowledge of each word do we need?

Word knowledge

Stahl and Kapinus provide a good initial definition of word knowledge, suggesting that:

> When children 'know' a word, they not only know the word's definition and its logical relationship with other words, they also know how the word functions in different contexts.

> (Stahl and Kapinus, 2001)

Being able to understand or use a word in context is the key factor, and for this to happen there are several concepts that can be useful in the classroom:

- Orthography
- Morphology
- Etymology

Orthography

Orthography is the set of conventions for how a spoken language is written down. It includes spelling, punctuation, and use of language features such as capital letters, word spacing and emphasis. Making sense of English orthography is often a gradual process, with a combination of elements taught at school (punctuating different sentences with capital letters and full stops, for example) and learning through experience (such as learning that the /eɪ/ sound from 'bay' and 'make' is often spelled –*ay* at the end of a word, but is more likely to be represented with a split digraph *a_e* or with *ai* elsewhere in a word). While this knowledge could be taught explicitly, it is more likely to be worked out through repeated exposure to print, first in reading and then writing (Landauer and Dumais, 1997; Seidenberg, 2013). As discussed later in the chapter, quantity and diversity in print exposure are important factors in both reading and vocabulary development.

Morphology

Morphology is the study of words, analysing their structure. *Morpheme* is the name given to the smallest units of meaning in a language, the units of grammar and syntax. Every word in English is made up of one or more morphemes. A morpheme can be an individual root word, such as 'fox' or 'jolly'. These are called *free morphemes* – they make sense on their own.

In contrast, *bound morphemes* need to be attached to other morphemes to make sense. These might be a root (the *bio* in *biological*, for example), or prefixes or suffixes that join onto a root (the *un* in *unhappy*, say). Each bound morpheme has its own meaning, but it needs to join together and work with another morpheme. Adding two morphemes together might produce an *inflection* (a modification of the word to change its grammatical purpose) of the original word – such as adding *-es* to turn *fox* into *foxes*. Adding the *-es* suffix changes the meaning, pluralising the word. Or a suffix could be added to change the tense, telling when something takes place: *appear* can become *appears, appearing,* or *appeared.* Combining morphemes can also create a *derivation* (where a word with a new meaning is formed from another base or root word altogether – adding *un-* to change *happy* to *unhappy* or creating *appearance* or *reappear* from *appear*).

Brysbaert et al. (2016) estimate that an adult has an average receptive vocabulary of approximately 70,000 words. Even if, for the great majority of children, these words are learnt naturally through conversation and then later, reading (Nagy et al., 1985), building a vocabulary of this size is still a daunting task. However, Brysbaert et al. (2016) note that if *inflections* are not counted as unique, the number of words falls to 42,000. Once *derivations* are adjusted for the number drops further to 11,100; a far more manageable number. As Rastle and Davis (2008) note, the relatively reliable patterns of morphemes in English allow learners to generalise about new words, drawing conclusions about their meaning and making links with other, already familiar words. This appears to be the key way that our vocabulary can grow without having to learn each word as a distinct item. James et al. (2020) suggest that morphological awareness makes a unique contribution to children's comprehension and that an awareness of inflections and derivations can support reading development.

Etymology

Etymology is the study of the history of words. English has evolved over time, absorbing words and phrases from other languages. Learning about the origins of words and how their meaning has changed can support children to learn the meaning of a new word, make connections to other words and understand the reasons behind some of English's more opaque spellings. For example, knowing that *science* originates from the Latin word *scire* (to know) helps to explain the *s* and *c* representing the initial /s/, supporting a tricky spelling. This knowledge might also support children to understand the meaning of words such as *prescience, conscious, conscientious,* and *conscience.*

Spelling – applying word knowledge

Even in this age of spellcheckers and predictive text, being able to spell the words we wish to use to communicate is important. Fluent spelling enables fluency in writing. The child who does not have to pause to consider how a word is spelled will be able to focus more on the act of composition. Rightly or wrongly, judgements about the quality of a piece of writing are often formed based on spelling – it can be hard to have trust in the content of the message if there are errors in the transcription.

In addition to its importance to writing, spelling has a reciprocal relationship with reading: the ability to match sounds to graphemes provides a foundation for word-reading (e.g. Melby-Lervåg et al., 2012) where a word that has been decoded is matched with an existing word in a child's vocabulary.

In most schools, the teaching of spelling will initially begin with the teaching of grapheme-phoneme-correspondences linked to early reading. Alongside this, mirroring the pathways to word reading explored in Chapter 7, the concepts of orthography, morphology and etymology outlined in the section above will become increasingly important. While the English spelling system is more regular than sometimes thought, English has a relatively deep orthography, meaning that spellings do not always correspond with the phonemes children might be expecting (Katz and Frost, 1992). Morphology and etymology give children the chance to make links between spelling and meaning, supporting vocabulary development as well as spelling, as illustrated in the case study below.

CASE STUDY 14.1

A Year 5 teacher timetables two short whole-class spelling sessions each week. The content for these discrete sessions is taken from the spelling appendix of the National Curriculum. Over the course of the year, children will have the opportunity to return to each pattern or rule many times, helping them to remember what they have been taught.

(Continued)

In this session, the class is learning about word endings which sound like /ʃəs/, spelled –cious or –tious. Before they consider these new spellings, the class looks at a set of words featuring the suffix –ous from Year 4 and work in pairs to suggest the meaning of the suffix:

- famous
- jealous
- ambitious
- nutritious
- cautious
- poisonous

This process of analysing and discussing the words makes it much more likely that children will remember the meaning than if they had simply been told. The class reaches the conclusion that the suffix often means 'being a lot like something or having a lot of something', and the teacher refines their definition to explain that it means being in possession or full of a certain quality, so suspicious is full of suspicion.

The class then quickly revises the Year 4 requirement for –ous. In pairs, the children write as many words as they can using -ous on their mini-whiteboards. As a class, they check their spelling of these words.

The teacher then explains that some words with this meaning have endings which sound like /ʃəs/, spelled –cious or –tious and the root word can help to decide which to use: -cious is used if the root word ends in –ce (such as space – spacious, and malice – malicious). The children then work in pairs to test this approach by looking at a list of words with these three suffixes (-ous, -tious and –cious) alongside their root words.

Before the next spelling session, the teacher asks the class to look for any words from their reading that end with the /ʃəs/ suffix but that don't fit with the spelling patterns studied today. They can then note these down and bring them along to share with the class. One girl finds the word anxious in her book. One boy sees aliens being described as fictitious in his book and is able to work out that they are 'full of fiction' or made up.

Vocabulary – breadth and depth

There are two aspects to vocabulary knowledge: breadth and depth (Tannenbaum et al., 2006). Breadth of vocabulary is the number of words a person knows, regardless of how well they know them. Of course, '...vocabulary knowledge is not all or none, i.e. there are different degrees of knowledge of the meanings of a word. The amount and detail of knowledge of words is often referred to as depth of vocabulary knowledge' (Oakhill et al., 2015).

Perhaps not surprisingly, research suggests that a deeper knowledge of words and their meanings is important for comprehension (Ouellette, 2006). This depth of knowledge includes being able to understand and use words across different contexts and their theoretical definitions. For example, a shallow knowledge of the word *temperate* might equate it with *warm* or *mild*. Deeper knowledge would be that the word denotes a mild or warm climate in an area or region, free from extremes of temperature. A user might be able to use it in a sentence:

> *The temperate climate of Suffolk makes it an ideal place for growing a wide range of crops.*

and know that it cannot always be used as a synonym for *warm* (*I'm nice and temperate in my new jumper*). A deeper knowledge of the word means that it is more likely to be used in formal or technical contexts than informal situations (*What a lovely, temperate morning for a walk!* might be slightly stiff way of proposing a family walk).

A broad and deep receptive vocabulary enables readers to take new ideas and fit them into their existing knowledge. This is true whether the words come from a text that children read for themselves or if they are listening to one being read aloud. One reason for the strong relationship between vocabulary and comprehension is that a rich knowledge of word meanings supports children to make inferences (Cain et al., 2003), through carefully building a mental model of the text (see p. 122).

The relationship between vocabulary and language comprehension is reciprocal, with the two aspects supporting one another. Children with a well-developed vocabulary are able to understand more-complex texts and spoken language forms, which in turn introduces them to new words, further enriching their vocabulary. This virtuous circle is often referred to as 'the Matthew Effect', a term first borrowed from sociology and applied to vocabulary by Stanovich (1986). It is based on the Parable of the Talents told in the Gospel of St. Matthew, with a message often paraphrased as 'the rich get richer, while the poor get poorer'.

This concept of 'word rich' and 'word poor' is often linked to economic and social wealth through the concept of the 'word gap'.

The 'word gap'

The 'word gap' is a key concept in discussions around vocabulary development. This idea originates from an influential US study by Hart and Risley (1995) that suggested children growing up in what they termed 'low socio-economic' households were exposed to far fewer words than their peers growing up in 'high socio-economic groups'. They estimated a gap of 30-million words, a figure that has drawn much attention, and the word gap and its possible implications have been repeated widely in popular debate from politicians to the popular press (e.g. Greening, 2017b; Ward, 2017; Adams, 2018).

Hart and Risley's research has also prompted criticism, with arguments suggesting that the number of words a child hears is not a valid measure of the richness of a child's linguistic environment. It has been suggested that evidence does not exist to indicate that lack of exposure to a certain quantity of words has a directly causal link with a child's cognitive development or that the number of words heard is the primary reason for the correlation between household income and academic achievement, simplifying a complex issue (Johnson, 2015; Avineri et al., 2015). Hart and Risley, and other researchers following a similar line of enquiry, have been accused of promoting a deficit model, where 'blame is afforded to families living in poverty for not living up to the standards of the middleclass rather than on the ideologies and practices of institutions responsible for the material conditions of families living in poverty' (Kuchirko, 2019).

Hart and Risley's methodology has also been criticised, with suggestions that the presence of an observer might affect the conscious language use of different groups and that the language practices of participants drawn from different ethnic groups might have affected their findings (Dudley-Marling and Lucas, 2009; Johnson, 2015).

Subsequent studies have also explored potential language gaps (e.g. Rowe, 2008; Huttenlocher et al., 2010; Levine et al., 2020), finding both significant differences in children's exposure to language in different homes and noting a correlation between these differences and household income and the level of parents' education. Gilkerson et al. (2017) collected language data from 329 families using an automated recording system to address one of the methodological criticisms of Hart and Risley's original study. This study found a significant language gap between the highest and lowest socio-economic groups, although there was also great variation within the groups too, reflecting the complicated nature of the relationship between language environment and socio-economic background. Sperry et al. (2019) also reported significant differences in children's home language environments, but in their study the differences were spread across different socio-economic groups: where observed 'gaps' existed they didn't correlate neatly with socio-economic status. They also suggested that ambient language – speech not directed at a child specifically, such as overheard conversations or speech from radio or television – might be an overlooked factor in the number of words children were exposed to. Criticisms of Sperry et al.'s study point out that it did not include a directly corresponding group for Hart and Risley's 'high socio-economic group', and that claims that ambient language is a significant factor in language development are not borne out by research (Golinkoff et al., 2019).

Where studies in this contested area agree is that some children begin school with fewer words to express themselves than others and some have less experience with the words and phrases, syntax and language patterns that are especially useful to access school life. As Nation observes:

> Language variation in children is complex and difficult to attribute to a single cause. Regardless of the causes, low levels of vocabulary set limits on literacy, understanding, learning the curriculum and can create a downward spiral of poor language which

begins to affect all aspects of life. The prospects for children entering school with low levels of vocabulary are a compelling reason for us to work to understand the way children learn in order to try and find solutions.

(Nation in OUP, 2018)

So, how can teachers go about supporting children to develop their vocabulary and word knowledge?

Building vocabulary and word knowledge – practice

There are three principal sources for learning new words at school:

- Through spoken language
- Through explicit teaching of new words
- Through reading

This section will explore each of these interlinked strategies that provide an opportunity for teachers to support children's vocabulary development.

Vocabulary development and spoken language

A classroom which supports vocabulary development is likely to be one in which children have the opportunity to hear language being modelled in context by other skilled users, with opportunities for guided participation, where support and scaffolds are provided for children to learn about and rehearse different language patterns (Alexander 2010; Littleton and Mercer, 2013). Ideally, this will be an environment where children feel free to be ambitious with language, with mistakes being acknowledged as part of the learning process (Broadfoot et al., 1999).

Alexander (2001) organises classroom talk into five categories: rote, recitation, instruction and exposition, discussion, and dialogue (see p. 73). While each is important for different purposes in the classroom, it is genuine discussion and dialogue that are likely to be useful for both children's language development and their wider learning (Murphy et al., 2009; Siraj-Blatchford et al., 2011; Mercer, 2016). Research with younger children suggests that turn-taking interactions may be a more significant factor than the overall amount of vocabulary exposure, further reinforcing the importance of genuine dialogue with adults who can model language effectively (Sameroff and Fiese, 2000; Romeo et al., 2018). Building opportunities for children to talk to one another, using new vocabulary and practising existing words and language patterns, is likely to be an important way of developing children's vocabulary.

CASE STUDY 14.2

An English subject leader was keen to provide scaffolds to support children to use new words and language patterns across the school.

The staff team worked together using *A Progression in Language Structures* (Tower Hamlets Learning and Achievement Team, 2009) to identify what development in language use might look like and the types of language patterns children might deploy in different year groups. The team used these to create their own sentence stems for different purposes unique to their class. For example, when asking children to use predictive language, younger children might have the phrase:

I predict that… because….

While older children would be given the scaffold:

Because _____ and _____ are similar, I predict that…

These were displayed prominently in each class, referred to by adults during lessons and children were encouraged to use them when discussing.

They then decided on some key approaches to everyday modelling and promoting new words that would be employed across the school, ensuring a consistent experience for children. The key approaches were:

Modelling ambitious vocabulary

An adult would explicitly model the use of potentially new words in conversation, either with the class, a group or an individual: 'the pattern *alternates* between red and yellow – it switches back and forward between red and yellow.'

Recasting language

Adults would repeat a word or phrase back to children using slightly more mature language, introducing a new word or gently correcting an error: 'Yes, he's very tired, isn't he? He's *exhausted*.'

Call and repeat

The teacher would introduce a new word and explain its meaning, sharing an example of the word in context. They would then say the word aloud and ask children to repeat the word. The emphasis, volume and pitch would be changed so the word was said several times and then children would be invited to say the word individually.

Planning for talk

Teachers were asked to explicitly plan opportunities for children to talk in pairs (*talk partners*) and in small groups (*think-share-pair*, to move from pairs to small groups, or *jigsawing*, where a group who have discussed something split up and regroup to share their discussions with others). Each of these would feature key words that the children would then share with their new partners.

In addition to the language requirements of learning in the English classroom, effective practical stimuli for discussion that can support children's vocabulary development include:

- shared book reading (Roche, 2015; Dickinson et al., 2019)
- images and multi-modal texts (Christen and Murphy, 1991; Marsh and Millard, 2000)
- play (Toub et al., 2018)
- drama (Winston, 2012; Lendvay, 2016)
- children's own interests (Callanan et al., 2017)
- the opportunity to play with language – jokes, puns and rhymes (Grainger et al., 2005)

CASE STUDY 14.3

A Year 2 class read *Bear and Wolf* by Daniel Salmieri, before taking part in a drama session.

In the spirit of playful collaborative drama (e.g. Winston and Tandy, 1998), the children took the role of a wolf pack and the teacher took the role of Wolf returning to see them. She told the children about her walk through the forest with Bear and the things that she saw. She described the scene, modelling rich language, including words and phrases that might have been unfamiliar to the children. The children were encouraged to repeat some of the words back, making a simple repeating poem.

She then asked the wolf pack if they would like to explore the forest. The children worked with a partner to walk around the space, describing what they could see. The teacher was delighted that many children tried to use the words and phrases she had introduced. Once they had explored, the pack came back together and shared what they had seen. The teacher praised children when they used interesting words to describe the scene, either language that had originated from her introduction or from their own word knowledge.

Back in the classroom, the children used pictures from the book to write their own descriptions of the woods in winter, drawing on the language they had learnt in the drama session.

For further discussion of the importance of spoken language development, see Chapters 5 and 6.

Discrete teaching of specific words

In addition to the new words that children will encounter through conversation both at home and at school, there is a well-established body of research that suggests that teaching children new words explicitly can be effective for growing children's vocabulary (e.g. Beck et al.,1982; Stahl and Fairbanks, 1986; Curtis et al., 1987).

Beck et al.'s *Bringing Words to Life* (2013) is an influential text on explicit vocabulary teaching. In the book, a carefully researched approach to vocabulary teaching is suggested (illustrated below with examples):

1. **Introduce words through explanations in everyday language rather than dictionary definitions**

    Triumphant means that you have won. France were triumphant in the 2018 Football World Cup. You can also feel triumphant after you've won something – it's a feeling of pride and happiness.

2. **Provide several contexts in which the word can be used**

    The general surveyed the battlefield and allowed himself a triumphant smile. Serena Williams stood triumphant, having won yet another tennis tournament.

3. **Get students to interact with word meanings right away**

    Can you think of a time when you have felt triumphant?

4. **Develop activities that require students to process the meanings of words in deep and thoughtful ways**

    How is the word triumphant different from the word successful? Can you think of a situation when someone might be triumphant but not successful? What about successful but not triumphant?

5. **Provide examples, situations and questions that are interesting**

    'I fell to the floor. My enemy stood over me, triumphant.' What could have happened in the scene above? Work with a partner to invent a story that features these lines.

    (Adapted from Beck et al., 2013)

Supporting Beck et al.'s approach, Nash and Snowling (2006) found that using a contextual approach to instruction provided greater vocabulary gains than lessons focused purely on word definitions. The context did not need to be in the body of a whole book or text, just in an example where the word meaning depended on understanding it. For example, the sentence:

The seagull swooped down to snatch the man's chips.

is likely to be more illustrative and memorable than:

The seagulls were swooping in the sky.

and far more useful than:

Swooping (verb): moving very quickly through the air.

STOP AND REFLECT

Can you think of meaningful examples for each of these words?

- consistent
- interpret
- journal
- adjacent
- behalf

Did you find it harder to think of examples for any of the words? Why do you think this was? What might the implications of this be for teaching children that word?

Choosing the words to teach

With limited teaching time available, choosing the most useful words to teach explicitly is important. In secondary school, the choice of words might be drawn from words judged to be useful for academic discourse, such as *Coxhead's Academic Word List* (Coxhead, 2000) or those drawn from examination syllabuses. At primary level, where the curriculum should be broader, teachers are faced with a wide choice of words to teach. Beck et al. (2013) suggest dividing words into three tiers:

- Tier 1 words are commonly used in spoken language (e.g. *pet, stop, pencil, fast*)
- Tier 2 words are found more often in written texts (*fragile, analyse, spiral*)
- Tier 3 consists of technical vocabulary; the language of the curriculum or specific topics (*alliteration, Jurassic, inlet*)

Tier 1 words are commonly learnt through speech, while tier 3 words are often taught explicitly in subject lessons at school. If explicit vocabulary teaching can focus on tier 2 words, children will have access to these words, supporting them as writers and readers. Tier 2 words might be chosen and mapped across a school curriculum or individual teachers might choose the tier 2 words they choose to teach, based on the texts they teach, the curriculum areas children will be learning about or their knowledge of their class.

STOP AND REFLECT

Read the extract below from *Outlaw* by Michael Morpurgo:

'There had never been a storm like it. The wind roared in from the west one evening in early October. No one was expecting it, least of all the forecasters. The ground, already saturated by a week of continuous rain, could not hold the trees in place. They too had been caught unawares. I watched all evening long, face pressed up against my bedroom window. Still top heavy in leaf, the trees were like clippers in full sail caught in a hurricane. They keeled over and could not right themselves. Great branches were torn off like twigs. Roots were wrenched from the earth, and towering oaks and beeches sent crashing to the ground.'

Which words would you identify as Tier 2 words? Now share the extract with someone else and ask them to repeat the task. Have you both chosen the same words? If not, where do your choices differ? Why might that be?

A second attribute to consider is the utility of words. While learning rich and beautiful adjectives (resplendent, austere, vivid, portly) might provide children with a rich palette of words to communicate with, and is likely to make for an interesting and engaging teaching session, these are words that are likely to be used infrequently by children and might be better encountered through reading or being taught as part of English lessons. Castles et al. (2018) suggest that a focus on words that act as cohesive ties is crucial as they play an important role in building a mental model when children read. An understanding of the subtle meaning conveyed by conjunctions (*unless, since*) or modal verbs (*must, may, should*) allow children to understand and communicate subtle messages, building a robust mental model of a text.

Vocabulary development and reading

Once children are able to read, the majority of new vocabulary they learn comes through reading rather than spoken language (Nagy et al., 1985). In addition to the words encountered, written language has different lexical qualities and a different syntax too, explaining the link between reading and the development of written and spoken communication (Montag et al., 2015; Montag and MacDonald, 2015). Therefore, the amount children read matters a great deal, with reading volume closely linked to long-term vocabulary development (Cunningham and Stanovich, 1998). A rich vocabulary is as much an outcome of wide reading and talk as it is a necessary factor in comprehension.

As discussed in Chapter 7 (p. 109), research suggests that the visual word recognition element of reading isn't solely based on phonological spelling-to-sound correspondences. Instead, it relies on two pathways: the phonological route that maps words on a page or screen into ideas via sounds and another orthographic route that maps from word to meaning directly (Coltheart et al., 2001; Harm and Seidenberg, 2004). As children read, they encounter the same words again and again. This process, called *orthographic learning*, arises where experience of printed text builds over time, embedding the words met in children's memories, allowing for rapid and efficient processing during reading (e.g., Castles and Nation, 2006; Nation, 2017) leading to self-teaching (Share, 1995).

In addition to supporting visual word recognition, this process could also support vocabulary learning. In both the texts children read to themselves and the books that are read aloud to them, children encounter words in context, rather than in isolation. This context – the relationship between words – provides a valuable source of information about the individual words. As a reader meets the same word or phrase across many different contexts, they can amass sophisticated knowledge about the meaning of that word and how it relates to other words. Children who read more widely will not just meet more words, they will encounter them in different contexts, explaining why they are likely to have a broader and deeper vocabulary.

A useful concept for teachers is that of semantic diversity. This refers to 'the degree to which the different contexts associated with a given word vary in their meanings' (Hoffman et al., 2013). This measure of the variation in words' meanings encompasses two aspects. First, it can refer to *polysemous* words where the same word has two or more different meanings:

novel might refer to a type of book or something new or unusual

It can also refer to the variety of different contexts the words might be found in:

impede, meaning to delay or prevent, is a verb that might be used across many different contexts
aerocapture is a verb that refers to a specific manoeuvre a space shuttle can perform to slow down and is likely to only occur in very specific contexts linked to spaceflight

Although impede and aerocapture are both *monosemous* – words with one meaning – impede has a greater semantic diversity because it is likely to be encountered in many more contexts.

Recent research suggests that in reading, semantic diversity is linked to children's word knowledge, with children learning to recognise, read and understand words with a higher semantic diversity more quickly (Hsiao and Nation, 2018). This suggests that variation in context contributes to children's word knowledge: children's vocabulary will benefit not just from reading widely, but from reading across a diverse and varied range of reading material.

Cunningham (2005) suggests a combination of structured read-alouds, book-based discussion sessions and independent reading experiences at school and home to encourage vocabulary growth in children. In practice, teachers, schools and school librarians can support this through:

- building in ring-fenced time for children to read independently at school
- encouraging children's reading at home
- reading aloud to children every day, including texts that children might not choose to read themselves
- taking time to promote and share recommendations from the teacher and from peers
- supporting children to read a wide range of books, sometimes taking a chance on an unfamiliar author, genre, or subject

For a range of practical approaches to encourage children to read widely, see Chapter 9.

Conclusion

Vocabulary development correlates with so many other important aspects of education. It is little surprise that it has captured the imagination of politicians and policy-makers as a silver bullet for raising educational standards and addressing perceived inequality. As teachers, helping children to develop their word knowledge and equipping them with a rich vocabulary is one of the most useful things we can do. This can be achieved through creating a language-rich classroom environment, judicious teaching of words and promoting wide reading.

All children join school from different starting points, with a wide range of language and experiences. The challenge is to provide both focused teaching and a classroom environment that does not reflect a deficit model. Instead it builds on the 'hidden funds of family knowledge' that all children begin school with (Fránquiz et al., 2011).

IN SUMMARY

- A child's vocabulary correlates closely with a variety of different educational outcomes, most notably reading comprehension. While this relationship is likely to be reciprocal with both elements supporting one another, helping children to develop a wide and rich receptive and expressive vocabulary is an important part of primary English teaching.
- Some models of vocabulary teaching can promote a deficit model, where some social groups have historically been viewed as being 'word poor'. In reality, the picture is likely to be more complex. However, for a number of reasons, children can arrive at school still needing support to develop the language of the classroom that will help them to access the curriculum.
- Orthography, morphology and etymology are concepts that can be usefully employed to support vocabulary development and spelling knowledge in the primary classroom.

FURTHER READING

- For a rigorous and principled guide to vocabulary development, read *Bringing Words to Life: Robust Vocabulary Instruction* by Isobel Beck, Margaret McKeown and Linda Kucan.
- For an accessible overview of orthographic learning and its impact on reading development and vocabulary development read *Language at the Speed of Sight* by Mark Seidenberg.
- To find out more about spoken language development and discover practical approaches for embedding a culture of talk and vocabulary development in the primary school, read *Time to Talk* by Jean Gross and *Word Aware* by Stephen Parsons and Anna Branagan.

REFERENCES

Adams, R. (2018) Teachers in UK report growing 'vocabulary deficiency'. *The Guardian*. Available at: www.theguardian.com/education/2018/apr/19/teachers-in-uk-report-growing-vocabulary-deficiency

Alexander, R.J. (2001) *Culture and Pedagogy: International comparisons in primary education.* Oxford: Blackwell.

Alexander, R.J. (Ed.) (2010) *Children, their World, their Education: Final report of the Cambridge Primary Review.* London: Routledge.

Avineri, N., Johnson, E. J., Brice-Heath, S., McCarty, T., Ochs, E., Kremer-Sadlik, T. and Paris, D. (2015) Invited forum: Bridging the 'language gap'. *Journal of Linguistic Anthropology*, 25(1): 66–86.

Baumann, J. F. and Kame'enui, E. J. (1991) Research on vocabulary instruction: Ode to Voltaire. In J. Flood, J.D. Lapp and J.R. Squire (Eds.), *Handbook on Research on Teaching the English Language Arts* (pp. 604–32). New York: MacMillan.

Beck, I., McKeown, M. and Kucan, L. (2013) *Bringing Words to Life: Robust Vocabulary Instruction* (2nd ed.). New York: Guildford Press.

Beck, I., Perfetti, C. and McKeown, M. (1982) Effects of long-term vocabulary instruction on lexical access and reading comprehension. *Journal of Educational Psychology*, 74(4): 506–21.

Broadfoot, P., Daugherty, R., Gardner, J., Gipps, C., Harlen, W. and James, M. (1999) *Assessment for Learning: Beyond the black box.* Cambridge: Universty of Cambridge School of Education.

Brysbaert, M., Stevens, M., Mandera, P. and Keuleers, E. (2016) How many words do we know? Practical estimates of vocabulary size dependent on word definition, the degree of language input and the participant's age. *Frontiers in Psychology*, 7: 1116.

Cain, K., Oakhill, J.V. and Elbro, C. (2003) The ability to learn new word meanings from context by school-age children with and without language comprehension difficulties. *Journal of Child Language*, 30: 681–94

Cain, K., Oakhill, J. and Lemmon, K. (2004) Individual differences in the inference of word meanings from context: The influence of reading comprehension, vocabulary knowledge, and memory capacity. *Journal of Educational Psychology*, 96: 671–81.

Callanan, M., Anderson, M., Haywood, S., Hudson, R. and Speight, S. (2017) *Study of Early Education and Development: Good Practice in Early Education*. London: DfE and NatCen.

Castles, A. and Nation, K. (2006) How does orthographic learning happen? In S. Andrews (Ed.), *From Inkmarks to Ideas: Current issues in lexical processing*, (pp. 151–79). New York: Psychology Press.

Castles, A., Rastle, K. and Nation, K. (2018) Ending the reading wars: Reading acquisition from novice to expert. *Psychological Science in the Public Interest*, 19(1): 5–51.

Chang, Y-N., Taylor, J., Rastle, K. and Monaghan, P. (2020) The relationships between oral language and reading instruction: Evidence from a computational model of reading. *Cognitive Psychology* (In press). Available at: https://doi.org/10.1016/j.cogpsych.2020.101336.

Christen, W., and Murphy, T. (1991) *Increasing Comprehension by Activating Prior Knowledge*. Bloomington, IN: Indiana University Press.

Coltheart, M., Rastle, K., Perry, C., Langdon, R. and Ziegler, J. (2001) DRC: A dual route cascaded model of visual word recognition and reading aloud. *Psychological Review*, 108: 204–56.

Coxhead, A. (2000) A new academic word list. *Tesol Quarterly*, 34(2): 213–38.

Cunningham, A.E. (2005) Vocabulary growth through independent reading and reading aloud to children. In E.H. Hiebert and M L. Kamil (Eds), *Teaching and Learning Vocabulary: Bringing research to practice*. Mahwah, NJ: Erlbaum.

Cunningham, A.E. and Stanovich, K.E. (1998) Early reading acquisition and its relation to reading experience and ability 10 years later. *Developmental Psychology*, 33: 934–45.

Curtis, M., McKeown, M. and Curtis, M. (1987) Vocabulary testing and instruction. In *The Nature of Vocabulary Acquisition* (pp. 37–51). Hillsdale, NJ: Erlbaum.

Dickinson, D., Nesbitt, K., Collins, M., Hadley, E., Newman, K., Rivera, B., Ilgez, H., Nicolopoulou, A., Golinkoff, R. and Hirsh-Pasek, K. (2019) Teaching for breadth and depth of vocabulary knowledge: Learning from explicit and implicit instruction and the storybook texts. *Early Childhood Research Quarterly*, 47: 341–56.

Dudley-Marling, C. and Lucas, K. (2009) Pathologizing the language and culture of poor children. *Language Arts*. 86(5): 362–70.

Fránquiz, M. E., Martínez-Roldán, C. and Mercado, C. (2011). Teaching Latina/o children's literature in multicultural contexts. In S. A. Wolf, K. Coats, P. Enciso and C. A. Jenkins (Eds.), *Handbook of Research on Children's and Young Adult Literature* (pp. 108–20). New York: Routledge.

Gilkerson, J., Richards, J. A., Warren, S. F., Montgomery, J. K., Greenwood, C. R., Kimbrough Oller, D., Hansen, J. and Paul, T. D. (2017) Mapping the early language environment using all-day recordings and automated analysis. *American Journal of Speech-Language Pathology*, 26(2): 248–65.

Golinkoff, R.M., Hoff, E., Rowe, M.L., Tamis-LeMonda, C.S. and Hirsh-Pasek, K. (2019) Language matters: Denying the existence of the 30-million-word gap has serious consequences. *Child Development*, 90: 985–92.

Grainger, T., Goouch, K. and Lambirth, A. (2005) *Developing Voice and Verve in the Classroom*. London: Routledge.

Graves, M. (2006) *The Vocabulary Book*. New York: Teacher's College Press.

Greening, J. (2017a) Speech made by the Secretary of State for Education, at the Reform social mobility conference on 14 December 2017. Available at: www.ukpol.co.uk/justine-greening-2017-speech-on-social-mobility/

Greening, J. (2017b) Education and skills will unlock our nation's talent. *Speech made by the Secretary of State for Education to the Conservative Party Conference on* 1 October 2017. Available at: www.conservatives.com/sharethefacts/2017/10/justine-greening-education-and-skills-will-unlock-our-nations-talent

Harm, M.W. and Seidenberg, M.S. (2004) Computing the meanings of words in reading: Cooperative division of labor between visual and phonological processes. *Psychological Review*, 111: 662–720.

Hart, B. and Risley, T.R. (1995) *Meaningful Differences in the Everyday Experience of Young American Children*. Baltimore: Paul H. Brookes.

Hirsch, E.D. (2013) A Wealth of Words. *City Journal*. New York: Manhattan Institute for Policy Research.

Hoffman, P., Lambon Ralph, M.A. and Rogers, T.T. (2013) Semantic diversity: A measure of semantic ambiguity based on variability in the contextual usage of words. *Behavior Research Methods*, 45: 718.

Hsiao, Y. and Nation, K. (2018) Semantic diversity, frequency and the development of lexical quality in children's word reading. *Journal of Memory and Language*, 103: 114–26.

Huttenlocher, J., Waterfall, H., Vasilyeva, M., Vevea, J. and Hedges, L. (2010) Sources of variability in children's language growth. *Cognitive Psychology*, 61: 343–65.

James, E., Currie, N., Tong, S.X. and Cain, K. (2020) The relations between morphological awareness and reading comprehension in beginner readers to young adolescents. *Journal of Research in Reading* (Advance online publication).

Johnson, E. (2015) Debunking the 'language gap'. *Journal for Multicultural Education*, 9: 42–50.

Katz, L. and Frost, L. (1992) The reading process is different for different orthographies: The orthographic depth hypothesis. In R. Frost and L. Katz (Eds), *Orthography, Phonology, Morphology, and Meaning* (pp. 67–84). Amsterdam: Elsevier.

Kuchirko, Y. (2019) On differences and deficits: A critique of the theoretical and methodological underpinnings of the word gap. *Journal of Early Childhood Literacy*, 19(4): 533–562.

Landauer, T.K and Dumais, S.T. (1997) A solution to Plato's problem: The latent semantic analysis theory of acquisition, induction and representation of knowledge. *Psychological Review*, 104(2): 211–40.

Law. J., Rush, R., Schoon, I. and Parsons, S. (2009) Modeling developmental language difficulties from school entry into adulthood: literacy, mental health, and employment outcomes. *Journal of Speech Language and Hearing Research*, 52, 1401–16.

Law, J., Charlton, J. and Asmussen, K. (2017) *Language as a Child Wellbeing Indicator*. London: Early Intervention Foundation/Newcastle University.

Lendvay, G. (2016) Unleash the drama! Make vocabulary and content come to life. *Kappa Delta Pi Record*, 52(3): 121–5.

Levine, D., Pace, A., Luo, R., Hirsh-Pasek, K., Golinkoff, R., Villiers, J., Iglesias, A. and Wilson, M. (2020) Evaluating socioeconomic gaps in preschoolers' vocabulary, syntax and language process skills with the Quick Interactive Language Screener (QUILS). *Early Childhood Research Quarterly*, 50(1): 114–28.

Littleton, K. and Mercer, N. (2013) *Interthinking: Putting talk to work*. Abingdon: Routledge.

Marsh, J. and Millard, E. (2000) *Literacy and Popular Culture: Using children's culture in the classroom*. London: Chapman.

Melby-Lervåg, M., Lyster, S.-A. H. and Hulme, C. (2012) Phonological skills and their role in learning to read: A meta-analytic review. *Psychological Bulletin*, 138: 322–52.

Mercer, N. (2016) Education and the social brain: Linking language, thinking, teaching and learning. *Éducation et didactique*, 10: 9–23.

Montag, J.L. and MacDonald, M.C. (2015) Text exposure predicts spoken production of complex sentences in 8-and 12-year-old children and adults. *Journal of Experimental Psychology*, 144: 447–68.

Montag, J L., Jones, M.N. and Smith, L.B. (2015) The words children hear: Picture books and the statistics for language learning. *Psychology of Science*, 26: 1489–96.

Murphy, P.K., Wilkinson, I.A., Soter, A.O., Hennessey, M.N. and Alexander, J.F. (2009) Examining the effects of classroom discussion on students' comprehension of text: A meta-analysis. *Journal of Educational Psychology*, 101(3): 740.

Nagy, W.E., Herman, P.A. and Anderson, R.C. (1985) Learning words from context. *Reading Research Quarterly*, 20: 233–53.

Nash, H. and Snowling, M. (2006) Teaching new words to children with poor existing vocabulary knowledge: A controlled evaluation of the definition and context methods. *International Journal of Language and Communication Disorders*, 41(3): 335–54.

Nation, K. (2017) Nurturing a lexical legacy: Reading experience is critical for the development of word reading skill. *NPJ Science of Learning*, 2(1): 3.

Oakhill, J., Cain, K. and Elbro, C. (2015) *Understanding and Teaching Reading Comprehension*. Abingdon: Routledge

Ouellette G.P. (2006) What's meaning got to do with it: The role of vocabulary in word reading and reading comprehension. *Journal of Educational Psychology*, 98: 554–66.

Oxford University Press (OUP) (2018) *Why Closing the Word Gap Matters: Oxford language report*. Oxford: OUP

Pace, A., Luo, R., Hirsh-Pace, K. and Golinkoff, R.M. (2017) Identifying pathways between socioeconomic status and language development. *Annual Review of Linguistics* 203(1): 285–308.

Quinn, J.M., Wagner, R.K., Petscher, Y. and Lopez, D. (2015) Developmental relations between vocabulary knowledge and reading comprehension: A latent change score modeling study. *Child Development*, 86: 159–75.

Rastle, K. and Davis, M.H. (2008) Morphological decomposition based on the analysis of orthography. *Language and Cognitive Processes*, 23: 942–71.

Roche, M. (2015) *Developing Children's Critical Thinking through Picturebooks*. Abingdon: Routledge.

Romeo, R.R., Leonard, J.A., Robinson, S.T., West, M.R., Mackey, A.P., Rowe, M.L. and Gabrieli J.D.E. (2018) Beyond the 30-million-word gap: Children's conversational exposure is associated with language-related brain function. *Psychological Science*, 29(5): 700–10.

Rowe, M. (2008) Child-directed speech: Relation to socioeconomic status, knowledge of child development and child vocabulary skill. *Journal of Child Language*, 35(1): 185–205.

Sameroff, A. J. and Fiese, B.H. (2000). Models of development and developmental risk. In C.H. Zeanah, Jr. (Ed.), *Handbook of Infant Mental Health* (pp. 3–19). New York: The Guilford Press.

Seidenberg, M.S. (2013) The science of reading and its educational implications. *Language Learning and Development*, 9: 331–60.

Share D.L. (1995) Phonological recoding and self-teaching: Sine qua non of reading acquisition. *Cognition*, 55: 151–218.

Siraj-Blatchford, I., Shepherd, D., Melhuish, E., Taggart, B., Sammons, P. and Sylva, K. (2011) Effective Primary Pedagogical Strategies in English and Mathematics in Key Stage 2: A study of Year 5 classroom practice drawn from the EPPSE 3–16 longitudinal study. Available at: https://assets.publishing.service.gov.uk/government/uploads/system/uploads/attachment_data/file/183324/DFE-RR129.pdf

Spencer, M., Quinn, J.M. and Wagner R. K. (2017a) Vocabulary, morphology, and reading comprehension. In K. Cain, D.L. Compton and R.K. Parrila (Eds), *Theories of Reading Development* (pp. 239–56). Amsterdam: John Benjamins.

Spencer, S., Clegg, J., Stackhouse, J. and Robert Rush, R. (2017b) Contribution of spoken language and socio-economic background to adolescents' educational achievement at age 16 years. *International Journal of Language and Communication Disorders*, 52: 2.

Sperry, D.E., Sperry, L.L. and Miller, P.J. (2019) Reexamining the verbal environments of children from different socioeconomic backgrounds. *Child Development*, 90: 1303–18

Stahl, S. and Fairbanks, M. (1986) The effects of vocabulary instruction: A model-based meta-analysis. *Review of Educational Research*, 56(1): 72–110.

Stahl, S.A. and Kapinus, B. (2001) *Word Power: What every educator needs to know about teaching vocabulary*. Washington, DC: National Education Association.

Stanovich, K.E. (1986) Matthew effects in reading: Some consequences of individual differences in the acquisition of literacy. *Reading Research Quarterly*, 22: 360–407.

Tannenbaum, K.R., Torgesen, J.K. and Wagner, R.K. (2006) Relationships between word knowledge and reading comprehension in third grade children. *Scientific Studies of Reading*, 10: 381–98.

Toub, T.S., Hassinger-Das, B., Nesbitt, K.T., Ilgaz, H., Weisberg, D.S., Hirsh-Pasek, K., Golinkoff, R.M., Nicolopoulou, A. and Dickinson, D.K. (2018) The language of play: Developing preschool vocabulary through play following shared book-reading. *Early Childhood Research Quarterly*, 45: 1–17.

Tower Hamlets Learning and Achievement Team (2009) A Progression in Language Structures. London: THLAT.

Ward, H. (2017) Social mobility: £120m pledged to tackle early years 'word gap'. *Times Educational Supplement*.

Westrupp, E.M., Reilly, S., McKean, C., Law, J., Mensah, F. and Nicholson, J.M. (2019) Vocabulary development and trajectories of behavioural and emotional difficulties via academic ability and peer problems. *Child Development* (Advance online publication).

Winston, J. (Ed.) (2012) *Second Language Learning Through Drama: Practical techniques and applications*. New York: Routledge.

Winston, J. and Tandy, M. (1998) *Beginning Drama 4–11*. London: David Fulton.

Wright T. S. and Cervetti G. N. (2017) A systematic review of the research on vocabulary instruction that impacts text comprehension. *Reading Research Quarterly*, 52, 203–226.

LITERATURE

Bear and Wolf by Daniel Salmieri

Outlaw by Michael Morpurgo

PART 6

CURRICULUM, PLANNING AND ASSESSMENT

15

CURRICULUM AND PLANNING IN PRIMARY ENGLISH: THEORY

THIS CHAPTER WILL

- Outline some key theoretical principles around curriculum design and implementation in the primary school

- Explore some of the key drivers for curriculum design, including the national curriculum, national assessment and school inspection

- Consider the link between curriculum and planning for teaching and learning

- Share practical examples of curriculum planning and models from the primary classroom, illustrating the theory sections of the chapter

Introduction

In recent times, the curriculum has become a topic for vigorous debate, sitting at the heart of discussion around educational reform. Across the world, governments and educators are grappling with the demands of preparing students for a global world where rapid techno-logical advances have changed much of daily life.

In England, a new national curriculum, changing assessment systems and a renewed focus on curriculum from the inspectorate Ofsted have fed into the debate surrounding what children should be taught and how this might be best structured. Exactly who has responsibility for curriculum provision and planning will vary greatly in different schools and the levels of autonomy over planning that individual teachers have will differ, but an appreciation of issues surrounding this contested area of education is likely to be of benefit to all, from experienced managers to those new to the classroom.

This chapter introduces the key theoretical ideas underpinning the curriculum, before exploring the external factors that can serve to drive a school's curriculum model for English and literacy. Chapter 16 will then share a range of case studies to suggest how different curriculum structures might work in practice and will focus on teachers' and schools' planning processes.

The nature of curriculum: an introduction

The first section of the chapter will consider theory and research surrounding curriculum and planning in primary education.

Defining curriculum

For such a commonly used word in education, pinning down an exact definition of *curriculum* is difficult. Kelly (2009) suggests that rather than being a body of knowledge and skills that children will be taught, curriculum refers to 'the totality of the experiences the pupil has as a result of the provision made'. This includes both the planned areas of learning in lessons (often termed 'the planned curriculum' or 'the intended curriculum'), what children actually take from these planned learning opportunities (called 'the received curriculum' or 'the implemented curriculum') and the hidden curriculum, the aspects of education that children will encounter while in education but which have not been specifically planned for, including behaviours and values. As Hyman notes:

> The curriculum – informal and formal – is what students will do in their 15,000 hours in school. The curriculum is about the allocation of time; what we think matters. It embodies our values.
>
> (Hyman in Blatchford, 2019)

Other definitions of curriculum go beyond these '15,000 hours', taking into account what children do at home at the suggestion or requirement of the school. In primary English, home reading, writing or other suggested activities to build literacy would form part of the curriculum.

It is clear that a school's curriculum is more than just the things we would like children to know: it encompasses values, decisions about pedagogy and the allocation of time for different elements.

Drawing on a body of work about curriculum going back 70 years, including that of Tyler (1949), Taba (1962) and Ausubel (1968), Wiliam (2013) outlines three levels that are useful to consider:

1. The intended curriculum: this is the specified knowledge, topics, ideas and content that schools plan to teach children. It is likely to be the elements prescribed by a national curriculum which is then interpreted by a school.
2. The implemented curriculum: the schemes of work, lesson plans and taught content that is planned, based on the intended curriculum.
3. The achieved curriculum: how the planned units of work or schemes are implemented in the classroom – what Wiliam terms 'the lived daily experience of young people in classrooms'.

For most primary schools, the intended curriculum is likely to be driven by a number of factors:

*   The needs of the pupils/community
*   The requirements of any national curriculum or core standards
*   The demands of national assessment
*   Any existing approaches or published schemes used by the school
*   The school's culture, as well as teachers' and school leader's ethos and beliefs
*   Time, money and resources

In the reality of the primary classroom there is likely to be tension between these different factors. This may be due to finite resources such as money or teacher time, or to conflicting priorities between different drivers. In England, for example, an assessment system that seeks to measure children's knowledge of grammar as a decontextualised body of knowledge might be at odds with schools' belief that grammar teaching should be linked to expression and communication (Wyse and Torgerson, 2017). It can be a challenge for teachers and school leaders to navigate these tensions. Ultimately, much of curriculum design is about choice: choice about which skills and knowledge to prioritise, which experiences might be most valuable for our students to have, which texts our children should have the chance to read, discuss and enjoy. Curriculum is as much about a school's values as it is about the pragmatic business of organising what to teach and when to teach it.

Curriculum: Underlying principles and ideologies

In recent times, there has been a renewed interest in the concept of curriculum as a driver for educational change, viewing the content that children are expected to learn as a call for social change, and a means for raising educational achievement in preparing children for life in a changing world.

Renewed attention has led to tensions between differing beliefs about what might best inform the curriculum and the ideologies that might underpin it. This section will consider three of these contrasting ways of thinking: 'the knowledge-rich curriculum', '21st-century skills' and 'child-centred progressivism'.

'Cultural literacy' and 'powerful knowledge'

In recent years – in England and the USA particularly – an increasingly influential theory has been that of the 'knowledge-rich curriculum'. This concept builds on Hirsch's concept of 'cultural literacy' (1988, 2016) – the knowledge required by members of a society in order to be able to participate fully in its culture. Hirsch argues that a curriculum built on a body of shared knowledge is a way of ensuring that all children are able to be 'culturally literate':

> Breadth of knowledge is the single factor within human control that contributes most to academic achievement and general cognitive competence. Breadth of knowledge is a far greater factor in achievement than socioeconomic status… That is to say, being 'smart' is more dependent on possessing general knowledge than on family background. Imparting broad knowledge to all children is the single most effective way to narrow the gap between demographic groups through schooling.

> (Hirsch, 2016)

That *some* types of knowledge are of greater value to children if they are going to be able to take an active part in society (such as understanding different texts and navigating the world), is reflected in the early work of Young (1971). Young argued that the curriculum is socially constructed and, as a result, certain types of knowledge are key in maintaining power relationships in education and wider society. Access to this knowledge allows for conversations to include those who had previously been excluded.

In more recent work, Young (2009) makes a distinction between 'knowledge of the powerful' and 'powerful knowledge'. 'Knowledge of the powerful' refers to knowledge that is deemed to have greater value than other ideas or aspects of culture. It has been *chosen* by groups that have power, whether institutional power like governments or schools, or influencers such as particular high-status socio-economic groups. Entwined in this concept are questions around who decides who has access to it and how this knowledge is used both directly and indirectly to include or exclude groups from positions of influence. 'Powerful knowledge', on the other hand, refers to knowledge that allows an understanding of the world or useful ways of thinking that may take a student beyond their lived experience.

In England, the education inspectorate Ofsted have put the idea of 'cultural capital' at the centre of their curriculum-focused inspection framework, stating that 'as part of making the judgement about the quality of education, inspectors will consider the extent to which schools are equipping pupils with the knowledge and cultural capital they need to succeed in later life' (Ofsted, 2019). Ofsted draws their definition of cultural capital from the 2014 National Curriculum, stating that:

> It is the essential knowledge that pupils need to be educated citizens, introducing them to the best that has been thought and said and helping to engender an appreciation of human creativity and achievement.

> (DfE, 2013)

In the context of primary English, it is easy to see how the decisions that teachers and school leaders make about curriculum structure and content might reflect these ideas of cultural capital and powerful knowledge. The chance to encounter new ideas or ways of thinking from literature relies on the choice of texts schools decide to study and the wider curriculum in which these texts sit. If children are given opportunities to write for audiences and purposes that require formal language and 'language that we all understand' (see p. 89), they have the chance to learn to communicate in ways that are likely to be valuable in their ongoing education and in many professional contexts in later life. Perhaps more so than any other subject, the English curriculum can support children to acquire this powerful knowledge through the curriculum choices schools make.

However, there are potential difficulties when applying these ideas to primary English.

The first question we should ask is who gets to decide what constitutes powerful knowledge? Whether a particular item should be included will always be a subjective decision: which books are promoted over others (after all, the curriculum is always a matter of choice) and, as a result, whose story gets to be told? Whose voice is represented as the 'best that has been thought and said'?

The second challenge is the concern that a full and rounded picture of this 'powerful knowledge' might be diluted to become a set of discrete facts to be delivered by a teacher to then be memorised by pupils. Applebee (2002) suggests that the concept of 'interconnectedness' flows through effective English classrooms and that ideas and principles form a web, reinforcing and supporting one another:

> Interconnectedness is an important feature of effective curriculum and instruction at virtually every level, from the coherence and interconnectedness of classroom discussion on a particular day, to the connections across school experiences and between school and home, to the interweaving of reading, writing, and discussion throughout a unit, to the exploration of key concepts and questions over the course of a semester or year.

> (Applebee, 2002)

It is easy to teach children that William Shakespeare wrote *Macbeth* and that the play was probably first performed for King James I in 1606. Children might also learn the story, about the relationships between the characters and even the meaning of some new words, but would this constitute 'powerful knowledge'? Certainly, knowing who Shakespeare was and having some knowledge of one of his most famous plays provides some cultural capital: the 'being smart' that Hirsch talks about. However, in the English classroom we want more. We might want to study *Macbeth* in order to explore those universal themes that reflect on what it is to be human: ambition, hubris, fate. We might want to consider how a character can be conflicted, or the capacity of power to corrupt. We might explore how beautiful language can be used to articulate great ideas: 'Tomorrow, and tomorrow, and tomorrow…'. We might even want to forge links from one text to another, thinking about *Macbeth* in relation to *Julius Caesar* or a Greek tragedy. This web of ideas and knowledge, interlinked and built slowly over time, is surely the rich knowledge that studying English can provide.

'21st-century skills'

While Hirsch (1988, 2016) suggests that introducing children to a foundation of shared knowledge is key to them becoming culturally literate and equipped to play their part in the modern world, other theorists suggest that the changing nature of this modern world requires the curriculum to be constructed with a very different approach at its heart. OECD Education Director Andreas Schleicher outlines a view of the changing nature of education in modern times:

> Today, because of rapid economic and social change, schools have to prepare students for jobs that have not yet been created, technologies that have not yet been invented and problems that we don't yet know will arise…educational success is no longer about reproducing content knowledge, but about extrapolating from what we know and applying that knowledge to novel situations.

(Schleicher, 2010)

This view of the role and requirements of education contrasts sharply with that of Hirsch. In a world of AI and search engines, skills and dispositions become more important than knowledge. With specific regard to literacy, Schleicher continues:

> Rather than just learning to read, 21st century literacy is about reading to learn and developing the capacity and motivation to identify, understand, interpret, create and communicate knowledge.

(Schleicher, 2010)

There have been many attempts to articulate what these 21st-century skills are. Trilling and Fadel (2009) provide one of the most widely accepted models:

Learning and innovation skills:

- Critical thinking and problem solving
- Communication and collaboration
- Creativity and innovation

Digital literacy skills:

- Information literacy
- Media literacy
- Information and communication technologies literacy

Career and life skills:

- Flexibility and adaptability
- Initiative and self-direction
- Social and cross-cultural interaction
- Productivity and accountability
- Leadership and responsibility

Primary English would seem the perfect place to address many of these aspects of learning. It provides a medium in which to work with others, be creative and think critically. In addition, many digital literacy skills depend on the conventional literacy skills that are developed in English: being able to read and think critically about online texts relies on fluent word-reading and comprehension. Writing and creating multi-modal texts such as webpages rely on a sense of audience and purpose and the ability to craft language that is developed through spoken language and traditional writing lessons.

To be literate in the modern world might depend on more than 'just learning to read' as Schleicher (2010) puts it, but without traditional literacy other skills become impossible. Reading fluently and being able to communicate well in both speech and writing are the foundations on which the 21st-century skills can be built. Being literate in the broadest sense is crucial in this century as much as any other.

Criticisms of 21st-century skills often focus on the fact that many of them are not particular to the present age. Constructing the ancient city of Petra would have involved considerable creativity, teamwork and communication, for example. Arguably, the skills are the same even if the medium in which they are expressed is quite different from today. The other criticism levelled at a skill-based curriculum model is that it is not possible to learn and practise these skills in a vacuum. They need a context and that context itself matters. As Willingham suggests:

> Thinking well requires knowing facts, and that's true not simply because you need something to think *about*. The very processes that teachers care about most – critical thinking processes such as reasoning and problem solving – are intimately intertwined with factual knowledge that is stored in long-term memory.

(Willingham, 2009)

Creativity, for example, is very difficult without a sound knowledge of the field in which you are producing ideas. When writing an adventure story, children will draw on their knowledge of that genre of writing and the stories they know already, their understanding of the structure these texts often employ, and the different language patterns that are likely to be useful to express their ideas effectively. The relationship between skills and knowledge is reciprocal.

Starting with the child

Both approaches to curriculum – powerful knowledge or 21st-century skills – take what is to be learnt as the starting point. Other traditions in education suggest that learning should begin with the child instead.

'Child-centred progressivism', often shortened to 'progressivism' or 'a progressivist approach', has its roots in the ideas of the 18th-century philosopher Rousseau, although it is Dewey who most famously applied these ideas to education at the start of the 20th century. Dewey (1902) argued that children were not passive recipients of education, there to be shaped and moulded by teachers with a curriculum detached from their lives and wider society. Working from the assumption that a child has no existing knowledge, skills or interests prior to being introduced to the curriculum was doing them a disservice:

> To retain the belief that the child understands nothing important about mathematics, language, history, art, music, and science is a prejudice or prejudgement that needs to be abandoned. We find in the experience of children the rudiments of ideas that leads to a formal study of nearly all subjects.

> (Dewey, 1902)

To Dewey, the child and their knowledge and their interests provided the starting point for learning. This was not just because their interests were likely to be motivating and engaging, but because they form a bridge between human knowledge and a child's lived experience. Schooling is not merely preparation for life; it *is* part of life.

Building on this desire to put children at the centre of curriculum planning, in his later writings Dewey championed the key role teachers had to play in linking children's interests to their educational development and experiences, seeking to reframe the relationship between the knowledge and skills shared by the curriculum and the interests of children (Dewey, 1938). Rather than be seen as divergent starting points set in opposition, these were areas which could mutually strengthen one another.

In primary English, the benefits of planning learning, building on the interests of children, would appear obvious. In reading, research has shown that choice plays an important factor in children's motivation to read, and, in turn, motivation is correlated strongly with achievement (Clark and Rumbold, 2006; Gambrell, 2011). While there is a need to introduce children to new texts, authors and ideas, the use of texts that they have knowledge of already – familiar authors, non-fiction and multi-modal texts about subjects that reflect their interests – is likely to play an important part in the classroom diet of reading aloud, independent reading and even the books studied in English or reading sessions. With writing, skilful communication often depends as much on the *what* (the subject matter) as it does on the *how* (the writer's craft). Giving children a chance to write about their interests or areas in which they are knowledgeable allows them to draw on their existing schema of ideas and language. Building opportunities for children to write about their interests also helps them to see themselves as writers, people with an authentic voice that deserves to be heard (see Chapters 11 and 12).

However, critics of the progressivist approach argue that it has led to declining standards in education:

> ...for the idealistic teacher, it seems axiomatic that granting our pupils more freedom, more independence and more autonomy will result in improved learning. However, this victory in the intellectual battle has been matched only by failure in practice.

> (Peal, 2014)

The principal criticism is that starting from children's own interests leads to low expectations for children as they are confined to their current field of experience without having the opportunity to experience new spheres of knowledge. As Amis famously wrote in the *Black Papers*:

> A student, being (if anything) engaged in the acquiring of knowledge, is not in a position to decide which bits of knowledge it is best for him to acquire, or how his performance in the acquisition of knowledge can most properly be assessed, or who is qualified to help him in this activity... Who can understand the importance of Roman law, or anatomy, or calculus, if he has not mastered them?

> (Amis, 1967)

The tension between a progressivist, child-centred approach to education and a more traditional approach (with the teacher and intended curriculum at the centre) has been a feature of education debate for more than a century. The same is true of discussion around a curriculum built on a body of knowledge or a set of transferable skills.

STOP AND REFLECT

After reading the sections above about rich knowledge, 21st-century skills and progressivism, consider the following questions:

- Is there one view that resonates with you particularly?
- What would someone who held the opposite belief say to you?
- Do you disagree strongly with any of these perspectives on curriculum?
- Are the three viewpoints necessarily in opposition? Would it be possible to design a curriculum based on rich knowledge and 21st-century skills? Could a curriculum be child-centred and progressive, yet also designed to build cultural capital?

Planning: the curriculum in practice

These theoretical starting points, whether explicitly stated or working below the level of conscious planning, will inform the decisions a teacher or school leader will make around the structure of their curriculum model. However, it is the classroom execution, the planning of *how* the curriculum will be organised for teaching that is often discussed. This is the focus of the next section.

Curriculum vehicles

One way to consider the English curriculum is to think of it as a set of 'vehicles' that can be used to introduce children to key knowledge, skills and characteristics from the intended curriculum and then practise these. The vehicles used to structure English in the primary classroom will often include:

- English lessons
- small group reading
- whole-class shared reading
- children's independent reading
- reading aloud to children
- discrete phonics sessions
- drama and structured play
- one-to-one reading
- shared writing
- guided writing
- discrete grammar and punctuation teaching
- standalone spelling teaching
- cross-curricular links to English
- homework

STOP AND REFLECT

Look at the list of different vehicles used for teaching primary English above.

- Which do you currently use successfully in your classroom?
- Which are under-used or not used at all?
- Do the vehicles you employ to teach English work together as a cohesive whole?

These individual vehicles can be planned separately; however, for them to work as a cohesive curriculum, they benefit from being thought about as an integrated whole. A well-planned curriculum functions like an ecosystem, with the success of each element depending on its relationship with other parts.

Planning for primary English

In schools, the process of planning is usually divided into three tiers: long-term planning, medium-term planning and short-term planning.

Long-term planning, in conjunction with a school's English policy, sets the vision for English teaching and outlines the aspects of the curriculum that will be covered in each year group. This long-term plan may be built around:

- different genres of writing that children will read and write (instructional writing; non-chronological reports; narrative poetry)
- different texts children will study (*The Iron Man*; a study of the poet Joseph Coelho)
- key skills that children will master (aspects of reading, writing, spoken communication, etc.)
- experiences that children should have (performing a poem aloud, making a book of an adventure story, visiting a theatre and watching a play, etc.)

In most schools, long-term planning is built around a combination of these. Chapter 16 provides examples of long-term plans for English to compare.

Medium-term planning is the level of individual units of teaching. These units might last anywhere between a week and half a term. They could be built around:

- a broad area of English learning (e.g. researching a topic, preparing arguments, and then holding a debate)
- a genre or text type (e.g. learning the features of newspaper reports and then writing one)
- a book, poem or other text (e.g. reading *Fireweed* by Jill Paton Walsh and then writing an adventure story set during the blitz)
- a particular purpose (e.g. writing to persuade)
- a cross-curricular link (e.g. reading and writing about life in Roman Britain)
- an event or occasion (e.g. thank you letters to be sent to an author who has visited the school)

The level of detail in medium-term plans will differ depending on their precise use and the teacher's planning style. They may present a broad overview of the elements to be taught, which will then inform short-term planning such as weekly plans or even individual lesson plans. It may be that the medium-term unit plans are the lowest level of planning for a school and teacher's teach directly from them.

The need for short-term planning, whether weekly plans or lesson plans, will depend on the school's expectations and individual teachers' preferences. Many teachers prefer to teach directly from a unit plan, spending the time on lesson preparation and resourcing. For other teachers, especially those less experienced in an area, short-term planning is invaluable. In England, the Department for Education and Ofsted have identified producing detailed lesson plans as a significant factor in teacher workload and both have confirmed that creating short-term plans is not expected and only undertaken if the teacher feels it will help them in the classroom (DfE, 2018; Ofsted, 2018). While this has been broadly well received by the teaching profession (NEU, 2018), the argument has been made that teachers who are still developing their practice, most notably ITT students or newly qualified teachers, may well benefit from short-term planning, thinking through the aims and strategies that will be employed in the lesson (Daly, 2018).

While the specific structure and the relationship between long-, medium- and short-term planning will vary from school to school, the underlying principles that underpin them is likely to be similar. Planning begins from an intention (what we want children to learn or practise), before considering how teaching and learning can be structured to ensure this happens as effectively and meaningfully as possible. This practical process for planning forms the basis of Chapter 16.

Conclusion

The curriculum – the *what* of teaching – is intrinsically linked with pedagogy – the *how*. Together, these two elements provide the structure that the day-to-day business of teaching is built upon. This chapter has introduced key elements of theory around curriculum, offering a definition for curriculum and then exploring some of the principal ideologies and viewpoints that inform current curriculum debate.

Chapter 16 will apply this theory to classroom practice, sharing examples of differing curriculum models and planning, whilst exploring the factors that support successful planning for English.

IN SUMMARY

- The planning of a school's curriculum involves choices around what will be included, what must be omitted, how teaching and learning will be structured, and around the perceived priorities for the children the school serves.
- Three ideological starting points for thinking about curriculum are: 'powerful knowledge', where a certain body of knowledge should be prioritised because it allows children to make sense of the world and join in national and international conversations; '21st-century skills',

where the transferable skills that may be needed for life in the modern world are seen as the most important aspects of education; and 'child-centred progressivism', where the starting point for the curriculum is not external content such as knowledge or skills, but the interests and current knowledge of the children themselves.

- In practice, the curriculum can be viewed as a set of interlinked vehicles that work together to enable the curriculum. These will be planned for through long-term plans which provide a curriculum overview, medium-term plans that translate this into units of work and short-term plans at the level of individual lesson or weekly plans.

FURTHER READING

- To find an overview of curriculum research and a set of principles for effective curriculum planning, read Dylan Wiliam's *Redesigning Schooling: Principled Curriculum Design.*
- To hear the case for the knowledge-rich curriculum, read E.D Hirsch's *The Schools We Need: And Why We Don't Have Them.* For information about 'powerful knowledge', see *Bringing Knowledge Back In* by Michael Young. *21st Century Skills: Learning for life in our times* by Trilling and Fadel provides an introduction to this school of thought. See *Progressive Education: A critical introduction* by John Howlett for a thorough overview of the history and ideas that underpin progressivism and Robert Peal's *Progressively Worse* for a critique of progressive education.

REFERENCES

Applebee, A. (2002) Engaging students in the disciplines of English: What are effective schools doing? *The English Journal*, 91(6): 30–6.

Amis, K. (1967) Pernicious participation. In C.B. Cox and A.E. Dyson (Eds), *Black Paper 1: The Fight for Education*. London: Critical Quarterly Society.

Ausubel, D.P. (1968) *Educational Psychology: A cognitive view*. New York: Holt, Rinehart & Winston.

Blatchford, R. (Ed) (2019) *The Primary Curriculum Leader's Handbook*. Woodbridge: John Catt.

Clark, C. and Rumbold, K. (2006) *Reading for Pleasure: A Research Overview*. London: National Literacy Trust.

Daly, C. (2018) *DFE advice on student teacher workload misses what is learnt by planning lessons.* Available at: https://ioelondonblog.wordpress.com/2018/11/09/dfe-advice-on-student-teacher-workload-misses-what-is-learnt-by-planning-lessons/ (accessed 31/10/19).

Dewey, J. (1902) *The Child and the Curriculum*. Chicago. University of Chicago Press.

Dewey, J. (1938) *Experience and Education*. New York: Macmillan Company.

Department for Education (DfE) (2013) *National Curriculum in England: Primary Curriculum*. London: DfE.

Department for Education (DfE) (2018) *School Workload Reduction Toolkit*. London: DfE.

Gambrell, L. (2011) Seven rules of engagement: What's most important to know about motivation to read. *The Reading Teacher*, 65(3): 172–8.

Hirsch, E.D. (1988) *Cultural Literacy: What every American needs to know*. New York: Vintage Books.

Hirsch, E.D. (1999) *The Schools We Need: And Why We Don't Have Them*. New York: Anchor Books.

Hirsch, E.D, (2016) *Why Knowledge Matters*. Cambridge, MA: Harvard University Press.

Howlett, J. (2013) *Progressive Education: A critical introduction*. London: Bloomsbury Academic.

Kelly, A. V. (2009) *The Curriculum: Theory and Practice* (6th Ed.). London: Sage.

National Education Union (2018) *Ofsted guidance on Ofsted myths*. Available at: www.teachers.org.uk/education-policies/ofsted-estyn/clarification-schools (accessed 31/10/19).

Ofsted (2018) *Ofsted Inspections: Myths*. London: HMSO.

Ofsted (2019) *School Inspection Handbook*. London: HMSO.

Peal, R. (2014) *Progressively Worse: The burden of bad ideas in British schools*. London: Civitas.

Schleicher, A. (2010) The case for twenty first century learning. Available at: www.oecd.org/general/thecasefor21st- centurylearning.htm (accessed 29/10/19).

Taba, H. (1962) *Curriculum Development: Theory and practice*. New York: Harcourt Brace Jovanovich.

Trilling, B. and Fadel, C. (2009) *21st Century Skills: Learning for life in our times*. San Francisco, CA: Jossey-Bass.

Tyler, R.W. (1949) *Basic Principles of Curriculum and Instruction*. Chicago, IL: University of Chicago Press.

Wiliam, D. (2013) *Redesigning Schooling: Principled Curriculum Design*. London: SSAT.

Willingham, D. T. (2009) *Why Don't Students Like School?* San Francisco, CA: Jossey-Bass.

Wyse, D. and Torgerson, C. (2017) Experimental trials and 'what works?' in education: The case of grammar for writing. *British Educational Research Journal*, 43(6): 1019–47.

Young, M.F.D. (1971) *Knowledge and Control*. London: Collier Macmillan.

Young, M.F.D. (2009) *Bringing Knowledge Back In: From social constructivism to social realism in the sociology of education*. London: Routledge.

LITERATURE

Macbeth by William Shakespeare

Fireweed by Jill Paton Walsh

The Iron Man by Ted Hughes

16

CURRICULUM AND PLANNING IN PRIMARY ENGLISH: PRACTICE

THIS CHAPTER WILL

- Illustrate the key theoretical concepts from Chapter 15 with regard to classroom practice

- Introduce the different levels of planning, considering key factors for each

---

Introduction

The curriculum, the *what* of primary English, is closely linked to pedagogy, the *how* of different approaches to ensure children learn. As discussed in Chapter 15, curriculum is not merely a body of knowledge or a set of skills, it represents the values and beliefs that we have about the purpose of education. A school's curriculum (and the body of planning which brings it to life in the classroom) is likely to be organic, changing to meet the demands of the national picture, educators' own ideas, research which informs classroom practice and, most importantly, the needs of the children that we teach.

This chapter will consider the practical business of designing and implementing a curriculum, brought to life through the planning process. While many sources of off-the-shelf planning exist – published schemes from professional companies, downloadable plans shared by other teachers online, or books detailing a specific approach – the process of planning is likely to be a personal one.

Curriculum intent

The *intended curriculum* (Wiliam, 2013) refers to knowledge and skills that schools wish children to leave with, the experiences they would like them to have and the behaviours and dispositions they will develop. These are often expressed as a set of broad aims (often laid out in an English policy or vision statement), before being applied in long-term and medium-term plans.

These curriculum aims will often be unique to the school; however, they should reflect the demands of the national curriculum for the region the school serves. The 2014 National Curriculum for English states that all pupils in England should:

- read easily, fluently and with good understanding
- develop the habit of reading widely and often, for both pleasure and information
- acquire a wide vocabulary, an understanding of grammar and knowledge of linguistic conventions for reading, writing and spoken language
- appreciate our rich and varied literary heritage
- write clearly, accurately and coherently, adapting their language and style in and for a range of contexts, purposes and audiences
- use discussion in order to learn; they should be able to elaborate and explain clearly their understanding and ideas
- be competent in the arts of speaking and listening, making formal presentations, demonstrating to others and participating in debate

(DfE, 2013)

STOP AND REFLECT

Look at the aims stated for the English National Curriculum.

- To what extent do you think these aims reflect your vision of English learning in primary schools?
- Are there any aims that you think are missing from the list that you would wish to see in your school?
- Are there any aims that you would amend to include another focus or express differently?
- If a child met all of these aims, to what extent would they be ready for secondary school and later life?

Long-term planning

Once the aims of the curriculum have been decided, they can be plotted onto a long-term curriculum map. The composition of these maps will vary greatly from school to school, both in detail and structure. For example, a small village school with mixed classes will require a rolling structure so children do not cover the same content and experiences each year. Some long-term plans cover only English lessons, while others seek to map all of the *curriculum vehicles* through which English is taught (see Chapter 15).

Long-term plans might begin with the types of writing children will learn about: different types of fiction, a variety of non-fiction genres, and different types of poetry. Figure 16.1 gives an example of this common approach.

Table 16.1   Example long-term English plan using types of writing

Year Three

	Autumn	Spring	Summer
Fiction	Fables (2 weeks) Stories Set in the Past (2 weeks)	Stories Set in Our Community (2 weeks) Playscripts (2 weeks)	Stories From Across the World (3 weeks) Myths and Legends (2 weeks)
Non-fiction	Instructions and Explanations (2 weeks) Information Texts (2 weeks)	Recounts (2 weeks) Reports (2 weeks)	Persuasive Writing (3 weeks)
Poetry	Creating Images (2 weeks) List Poems and Kennings (1 week)	Narrative Poems (3 weeks) Poems to Perform (1 week)	Performance Poetry (2 weeks)

Alternatively, in a text-based curriculum, long-term planning might specify the texts to study. With this approach there is often a tension surrounding who decides which books should be on the curriculum. If the texts to be studied in each year group are chosen by school leaders, it allows for progression across year groups and ensures that the texts children read have been carefully chosen with a clear rationale. However, this level of control can be counter-productive to good teaching as it could prevent knowledgeable, skilful and enthusiastic teachers from using texts that they know well and are excited about using.

Curriculum models built on Hirsch's concept of 'cultural literacy' (1987, 2016) have grown in popularity in England and the USA in recent years (see Chapter 15). This approach tends to emphasise the need for subjects to be taught as distinct domains of knowledge, each with its own traditions, ways of thinking and body of knowledge. Subjects such as the humanities and science are broken into detailed schemes covering the concepts and information teachers wish children to learn. In English, a knowledge-rich curriculum often manifests around two areas: the choice of literature children read and study, with schools attempting to introduce 'the best that has been thought and said' (Arnold, 1875), and through traditional approaches to teaching English language, especially grammar, punctuation and standard dialect forms (often presented as 'Standard English'). With regard to the choice of texts children will read and study, pinning down 'the best...' can be a challenge. Chapter 10 addresses choice of texts comprehensively, but when considering the texts that might be selected for reason of cultural capital, these might fall into three broad categories:

Literary heritage texts

These are 'famous writings from the past which still influence the present' (Cox, 2014) and are often the texts that are thought of when discussing cultural capital. In the primary classroom, this could mean poems such as *The Eagle* by Tennyson; children's classics such as *Treasure Island* or *Tom's Midnight Garden*; retellings of classics for older readers such as Leon Garfield's *Shakespeare Stories* or Geraldine McCaughrean's retelling of *Moby Dick*, or myths and legends from across the world such as the stories from India in *A Jar of Pickles and a Pinch of Justice* by Chitra Soundar or the British and Irish folktales collected in Kevin Crossley-Holland's *Between Worlds*. These texts resonate beyond the books themselves, and readers will find them referenced in other media, encountering the ideas, narrative structures and characters again and again in other books, in films and on television. Giving children access to these stories gives them access to a world of rich knowledge and allows them to make sense of and accumulate a greater understanding of the world.

Books that support an understanding of the world

These are texts that introduce children to the 'powerful knowledge' (Young, 2009) that is useful to make sense of the world and to be able to understand references from many different sources. This might include books that develop knowledge of the humanities, such as *Little People, Big Dreams: Emmeline Pankhurst* by Lisbeth Kaiser and Ana Sanfelippo; the illustrated edition of *The Silk Roads* by Peter Frankopan and Neil Packer or books that make key theories accessible such as *On the Origin of Species* retold by Sabina Radeva.

Books that introduce a big idea

While the first two categories are probably well established as texts for building cultural capital, the third is perhaps less obvious. These are the texts that do what great literature in all of its forms does: it introduces readers to universal themes and truths, to ideas that are new, takes them out of their scope of experience and allows them to see the world in a different way. *Louis I, King of the Sheep* by Olivier Tallec, is about a sheep who finds a paper crown and decides to become king, but, like *Macbeth*, it is also about the ability of power to corrupt absolutely. Books in this category are also the texts that allow for a communal moment, a piece of shared humanity such as *Charlotte's Web* by E.B. White or *Raymie Nightingale* by Kate DiCamillo. These are texts that allow us to make sense of the world in the deepest and truest sense and they deserve a place on any curriculum that purports to be concerned with cultural capital.

STOP AND REFLECT

Think about the three categories of 'texts for cultural capital' outlined above.

- Can you think of books you have read or taught using that would fit into each category?
- Can you think of any books that might fit into more than one category?
- What might the impact of encountering these books be on a child's knowledge?
- What part might these books play in fostering a love of reading?

One way of mediating the challenge of who selects the texts to be studied is for a school to centrally plan the broad text-based units and make suggestions for texts, offering teachers a choice. If individuals or year group teams have alternative ideas, they can use these instead. The long-term planning provides a framework for those teachers who need support and allows freedom for those who will flourish. Table 16.2 illustrates this model of long-term planning. In this case, outcomes are organised not by genres or text types, but by purposes for writing (see Chapter 11).

Table 16.2   Example text-based long-term English plan

Year 4 Autumn Term

Unit	Example Texts	Writing for Purpose
Classic Narratives (3 weeks)	Choices from: *The Labours of Heracles* *Greek Heroes* by Geraldine McCaughrean *The Twelve Labours of Heracles* by James Ford *Greek Myths* retold by Marcia Williams *Tales from 1001 Nights* *One Thousand and One Arabian Nights* retold by Geraldine McCaughrean	Entertain: Extended narrative – retelling the story as first-person narrative, with own adventures Extended narrative – using story as a frame for own stories (e.g. new stories for Shahrazad to tell) Playscript – retelling a story as a playscript (and then performing it) Describe: Detailed description of one character from a text (e.g. Heracles or Shahrazad)

Year 4 Autumn Term

Unit	Example Texts	Writing for Purpose
	The Arabian Nights by Michael Foreman	Inform:
		A short non-fiction text about a country or time in history from one of the books studied
	The Thousand Nights and One Night retold by David Walser and Jan Pienkowski	
Picturebooks and Graphic Novels (2 x 1–2 weeks)	*Flotsam* by David Weisner	Entertain:
	Up the Mountain by Marianne Dubuc	Narrative – using wordless picturebook as frame for writing own narrative
	Professional Crocodile by Giovanna Zoboli and Mariachiara Do Giorgio	Narrative – creating own picturebook or graphic novel, using illustrations and text to tell story
	Night of the Gargoyles by Eve Bunting and David Wiesner	
	Azzi in Between by Sarah Garland	
Biography (2 weeks)	A range of published biographies (books and online) linked to foundation subjects/science:	Inform:
		A short, illustrated biography of a significant character from history, based on research
	On a Beam of Light by Jennifer Berne and Vladimir Radunsky	
	Hidden Figures by Margot Lee Shetterly and Laura Freeman	
	Star Stuff by Stephanie Roth Sisson	
	Enormous Smallness by Matthew Burgess and Kris Di Giacomo	
Recounts (Ongoing)	Linked to educational visits and visitors to school/workshops or from imaginative work in drama	Inform:
		Recounts from real experiences or imagined worlds of drama
Poetry (2 x 1 week)	A broad range of different types of poems from:	Discuss:
		Personal responses to a range of poems using different language forms showing understanding of ideas, language and themes (including poems written in different dialect forms, such as: *Talking Turkeys* by Benjamin Zephaniah or *Don't Call Alligator...* by John Agard and older poems such as *Snake* by D.H. Lawrence or *The Eagle* by Alfred, Lord Tennyson)
	The Rattle Bag compiled by Seamus Heaney and Ted Hughes	
	The Nation's Favourite Children's Poems	
	The Ring of Words edited by Roger McGough	
	iF Poems (as a book or app)	
	Please Mrs Butler by Allan Ahlberg	

Another aspect of long-term planning is the weekly timetable for a class, showing where the different vehicles for teaching English sit. While this can be thought of as short-term planning as it details a short space of time, in fact, if the timetable stays broadly the same each week, it is better thought of as long-term planning but for the allocation of time rather than areas of learning. Again, timetables will vary widely from school to school, from year group to year group and from class to class. Table 16.3 gives an example timetable for a Year 3 class with English sessions highlighted in bold.

Table 16.3 Example weekly timetable

Weekly Timetable for Class 3H

Time	Monday	Tuesday	Wednesday	Thursday	Friday
09.00	**Spelling**	**Library**	Circle Time	**Handwriting**	**Spelling Test**
09.30	Mathematics	**English**	Mathematics	**English**	Mathematics
10.30	Assembly	MFL	Assembly	**Spelling**	Assembly
10.50	Break				
11.05	**English**	Mathematics	**English**	Mathematics	English
12.00	**Group Reading**	**Group Reading**	**Group Reading**	**Group Reading**	Group Reading
12.30	Lunch				
13.30	**Reading Time**	**Reading Time**	**Reading Time**	**Reading Time**	**Reading Time**
13.45	Foundation Curriculum	PE	Science	Foundation Curriculum	MFL
14.40	Computing	Science	Foundation Curriculum	RE/PHSE	PE
15.30	Home				

The timetable shows a number of different curriculum vehicles for teaching different aspects of English. While these have been allocated separate spaces on the timetable, in an effective classroom the separate vehicles work together towards the same aims.

CASE STUDY 16.1

One of the best ways that children can develop as readers is by reading independently, building up the print experience discussed in Chapter 9. Research suggests that after the age of seven, the majority of new words children learn come from the material they read, and vocabulary development is closely linked to reading comprehension

(Cunningham, 2005). However, this aspect of reading, along with reading aloud to Key Stage 2 children, is often missing from school timetables. Instead, it remains reserved as an ad-hoc activity for when children have finished their work.

At one school, there were concerns about how little the children were reading at home. As the children moved into Key Stage 2, staff and parents found that other activities such as afterschool clubs, playing out with friends, and television and computer games began to compete for children's time. The decision was made that children would have time to read independently, so if it wasn't happening at home, it was happening at school.

Opportunities for independent reading are built into the timetable for all classes across the school. This is time for children to sit quietly and read a book of their choice for a sustained period of time. Although children have a free choice of the book that they are reading, the teacher monitors this closely and is on hand to support the class and to make recommendations. The children have the opportunity to talk about the books they have read and make recommendations to one another. The idea was to continue to champion a positive pedagogy around reading and books in the hope that it would filter outside of the classroom.

Medium-term planning

Medium-term or unit planning for English will begin with overarching learning aims (drawn from the long-term curriculum map), before adding in detail with specific intentions or objectives within the unit and a context for the learning. Table 16.4 gives an example of this for a unit on instructional writing.

Table 16.4 Learning aims, specific learning intentions and the context for learning

Wider learning aim	Specific learning intentions	Context for learning
To learn to write effective instructional texts	To learn different ways instructional texts can be structured and choose the most appropriate for audience and purpose	Instructions for a new board game Recipe for a healthy snack created in DT
	To learn to use language features commonly employed in instructional texts (adverbials of time, imperative form)	Quest story told as set of directions in the style of *Instructions* by Neil Gaiman
	To recognise the likely knowledge of the audience and tailor writing accordingly	

When creating a medium-term unit plan, there are a number of factors to be considered:

Time allocation

How many days or weeks will be spent on this unit of work? In an effective English classroom, there will be some flexibility to this, with teachers monitoring children's understanding and adapting their planning accordingly.

Consideration of children's likely starting points

There are two aspects to this factor: the knowledge and experience children already have and that which they will need to access the unit. For example, if children are working on a unit culminating in writing a playscript, the teacher will assess what they know about this type of writing before planning the unit. If children have some experience in this area, perhaps due to a unit in a previous year, then there is the opportunity to briefly recap and then begin looking at more advanced features. If children are not familiar with the genre, then the unit needs to begin from a very different point. The second aspect is key knowledge that will be useful before beginning. For example, a text-based unit using *Ruby in the Smoke* by Philip Pullman might benefit from some understanding of Victorian London, even if it is just watching a short video clip and discussing what children know about life for the poor in the Victorian Era. It should be stressed that this pre-teaching of key knowledge is not always necessary; studying a text can be a valuable source of new knowledge and the relationship between new knowledge and reading is a reciprocal one.

Intended outcomes

Outcomes will include the product that the unit is building towards, perhaps a piece of writing, a presentation, or a performance or a debate. There are other aims which may not result in a physical product or experience, however. A teacher may have in mind longer-term objectives drawn from the curriculum which cannot be achieved in one lesson. Instead, they need to be taught continuously over time. Statements from the curriculum such as 'develop positive attitudes to reading and understand what they have read' or 'increase their familiarity with a wide range of key texts, including myths and legends' will be met over the course of a unit and need to be planned for accordingly, even if these statements will not be objectives for individual lessons.

Clear learning intentions/objectives

Below the level of outcomes sit the individual objectives for each teaching session. These provide a focus for the lesson, ensuring planning is centred on what children are learning or practising, rather than the activity. See Chapters 17 and 18 (p. 328) for a detailed discussion about the successful use of learning objectives.

How *all* children will be supported to make progress

Every primary class is made up of individuals with different starting points and different needs. Some children will be beginning the unit from a strong foundation, with excellent prior knowledge and understanding; others may lack understanding or confidence of the topic at that moment. Some will have specific barriers around language development, fluency in English or current levels of reading achievement. Good English teaching is structured so that potential barriers are anticipated and ways round them are planned for, so all children can make progress towards the aims of the unit. This could involve additional pre-teaching of a key section of text so that a small group of children who could struggle feel confident taking part in a whole-class discussion. It could involve additional teacher support for an individual when writing, the use of writing frames or the chance for a child to write in their home language.

Meaningful cross-curriculum links

Where possible, links can be made from English to other subjects, strengthening the link between both. It may be that the English unit links to an area from the wider curriculum, for example, a Year 3 class reading *Starry Skies* by Samantha Chagollan and Nila Aye and then writing a new page for the book when learning about space in science. It may also be that learning in English links to learning in other curriculum areas, for example, Year 1 reading *Odd Dog Out* by Rob Biddulph and then discussing the differences between people and how this can make people feel in a PHSE lesson.

Thought about resources, including adults

Classroom resources include physical objects such as: sugar paper and pens for group note-taking; ICT resources, for example, school laptops for recording podcast poetry reviews; the books and text that will be studied; artefacts to support making predictions in a comprehension lesson; or props for a drama session where children will work in role. Successful planning also relies on considering how human resources such as the teacher and any additional adults might best be deployed. Will they be working with a specific group of children/child, circulating round the classroom offering feedback and support or positioned as part of a carousel, where every child will have the chance to speak to them over the course of the session (see p. 215)?

CASE STUDY 16.2

In a Year 6 class, the teacher felt there was a tension between sticking to the unit plan and working at the speed that the children in her class needed to ensure genuine learning. Often, she found that although the plan was ready to move onto the next stage of learning, some children in the class needed additional time to master an objective. To take this additional time threw the unit plan out of sync and meant that other units no longer fitted into the time allocated. As a result, the school made two changes to ensure that teaching was effective and about more than simply ticking off objectives and activities as 'done':

- Two units were removed from the long-term plan for each year group, meaning that the curriculum now covered 33 weeks. This left six 'free' weeks across the year for teachers to return to topics or areas that children needed more time on.
- Each unit had three or four lessons without any prescribed or planned content spread throughout the unit. This meant that teachers could use these sessions to stop and reteach a particular element or spend additional time practising something if they felt children would benefit from it without having to remove something from the unit or going over their allocation of time. These were known colloquially as 'fire-break lessons' because they stopped children's potential confusion spreading any further.

Conclusion

A rich, cohesive curriculum and a carefully planned model for supporting children's learning sit at the heart of good English teaching. While a good curriculum may grow organically taking in new elements and ideas, at its heart lies principled and strategic planning aligned to the school's ethos and beliefs. Through the process of planning, a skilful teacher decides best how to structure the learning, building the foundation on which great teaching and learning stands.

Chapters 15 and 16 have covered the theory and practice surrounding curriculum and planning; the next two chapters will consider how the curriculum, and the learning that is built upon it, can be assessed.

IN SUMMARY

- The overarching aims of a school's curriculum will provide the guiding principles to inform curriculum planning. These will be informed both by concrete objectives, the things schools wish children to know and be able to do, as well as the school's ethos and beliefs about how learning might best be approached.

- In practice, the curriculum will be planned for through the process of long-term planning which provides a curriculum overview, structured around the types of texts children will study, the books and other stimuli for learning, and the experiences the school wishes them to have.
- Medium-term plans then translate the principles, aims and long-term maps into units of work at the level of unit plans.

FURTHER READING

- To read more about a text-based curriculum and the implications for planning for this in school, read *Teaching English by the Book* by James Clements.
- For examples of process-based planning featuring rich cross-curricular links, see Mat Tobin's padlet of planning (search online for *Mat Tobin picturebook padlet*).

REFERENCES

Arnold, M. (1875) *Culture and Anarchy with Friendship's Garland and Some Literary Essays*. In R.H. Super (Ed.) (1965) *The Complete Prose Works of Matthew Arnold in eleven volumes*. Ann Arbor, MI: The University of Michigan Press.

Cox, B. (2014) *Opening Doors to Famous Poetry and Prose: Ideas and resources for accessing literary heritage works*. Carmarthen: Crown House.

Cunningham, A. E. (2005) Vocabulary growth through independent reading and reading aloud to children. In *Teaching and Learning Vocabulary: Bringing research to practice*, 45–68.

Department for Education (DfE) (2013) *National Curriculum in England: Primary Curriculum*. London: DfE.

Hirsch, E.D. (1987) *Cultural Literacy: What every American needs to know*. New York: Vintage Books.

Hirsch, E.D. (2016) *Why Knowledge Matters*. Cambridge, MA: Harvard University Press.

Wiliam, D. (2013) *Redesigning Schooling: Principled Curriculum Design*. London: SSAT.

Young, M.F.D. (2009) *Bringing Knowledge Back In: From social constructivism to social realism in the sociology of education*. London: Routledge.

LITERATURE

A Jar of Pickles and a Pinch of Justice by Chitra Soundar

Azzi in Between by Sarah Garland

Between Worlds by Kevin Crossley-Holland

Charlotte's Web by E.B. White

Don't Call Alligator... by John Agard

Enormous Smallness by Matthew Burgess and Kris Di Giacomo

Flotsam by David Weisner

Greek Heroes by Geraldine McCaughrean

Greek Myths retold by Marcia Williams

Hidden Figures by Margot Lee Shetterly and Laura Freeman

iF Poems (as a book or app)

Instructions by Neil Gaiman

Little People, Big Dreams: Emmeline Pankhurst by Lisbeth Kaiser and Ana Sanfelippo

Louis I, King of the Sheep by Olivier Tallec

Macbeth by William Shakespeare

Moby Dick retold by Geraldine McCaughrean

Night of the Gargoyles by Eve Bunting and David Wiesner

Odd Dog Out by Rob Biddulph

On a Beam of Light by Jennifer Berne and Vladimir Radunsky

On the Origin of Species retold by Sabina Radeva

One Thousand and One Arabian Nights retold by Geraldine McCaughrean

Please Mrs Butler by Allan Ahlberg

Professional Crocodile by Giovanna Zoboli and Mariachiara Do Giorgio

Raymie Nightingale by Kate DiCamillo

The Ruby in the Smoke by Philip Pullman

Shakespeare Stories by Leon Garfield

Snake by D.H. Lawrence

Star Stuff by Stephanie Roth Sisson

Starry Skies by Samantha Chagollan and Nila Aye

Talking Turkeys by Benjamin Zephaniah

The Arabian Nights by Michael Foreman

The Eagle by Alfred, Lord Tennyson

The Nation's Favourite Children's Poems

The Rattle Bag compiled by Seamus Heaney and Ted Hughes

The Ring of Words edited by Roger McGough

The Silk Roads by Peter Frankopan and Neil Packer

The Thousand Nights and One Night retold by David Walser and Jan Pienkowski

The Twelve Labours of Heracles by James Ford

Tom's Midnight Garden by Philippa Pearce

Treasure Island by Robert Louis Stevenson

Up the Mountain by Marianne Dubuc

17

ASSESSMENT IN ENGLISH: THEORY

THIS CHAPTER WILL

- Consider the principal purposes for assessment and how these are linked to different assessment structures; illustrating them with examples from primary English

- Explore the key concepts around educational assessment and measurement, including validity, reliability, bias and measurement error

- Outline the current system of national assessment in English schools

Introduction

Assessment remains a complicated and contested area of education and few areas of policy generate as much discussion. While this discourse often surrounds the role of national assessments and the impact these can have on children's, teachers' and schools' experience of education, assessment is a broad field, ranging from tests designed to monitor standards across the education system to questioning in class designed to elicit children's understanding and enable future planning.

This chapter introduces the theoretical background to educational assessment, before exploring this body of knowledge. It is intended to be read in conjunction with Chapter 18, where the ideas will be explored through the prism of English teaching in the primary classroom, drawing on a range of case studies to suggest how assessment and feedback can work in practice. While concepts and approaches are introduced here as discrete elements, it is through links with other areas of English, and other chapters of this book, that they are most valuable.

A commonly cited definition of assessment employed by Black (1998) is:

> A general term embracing all methods customarily used to appraise performance of an individual or a group. It may refer to a broad appraisal including many sources of evidence and many aspects of a pupil's knowledge, understanding, skills and attitudes; or to a particular occasion or instrument.

Accurate assessment relies on measuring or sampling an aspect of learning, often whether a child has understood a concept or can perform a particular behaviour. Assessment in schools can serve many different purposes, but the assessments teachers most often encounter can be said to have three broad and interlinked functions:

- **Assessment for summative purposes**: assessments used to evaluate children's learning, proficiency in an area, and academic achievement at the end of a period of teaching – often at the end of a project, unit of work, term or academic year.
- **Assessment for formative purposes**: assessments used to inform the next steps for future learning. Assessments for this purpose often take place during day-to-day classroom practice and while pupils are engaged in learning. Assessments used formatively should aim to give children an active role in the assessment process.
- **Assessment for diagnostic purposes:** assessments used to understand a child's current position or understanding. This might refer to assessments conducted at the start of learning to identify pupils' strengths and areas for improvement. It also refers to assessments used to identify potential learning difficulties and form the basis for interventions to address these.

To be useful, assessments need to be 'dependable' (Wiliam, 1993), providing trustworthy information that can be used for whatever purposes it is needed. For formative purposes, this is so future learning opportunities can be planned to address gaps or misconceptions. For summative purposes, dependability is vital if judgements or awards are to be made based on the assessment: qualifications, judgements about standards of education or of teacher efficacy. Dependability is comprised of two key characteristics of any measurement procedure: 'reliability' and 'validity'.

Reliability and validity

Reliability 'refers to the degree of consistency with which instances are assigned to the same category by different observers or by the same observer on different occasions'

(Hammersley, 1992). Reliability is a measure of the internal consistency and stability of an assessment: if the assessment were repeated, would the second result agree with the first? For a set of scales to be considered reliable, the scale would need to show 1kg each time a 1kg bag of flour was weighed.

Validity relates to whether the measuring device actually measures what it is supposed to. If the set of scales added ½kg to the display each time an object was put on it, it would be reliable, but it would not be valid as a measuring device.

The concept of validity originates from the field of psychometric testing where it refers to:

> An integrated evaluative judgement of the degree to which empirical evidence and theoretical rationales support the adequacy and appropriateness of inferences and actions based on test scores or other modes of assessment.
>
> (Messick in Linn, 1989)

The two concepts are interlinked, with reliability *necessary* but not *sufficient* for validity. For something to be valid it must be reliable, but it must also measure what it is intended to. Reliability and validity depend on the concept of a *true score* that underlies each measurement, the score in a test that a child *should* get or the correct judgement that could be made about a child's proficiency in a particular area. While a true score is a straightforward concept when weighing a bag of flour (a 1kg bag of flour has a true score of 1kg), the concept of a true score regarding a child's proficiency in an area of English, such as reading or writing, is far more difficult.

If we are assessing writing for example, before we can design a dependable assessment, we need to accept that an individual has a distinct trait such as 'writing ability' that can be measured through our assessment. Of course, whether there is a single concept such as writing ability is a matter for debate. Writing ability certainly corresponds to a concept that can be recognised – that some people are *better* at writing than others and it is likely that a child will become a *better writer* as they get older and move through school, but pinning this down to something that can be subjectively measured provides a challenge. As noted in Chapter 11, the process of writing is composed of a number of different elements. Does our assessment take into consideration the content, the style, the handwriting, the use of grammar and punctuation, how well the writing achieves its purpose? What about that sense of originality, entertainment and flair? Different individuals with different strengths will perform better or worse depending on what a specific assessment rewards or when judgements are made in different contexts.

For the assessment of complicated and multi-faceted areas such as writing, often specific measurable elements are deliberately chosen to assess against in order to organise a complex experience into smaller, assessable units. So, for writing, perhaps some criteria are given for what an effective piece of writing might look like in response to a given task or for a child of a particular age. Whether these elements truly reflect the attribute being assessed is the concern of *construct validity* (Messick, 1989). The term *construct* is helpful as it highlights the idea that the assessment task itself, and what it means to succeed at this task, have been created. They stand as proxies for a much wider set of competencies. For example, if a child can successfully write a short story based on a drama lesson they have taken part in, then the person measuring it is using this as a proxy to make broader judgements about the child's current levels of achievement in writing.

Measurement error and bias

In reality, no assessment can give a perfect measure. As Harlen (2007) notes, each measurement inevitably contains some error, causing the score or judgement to differ from the hypothesised true score. Black and Wiliam (in Gardner, 2006) suggest three particular potential sources of error, termed 'threats to reliability'. Table 17.1 outlines these and provides an illustration of each from the primary English classroom.

Table 17.1 Illustration of Black and Wiliam's threats to reliability

Threat to reliability	Illustration
The specific items chosen for the assessment might affect a student's performance	A reading assessment uses a text about turtles followed by a set of questions to check comprehension. One girl, who is very knowledgeable and passionate about animals, has an advantage as she is able to draw on her background knowledge. She does significantly better than she did in last half-term's reading test, based on a text about steam trains.
An individual's performance may vary from day-to-day	A Year 3 class are given 45 minutes to write a report about an educational visit to a local castle they went on. After a bad night's sleep and missing his breakfast due to an argument at home, one pupil arrives late to school. Naturally, he finds it difficult to concentrate on the writing that he is asked to produce and the end product is far from representative of his best work.
Different markers might reach different conclusions	In a grammar and punctuation test, children need to score 26/40 to pass. One of the questions asks children to insert a comma into a piece of text. A girl does this, but as she rushes her comma inclines to the side, looking like a dash. She isn't awarded the mark and scores 25/40. In another school, on the same test, a marker gives the benefit of the doubt to another boy who does exactly the same and he achieves the pass mark.

An additional source of error is through bias. This can be an issue with assessments made by teachers, whether looking holistically at a child's performance in a subject area or when considering a child's performance against a set of criteria (Harlen, 2004a). Harlen (2004b) notes: 'teachers' judgements can be biased by behaviour (for young children), gender and special educational needs; students' overall academic achievement and verbal ability may influence judgement when assessing specific skills'. These conclusions are confirmed by recent research too (Burgess and Greaves, 2013; Campbell, 2015).

These key concepts of *validity, reliability, measurement error* and *bias* are useful for considering the purposes of assessment, including English in the primary school.

Assessments for summative purposes

Assessment for summative purposes (assessments that are used to evaluate children's learning at the end of a period of teaching) consist of in-school summative assessments, organised by individual teachers and schools and national summative assessments, colloquially called *SATs* in England.

National summative assessments in England

A system of national assessment at primary level was first introduced in England as part of the 1988 Education Reform Act, which also introduced a national curriculum to England. At first, there were no national tests. Instead, judgements were made through the use of Standard Assessment Tasks, a framework based on teacher assessment moderated by externally set, teacher-marked tasks proposed by the Task Group on Assessment and Testing (DES, 1988). In 1995, the tasks were replaced by externally marked tests for reading and writing which were supplemented with a system of teacher assessment to ensure the breadth of the curriculum was assessed. For a comprehensive overview, see Stobart (2001).

In 2015, in response to a new national curriculum, new national assessments were introduced. These consisted of teacher assessments for reading and writing at Key Stage 1 and an externally marked reading test as well as a grammar, punctuation and spelling test. Finally, there was a nationally moderated teacher assessment of writing, based on 'interim teacher assessment frameworks'. After much criticism of their overemphasis on technical aspects of writing (e.g. DfE and STA, 2017; House of Commons Education Committee, 2017), the frameworks were replaced with 'teacher assessment frameworks' for 2018/19.

The current national assessment framework for England is summarised in Table 17.2.

Table 17.2 Current statutory national assessments in England (adapted from DfE and STA, 2017)

Key Stage 1 (5–7)	
Phonics Screening Check (Year 1)	**Phonics screening check:** A statutory screening check administered by teachers. The check assesses a pupil's phonics decoding ability in order to identify pupils needing additional support. School-level data is not published, while national and local authority level results are. Pupils who do not meet the required standard are required to re-sit the check in Year 2.

Key Stage 1 (5–7)	
End of Key Stage 1 (Year 2)	**End of Key Stage 1 national curriculum assessments:** Teacher assessment judgements are currently made using interim teacher assessment frameworks for reading (informed by internally marked national curriculum tests), and writing. These teacher assessments are externally moderated by local authorities, who sample 25% of schools each year. These assessments form the baseline for measuring progress made between Key Stage 1 and Key Stage 2. The proportions of pupils achieving the expected standard in English reading and writing are published at national and local authority level, but not at school level.
	There is currently an optional test in English grammar, punctuation and spelling at the end of Key Stage 1. All papers are optional from 2023.

Key Stage 2 (7–11)	
End of Key Stage 2 (Year 6)	**End of Key Stage 2 national curriculum assessments:** Pupils sit externally marked tests in reading, and grammar, punctuation and spelling. Teacher assessment judgements are made in reading and writing. The proportions of pupils achieving the expected standard in both reading (based on test data) and writing (based on teacher assessment judgements) are published at national, local authority and school level and are used to calculate the progress that pupils make between Key Stage 1 and Key Stage 2. Progress and attainment measures form part of the floor standard, which is used as the starting point for a conversation about whether a school might require additional support.
	National curriculum test data in reading and grammar, punctuation and spelling, and teacher assessment judgements in writing are published at national and local authority level.

National tests and measurement error

National testing plays an important part in the discourse around 'educational standards', which has its origins in the late 1970s where political attention was directed on the link between education and economic success (Wolf, 1995). Support for national testing focuses on the link between testing and the curriculum, arguing the role it has played in raising attainment in tested subjects and teachers' expectations (Sammons, 2008; Oates, 2010) and suggesting that the system is vital for monitoring and maintaining educational standards:

> Statutory assessment plays an important role in ensuring that every child is supported to leave primary school prepared to succeed...to help teachers to raise standards, and to give every child the best chance to master reading, writing and arithmetic, which are fundamental in preparing them for secondary school. We believe that it is right that the government sets a clear expected standard that pupils should attain by the end of primary school, and that this standard is ambitious, to ensure schools support all pupils to achieve their potential, regardless of their background.
>
> (DfE and STA, 2017)

One potential issue with measuring standards in education, whether the achievement of individual pupils or the effectiveness of particular schools, is a misunderstanding about the reliability of tests. Tests and examinations, drawing as they do on 'scientific principles', are portrayed as being 'fair, objective and reliable' for every candidate (Lawlor, 1995).

In reality, this may not be the case. Statistical modelling has suggested that the percentage of individual pupils awarded an incorrect level at Key Stage 2 could be around 30%, although over the large number of children who take the national tests each year, the number that achieve a standard higher than their hypothesised 'true score' and those that are awarded a lower level might be expected to be approximately equal, meaning scores for large groups (e.g. the national cohort) are likely to be accurate (Wiliam, 2001). While other explorations of the data suggest more modest levels of misclassification of around 15%, that is still four or five children in every class of thirty (NFER, 2007 in Newton, 2009; MacCann and Stanley, 2010). As Newton notes:

> Even if Wiliam's 30% is an over-estimate of error related to random causes, there is a substantial amount of error related to systematic causes that also needs to be taken into account. Were it possible to quantify overall inaccuracy, misclassification rates might indeed be as high as 30% or even higher. We simply do not know.
>
> (Newton, 2009)

These problems with inherent error within educational measurement are rarely discussed by politicians or the media and it has been argued that unless they are explained and understood by the public, there is the threat of unrealistic expectations being made of the system (Newton, 2005). While a system of national testing might give useful information about the education system as a whole, due to the inherent error present in all measures, using national tests as a way of judging individual pupils, teachers or schools might present a problem.

The national assessment system is also criticised on the grounds that tests only measure a narrow part of the curriculum. Wiliam (2001) illustrates this using the analogy of stage lights:

> One can use a spotlight to illuminate a small part of the stage very brightly, so that one gets a very clear picture of what is happening in the illuminated area (high reliability), but one has no idea what is going on elsewhere, and the people in darkness can get up to all kinds of things, knowing that they won't be seen (not teaching parts of the curriculum not tested).
>
> (Wiliam, 2001)

In a high-stakes system, where judgements are made about schools and teachers based on national assessment outcomes, concentrating on those areas that will be assessed is incentivised. This leads to the concern that assessments can undermine the breadth of the curriculum with schools focusing on the tested elements that inhabit 'the illuminated area'. Reading assessments, for example, assess only part of what it means to be a reader in its broadest sense, concentrating on the measurable aspects of reading such as decoding using phonics in

Year 1, or a narrow range of comprehension responses in Years 2 and 6. The assessments neglect children's emotional responses to a text, their ability to act on individual preferences and tastes, their reading stamina and the range of their reading (Bearne and Reedy, 2018).

What is certain is that navigating the demands of a high-stakes national assessment system, while keeping the wider development of children as confident and keen users of English, takes skill and a strong moral compass.

In-school summative assessments

Each school is likely to have its own model for in-school summative assessments. These might take the form of tests (e.g. a weekly spelling test or an annual test of reading age); teacher assessments such as a writing assessment at the end of a unit of teaching; or observations, for example hearing a child read to assess fluency or observing a group of Reception children building a model together to consider their spoken communication. While each of these assessments could be used formatively (e.g. a spelling test used to choose the spelling patterns that could be taught next), in this context they are designed to make judgements about children's achievement for reporting or accountability purposes, rather than to inform future learning.

STOP AND REFLECT

The Commission on Assessment Without Levels (2015), convened by the DfE after systemic changes in national assessment were made, suggests six questions that form 'principles for in-school summative assessment':

1. Who will use the information provided by this assessment?

2. Will it give them the information they need for their purposes?

3. How will it be used to support broader progress, attainment and outcomes for the pupils?

4. How should the assessment outcomes be communicated to pupils to ensure they have the right impact and contribute to pupils' understanding of how they can make further progress in the future?

5. How should the assessment outcomes be communicated to parents to ensure they understand what the outcomes tell them about their child's attainment, progress and improvement needs?

6. How should the assessment outcomes be recorded to allow the school to monitor and demonstrate progress, attainment and wider outcomes?

(Commission on Assessment Without Levels, 2015)

(Continued)

Think of an in-school assessment you have used in class – perhaps a test or assessment task – and then apply the questions above to your assessment:

- How well are you able to answer the questions above?
- Do they raise any issues with the assessment itself?
- Considering the ideas of *validity* and *reliability* and *bias* introduced earlier in the chapter, are there any potential threats concerning the assessment and these concepts? If so, how could these be mitigated?

In-school summative assessments of reading

The main ways of assessing reading for summative purposes are through tests and ongoing teacher assessments:

Reading tests

The most common reading tests are those that use a short piece of text, often an extract from a longer text, followed by questions to test comprehension. As these assessments involve children reading the texts independently, they serve as a way of assessing the word-reading element too. If a child can answer questions successfully, it can be assumed that they have been able to read the words, understand the language and comprehend the text. While it is not unusual for teachers to create these tests themselves, *standardised assessments* are likely to provide a more objective measure. Standardised assessments, such as the NfER's New Group Reading Test, feature a bank of test items that are the same for a nation-wide cohort and are unchanged over a number of years so as to allow for wide-ranging comparisons. Standardised reading tests are norm-referenced, meaning a child's score is placed relative to the distribution of results amongst the performance of other children who have sat the test in the past. The scale is calibrated to a broad spread of other children rather than a predetermined standard of what children *should* achieve.

Even the most widely used standardised tests are likely to be used for monitoring purposes, rather than diagnostically to provide detailed information about children's strengths and weaknesses. If children are unable to answer the questions, it is not always clear what the barrier to meaning is. And, as noted in Chapter 7, the challenge might not come from the child's ability to read and understand, but from the context of the text itself. In Recht and Leslie's widely cited US study (1988), when given a text about baseball, children who were weaker readers with a good knowledge of the game appeared to achieve higher scores than those who were confident readers but didn't know much about this sport (although their findings did not reach a level of statistical significance, so this cannot be viewed as definitive – see Seidenberg and Farry-Thorn, 2020). However, this, combined with the issues surrounding measurement error addressed earlier, means that using a reading test to make decisions about the performance of a group of children is more complicated than it might appear.

On occasion, it may be useful for a child to sit an individual diagnostic test, especially if they are struggling with an aspect of reading. Tests of word-reading such as the Diagnostic Test of Word Reading Processes or comprehension tests such as The York Assessment of Reading for Comprehension or the Neale Reading Analysis can help to identify specific areas of difficulty for children, allowing the teacher and school to plan targeted support.

Ongoing teacher assessment

In many schools, assessments of reading are based on a teacher's own assessments, either through regularly hearing each child read aloud and then discussing the text, or through small-group reading sessions. These assessments might be carried out against a set of criteria, or they may make use of specific techniques such as miscue analysis (Goodman, 1973) or running records (Clay, 1985). While time-consuming, the benefits of assessing children as they read is that it allows for interaction between teacher and child. A teacher is able to use follow-up questions to explore any misconceptions. In addition to the same challenges with selecting the text that reading tests provide, teacher assessment is open to bias, as seen earlier in the chapter.

In-school summative assessments of writing

Assessments of writing are often made through standalone writing tasks or tests, usually within a set time or through judgements drawn from the writing children collated from their written work in class.

Assessment of written work is far more likely to be *criterion referenced*. These assessments locate a child's position on a scale of development or skill without reference to other individuals. This involves assessing an individual by comparing their achievements with a set of criteria for particular levels of performance. Unlike norm referencing, criterion referencing does not involve the allocation of marks to normal distributions and, therefore, an individual's mark is not influenced by the performance of others.

Potential difficulties relating to using criteria for assessing writing are that it can reduce the assessment of complex concepts and ideas into a series of discrete boxes to be ticked off (Morgan and O'Reilly 1999; Hodgen and Marshall, 2005) and that it can be unreliable because it involves inference and subjective judgement (Black, 1998).

There are also difficulties in expressing a difficult concept in words. The phrasing of an objective could be interpreted differently by different people, leading to very different outcomes being accepted as successfully meeting the criteria (Koretz, 1998). As Marshall observes, meeting a set of criteria does not necessarily mean a good piece of English work (Marshall in Cremin and Dombey, 2007). A set of tight criteria can be limiting, especially in an area such as writing, where a number of choices could be equally valid ways of creating a desired effect. However, there is also the danger that ideas or techniques not referenced in the criteria might be ignored as they cannot be measured against (Kohn, 2006).

STOP AND REFLECT

As an introduction, before they begin reading Leon Garfield's retelling of *Julius Caesar*, a Year 5 class have been shown an illustration of Caesar's legions assembled about to cross the Rubicon and march towards Rome. Their task is to write a sentence that describes what they can see. The success criteria remind them to use 'descriptive language, such as carefully chosen adjectives and figurative language such as similes or metaphors'.

One child writes:

'The Roman soldiers lined up like vehicles in a traffic jam. Their bright red cloaks are like fire in the hot sunshine.'

Another child writes:

'The air is filled with the sound of spears clattering and swords crashing against shields. Veterans of a hundred battles, Caesar's troops are ready to begin their march towards the city.'

Consider:

- Are these two pieces of writing both valid descriptions of the scene?
- Which might be considered the more mature, accomplished description?
- Which is the best fit for the success criteria?

When thinking about giving children criteria to judge their success against, care needs to be taken to allow some freedom to meet the objective in varied or unexpected ways. Especially in the teaching of writing where overly prescriptive criteria can limit children's responses. An effective moderation process (Shapley and Bush, 1999), in which a set of fixed criteria is applied to a broad range of written work rather than a single piece (Wiliam, 2001), could invite a truer and more realistic assessment.

A final criticism of criterion referencing is that teachers have been observed to rely on intuition rather than deliberate analysis, opting for what 'feels right', rather than seeking to consider the criteria objectively (Gipps and Clarke, 1998). In fact, rather than representing a challenge to dependability, this holistic approach to judging quality of writing could form a reliable way of making judgements. *Comparative judgement* is a method of assessing writing without stated criteria. It relies on a pairwise analysis of two items, with an assessor simply deciding which is the better of the two items. In the case of writing, it would involve looking at two pieces of writing, with no criteria, and then deciding which piece is better. This process, repeated a number of times by different assessors, creates a scaled ranking of the pieces of writing. This can be anchored against other pieces of writing to provide a judgement of which pieces meet an agreed standard or to compare the quality of writing produced over time (see Heldsinger and Humphry, 2010).

Studies of comparative judgement in primary writing have shown good levels of reliability (Whitehouse and Pollitt, 2012; McMahon and Jones, 2014) and this appears to be an area of assessment that shows promise, although the reliance on software to perform the statistical analysis means it is not an option easily available to individual teachers.

Criticisms of comparative judgement reflect those of norm referencing in general: a perceived unfairness within the process because the score of any individual is dependent not only on their own performance, but on that of everyone else being assessed (Gipps, 1994). As an individual cannot control the performance of others, they therefore have limited control over their own individual result. Other arguments suggest that the absence of criteria makes the process of awarding a particular standard opaque, and it is not possible to show a child where they have not reached the required standard as it would be using a set of criteria. As previously noted, this criticism relies on a confidence in the consistent application of criteria that may well be unfounded. The use of comparative judgement in educational assessment is an expanding field and work has begun in looking at how the technique might support informing children's future learning. This remains an area in which further research is required (Van Gasse et al., 2017).

Selecting an approach for in-school summative assessment of reading and writing requires care, as each will have strengths, but with potential drawbacks to consider. As with all methods of educational assessment, it is important to note the limitations of the methodology and not to assign disproportionate value to the findings of an individual assessment.

Assessment for formative purposes

If assessment for summative purposes is concerned with measuring and recording what learners can do at any one time, assessment for formative purposes, often termed *assessment for learning*, is concerned with shaping future learning:

> Assessment for learning is the process of seeking and interpreting evidence for use by learners and their teachers to decide where the learners are in their learning, where they need to go and how best to get there.
>
> Assessment Reform Group (2002)

This is the type of assessment that lies at the heart of good classroom teaching, with a teacher using assessment to change the direction and focus of instruction, like a skilful sailor adjusting the sails of a boat in response to the changing winds and tide to guide their vessel to shore.

This broad purpose for assessment has been referred to by a number of different names: *formative practice* (Sadler, 1989), *assessment for learning* (Broadfoot et al., 1999) and *responsive teaching* (Wiliam in Fletcher-Wood, 2018).

Broadfoot et al. (1999) share five key factors where assessment can help to improve learning:

1. Providing effective feedback to pupils
2. Actively involving pupils in their own learning
3. Adjusting teaching to take account of the results of assessment
4. Recognising the profound influence assessment has on the motivation and self-esteem of pupils, both of which are crucial to learning
5. Considering the need for pupils to be able to assess themselves and to understand how to improve

These factors form some useful principles for effective formative assessment. Investigating how these principles might be applied to classroom teaching, Black et al. (2002) organise their main findings under the following four headings:

- **Questioning:** the type and frequency of questions teachers ask and the way responses are structured are a key aspect of formative assessment, promoting children's learning as well as eliciting information about their current understanding of a topic.
- **Feedback**: this refers to information that is shared about performance in a specific task or learning in general, relative to specific aims or objectives.
- **Peer- and self-assessment:** peer-assessment relates to children working together, making judgements or offering feedback or ideas towards a shared aim. Self-assessment is the process of children developing sufficient insights into their own learning and how to improve it.
- **The formative use of summative assessments**: tests or tasks that are concerned with measuring and recording what learners can do at any one time can play a positive part of the learning process, providing information to both teachers and children. Using these assessments to help children to reflect on the areas in which they still need to make progress can have a positive effect on their self-esteem and future learning.

These four areas provide a useful model for considering the interrelated strands that make up formative assessment in practice (this is pursued further in Chapter 18).

The relationship between formative and summative assessments

The labels *summative* and *formative* refer not to assessments themselves, but to the purposes to which they are put. Tests can be used formatively while a conversation with a child based on their favourite book can help to form a summative judgement. There are well-founded arguments about the possible negative impact of blurring of assessments for formative and summative purposes:

...teachers are subject to conflicting pressures: trying to make appropriate use of assessment as part of the day-to-day task of classroom teaching, while at the same time collecting assessment data which will be used in very high stakes evaluation of individual and institutional performance. These conflicted purposes too often affect adversely the fundamental aims of the curriculum, particularly regarding breadth of content and depth of learning.

(Commission on Assessment Without Levels, 2015)

Being clear about the purpose to which an assessment is to be put is vital if it is to be valid and reliable. However, as Harlen notes: 'There seems to be value in maintaining the distinction between formative and summative purposes of assessment while seeking synergy in relation to the process of assessment' (2005).

One way this 'synergy' can be formed is by ensuring that an assessment is used formatively once it has fulfilled its summative purpose. In English, this might mean children producing a piece of writing as a snapshot assessment of their proficiency in writing. However, rather than this piece being left in a folder as evidence, the teacher would make use of it, perhaps through drawing a new teaching point or offering the child some feedback.

Chapter 18 will explore the relationship between assessments for summative and formative purposes, as well as illustrating how different assessments might be used effectively in the primary classroom.

Conclusion

The conversation around educational assessment is often driven by differing attitudes to national testing, focusing on the use of these to measure standards in education and the impact of high-stakes assessment on the taught curriculum, teachers and children. However, under the broad umbrella of assessment sit the diverse strands of assessment used for different purposes described in this chapter.

For both teachers in the classroom and for policy-makers, navigating the different features of assessments for summative and formative purposes and understanding the relationship between them presents challenges, but also opportunities: it is through understanding what children understand and can do that teachers are able to plan for future learning. Good assessment sits at the heart of good education.

IN SUMMARY

- Assessments can have a number of purposes. *Assessments for summative purposes* are used to make judgements about a child's learning at the end of a period of teaching while *assessments for formative purposes* are used to plan for future teaching and learning.

- In England, a national system of summative national assessments collect data at the end of key stages on the performance of schools and the education system as a whole.
- Formative assessment is the collective name given to a raft of approaches built around the principle that assessment can support future learning. Repeated research suggests that formative assessment techniques, implemented consistently, can have a significant impact on children's learning.
- In order to be useful, all assessments must be *valid* and *reliable*. *Validity* refers to whether the assessment measures what it purports to measure. *Reliability* relates to whether an assessment will produce the same measurement each time it is used.

FURTHER READING

- For an account of issues surrounding the relationship between assessments for summative and formative purposes and how these might be implemented in school, read *The Final Report of the Commission on Assessment Without Levels*, available freely via an online search.
- For a thorough introduction to assessment for summative purposes (including testing), read *Testing: Friend or Foe?* by Paul Black or *Assessment of Learning* by Wynne Harlen.
- For a current and practical overview of the field of formative assessment, read *Embedded Formative Assessment* by Dylan Wiliam.

REFERENCES

Assessment Reform Group (2002) *Assessment for Learning: 10 principles: research-based principles to guide classroom practice.* Assessment Reform Group.

Bearne, E. and Reedy, D. (2018) *Teaching Primary English: Subject knowledge and classroom practice.* Abingdon: Routledge.

Black, P. (1998) *Testing: Friend or Foe? Theory and Practice of Assessment and Testing.* London: Falmer.

Black, P., Harrison, C., Lee, C., Marshall, B. and Wiliam, D. (2002) *Working Inside the Black Box: Assessment for learning in the classroom.* London: King's College.

Broadfoot, P., Daugherty, R., Gardner, J., Gipps, C., Harlen, W. and James, M. (1999) *Assessment for Learning: Beyond the black box.* Cambridge: Universty of Cambridge School of Education.

Burgess, S. and Greaves, E. (2013) Test scores, subjective assessment, and stereotyping of ethnic minorities. *Journal of Labor Economics,* 31(3): 535–76.

Campbell, T. (2015) Stereotyped at seven? Biases in teacher judgement of pupils' ability and attainment. *Journal of Social Policy*, 44(3): 517–47.

Clay, M. (1985) *The Early Detection of Reading Difficulties*. Portsmouth, NH: Heinemann.

Commission on Assessment Without Levels (2015) *Final Report*. London: DfE.

Cremin, T. and Dombey, H. (Eds) (2007) *The Handbook of Primary English in Initial Teacher Education*. London: NATE/UKLA.

Department for Education and Standards & Testing Agency (2017) Primary assessment in England Government consultation, launch date 30 March 2017, closing date 22 June 2017. Available at: https://consult.education.gov.uk/assessment-policy-and-development/primary-assessment/supporting_documents/Primary%20assessment%20in%20England.pdf (accessed 11/11/ 2018).

DES (1988) *Task Group on Assessment and Testing: A Report*. London: HMSO.

Fletcher-Wood, H. (2018) *Responsive Teaching: Cognitive science and formative assessment in practice*. Abingdon: Routledge.

Gardner, J. (Ed.) (2006) *Assessment and Learning*. London: Sage.

Gipps, C. (1994) *Beyond Testing: Towards a Theory of Educational Assessment*. London: Falmer Press.

Gipps, C. and Clarke, S. (1998) *Monitoring the Consistency in Teacher Assessment and the impact of SCAA's Guidance Materials at KS1, 2 and 3*. London: QCA.

Goodman, K. (Ed.) (1973) *Miscue Analysis: Applications to reading instruction*. Urbana, IL: NCTE.

Hammersley, M. (1992) *What's Wrong with Ethnography?* London: Routledge.

Harlen, W. (2004a) *A systematic review of the evidence of the impact on students, teachers and the curriculum of the process of using assessment by teachers for summative purposes*. London: EPPI-Centre, Institute of Education.

Harlen, W. (2004b) *A systematic review of the evidence of reliability and validity of assessment by teachers used for summative purposes*. London: EPPI-Centre, Institute of Education.

Harlen, W. (2005) Teachers, summative practices and assessment for learning – tensions and synergies. *The Curriculum Journal*, 16(2): 207–23.

Harlen, W. (2007) *Assessment of Learning*. London: Sage.

Heldsinger, S. and Humphry, S. (2010) Using the method of pairwise comparison to obtain reliable teacher assessments. *Australian Educational Researcher*, 37(2): 1–19.

Hodgen, J. and Marshall, B. (2005) Assessment for learning in English and mathematics: A comparison. *The Curriculum Journal*, 16(2): 153–76.

House of Commons Education Committee (2017) Primary Assessment: Eleventh Report of Session 2016–17 (Report, together with formal minutes relating to the report). Available at: https://publications.parliament.uk/pa/cm201617/cmselect/cmeduc/682/682.pdf (accessed 2/10/ 2018).

Kohn, A. (2006) The trouble with rubrics. *English Journal*, 95(4): 12–15.

Koretz, (1998) Large-scale portfolio assessments in the US: Evidence pertaining to the quality of measurement, *Assessment in Education: Principles, Policy & Practice*, 5(3): 309–34.

Lawlor, S. (Ed.) (1995) *An Education Choice: Pamphlets from the Centre 1987–1994*. London: The Centre for Policy Studies.

Linn, R.L. (Ed.) (1989) *Educational Measurement*. New York: Macmillan.

MacCann, R. and Stanley, G. (2010) Classification consistency when scores are converted to grades: Examination marks versus moderated school assessments. *Assessment in Education: Principles, Policy & Practice*, 17(3): 255–72.

McMahon, S. and Jones, I. (2014) A comparative judgement approach to teacher assessment. *Assessment in Education: Principles, Policy & Practice*, 1–22.

Messick S. (1989) Meaning and values in test validation: The science and ethics of assessment. *Educational Researcher*, 18(2): 5–11.

Morgan, C. and O'Reilly, M. (1999) *Assessing Open and Distance Learners*. London: Kogan Page.

Newton, P. (2005) The public understanding of measurement inaccuracy. *British Educational Research Journal*, 31(4): 419–42.

Newton, P. (2009) The reliability of results from national curriculum testing in England. *Educational Research*, 51(2): 181–212.

Oates, T. (2010) *Could do Better – Using international comparisons to define the National Curriculum in England*. Cambridge: Cambridge Assessment.

Recht, D.R. and Leslie, L. (1988) Effect of prior knowledge on good and poor readers' memory of text. *Journal of Educational Psychology*, 80: 16–20.

Sadler, R. (1989) Formative assessment and the design of instructional systems. *Instructional Science*, 18: 119–44.

Sammons, P. (2008) Zero tolerance of failure and New Labour approaches to school improvement in England. *Oxford Review of Education*, 34(6).

Seidenberg, M. and Farry-Thorn, M. (2020) Some context on context. Reading Matters: Connecting science and education. Available at: https://seidenbergreading.net/2020/09/10/some-context-on-context/ (accessed 11/9/20).

Shapley, K. and Bush, M. (1999) Developing a valid and reliable portfolio assessment in the primary grades: Building on practical experience. *Applied Measurement in Education*, 12(2): 11–32.

Stobart, G. (2001) The validity of National Curriculum assessment. *British Journal of Educational Studies*, 49(1): 26–39.

Van Gasse R., Mortier, A., Goossens, M., Vanhoof, J., Van Petegem, P., Vlerick, P. and De Maeye, S. (2017) Feedback opportunities of comparative judgement: An overview of possible features and acceptance at different user levels. In D. Joosten-ten Brinke and M. Laanpere (Eds), *Technology Enhanced Assessment*. TEA 2016. Communications in Computer and Information Science 653. CCIS.

Whitehouse, C. and Pollitt, A. (2012) *Using adaptive comparative judgement to obtain a highly reliable rank order in summative assessment*. Manchester: CERP.

Wiliam, D. (1993) Validity, dependability and reliability in National Curriculum assessment. *The Curriculum Journal*, 4: 335–50.

Wiliam, D. (2001) Reliability, validity, and all that jazz. *Education 3–13*, 29(3): 17–21.

Wolf, A. (1995) *Competence-Based Assessment*. Buckingham: Open University Press.

LITERATURE

Shakespeare Stories II by Leon Garfield

18

ASSESSMENT IN ENGLISH: PRACTICE

THIS CHAPTER WILL

- Explore the practical considerations of assessment in the primary classroom

- Consider approaches to assessments for both formative and summative purposes

- Address a range of levels of assessment, from school-level systemic assessment to teachers' own ongoing assessment

Introduction

Assessment is a crucial element of teaching, both when used for summative purposes to capture information about children's learning and for formative purposes, where assessments inform future teaching and learning. Chapter 17 introduced the key theoretical concerns of educational assessment, focusing on the broad principles before considering the purposes to which assessment is put in schools and the wider education system. As national summative assessment is beyond the control of teachers and schools, this chapter will focus on the practical uses of assessment, both for summative and formative purposes. As with previous paired chapters in this book, this chapter is intended to be read in conjunction with Chapter 17.

In-school assessments for summative purposes

In-school summative assessments are those that are used to measure and report on children's progress or achievement at a given point, such as the end of a unit of work, the end of an academic year or when children have finished studying a particular text.

In order to be effective, any in-school assessment must be matched to its purpose, providing schools with information they can use to monitor and support pupils' progress, attainment and wider outcomes. Before designing or selecting an assessment method, teachers and schools should be clear about:

- why pupils are being assessed and what the assessment is intended to measure
- whether the assessment is as valid and reliable as it can be
- whether the likely bias and measurement error have been considered and how these will affect how the results are interpreted and used
- how the assessment information will be used, who it will be shared with and how

For a class teacher, there are likely to be two prompts for summative assessments: those designed and used by the teacher and those designated by the school as part of a whole-school system.

Whole-school assessment systems

Most schools have a system of assessment that allows them to track pupils' achievement as they move through the school. In England, this would have once been based on national curriculum levels, but the 2014 National Curriculum removed these levels and suggested that schools could replace them with a system of their own choosing (DfE, 2014). While many schools chose to purchase an assessment system, others designed their own based on their own principles.

CASE STUDY 18.1

One school formed a working group of staff and outside experts, drawn from the Local Authority, to devise the new assessment system. They began by drawing up a set of key features and principles that would underpin their system. After vigorous discussion, they agreed on the following key principles:

Formative at heart: it would be built around the idea that in addition to providing data for accountability purposes, it would actually support children to become more proficient in their learning.

(Continued)

> *Easy for teachers to use*: it would not mean lots of extra work for teachers. Instead, it should be part of the cycle of assessing, planning and teaching that teachers carry out constantly.
>
> *Based on children legitimately getting better at a subject*: rather than simply making progress in tests and colours changing on a spreadsheet, the system would be built around statements of attainment that could be easily understood by school staff, parents and children.
>
> *Rigorous moderation and validation of data*: the data used for accountability purposes is only useful if accurate data is put into the system. Moderation and the use of standardised tests would help to ensure any judgements we make about children's learning is as accurate as it can be.
>
> *Easy for parents and children to understand*: there would be no educational jargon when achievement and progress were reported. They wished to use easily understandable language, explaining where children had achieved well against the government's age-appropriate expectations and where they were still working towards them.
>
> If you were to develop an assessment system from scratch, what would your underpinning principles be? To what extent would they agree with those stated here?

Common features of assessment systems, either commercial or created by schools, are:

Tracker sheets

Either online as a set of statements to highlight when achieved or as a paper sheet to be highlighted, tracker sheets are a popular way of recording children's progress against set objectives.

There sheets are criterion-based and therefore contain the potential for bias with regards to interpretation of results (issues explored in Chapter 17). In addition, they can be cumbersome with regards to teachers' workload and the demands of inputting data.

Termly assessment tests and tasks

In many schools, children sit an assessment task so as to provide a summative assessment of achievement for reading and writing. This is usually marked by teachers before the results for each child is added to a tracker document, either a spreadsheet or a specialist software program. Again, data inputted into the system are only as dependable as the tests themselves, and caution needs to be taken not to infer too much from a stan-dalone assessment (see p. 301).

Standardised tests and assessment tasks

Standardised tests and tasks are often employed to support a school's assessment system, providing validation for teachers' assessment and ensuring bench-marking against a national or international set of standards. Tests such as those of reading age fit this category. The chal-lenge for schools is to remember that while these tests make comparisons with a large sam-ple, as snapshots they are still vulnerable to the differences in performance to be expected from children day-to-day (Black and Wiliam, in Gardner, 2006). This is especially true of younger children, where 'instability is more the case than not in early childhood develop-ment, and tests of accountability that overlook the implications of this variability will mislead policymakers, the public and children's teachers' (Meisels and Atkins-Burnett, 2008).

While no assessment system will provide certainty in terms of validity and reliability, combinations of different assessments can work together to provide useful information. Where there is concurrence between different assessments, they gave reassurance; where there is a difference, they can prompt further investigation.

Validity and reliability of teachers' own assessments

Chapter 17 discussed the inherent challenges with educational assessments due to reliability, validity, measurement error and bias (see p. 299). Assessments designed by individual teachers are likely to have the same or perhaps even greater margins for error within them as they are unlikely to have been subject to the same quality assurance and tests of internal validity as national assessments. This doesn't mean that these tests cannot provide useful information for teachers and schools, just that caution should be applied to any results and it might be wise not to base deci-sions, such as grouping of pupils or choices of reading material, solely on test results.

Assessment for formative purposes

Teachers are constantly carrying out assessments, making judgements about children's understanding or the effectiveness of a particular approach. This is an integral part of good teaching. Much of this assessment will be for formative purposes, to inform teaching or to plan provision for particular children. It may also feed back into curriculum design. If a cho-sen teaching activity wasn't judged to be effective then it may need to be changed or adapted in the future.

Black et al. (2002) suggest four particular aspects of formative practice:

- Questioning
- Feedback
- Peer- and self-assessment
- The formative use of summative assessments

Questioning

Research suggests that questioning is a key element of classrooms, with teachers spending between 30 and 50 per cent of their time posing questions (van Lier, 1998). However, it has been suggested that these questions are often either procedural (*Does everyone have a sharp pencil?*) or questions to prompt the recall of facts (*In which city was the story set?*), rather than open questions which might prompt genuine discussion (Wilen, 1991; Brualdi, 1998). Harrison and Howard (2009) suggest four ways to improve classroom questioning:

- Plan for and use a greater ratio of open to closed questions
- Increase the time children are given to consider the question and think of an answer (*wait time*)
- Promote a classroom ethos which values 'having a go' and where all children are encouraged to contribute even if they are not sure their answer is 'right'
- Invite other children to provide an answer or comment on another child's response, rather than immediately responding themselves

A greater ratio of open-ended questions

Samson et al. (1987) suggest that higher order questions, 'higher cognitive questioning strategies', can support children's learning. These are the rich open-ended questions that do not have a single correct answer. For example:

   'Was the Pied Piper right to take the children of Hamelin away?'

rather than:

   'What happened to the children of Hamelin in the story?'

While research (e.g. Harrison and Howard, 2009) suggests that a move towards more open-ended questions is the key factor in supporting children's learning in English, the 'authenticity' of the questions might also have an impact on children's engagement and learning.

In this context, authenticity refers not just to whether questions allow for more than one answer, but whether the answers have been already anticipated by the teacher (Tennent et al., 2016).

Wait time

Allowing children *wait time* to think before answering a question can have a positive effect on children's involvement in classroom discussion. Rowe (1974) found that the average wait time in primary classrooms was less than a second. This research suggested that when the teacher's questions were followed by at least three seconds of time for children to think carefully and then formulate a response, the question was more likely to be answered successfully. Later research indicates that regular use of wait time can have a positive impact on both children's and teacher's behaviours.

For children:

- An increase in successfully answered questions
- A decrease in children responding that they didn't know the answer
- The length and accuracy of answers increased
- A greater number of children volunteered an answer

For teachers:

- The questioning strategies they employed became more flexible and varied
- The quantity of questions asked decreased, while the quality and variety of questions increased
- The use of higher-order cognitive questioning questions increased

(Drawn from Brualdi, 1998; Condie et al., 2005; Ko and Sammons, 2013; Webb and Jones, 2009; Wiliam, 2018)

A 'have a go' ethos

The classroom culture plays a significant factor in the success of questioning and wider classroom talk. If children are unwilling to offer an opinion or an idea for fear of being wrong, formative assessment is unable to function effectively. Every classroom is different, but most take time and conscious effort to build this type of environment through careful modelling, reflection and reinforcement. Even after great care has been taken to establish a classroom ethos where everyone can make suggestions freely, there may be some children who are reluctant to offer suggestions they are unsure of.

Invite children to comment, rather than supply a teacher response

This strategy relies on conversation in the classroom being structured differently from the teacher-child-teacher tennis lesson of classroom questioning. Instead, a teacher might invite other children to comment on, expand or present a counter view to a child's answer.

CASE STUDY 18.2

The Year 2 teacher of Turtle Class used the resources from Cambridge University's *Thinking Together* project (Dawes and Warwick, 2012) to discuss the class' ground rules for talk. The children worked through some suggested ideas, discussing which they agreed with and which they didn't, before creating the 'Turtle Class Rules for Talk'. These were:

- We will take turns to talk and to listen.
- We will listen and think about each other's ideas carefully.
- We understand that talking is thinking aloud together.
- We know that we don't always get everything right when we are thinking aloud.
- We share our ideas and lend them to each other – we are a team.
- We ask each other for reasons why we think things.
- We don't always agree with each other and it is fine to have different ideas.
- We try to talk loudly enough so that everyone can hear, but not too loudly!
- We think it is fine to change your mind about something once you've thought about it.

These were displayed prominently in the classroom and referred to frequently when the children were talking together as a class or in groups. While the rules themselves were valuable for the teacher and children to refer to, so was the process of discussing them and devising them using the online *Thinking Together* resources (freely available by searching: 'Thinking Together Cambridge').

Feedback

Feedback refers to information that is shared about performance in a specific task or learning in general, relative to the aims or objectives of the teaching activity:

Feedback redirects or refocuses either the teacher's or the learner's actions to achieve a goal, by aligning effort and activity with an outcome. It can be about the learning activity itself, about the process of activity, about the student's management of their learning or self-regulation.

(Higgins et al., 2014)

Meta-analyses of education practice suggest that feedback is one of the most useful ways of developing children's learning (e.g. Hattie, 2008; Higgins et al., 2014), and this is true of teaching reading and writing. However, as feedback is often studied in relation to other aspects of formative assessment, detaching its effect can present a challenge (Tierney and Charland, 2007), as can ensuring that the effects of feedback last beyond the short term, leading to genuine learning and lasting performance (Kluger and DeNisi, 1996). It is important to note that while feedback can be a powerful factor in supporting learning, there are circumstances where it can lead to a lowering of performance (Kluger and DeNisi, 1996).

In the classroom, feedback can be synonymous with marking a child's written work, but effective feedback can be targeted at the level of the individual, group or whole class and it can be written or given as oral feedback. Whichever form it takes, research suggests that well-structured feedback is a powerful way of supporting children's learning. Wiliam (2018) refers to feedback as 'a recipe for future action', and it is this idea that should sit at the heart of feedback – it should lead to a child taking action to improve their performance or to address any misconceptions. Research from Boulet et al. (1990), suggests that this chance to take action is a more significant factor than whether feedback is written or oral in nature. The writing process case study in Chapter 12 (Case Study 12.3, p. 216) illustrates how feedback can be embedded into the teaching of writing which in turn will lead to 'future action'.

Feedback that gives comments only, rather than awarding a mark or grade, can have a greater impact than where marks have been given alone or alongside a comment (Butler, 1988), as children tend to focus on these, rather than the action they need to take to improve. There is also an emotional aspect to feedback: a low mark can be dispiriting, while a high mark can act as a disincentive to seek to improve further (Assessment Reform Group, 2002). As a result, emphasis needs to be given to the emotional response that feedback is likely to provoke as much as the possible impact on outcomes (Dweck, 1986, 2006; Kluger and DeNisi, 1996).

Hattie and Temperley (2007) suggest that feedback is most powerful when it is viewed as being directed from a student *to* a teacher: it shows a teacher what a child does or doesn't know, where there are possible misconceptions to address and the areas where a child might feels confident or less-confident.

Black et al. (2002) suggest that the key elements of effective feedback are:

- When comments recognise what has been done well and the next steps for improvement, providing guidance on how to make that improvement.
- When written and oral feedback encourages pupils to develop and show understanding of the key features of what they are learning.
- When opportunities for pupils to follow up comments are planned as part of the overall learning process and feedback causes thinking to take place.

CASE STUDY 18.3

Rather than have a set feedback policy for teachers to follow, the primary school Karra attends asks teachers to build in opportunities for written and oral feedback, depending on what the teacher thinks will be most effective. This could be delivered to an individual, a group of children or the whole class. Below are some examples of ways Karra has received feedback to help her develop in English over the course of one week in Year 4:

Whole-class oral feedback: the class have been writing stories based on their Ancient Egyptian topic. Together they have read Marcy and the Riddle of the Sphinx by Joe Todd-Stanton which has given them a model for their own tales. From the first draft of their stories, Karra's teacher notices that many children still have difficulty punctuating direct speech, so she teaches a session on this. She then extends the task, showing them how they can use dialogue to move the action forward in a story. The children are then asked to return to their stories and edit them in light of the teaching points. Karra matches her writing against the examples on the board, seeing where she is correct. She then goes back to add the comma in after each character has finished speaking and tries to use two characters talking about the 'Lost Crystal of Anubis' to set the scene of her story. For the teacher to feed back individually to each child, either orally or in writing, would have been extremely time-consuming.

Small group written feedback: the children have been divided into groups and have been preparing a presentation for the class on one aspect of Ancient Egyptian life. Karra and her group have chosen mummification. After the presentation, the teacher shares her notes with the group, focusing on the aspects that they have done well: excellent research and a loud, clear delivery. She also suggests an area for improvement: the possibility of some audience interaction. The group have time to discuss the feedback and put it into practice ahead of their presentations forming part of a class assembly for parents at the end of the week.

Individual oral feedback: Karra's teacher listens to her read Gawain and the Green Knight retold by Philip Reeve. Karra's teacher feeds back that she is delighted with Karra's reading, especially the voices she gives the different characters. As they reach the part where the Green Knight is about to behead Sir Gawain, Karra's teacher models how to slow the pace down for dramatic effect. Karra tries to copy her teacher and then goes home and reads the section to her mum using the same technique.

Individual written feedback: in a science lesson, Karra has written up the results of a class experiment on the permeability of different rocks. Her teacher notices that she uses different modal verbs interchangeably in her method section (you could add five drops of water to the beaker). In a brief comment, the teacher reminds Karra that she is giving instructions so she needs a stronger verb (you should add...) or no modal verb at all (add five drops...). Although this is a science lesson and the feedback focus would normally be linked to a science objective, here the teacher decides to take the opportunity to address an English misconception.

In each case, the elements Karra has done well are validated and then she is given comments or a model to show how she can improve her performance.

Peer-assessment and self-assessment

Peer-assessment relates to children working together, making judgements, offering feedback or ideas towards a shared aim. This might be a shared goal (in English lessons, a small group reading and building an understanding of a text together or creating a joint presentation), or supporting each other with their own individual pieces of work (two children taking it in turns to proofread and critique each other's work). This *cooperative learning* (Johnson et al., 1981; Johnson and Johnson, 2009) can be a powerful way of supporting children to develop as learners. Reviews of research by Slavin et al. (2003) and Hattie (2008) suggest that cooperative learning can have a significant effect on children's learning. However, meta-analysis of peer-assessment suggests that success is variable and children are more likely to benefit if they have been taught explicitly how to go about the process (Li et al., 2019). Peer-tutoring, where one child explains a concept to another child, has been found to be effective; indeed, Schacter (2000) suggests that it may be as effective as a one-to-one intervention from a teacher.

CASE STUDY 18.4

In a Year 3 class, children were paired up by the teacher as reading buddies for a 30-minute session each week while the teacher listened to particular children read aloud. The pairs were different each week, and children had time to read to their partner for ten minutes. After reading, the two children worked together through a proforma set of questions to evaluate the child's reading together. They would then repeat the process with the other child reading. They were prompted to discuss prosodic elements such as intonation, pace and expression; any difficulties with particular words and anything else that came up, particularly around comprehension. A long time had been spent modelling the conversations, so the children knew how to talk to one another, both offering and receiving criticism. Because children worked through the discussion points together, often the reader would lead the conversation, saying things like, 'I struggled a bit with that word. It took me three goes to get it right!'. This helped the children to reflect on their own reading as well as having a critical friend as support. The teacher reported that the children looked forward to the sessions immensely, as well as becoming increasingly aware of what makes a fluent reader. She felt strongly that a task like this was useful for children, whereas expecting them to feed back to a peer without support for the dialogue might be too challenging.

Getting peer-assessment right is not without its challenges. When following children's interactions in the primary classroom, Nuthall (2007) notes that while the majority of feedback children receive at school comes from a peer rather than an adult, much of that feedback is, in fact, incorrect.

Peer feedback is especially useful when children are able to explain *why* there is a misconception or error, rather than simply pointing out that something is incorrect. This can benefit both the child receiving the explanation and the child who gives the explanation (Webb, 1991). Since both children need to be secure in their own understanding, the process of expressing that understanding in a clear way helps them to clarify their thoughts. This form of *self-explanation* (being able to articulate to oneself how new information fits with existing knowledge) can have a significant impact on learning and understanding (Bisra et al., 2018).

As Wiliam (2018) notes, in the context of formative assessment, self-assessment is not concerned with children awarding themselves marks or grades, but 'whether or not students can develop sufficient insights into their own learning to improve it'. For example, a child being able to recognise if they have understood a section of a text, or if they need to re-read. One element of self-assessment is *self-evaluation*, 'setting standards and using them for self-judgement' (Hattie, 2012), which research suggests is an effective way of helping children to make progress (Lavery, 2008; Dunlosky et al., 2013). In primary English teaching, this might involve a child reading carefully over their writing to ensure it matches the intended purpose of the piece. Effective self-assessment relies on metacognition – an individual's understanding and regulation of their own thoughts and cognitive processes. Research suggests that metacognition can have a significant impact on children's learning (Butler and Winne, 1995; Dignath et al., 2008; Donker et al, 2014). Self-assessment is also likely to play a part in developing greater autonomy, allowing them to generalise ideas and concepts from one area of learning to another (Hacker et al., 1998). As with peer-assessment, self-assessment is not without its challenges; many students can find it difficult to think about their learning in relation to specific learning goals. Developing this ability can take time which teachers are sometimes reluctant to allocate (Black et al., 2010).

CASE STUDY 18.5

A primary school has the policy that self-assessment is the first assessment step when children create a piece of writing before receiving any feedback.

After a break from writing (usually the next day), children are given an opportunity to return to their work and look at it again with fresh eyes. Without sharing their writing with anyone else or any specific teacher feedback, they are asked to read over their piece and identify the elements they are pleased with. They then proofread, looking for any obvious errors or areas where improvements could be made. The class has been taught to read the words aloud under their breath one sentence at a time, so they read the actual words rather than the words they think they have written. They are reminded to focus on:

- missing words
- sentences or phrases that don't make sense
- common words spelled incorrectly
- how punctuation is used to communicate their ideas clearly

While the majority of the class work independently to try and make corrections, the teacher works with a small group of three children to mark their work in detail and give them comprehensive oral feedback.

The point of this checking time is to ensure that the children can self-correct the little errors that often slip into their writing when producing an extended piece of writing. If the teacher takes in and marks this first draft, she is likely to find she is addressing many secretarial errors rather than concentrating on improving the content of the writing. If children are taught to check their work, it means that any mistakes after this are likely to be conceptual errors that need to be retaught, rather than mistakes that children have made through rushing. This enables the teacher to use her limited time to teach the things that will have the greatest impact on children's development in writing. Learning to self-check is also useful for children to apply and regular practice is important in developing this skill.

Learning to self-check in this way takes time and not every child finds it easy. The school begins by encouraging children to look at their work and identify parts they are pleased with. Once this habit is established, they begin to look for elements that might not be correct or which could be improved. Finally, they are given time to try and make changes. While this is not always successful (sometimes children do not know what is wrong so they cannot identify it and sometimes they do not know how to make successful changes), this time is always given to every child to reinforce the idea that it is *their* writing and they have the responsibility for making it as good as it can be before the teacher offers feedback.

Research indicates that the success of peer- and self-assessment relies on specific criteria or examples for children to judge success against (e.g. Black and Wiliam, 1998; McDonald and Boud, 2003; Swaffield, 2011). In the context of English teaching, this could take the form of specific written criteria, such as learning intentions shared at the start of an activity:

Today we are learning to use the imperative to write clear instructions

Or

LO: To demonstrate you can draw conclusions about a character and support these with evidence from the text

Criteria might also take the form of success criteria used to judge a product against:

Success criteria:

- *Choose one character from the text and identify one of their key characteristics.*
- *Use the text that tells you about this aspect of their character.*

Remember, it may be a direct quote, or evidence might come from their actions or the words that they say.

While clearly stated learning intentions and success criteria are an integral part of formative assessment practice, and have become a mainstay of wider classroom teaching, constructing them and using them are not without challenges. Clarke has written widely on the potential difficulties of devising criteria that are about learning rather than context or activities (e.g. Clarke, 2005, 2008).

CASE STUDY 18.6

Teachers at a small rural primary school were concerned that they had fallen into a mechanistic pattern of sharing learning objectives with their two mixed-age Key Stage 2 classes: the teacher would share the objective, the children would write this down in their books and then they would return to it during a plenary session. The three teachers trialled some alternatives to sharing learning:

'Big questions': rather than beginning by telling the children what they were going to learn, some sessions began with a key question to explore. When studying The Eagle by Alfred, Lord Tennyson, instead of the objective 'to analyse how a poet creates a description using poetic devices', the big question would simply be:

'How do the author's language choices help the reader to picture the subject?' The teachers found children were engaged with trying to answer the question and lessons sometimes followed a more authentic, open-ended route.

Co-devising learning objectives: rather than the teacher providing children with an objective for them to meet, the objectives were discussed and created as a group – for example, thinking together about what might make a good character study. While this could be time-consuming, it helped the children to understand what the intention was and invited them to become intrinsically invested in the task.

'Guess the objective': one teacher suggested writing a lesson objective on a piece of paper and putting it in a sealed envelope. At the end of the lesson, children would be invited to guess what they were supposed to be learning. The teacher said this helped her to keep coming back to the learning intention throughout the lesson and making clear she used key language to share the purpose of her teaching.

Rather than written criteria, judgements can also be made against samples of work or specific examples. This is also a common approach in primary writing lessons, with teachers sharing 'what a good one looks like' (WAGOLL) with children before they write. These completed examples are used to help children identify successfully employed features from other children's work. Advocates of comparative judgement suggest that this method could help to produce annotated samples of writing to support children to see what effective writing looks like in different contexts, and because these samples would be chosen from a broad range of different versions of success, variety could be celebrated, rather than narrow adherence to one way of meeting the aim (Christodoulou, 2016).

The formative use of summative assessments

While assigning too many purposes to the same assessment can create tensions, using a test formatively once it has fulfilled its summative purpose is a useful way of bridging the gap between these two purposes for assessment and supporting children's learning.

CASE STUDY 18.7

A Year 6 teacher used three past papers for the Key Stage 2 national tests over the course of the year to help his class learn to navigate the tests and provide information about children's progress. He was determined that sitting the tests could play a positive part in children's learning, so he planned two practical approaches to using the reading tests formatively:

Redrafting the test: once the children had sat a test and their scores were recorded, they were given the opportunity to come back to it and redraft their

(Continued)

answers. Working with a partner or in a small group, the children went back to any questions that they did not answer fully or answered incorrectly, and redrafted them so that they received full marks instead. While the new score (ideally, full marks) couldn't be used for summative purposes, this process was useful in helping children to address any misconceptions they had. It also helped the children to see what a correct answer might look like (reinforcing the mindset that it wasn't that they couldn't get correct answers, just that they hadn't manage to achieve them yet).

Model answers: in conjunction with the children, the teacher selected five questions from the test that the cohort found challenging, and worked together as a class to write a model answer for each. The process of discussing what to include in the answer and how to phrase it proved to be a powerful way of supporting learning.

Research suggests that the different strands that make up formative assessment can have positive effects on student learning and achievement (e.g Wiliam et al., 2004; Condie et al., 2005; Ofsted, 2008), and while the degree of this impact has been challenged with a call for more evidence (Kingston and Nash, 2011), the strategies that form formative practice represent many of the elements that might be recognised in good English teaching. As a result, many of these ideas are weaved through other practice chapters of this book.

STOP AND REFLECT

Consider the four aspects of formative practice suggested by Black et al. (2002):

- Questioning
- Feedback
- Peer- and self-assessment
- The formative use of summative assessments

When considering your own teaching of English, which of these elements:

- are you aware of?
- do you make a conscious effort to include in your teaching?
- do you use well?
- have you seen have an impact on children's progress?

Conclusion

Few topics drive education with as much force as assessment. On a national level, a system of assessment is used to make judgements about schools, teachers and pupils which affects the structure of the curriculum and organisation of teaching in all but a few schools. These flow down into the in-school assessments used to track the achievement of pupils, inform decisions about education quality, make adjustments to the curriculum, and often to drive teaching and learning in classrooms. Finally, there is assessment for formative purposes: a set of practices that can potentially lead to substantial increases in children's achievement at school (e.g. Wiliam, 2006). And yet, it is often the summative assessments that become the day-to-day concerns in school and dominate the national discourse around educational assessment.

This chapter has focused predominantly on assessment for formative purposes, and these ideas weave through other sections of this book concerned with teaching reading, writing and spoken language. Assessment for formative purposes is integral to good teaching and it is the type of assessment that should be driving the teaching of English in primary schools.

IN SUMMARY

- The assessments employed in schools have a number of purposes. *Assessments for formative purposes* are used to plan for future teaching and learning, while *assessments for summative purposes* are used to make judgements about a child's learning at the end of a period of teaching.
- Assessments can be said to have two properties, *validity* (whether an assessment measures what it needs to measure) and *reliability* (whether an assessment will produce the same measurement each time it is employed).
- No assessment provides a perfectly dependable measurement. As a result, teachers need to exercise caution about how much faith is placed in the result of an individual assessment, especially when making decisions based on the outcome.
- The elements that make up formative assessment – questioning, feedback, peer-assessment and self-assessment and the formative use of summative assessments – have been shown to have a significant impact on children's learning. Developing this strand of assessment should be the principal concern of class teachers.

FURTHER READING

- For a current and practical overview of the field of formative assessment, see *Embedded Formative Assessment* by Dylan Wiliam.

- To find out more about practical applications for formative assessment, see the work of Shirley Clarke, including *Outstanding Formative Assessment: Culture and Practice* and *Active Learning Through Formative Assessment*.
- *The Final Report of the Commission on Assessment Without Levels*, available free through an online search, provides an overview of successful in-school assessment systems and the principles that sit behind them.

BIBLIOGRAPHY

Assessment Reform Group (2002) *Assessment for learning: 10 principles: research-based principles to guide classroom practice*. Assessment Reform Group.

Bisra, K., Liu, Q., Nesbit, J.C., Salimi, F. and Winne, P. (2018) Inducing self-explanation: A meta-analysis. *Educational Psychology Review*, 30(3): 703–25.

Black, P., Harrison, C., Lee, C., Marshall, B. and Wiliam, D. (2002) *Working Inside the Black Box: Assessment for learning in the classroom*. King's College, London.

Black, P., Harrison, C., Lee, C., Marshall, B. and Wiliam, D. (2010) *Assessment for Learning: Putting it into Practice*. London: Open University Press.

Black, P. and Wiliam, D. (1998) Assessment and classroom learning, assessment in education. *Principles, Policy & Practice*, 5(1): 7–74.

Boulet, M., Simard, G. and De Melo, D. (1990) Formative evaluation effects on learning music. *Journal of Educational Research*, 84(2): 119–25.

Brualdi, A. C. (1998) *Classroom Questions*. ERIC Clearinghouse on Assessment and Evaluation: Washington DC.

Butler, D.L. and Winne, P. H. (1995) Feedback and self-regulated learning: A theoretical synthesis. *Review of Educational Research*, 65(3), 245–81.

Butler, R. (1988) Enhancing and undermining intrinsic motivation: The effects of task-involving and ego-involving evaluation on interest and performance. *Journal of Educational Psychology*, 58(1): 1–14.

Christodoulou, D. (2016) *Making Good Progress?* Oxford: Oxford University Press.

Clarke, S. (2005) *Formative Assessment in Action: Weaving the elements together*. London: Hodder Murray.

Clarke, S. (2008) *Active Learning Through Formative Assessment*. London: Hodder Murray.

Commission on Assessment Without Levels (2015) *Final Report*. London: DfE.

Condie, R., Livingston, K. and Seagraves, L. (2005) *Evaluation of the Assessment for Learning Programme: Final report*. Glasgow: Quality in Education Centre, University of Strathclyde.

Dawes, L. and Warwick, P. (2012) *Talking Points: Discussion activities in the primary classroom*. Abingdon: Routledge.

Department for Education (DfE) (2014) *Assessing Without Levels*. London: DfE.

Dignath, C., Buettner, G. and Langfeldt, H. (2008) How can primary school students learn self-regulated learning strategies most effectively? A meta-analysis on self-regulation training programmes. *Educational Research Review*, 3(2): 101–29.

Donker, A.S., De Boer, H., Kostons, D., Dignath van Ewijk, C.C. and Van der Werf, M.P.C. (2014) Effectiveness of learning strategy instruction on academic performance: A meta-analysis. *Educational Research Review*, 11: 1–26.

Dunlosky, J., Rawson, K.A., Marsh, E.J., Nathan, M.J. and Willingham, D. T. (2013) Improving students' learning with effective learning techniques: Promising directions from cognitive and educational psychology. *Psychological Science in the Public Interest*, 14(1): 4–58.

Dweck, C. (1986) Motivational processes affecting learning. *American Psychologist*, 41(10): 1040–8.

Dweck, C. (2006) *Mindset: The new psychology of success*. New York: Random House.

Gardner, J. (Ed.) (2006). *Assessment and Learning*. London: Sage.

Hacker, D.J., Dunlosky, J. and Graesser, A.C. (1998) *Metacognition in Educational Theory and Practice*. London: Taylor & Francis.

Harrison, C. and Howard, S. (2009) *Inside the Primary Black Box: Assessment for learning in primary and early years classrooms*. London: GL Assessment.

Hattie, J. (2008) *Visible Learning*. Abingdon: Routledge.

Hattie, J. (2012) *Visible Learning for Teachers*. Abingdon: Routledge.

Hattie, J. and Temperley, H. (2007) The power of feedback. *Review of Educational Research*, 77(1): 81–112.

Higgins, S., Katsipataki, M., Coleman, R., Henderson, P., Major, L.E. and Coe, R. (2014) *The Sutton Trust-Education Endowment Foundation Teaching and Learning Toolkit*. London: Education Endowment Foundation.

Johnson, D.W. and Johnson, R.T. (2009) An educational psychology success story: Social interdependence theory and cooperative learning. *Educational Researcher*, 38(5): 365–79.

Johnson, D.W., Maruyama, G., Johnson, R. and Nelson, D. (1981) Effects of cooperative, competitive and individualistic goal structures on achievement: A meta-analysis. *Psychological Bulletin*, 89(1): 4–62.

Kingston, N. and Nash, B. (2011) Formative assessment: A meta-analysis and call for research. *Educational Measurement: Issues and Practice*, 30(4): 28–37.

Kluger, A. and DeNisi, A. (1996) The effects of feedback interventions on performance: A historical review, a meta-analysis, and a preliminary feedback intervention theory. *Psychological Bulletin*, 119 (2): 254–84.

Ko, J. and Sammons, P. with Bakkum, L. (2013) *Effective Teaching: A review of research and evidence*. Reading: CfBT Education Trust.

Lavery, L. (2008) *Self-regulated learning for academic success: An evaluation of instructional techniques*. PhD thesis, University of Auckland, New Zealand.

Li, H., Xiong, Y., Hunter, C.V., Guo, X. and Tywoniw, R. (2019) Does peer assessment promote student learning? A meta-analysis, *Assessment & Evaluation in Higher Education*, 45(2): 193–211.

McDonald, B. and Boud, D. (2003) The impact of self-assessment on achievement: The effects of self-assessment training on performance in external examinations. *Assessment in Education: Principles, Policy & Practice*, 10(2): 209–20.

Meisels, S. and Atkins-Burnett, S. (2008) Evaluating early childhood assessments: A differential analysis. In K. McCartney and D. Phillips (Eds), *Blackwell Handbook of Early Childhood Development* (pp. 533–49). Hoboken, NJ: Blackwell-Wiley.

Nuthall, G. (2007) *The Hidden Lives of Learners*. Wellington: New Zealand Council of Educational Research.

Ofsted (2008) *Assessment for Learning: The impact of National Strategy support*. London: Ofsted.

Rowe, M. (1974) Wait time and rewards as instructional variables, their influence on language, logic and fate control. *Journal of Research in Science Teaching*, 11: 81–94.

Samson, G., Strykowski, B., Weinstein, T. and Walberg, H. (1987) The effects of teacher questioning levels on student achievement: A quantitative synthesis. *American Educational Research Journal*, 80 (5): 290–5.

Schacter, J. (2000) Does individual tutoring produce optimal learning? *American Educational Research Journal*, 37(3): 801–29.

Slavin, R.E., Hurley, E.A. and Chamberlain, A.M. (2003) Cooperative learning and achievement. In W.M. Reynolds and G.J. Miller (Eds), *Handbook of Psychology* Volume 7: Educational Psychology, pp. 177–198. Hoboken, NJ: Wiley.

Swaffield, S. (2011) Getting to the heart of authentic Assessment for Learning. *Assessment in Education: Principles, Policy & Practice*, 18(4): 433–49.

Tennent, W., Reedy, D., Hobsbaum, A. and Gamble, N. (2016) *Guiding Readers: Layers of meaning*. London: UCL, Institute of Education.

Tierney, R.D. and Charland, J. (2007) *Stocks and Prospects: Research on formative assessment in secondary classrooms.* Paper presented at the annual meeting of the American Educational Research Association, Chicago, IL.

van Lier, L. (1998) The relationship between consciousness, interaction and language learning. *Language Awareness,* 7(2/3): 128–316.

Webb, M. and Jones, J. (2009) Exploring tensions in developing assessment for learning. *Assessment in Education,* 16(2): 165–84.

Webb, N. (1991) Task-related verbal interaction and mathematics learning in small groups. *Journal for Research in Mathematics Education,* 22(5): 366–89.

Wilen, W. (1991) *Questioning Skills for Teachers: What the research says to the teacher.* Washington: National Education Association.

Wiliam, D. (2006) Assessment: Learning communities can use it to engineer a bridge connecting teaching and learning. *Journal of Staff Development,* 27(1): 16–20.

Wiliam, D. (2018) *Embedded Formative Assessment.* Bloomington, IN: Solution Tree Press.

Wiliam, D., Lee, C., Harrison, C. and Black, P. (2004) Teachers developing assessment for learning: Impact on student achievement. *Assessment in Education: Principles, Policy & Practice,* 11(1): 49–65.

LITERATURE

Marcy and the Riddle of the Sphinx by Joe Todd-Stanton

Sir Gawain and the Green Knight retold by Philip Reeve

The Eagle by Alfred, Lord Tennyson

INDEX